GETTING AND SPENDING:
The Consumer's Dilemma

This is a volume in the Arno Press collection

GETTING AND SPENDING:
The Consumer's Dilemma

Advisory Editor
Leon Stein

*See last pages of this volume
for a complete list of titles*

CHAIN STORES

CHAIRMAN OF THE FEDERAL TRADE COMMISSION

ARNO PRESS
A New York Times Company
1976

Editorial Supervision: EVE NELSON

Reprint Edition 1976 by Arno Press Inc.

Reprinted from a copy in the University of Illinois Library

GETTING AND SPENDING: The Consumer's Dilemma
ISBN for complete set: 0-405-08005-0
See last pages of this volume for titles.

Manufactured in the United States of America

Library of Congress Cataloging in Publication Data

United States. Federal Trade Commission.
Chain stores.

(Getting and spending)
Reprint of Chain-store private brands, of Short weighing and over weighing in chain and independent grocery stores, and of Quality of canned vegetables and fruits under brands of manufacturers, chains, and other distributors, all published in 1933 by the U. S. Govt. Print. Off., Washington, and issued as Senate Documents 142, 153, and 170 respectively.
1. Food industry and trade--United States.
2. Branded merchandise--United States. 3. Food--Packaging. 4. Chain stores--United States. I. Title.
II. Series. III. Series: United States. 72d Congress, 2d session, 1932-1933. Senate. Document ; 142, 153, 170.
HD9005.U54 1976 381 75-39243
ISBN 0-405-08051-4

72D CONGRESS
2d Session

SENATE

DOCUMENT
No. 142

CHAIN STORES

Chain-Store Private Brands

LETTER

FROM THE

CHAIRMAN OF THE FEDERAL TRADE COMMISSION

TRANSMITTING

IN RESPONSE TO SENATE RESOLUTION NO. 224
SEVENTIETH CONGRESS, REPORT OF THE FEDERAL
TRADE COMMISSION RELATIVE TO
CHAIN-STORE PRIVATE BRANDS

Filed with the Secretary of the Senate
September 26, 1932

UNITED STATES
GOVERNMENT PRINTING OFFICE
WASHINGTON : 1933

SENATE RESOLUTION NO. 228

SUBMITTED BY MR. BROOKHART

IN THE SENATE OF THE UNITED STATES,
June 8 (calendar day, June 10), 1932.

Resolved, That the reports which may hereafter be filed with the Secretary of the Senate, pursuant to Senate Resolution No. 224, Seventieth Congress, first session, relative to the investigation by the Federal Trade Commission of chain stores, be printed, with accompanying illustrations, as Senate documents.

Attest:

EDWIN P. THAYER, *Secretary.*

Chain-store reports of the Federal Trade Commission so far submitted to the Senate are:

Title	Senate Document No.	Price per copy
SEVENTY-SECOND CONGRESS, FIRST SESSION		
		Cents
Cooperative Grocery Chains	12	15
Wholesale Business of Retail Chains	29	5
Sources of Chain-Store Merchandise	30	10
Scope of the Chain-Store Inquiry	31	5
Chain-Store Leaders and Loss Leaders	51	10
Coöperative Drug and Hardware Chains	82	5
Growth and Development of Chain Stores	100	10
SEVENTY-SECOND CONGRESS, SECOND SESSION		
Chain-Store Private Brands	142	10

These reports may be obtained at prices above noted from

THE SUPERINTENDENT OF DOCUMENTS,
WASHINGTON, D. C.

CONTENTS

APPENDIXES

TEXT TABLES

APPENDIX TABLES

ACKNOWLEDGMENT

For the general direction and supervision of the inquiry into the chain-store industry, the commission acknowledges the services of Mr. Francis Walker, chief economist, and Mr. W. H. S. Stevens, assistant chief economist. As contributing especially to the preparation of this report on Chain-Store Private Brands, the commission desires to mention Mr. Malcolm D. Taylor; Mr. Byron P. Parry, examiner in charge of the inquiry; Mr. Wilford L. White, in charge of statistical tabulations; and Mr. Martin A. Behrens.

LETTER OF TRANSMITTAL

FEDERAL TRADE COMMISSION,
Washington, September 26, 1932.

THE PRESIDENT OF THE SENATE,
United States Senate, Washington, D. C.

DEAR SIR: I have the honor to transmit herewith a report of the Federal Trade Commission, entitled, " Chain-Store Private Brands," submitted in pursuance of Senate Resolution 224, Seventieth Congress, first session. This is the eighth report of a series of reports covering a study on the subject of chain stores.

By direction of the commission.

W. E. HUMPHREY, *Chairman.*

LETTER OF SUBMITTAL

FEDERAL TRADE COMMISSION,
September 26, 1932.

To the Senate of the United States:

Under Senate Resolution 224, the Federal Trade Commission was directed to inquire into and report to the Senate regarding "the advantages or disadvantages of chain-store distribution in comparison with those of other types of distribution as shown by prices, costs, profits and margins, quality of goods, and services rendered by chain stores and other distributors or resulting from integration, managerial efficiency, low overhead, or other similar causes."

The importance of private brands in this connection lies in the possible effects of such brands upon the prices of chain stores, particularly with reference to their independent competitors. It is claimed that the gross profit or margin on private brand merchandise is relatively high. Because of this fact, the private brand owning chain stores, it is said, follow a policy of cutting the prices on standard brands of merchandise to a point where they yield little or no profit, making up this difference on the sale of the higher profit private brand goods to which they endeavor to switch their customers so far as practicable.

This report is primarily based on detailed information obtained from returns to two schedules, sent out by the commission in 1929 and 1931, respectively. Additional information was obtained by field agents from chain-store executives, and special reports on private brands were procured also from a limited number of chains. The report shows the extent and importance of private brands in different kinds of chains and the policies and practices which are used in merchandising them.

For the purposes of this report, a chain-store private brand of merchandise is defined as a commodity sold by the chain only through its own stores under its own distinctive mark of identification. Since some few companies have reported on private brands on the basis of a narrower definition, it is obvious that the private brand sales in this report are smaller and the other data somewhat less comprehensive than would be the case had the broader definition always been used.

ATTITUDE OF CHAINS TOWARD PRIVATE BRANDS

A large proportion of retail chain organizations, particularly the larger ones, are strong advocates of private-brand merchandise. Those favoring such brands give some 20 different reasons for their development and use. Perhaps the most important claim made is that private brands enable the chain store to give the consumer better values. Other claims include higher profits, lower purchase costs, and lower costs of distribution on private-label merchandise, the high quality of such merchandise and the ability of the chain to control, standardize, and improve this quality. The value of private-brand merchandise for advertising purposes and for the creation and promotion of good will and the development of repeat business are also frequently referred to.

Many of the chains, however, are comparatively indifferent to private brands. Some favor standard brands owned by manufacturers, in preference to private brands because among other reasons they claim that they turn faster. Other chains consider themselves too small to derive any advantage from engaging in the distribution of private-brand goods.

Perhaps the most frequently stated objection to private brands is the large amount of sales resistance which is encountered in their distribution. Extra selling effort and expense for advertising and promotion are necessary in order to build up consumer acceptance of such brands.

QUALITY OF CHAIN PRIVATE-BRAND PRODUCTS

Samples of canned fruits and vegetables, regarded as typical, were purchased in three cities (Des Moines, Memphis, and Detroit) covering four types of brand owners: Chain stores, cooperative chains, manufacturers, and wholesalers. These samples were submitted to the warehouse division of the Department of Agriculture for grading in order to have the quality of the product sold under each brand officially determined.

The grading tests showed that the chains were only slightly below nationally advertising manufacturers in the proportion of their cans of branded vegetables which graded "fancy," "extra standard," and "standard," respectively. They made a slightly better showing than nonnationally advertising manufacturers in the "fancy" grade, and showed a materially higher proportion for "extra standard." Compared with wholesalers, the chains showed a distinctly higher proportion in "fancy" and a somewhat lower proportion in "extra standard." Chains led cooperatives slightly in the proportions graded "fancy," but for the "extra standard" grade the cooperatives showed so high a ratio as to become the leader in the combined proportions of "fancy" and "extra standard."

In the proportion of their cans of branded fruits graded "choice" the chains substantially exceeded any other group, but a slightly better showing in the proportions of "fancy" grade was made by both nationally advertising manufacturers and wholesalers. The chain's proportion of cans graded "choice" and "fancy" combined was not only above the average, but it was appreciably higher than that of manufacturers, wholesalers, or cooperative chains. In canned fruits, none of the chain-store private brands graded "seconds."

EXTENT OF OWNERSHIP OF PRIVATE BRANDS

Four hundred and twelve chains, or about one-fourth of the 1,660 which furnished brand information in 1929–30, owned private brands. They operated 77 per cent of the stores, however, and transacted 75 per cent of the total business of all reporting chains. Twenty-eight per cent (or 351 chains) of the 1,247 chains reporting in 1931 owned private brands, but they operated over 81 per cent of the stores and transacted nearly 81 per cent of the total business. Private brand-owning chains operated more than ten times as many stores on the average as the nonbrand-owning chains.

The proportion of brand-owning chains in 10 groups (grocery, grocery and meat, confectionery, drug, tobacco, women's accessories, hats and caps, men's shoes, department store, and musical instruments) was above the average for all chains reporting. In fact, in each of these groups the proportion of brand-owning chains was over 37 per cent. Seven kinds of business, namely, meat, variety—$5 limit, variety—unlimited, women's ready-to-wear, men's and women's ready-to-wear, millinery, and furniture chains, showed low proportions of chains owning private brands, none exceeding 10 per cent.

Some private-brand merchandise, presumably, is sold in practically every store operated by chains owning private brands. If this assumption is correct, private brands are sold in about 97 per cent of the chain grocery and meat stores, in from 84 to 90 per cent of the chain grocery and department stores, in about 86 per cent of the confectionery stores, in from 63 to 81 per cent of the chain dry goods and apparel stores, and in from 62 to 75 per cent of the dollar-limit variety stores. The probability of a consumer being offered private brands in a chain hardware store is small, since chains owning private brands operated less than 9 per cent of such stores. It is also small in the following kinds of chains: Meat, women's ready-to-wear, furniture, unlimited price variety, and men's and women's ready-to-wear.

OWNERSHIP OF PRIVATE BRANDS BY SIZE OF CHAIN

The proportion of brand-owning chains varied directly with the size of the chain for all reporting chains combined, with one exception (the 501-1,000 stores group). The same general statement is also true, without exception, for four kinds of chains, namely, men's ready-to-wear, women's ready-to-wear, general merchandise, and musical instruments. It is true, with certain insignificant exceptions for five other kinds of chains: Grocery, grocery and meat, confectionery, drug, and women's shoes.

AMOUNTS AND PROPORTIONS OF SALES MADE IN PRIVATE BRANDS BY PRIVATE BRAND-OWNING CHAINS

Two hundred and fifty-five chains reported private brand sales aggregating $514,000,000 in 1929 and 274 chains reported a total of $520,000,000 for such sales in 1930. In each year private-brand sales represented approximately 28 per cent of the total sales of private-brand owning chains. If estimated private-brand sales of the Great Atlantic & Pacific Tea Co. and the Kroger Grocery & Baking Co. are included, the total for 1929 becomes $762,000,000 and for 1930 it is $770,000,000 and the proportion of total sales made in private brands becomes 24.3 per cent for each year.

Considered from the standpoint of dollar volume, the great bulk of the private-brand sales of these brand-owning chains, at least in recent years, has been made by chains in a limited number of lines of business. Excluding A. & P. and Kroger, nearly four-fifths of the total private-brand sales reported by the 274 chains in 1930 were made in 5 of the 26 kinds of chains, namely, dry goods and apparel, department store, men's and women's shoes, grocery, and grocery and meat. If A. & P. and Kroger are included, the private-brand sales of these five kinds of business represent nearly six-sevenths of the total. Approximately one-third of the private-brand sales of all private-brand chains reporting in 1930 was made by A. & P. and Kroger, and these two chains together with the J. C. Penney Co. accounted for more than half of the total private-brand sales reported in that year.

Based on the proportion of private-brand sales to total sales of private-brand owning chains, the private-brand business is apparently most important in confectionery and men's shoe chains and least important in hardware, unlimited variety, variety ($5 limit), and millinery chains.

TREND OF CHAIN-STORE PRIVATE-BRAND SALES

Figures for two groups of identical companies, one group of 48 chains for 1925, 1928, 1929, and 1930, and a larger group of 79 chains for 1928, 1929, and 1930, yield the following general facts regarding the trend of private-brand business in chain stores:

1. There has been an enormous increase in the dollar volume of private-brand sales in chain stores since 1925, both including and excluding The Great Atlantic & Pacific Tea Co. and the Kroger Grocery & Baking Co. figures.

2. Excluding the sales of The Great Atlantic & Pacific Tea Co. and the Kroger Grocery & Baking Co., there has been a considerable increase in the proportion of the sales of private-brand merchandise to total sales in both of the periods studied. Even including these two companies, there was an appreciable relative increase from 1928 to 1930 for the larger of the two groups of identical companies.

The following facts are indicated regarding the trend in individual kinds of chains: (1) The trend of private-brand business appears to be definitely upward in grocery and meat (excluding A. & P. and Kroger), drug, women's shoes, men's and women's shoes, and men's furnishings chains. It also was clearly upward from 1928 to 1930 in grocery and department-store chains. (2) The trend appears clearly to be downward in dollar limit variety chains and in the two hat and cap and one musical instrument chains reporting. The trend in tobacco chains, although not so definite, apparently is downward.

KIND OF MERCHANDISE SOLD UNDER PRIVATE LABELS

Based on an analysis of reports received from 70 grocery and grocery and meat chains operating over 30,000 stores as of December 31, 1928, coffee (52 chains) is the most frequently reported commodity sold under private labels, no other commodity except flour (29 chains) being reported by half as many chains. Tea, mayonnaise, canned milk, and butter follow in the order named.

The leading commodities sold under private brands in seven large chains handling grocery products (the Great Atlantic & Pacific Tea Co., the Kroger Grocery & Baking Co., the Grand Union Co., the National Tea Co., the First National Stores (Inc.), the H. C. Bohack Co. (Inc.), and the American Stores Co.) were canned beans, catsup, coffee, canned corn, flour, jelly, canned peaches, canned peas, sandwich spreads, canned tomatoes, and tea.

The largest number of commodities sold under private labels by any of the seven chains mentioned was 92 for the Kroger Grocery & Baking Co. The Great Atlantic & Pacific Tea Co. was second, with 69 commodities. Each of the remaining five chains reported more than 40 commodities sold under private labels.

Information received from 29 drug chains, operating more than 500 stores as of December 31, 1928, indicates that cough sirups, corn remedies, and tooth pastes are the most important commodities sold under private labels, based on the number of chains reporting.

MARK-UP ON PRIVATE AND STANDARD BRAND MERCHANDISE

Three hundred and four chains, operating a total of 34,016 stores on December 31, 1930, reported on their mark-up policy on private brands.

Most of the chain-store reports show that the per cent of mark-up on private and standard brands was approximately the same. One hundred and ninety-three, or about two-thirds of all the chains reporting, followed this policy, and these chains operated 19,418 stores, or more than one-half of those operated by the 304 chains reporting.

Ninety-three of the 304 chains, or about 31 per cent, reported that their mark-up on private brands was higher than on competing standard brands. These chains operated 7,157 or about 21 per cent of the stores operated by all chains reporting on mark-up policy. Only 18 chains, or about 6 per cent of the total reporting, sold their private brands at a lower mark-up than competing standard brands, but these chains operated slightly more stores (7,441) than the group marking up their private brands higher than standard brands.

In addition to the general statements on mark-up policy mentioned above, reports on the actual mark-up taken by individual chains on specific private brands and competing standard brands on March 30, 1929, were received from 10 groups of chains as follows: Grocery, grocery and meat, drug, tobacco, variety ($1 limit), men's ready-to-wear, women's accessories, women's shoes, dry goods and apparel, and department store.

A detailed analysis was made of the actual mark-up taken on 249 items sold under private brands and 294 items sold under competing standard brands by 59 chains handling grocery products. This analysis does not support the statements of policy made by the chains, most of which claim to mark up their private brands either the same or lower than competing standard brands. Reports of these grocery and grocery and meat chains show that the percentage of gross profit made on 37 of the 249 private-brand items was less than 16.1 per cent, which was the average cost of doing business in 1929 for all chains of these kinds which reported operating expenses to the commission. By way of contrast, the gross profit made on 96 of the 294 standard brand items on which reports were received was less than 16.1 per cent. Expressed in another way, only 14.8 per cent of the private brands reported were being sold on March 30, 1929, at less than the average cost of doing business as contrasted to 32.7 per cent of the standard brands.

The gross profit was 20 per cent or more on 73.9 per cent of the private brands as compared with only 48.2 per cent of the standard brands. Only 46.2 per cent of the private brands were sold at a gross margin of less than 25 per cent as compared with 71.5 per cent of the standard brands. At the other extreme, a gross profit of 40 per cent or more was made on 10 per cent of the private brands but on only 1.3 per cent of the standard brands.

An analysis of quotations received from 25 drug chains on private and competing standard brands of drug and miscellaneous products and toilet articles disclosed that the gross profit on only 1 of the 167 private brand articles on which quotations were received was less than 33.3 per cent, which was the average cost of doing business in 1929 for all drug chains reporting their operating expenses to the commission. In contrast, the gross profit made on over half of the 247 standard brands on which reports were received was less than 33.3 per cent. Stating this in another way, only about one-half of 1 per cent of the private brands, as contrasted to 54.3 per cent of the standard brands, was being sold on March 30, 1929, at less than the average cost of doing business in drug chains.

The gross profit was 65 per cent or more on 42.5 per cent of the items bearing private brands while the highest gross profit reported for any standard brand was 60.9 per cent.

These results are entirely consistent with the reports of the drug chains, nearly all of which, in contrast to grocery and grocery and meat chains, mark up their private brands higher than competing standard brands.

PRICING POLICIES ON PRIVATE AND STANDARD BRAND MERCHANDISE

Although the mark-up on private brands was equal to or higher than that on competing standard brands, according to a majority of the reporting chains, nevertheless private brands generally were priced lower than competing standard brands chiefly because of lower cost. Seventy-nine chains, or about one-third of the 248 reporting on their pricing policy, priced their private brands lower than competing standard brands, but this group operated 73 per cent (32,733) of the 44,853 stores operated by the 248 chains. The policy of 126 chains, or 51 per cent of those reporting, was to sell both private brands and standard brands at the same price. The remaining 43 chains, or 17 per cent of the 248 reporting, priced their private brands higher than competing standard brands, but these chains operated only 939 stores, or about 2 per cent of those operated by the 248 chains. The chains pricing private brands lower than standard brands averaged 414 stores per chain, those pricing private and standard brands the same were next with 89 stores per chain, while chains pricing private brands higher than standard brands averaged the smallest number of stores per chain, only 22.

The most frequently reported reason for pricing private brands higher than standard brands in the chains which followed this practice was that no retail price for private brands was established by competition. Three other important reasons were: First, because private brands were usually of higher quality than standard-brand products; second, because a larger profit on private brands was desirable in order to offset the small profit made on standard-brand merchandise; and, third, because more sales effort was required to sell private brands.

The most common reason reported for pricing private brands lower than standard brands, the policy followed by the majority, was that private brands cost less. Other reasons given were: That a low price is the chief sales argument in selling private brands; that a low price on private brands attracts customers to the store; and that a low price increases private-brand sales thus building up a repeat business on such brands.

The reason most frequently reported for making the prices on private brands the same as those on standard brands was that such a policy furnished a reasonable profit or a fair basis for profits. Other important reasons reported were that " the quality is the same, therefore the price should be the same," and " meeting competition of standard brands."

In addition to the general statements on pricing policies, reports were received on the actual selling prices, March 30, 1929, of private brands and competing standard brands which had the highest mark-up. A total of 212 usable comparative price reports on 44 different commodities was received from grocery and grocery and meat chains. If a hypothetical customer on March 30, 1929, had purchased all 424 commodities (212 under private brands and 212 under standard brands) from the grocery and grocery and meat chains reporting, his private brands would have cost him $92.22 and his competing standard brands would have cost $105.21. In other words, the private brands sold for $12.99, or 12.3 per cent, less than the standard brands. Of the total of 212 pairs of comparative price quotations, there were 173 in which the private brand was sold at a lower price than the competing standard brand item, 33 in which both were sold at the same price, and 6 in which the private brand was sold at a higher price than the standard brand.

In a comparison between the selling prices of private brands and competing standard brands which had the lowest mark-up, a total of 59 usable comparative price quotations was received from grocery and grocery and meat chains on 26 different commodities. If a customer on March 30, 1929, had purchased all 118 commodities (59 under private brands and 59 bearing standard brands) from the chains furnishing price information, the private brands would have cost $29.05 and the standard brands would have cost $31.74, or the private brands were 8.5 per cent lower than the competing standard brands. In 12 of the 59 individual price comparisons, the private brands were sold at higher prices than the standard brands with which they competed; in 44 cases they were lower; and in 3 instances both were sold at the same price.

In a comparison between private brands and competing standard brands having the highest mark-up, a total of 53 comparative price quotations was received from drug chains, 41 of them being on drug and miscellaneous products and 12 on toilet articles.

If a customer had purchased 82 drug and miscellaneous products (41 bearing private brands and 41 bearing competing standard brands) on March 30, 1929, from the drug chains reporting, the private brands would have cost $23.79 and the standard brands $28.23. In other words, the private brands were lower by $4.44, or 15.7 per cent. Private brands of toilet preparations on which quotations were received would have cost $5.44 on March 30, 1929, as contrasted to $7.40 for the competing standard brands. That is, the private brands were 26.5 per cent lower than the standard brands. Ten of the forty-one private brands of drug and miscellaneous products were sold at higher prices than competing standard brands, 28 were sold at a lower price, and in three cases both were the same price. Four of the twelve private brands of toilet articles were sold at higher prices than competing standard brands, five were sold at lower prices, and in three instances both were the same price.

In a comparison between private brands and competing standard brands having the lowest mark-up, a total of 23 comparative prices was received from drug chains, 15 of them being on drug and miscellaneous products and 8 on toilet preparations. All the drug and miscellaneous articles on which quotations were received would have cost $8.59 on March 30, 1929, as contrasted with $9.17 for the competing standard brands. In other words, the private brands were lower by 58 cents or 6.3 per cent. By way of contrast, the toilet articles bearing private brands would have cost $3.68 and those bearing standard brands would have cost $5.03, or the saving on private brands would have been 26.8 per cent.

NATIONAL ADVERTISING OF PRIVATE BRANDS

Only 34 chains, or about 9 per cent of all the chain systems which reported on national advertising of private brands, indicated that they advertised their private brands nationally. This relatively small number of chains, however, operated 18,176 stores, or nearly 37 per cent of the stores operated by chains reporting on this question. From the standpoint of the number of stores operated, the five most important kinds of chains doing national advertising were grocery and meat, dry goods and apparel, men's and women's shoes, department stores, and confectionery.

A comparison on the basis of the number of stores operated by chains doing national advertising is probably of greatest significance since advertised private brands are sold in most of these stores. A small chain, even though it should advertise its brands nationally, could not make serious inroads on the business of independent merchants selling merchandise of the same kind or on the business of manufacturers selling competing standard brands since the chain's brands are at best accessible only to consumers residing in the localities where it has stores. On the other hand, where a chain's nationally advertised private brands are readily accessible to large numbers of consumers in every part of the country, they approach the status of nationally advertised " standard " brands.

POLICY OF CHAINS IN RESPECT TO FUTURE DEVELOPMENT

Comments which could be classified were received from a number of chains as to their future policy in respect to private brands. Only three chains definitely favored curtailing their private brands, while 21 companies were inclined to favor their expansion, and 27 expected the ratio between the private and standard brands to remain the same. This would indicate that private brands will become of increasing importance in the majority of these chains provided the situation is favorable for their development. Replies of several of the chains indicated that this qualification was an important one. For example, one chain stated in part "* * * what the future has in store, we can not tell, for it rests largely with the public. Even our own policy, as we have pointed out, is dependent upon the acts of others and conditions not of our own creation."

By direction of the commission.

W. E. HUMPHREY,
Chairman.

CHAIN-STORE PRIVATE BRANDS

Section 1. Origin and scope of the report.

Under Senate Resolution 224, the Federal Trade Commission was directed to inquire into and report to the Senate regarding—

> The advantages or disadvantages of chain-store distribution in comparison with those of other types of distribution as shown by prices, costs, profits, and margins, quality of goods and services rendered by chain stores and other distributors or resulting from integration, managerial efficiency, low overhead, or other similar causes.

The importance of private brands in this connection lies in the possible effects of such brands upon the prices of chain stores particularly with reference to their independent competitors. It is claimed that the gross profit or margin on private-brand merchandise is relatively high. Because of this fact, the private-brand chains, it is said, follow a policy of cutting the prices on standard brands of merchandise to a point where they yield little or no profit to themselves or their independent competitors, making up this difference on the sale of the higher-profit private-brand goods to which they endeavor to switch their customers so far as practicable. Some assert that private-brand merchandise is priced higher than standard-brand merchandise while others claim the opposite. Conflicting claims are also made as to quality and as to the costs of distribution. It is contended in some quarters that chain-store private brands are increasing. On the other hand, others contend that there is a marked tendency for many chains to return to standard-brand merchandise.

This report is primarily based on detailed information obtained from returns to both the original and supplementary chain-store schedules, sent out by the commission in 1929 and 1931, respectively. Additional information was obtained by field agents from chain-store executives and special reports on private brands were procured also from a limited number of chains.

This report shows the extent and importance of private brands in different kinds of chains and the policies and practices which are used in merchandising them, including the pricing and mark-up polices on private brands. In the last connection, there is presented an analysis of the actual mark-ups and prices on private-label and competing standard-brand merchandise.

The use of private brands is not peculiar to chain stores. For many years, wholesalers, and in some lines retailers, have considered private brands to be an advantage. They have been widely used, for example, by large independent department stores.

Section 2. Definition of private brands.

The chain-store schedules did not contain any definition or explanation of the term "private brand." The majority of the chains which furnished information apparently reported as private brands all merchandise identified by their own labels. There are certain notable exceptions, such as the F. W. Woolworth Co. This company does not consider that the trade-mark "W" within a diamond, which is used as a distinguishing mark on a large number of commodities, is a private brand. A second chain, S. H. Kress & Co., limits the definition of private brands "to those brands which have actually been registered or copyrighted by us" and reported accordingly.[1] A third chain, Sears, Roebuck & Co., stated that its figures for private brand sales included only sales of "registered trade-marked brands"; brands which were used simply as a means of identifying articles were not included.

For the purposes of this report, a chain store private brand of merchandise is defined as a commodity sold by the chain only through its own stores under its own distinctive mark of identification. Since some few companies, as indicated above, have reported on private brands on the basis of a narrower definition, it is obvious that the private brand sales in this report are lower and the other data somewhat less comprehensive than would be the case had the broader definition been used.

Section 3. Reasons reported for the development and use of private brands.[2]

Better values for consumer.—A leading variety chain reported in March, 1932:

> Our principal motive and reason for the development of private brand merchandise was to give customers more for their money. (McCrory.)

Substantially identical with this report is that of one of the largest dry goods and apparel chains which gives as the reason for the development of its numerous lines of private brand merchandise—

> the desire and ability to give our customers better values for their money. (J. C. Penney.)

Based upon the emphasis placed upon this factor as well as the number of times it is reported, better values for consumers may be characterized as one of the leading, if not the most important, single motive for the ownership of private brands in the opinion of the chain-store companies. Though many answers are of the same general tenor and purport, there are considerable variations in the extent of quality superiority or consumer price saving claimed for the private brand by different chains. The strongest assertion of private brand superiority in both these respects is made by an eastern grocery chain of several hundred stores—

> Our principal motive for the development of our private brand merchandise is to supply our customers with merchandise of higher quality and at lower prices than similar nationally advertised merchandise. (D. Pender.)

Other chains are somewhat more moderate in their assertions. In a large grocery and meat chain also operating in the East:

---

[1]According to the company, the Kress name is often placed on merchandise simply to indicate that the quality has been approved and when so used it does not constitute a private brand. In explaining the chain's position on this point, the following example was given: "We have had steel knives etched 'Kress' on the blade. In this case we have approved the item, but the same item may be supplied to other chains and stamped or etched for them. Therefore, we hardly think such instances constitute what you really have in mind as 'private brands'."

[2] With very few exceptions the discussion in this section is based upon reports received in the spring of 1932. In a few of the quotations taken from these reports minor grammatical changes have been made which in no way affect the meaning.

Private brands are only considered by our company when we can offer a substantially greater value to the consumer in quality, price, or both. (First National.)

Another grocery and meat chain, one of the largest, uses private brands:

To deliver to the ultimate consumer merchandise of equal or better quality at a lower price. (Kroger.)

The report of one of the large grocery chains is that—

The principal motives and reasons for our development of the very few private brands of merchandise we carry was to supply the public with merchandise of as good, if not better, quality than the standard brands, at a lower price. (National Grocery.)

According to a small drug chain:

Having a private brand makes it possible to give the customer larger quantity of highest quality merchandise usually at a saving. (Schlegel.)

And an eastern grocery and meat chain, with between 500 and 1,000 stores, states that one of its purposes is—

To give the public merchandise of a high quality, reasonably priced. (Bohack.)

A somewhat more elaborate statement than any of the foregoing is that of a department-store chain with only a few stores but a huge sales volume:

Finally, if a retailer is to realize his true function as a community purchasing agent, he can not become a mere vending machine for nationally advertised merchandise. He must serve his public by giving equivalent or better values at lower prices to the consumer. The private brand is an effective means of accomplishing this purpose. (Macy.)

It should not be inferred, however, that this tenderness for the interest of consumers which is manifested in these statements of the chains proceeds from purely altruistic sentiments, nor would it be fair to the chains to say that they necessarily either expect or intend anyone to believe that it does. On the contrary, the reports of several chains make it clear that their regard for the interests of consumers is neither altruistic nor philanthropic. It is instead part and parcel of a more or less definite theory of merchandising, excellently summarized in the following report of one of the three largest grocery and meat chains with extensive lines of private brand merchandise:

The development of private brands is not an end with us, but merely a means adopted where such means were necessary to achieve the end. Our function as retailers, as we see it, is to give the public what it wants at the lowest practicable cost. That is the end that we have in mind, not for purely altruistic reasons, but, frankly, as an end which our intelligence tells us will in the long run be to our own best interests as well as the public's. (A. & P.)

Lower purchase cost.—Obviously lower consumer prices are dependent either upon lower buying prices, lower costs of distribution including net profit, or both. Private-label merchandise, it is asserted, can frequently be bought cheaper, a statement illustrated by the following quotation from the report of one of the four or five largest grocery and meat chains which incidentally claims not to be pushing its private-brand business—

For the past three years we have restricted our private-brand merchandise, rather than developed it. Our original motive in developing private brands was to secure as good or better a grade of merchandise at less cost than nationally advertised brands. (Safeway.)

Still another grocery and meat chain mentions as its fourth reason for the development of private brands:

To enable us to offer the consumer merchandise, such as bread and coffee, at lower prices than would be possible if we did not manufacture them ourselves. (Kroger.)

According to a company operating a number of shoe chains—

We are in a much more favorable position in negotiating for purchases, through the elimination of factory selling expense and standard brand advertising expense.

The same point of view is expressed by a leading women's ready-to-wear chain in referring to its private brand of hosiery:

Although the standard once adopted for a style is not varied, we frequently find manufacturers willing to make some standard hose at a lesser price because of some pressing need on their part for cash or business, which generally is not the case when you are buying standard or national brand hose. (Mangel's.)

"Again, ofttimes," says a 35-store furniture chain, "there is an advantage in buying private brands over standard brands." (Leath & Co.)

Lower cost of distribution.—The other angle of lower consumer prices is lower distribution costs. According to the largest grocery and meat chain—

We have found that upon numerous items the cost of distributing the merchandise to the consumer was too high, and we have endeavored to develop methods to reduce this cost. In many types of merchandise which we handle, the consuming public has gradually reached the point where it prefers to order or buy on the basis of brands or trade names. This has probably been accentuated by large expenditures in the advertising of trade names; it is probably due also to the greater ease to the customer in making his wants known and being sure of getting the same thing every time he uses that certain trade name or brand. When he wants a certain article, he knows that if he calls for it by that name he will get it; conversely, if he calls for an article under that brand he knows what he will get. (A. & P.)

Another chain in the same field with over 1,000 stores says:

Because of excessive advertising expenditures placed upon some manufacturers' merchandise we are able to offer the same grade and quality of merchandise to the consumer at a much greater advantage to them than the sale of excessively advertised merchandise permits us doing. (National Tea.)

To a similar effect are the statements of a well-known variety chain and one of the largest department store chains:

We believe our customers, in most instances, do not wish to pay for the cost of advertising standard brands which is reflected in a higher cost and retail on these articles, and our experience bears this out. (Grant.)

Private-brand merchandise of equal quality can generally be distributed at a lower cost than national merchandise due to the heavy overhead and selling cost incident to the distribution of nationally advertised brands. (Montgomery Ward.)

Another reason for the handling of private brands which is intimately connected with the question of lower consumer prices appears in the following statement of a large variety chain:

During times of business readjustment such as 1930 and 1931 we find it easier to adjust commodity prices to consumer demand through our private brands. (Grant.)

Of similar purport is the report of a department store chain with a few units but large sales volume:

In the present depression wholesale costs of many nationally advertised brands have been very slow to reflect lower production costs. When commodity trends are upward, we find many national brands are either advanced directly or the package content is changed to meet the situation. In short, this system tends to freeze wholesale costs and shuts out much healthy competition. (Macy.)

"Of late," states a grocery and meat chain of several hundred stores, "with radically lower markets on raw materials, nationally advertised goods have failed to show any appreciable declines in list prices, with the consequent result that many items can be purchased under other labels at much lower prices." (Sanitary.)

Alleged high quality of private brands.—There are, however, certain aspects of quality which are stressed by the chains more or less independently of price. One of these is the intrinsic equality or superiority of the articles sold under their private brands in comparison with other brands, particularly nationally advertised goods. For example, in one of the large drug chains which, as it happens, is not only a strong advocate of private brands but also manufactures [3] them to a considerable extent—

* * * the principal motive and reason for the development of our own line of merchandise, which started about 20 years ago, was, and still is, to manufacture products of the highest quality that could be sold in our stores.

As a matter of fact we pay the head of our laboratory three times as much salary as one of the very large companies in the East which is one of the best known manufacturers of so-called nationally advertised lines. I think some of our stuff is actually better than some of these other people's and that we have better people producing it. That may be merely conceit on our part, but we think it is so.

Similarly, one of the largest grocery and meat chains reports that—

We have a "Country Club" brand for practically everything we have in the store and nationally advertised products such as peas, corn, asparagus, and so on. We do not do any packing ourselves. It is always a protection to have private brands comparable in quality with nationally advertised products.

We might purchase "Country Club" items from some manufacturer from whom we also buy a nationally advertised article. All are made under our own specifications, which are usually on a comparative basis with nationally advertised articles. We believe our "Country Club" items are just as good as anything you will find on anybody's shelves of the highest quality, and we advertise them and push them and believe in them. (Kroger.)

In another less important though large grocery and meat chain one of the chief executives compares certain of his private brands with packers' label goods:

The whole object of private brands is to get a better grade of product. Where a packer of canned goods uses standard or choice grades, a chain will use choice or fancy, keeping one step ahead. (Bohack.)

Control and standardization of quality.—Other aspects of quality which lead to the adoption of private brands are the ability of the chain (1) to control and standardize quality and (2) to improve quality. The first does not necessarily mean an intrinsically superior product and the second may or may not imply it.[4] One of the

[3] Cf. Report on Chain-Store Manufacturing.

[4] The fact that some chains carry not one but two or more grades of the same commodity under private labels is sufficient to indicate the accuracy of this statement. (See section 11.)

largest private brand grocery and meat chains says that the real purpose of private brands is to insure a definite quality year in and year out. Another large chain in the same business indicates that private brands are hard to establish, but that they have the advantage of quality and uniformity. In a large department store chain—

The matter of the few private brands in use has been confined very largely to items of wearing apparel. The principal motive for the use of these brands has been to maintain a standard of quality for that particular type of apparel inasmuch as the merchandise is usually purchased from different sources and the manufacturers had no brand or label of their own. In the case of men's shirts, a private brand was placed upon a shirt where we could maintain a standard of quality by insisting upon a fabric from a specific mill, finished at a certain finishing plant, and made by a shirt manufacturer in accordance with our own specifications. (Mercantile Stores.)

Another department store chain with more than 30 units made the following statement:

Our principal reason for developing private-brand merchandise was to assure our customers of products made according to our own specifications wherever possible. (Interstate Department Stores.)

A 13-store men's ready-to-wear chain (Strauss) uses private brands "to identify our standard of quality" and an 18-unit tobacco chain "to better control the quality of the brand manufactured since the material is selected by this company." (Seidenberg Co.)

While much of this is no doubt true, it is interesting to find that such points of view are not held by all chains. A small grocery chain reports as one of the disadvantages of private brands "danger in having one lot go bad, and thereby spoiling the reputation of our entire line with customers." One of the largest grocery and meat chains likewise reports as one of four disadvantages of private brands "difficulty in securing constant quality." (Safeway.)

Improvement of quality.—A 35-store furniture chain says that by having furniture "built to our own specifications we are in a position many times to embody qualities and selling features that are not found in standard brands." (Leath & Co.) Likewise in one of the largest of the department store chains, one of the reasons assigned for the development of its private brands "is the ability in this manner to develop our own standards and specifications for merchandise inasmuch as we are constantly striving to improve upon accepted standards." (Sears, Roebuck.)

Creation and promotion of good will.—One of the reasons for the development of private brands which is cited by a number of chains is the creation and promotion of good will. One of the principal organizations in the shoe field which operates more than one chain selling only private brands reports that—

As specialists, we believe our position in the merchandise field is greatly strengthened by selling practically all our merchandise under the same name as that of the store. We stand behind our merchandise ourselves * * *, we believe that in selling our merchandise under our own brands we have developed good will that is of considerably more value than would be our good will had we sold standard brands either wholly or in part.

Similarly, another large shoe chain says:

We retail our entire product through our own stores and do not handle any other make of shoes. We handle slippers, hosiery, and other shoe store accessories, of course.

Our idea in having our own private brand is simply to identify our product and build a name and good will on such a brand. (Sheppard & Myers.)

A 9-store men's ready-to-wear chain points out that—

Any advertising development or promotion by the retailer is a capitalization of his own product and not a promotion of a trade-mark owned by some one else. (Kibler.)

"Private brands help to promote our store name and good will," according to a 6-unit department store chain with a large sales volume. (Gimbel.)

And in an important grocery and meat chain one of the reasons for private brands is:

Public appreciation of the better value under our private brand and consequently increased good will for our company. (Bohack.)

A somewhat more detailed statement along the same line is made by a prominent drug chain:

Suppose that milk of magnesia tooth paste sells for 50 cents and that it costs you 31 cents after all discounts, and everybody has that for sale and most of them can buy it for that price. Now suppose you can sell an identical article which instead of costing you 31 cents you can make for 20 cents or less. Now if you price that item, say, at 33 cents, you are making a little higher ratio of profit and if the public becomes seized of the idea that it is a good tooth paste and is a good bargain to them it is not only a question of making that profit but it is a question also of making good friends. In other words, if one can save 17 cents on his tooth paste which he buys in our stores and takes it to his dentist who tells him that it is absolutely as good as he can buy anywhere we have made a friend, and that is, after all, the only basis on which business is done. (Walgreen.)

Exclusive product.—A large chain of women's ready-to-wear stores (King & Applebaum) reports that—

Our principal motive for the development of a private brand was to have a brand that was exclusive with us in selling style merchandise.

The statement of a 35-store furniture chain is to the same effect:

Please be advised that we have developed private-brand merchandise for the reason that it gives us an exclusive article to sell our customer. (Leath & Co.)

"We are the sole source of supply on our own branded items," according to a thirty-odd unit department store chain (Interstate), and a company operating a number of private brand shoe chains says:

In brief, as specialists we believe that our strength with the public lies in the good will established by our own brands which we control and which are not sold in any other stores or through agents or dealers.

None of these last four reports explains very clearly the importance of an exclusive product. The replies of other chains, however, reveal that at least four distinct factors play a more or less important part in this desire for exclusive brands. The first of these is the advertising value of the private brand, the second is repeat business, the third is control of price, and the fourth is increased profit. Inferentially, however, all four motives may be actuating chains reporting only one of them.

Advertising.—Only one chain directly relates the exclusiveness of the private brand to its advertising value. This company, however, one of the largest grocery and meat chains, gives as the second of its four reasons for selling private-brand merchandise, "to attract customers to our stores to obtain merchandise which can be purchased only at our stores." (Kroger.)

In the case of two additional chains which mention advertising as a reason for developing or an advantage of handling private brands, the relation of this advertising value to the exclusiveness of the private brand, though obvious, must be inferred. A grocery chain, with under 500 stores reports—

It has been our experience that private brands, if properly priced and if of good quality, give the company which sells them a certain drawing power in so far as customers are concerned which does not accrue from the handling of nationally advertised brands. (Pender.)

A grocery chain with between 500 and 1,000 stores which handles only its own private label brands of coffee, tea, spices, and a few condiments, gives as the sole reason for their development the succinct statement, "advertising purposes." (C. F. Smith.)

In the women's ready-to-wear field, a large chain reports that—

We have every reason to believe that the name "Lerner" stamped on a piece of merchandise has as much selling value as any standard-brand name that we know of in the market to-day. (Lerner.)

Rather closely related to the reported advertising advantages of private-brand merchandise is the development of repeat business.

Repeat business.—A small tobacco chain points out the connection between the exclusiveness of the private brand and repeat business in the following language:

Our concern has only 11 stores or stands and we have only one private brand of any importance, which is a stogie.

The principal motive for developing this brand is to have an item which can be purchased only at our stores. It keeps customers coming back to us, whereas other stogies we sell can be purchased at all cigar stores. (R. Russell.)

"Satisfied customers return to repurchase and in turn buy other merchandise on display," according to a medium sized variety chain. (F. & W. Grand-Silver.) After stating that the principal cause for the development of its few private brands is to supply the public with as good or better merchandise at a lower price than the standard brands (supra) one of the grocery chains, operating nearly 1,000 stores, observes that "this would be advantageous to the consumer and the advantage to us would be that in order to purchase merchandise at that quality and price the consumer had to come to our stores." (National Grocery.)

Another grocery chain with less than 100 stores gives as its third reason for private brands "development of repeat business such as will compel purchaser to come only to our stores to make the purchase" (Busy Bee), while in a tobacco chain with nearly 100 stores the "principal motive for the development of private-brand merchandise is to establish repeating business for all establishments." (Barkalow.)

Some of the replies received from chains indicate, of course, that such repeat business must be founded upon quality, price, or both. For example, a variety chain with nearly a hundred stores reports that—

We develop private-brand merchandise in order to build up price and quality values and create a steady clientele. In other words, we want to have our customers return to us for the same items over and over again. (F. & W. Grand-Silver.)

Similarly, after citing as the first reason for private brands the ability to give a larger quantity of highest quality merchandise usually at a saving (supra), a small drug chain adds:

> Secondly, having sold the merchandise to the customer he would of necessity be forced to return to our store to secure more. (Schlegel.)

In the following statement of a one hundred and sixty-odd unit grocery chain, moreover, it is indicated that this repeat business is limited to grades essentially superior to those of standard brands:

> Private brands, of grades superior to the standard, create a steady market among our discriminating retail trade. (Gristede.)

Control of price.—Since the private brand is the property of the chain, it is possible to control its price. This is not practicable in the case of many of the standard brands, particularly those that are nationally advertised.

"Nationally known brands are largely used as 'leaders,'" declares a well-known department-store chain operating only a few units but having a huge sales volume. (Macy.)

According to a small drug chain—

> In highly competitive markets it is very rarely that one can make profit covering overhead expense and investment return on a popularly advertised and merchandised product. (Reznor Drug.)

Similarly, an important variety chain stated to an agent of the commission that—

> Nationally advertised lines, taken as a whole, and it is particularly true on toilet lines, are not very profitable because certain stores, especially drug chains, have cut the retail prices radically, and we have to meet competition—that is, we are trying to find a way to meet it.

To the same effect, though in somewhat greater detail, are the replies of other chains. For example, among the reasons given by a 5-unit drug chain for the use of private brands is the fact "that preparations of this type because of their exclusiveness with our stores are price protected." (Reznor.)

More specifically, a well-known though moderately sized department store chain says:

> The fact that standard nationally advertised brands have so frequently become the subjects of predatory price cutting by those merchants who use them as "leaders," an advertising device, and thereby have destroyed the opportunities for legitimate profit on such items, has led many merchants to establish brands of their own. (Associated Dry Goods.)

Hence the private brand serves "to take us out of destructive competition," according to a 6-unit department store chain with a large sales volume (Gimbel) and "to get away from the cut-price methods so widely used by many concerns in merchandising nationally advertised goods," according to a large and well-known variety chain. (McCrory.) More specifically a department store chain with about 25 units reports:

> We have a few private brands in such lines as are highly competitive in order to control the item against ruthless competition. (National Department Stores.)

Increased profits.—Where the competition on standard-brand items is so severe that there is no profit or perhaps a loss in selling them, the private brand on which the price can be controlled affords a means of profit, according to some of the chains. As a 15-store grocery and meat chain puts it:

Our reason for labeling merchandise under our private brand is that we can control the sale of such items and thereby protect our gross profit against competition. One of the first items we put under our private brand was coffee and, as mentioned above, national advertised brands of coffee were being sold at a gross profit which was less than our cost of operating. Therefore, we took this step to protect our profit. (J. E. George Grocery Co.)

According to a grocery chain with over 160 stores, private brands—

being noncompetitive, yield a more reasonable profit than do many standard advertised lines generally used by the trade as low-priced leaders and features. (Gristede.)

One of the largest grocery and meat chains, and a fifty-odd store grocery chain report more briefly but to the same effect:

To insure a better profit than can be obtained through the sales of highly competitive brands. (First National.)

Our principal reason in developing our private-brand merchandise has been larger profits than on advertised merchandise. (Busy Bee.)

Another grocery and meat chain, even larger than the one just mentioned, gave a somewhat more detailed explanation of this subject:

Our per cent of profit on our private brands is much better than on the nationally advertised brands for the reason that you do not encounter any competition. For instance, take the Del Monte brands. The Kroger Co. will have a sale on Del Monte goods this week and A. & P. will have a sale on them the following week and you are almost forced to keep your price down so you have reduced your mark-up for two weeks instead of only one week that you had planned. When you reduce private label merchandise you can immediately raise the price as soon as the sale is completed. For that reason your private label mark-up is much higher than it is on nationally advertised products. (Kroger.)

According to a variety chain with not far from 100 stores:

A great amount of money is spent on advertising of standard-brand products which of necessity forces us, the chain store, to pay more for the product and in turn work on a smaller mark-up as these items invariably have standard selling prices. (F. & W. Grand-Silver.)

Moreover, as a department store chain with a large sales volume adds:

Once a national brand is firmly established, the retailer's original profit margins are frequently reduced. The manufacturer often feels that his advertising expense warrants the raising of wholesale costs. The retailer often finds he must carry the article although the profit margin is less. (Macy.)

Restrictive price policies of manufacturers.—As noted in the preceding subsections, numerous chains claim that their development of private brands is the result either in whole or in part of the price cutting on standard brand or nationally advertised articles to a point where there is little or no profit obtainable. In view of these reports, it is particularly interesting to note that there are other chains which claim that one of the reasons for private brand development is because manufacturers will not permit the cutting of prices. For example, referring to its reasons for the development of private brands, one of the largest of the department store chains says:

The principal reason on our part has been to avoid conflict with established sales policies of manufacturers distributing goods under their own standard brand. * * *

If goods of standard manufacture were sold by us under the manufacturer's trade name at as great reduction in selling price, as our manner of doing business would justify, it would be difficult for him to maintain his outside distribution through other channels without considerable friction. Therefore, we avoid this issue by developing equal or similar products under our own name.

An important women's ready-to-wear chain furnishes a report to the same effect:

"National brand" hosè manufacturers restricted us from selling at free prices because of contracts with other retailers throughout the United States. A private brand enabled us to sell at any price policy or competition dictated.

More than one source of supply.—A large department store chain say that—

A firm engaged in the nation-wide distribution of all kinds of merchandise as we are (except groceries), would find it very difficult to confine its operations in any important line of merchandise to a given manufacturer's brand. (Sears-Roebuck.)

This sentiment is echoed by a variety chain with a few hundred stores:

On some lines of merchandise our quantity requirements may be such that nationally advertised brand manufacturers can not always be expected to supply us, so we have several sources for those lines, one or more of which may be standard-brand manufacturers. (Grant.)

Referring to its private brand of hosiery, a large women's ready-to-wear chain reports:

Although concentration on one national brand hose would apparently give the same advantages, we found no single manufacturer who would sign a contract guaranteeing uninterrupted delivery. By concentrating on our own private brand, once the standards for each particular style hose are set, we can always find any number of hosiery manufacturers that will make according to specifications and put our own brand name thereon. Our hose is not made in our mills. It is made for us by different hose manufacturers. (Mangel's.)

Similarly, one of the largest grocery and meat chains gives as one of its reasons for the development and handling of private brands, "to simplify the problem with which we are confronted when individual packers can not furnish sufficient quantity of one brand." (Kroger.)

Assumption of responsibility by chain.—In the case of private brands, according to a company operating private brand shoe chains—

There is never any question of dodging responsibility for defective goods nor is there any occasion for sharing the credit for quality with the manufacturer.

This may be regarded either as an advantage or a disadvantage depending upon the point of view. A large women's ready-to-wear chain reports—

Whenever a weakness is found in our hose in any section of the country, it is quickly rectified and improved in the following orders placed for the entire chain, and the entire country gets the immediate advantage in that we carry only a quick turn-over inventory as compared to a plan of having to wait for a national brand or standard manufacturer to adjust the weakness for his total output for the entire country. (Mangel's.)

Guaranty of satisfaction.—A large women's ready-to-wear chain reports that—

We insisted on selling hosiery with an absolute guaranty of satisfaction which manufacturers would not undertake. With our own private brand we have sold and are selling our hosiery with an unlimited guaranty of satisfaction. (Mangel's.)

Flexibility in changing line.—An important shoe chain points out that the private brand renders it easier for a chain to change its line of hosiery:

It sometimes becomes very necessary to change our line and, when it is built up on some one else's brand, it is frequently quite difficult to do; but if it is under your own brand, it is not so difficult, as you can get a similar hose from other people. (Sheppard & Myers.)

Similar considerations apparently are responsible for the following statement of a leading department store chain:

The motives and reasons for developing private-brand merchandise are simple. The development of national brands—in a certain sense—tie you up with the concerns producing those particular items, whereas the development of private brands enables you to promote and protect your own product in a way that is not possible with national names. (Montgomery Ward.)

Instruction value.—A department store chain asserts that private brands possess a certain teaching or instruction value—

In a trade-named dress, for instance, the specifications as to workmanship and material are definite and are taught not only to the departmental executives and general executives but to sales people. Many of these employees take an active interest and make suggestions and join in the discussions before the design is decided upon, and when the goods arrive, check the material and workmanship, the methods of advertising, etc. The care with which all this is supervised has a great teaching value and results in the formation of good habits that are of great benefit in handling all of our problems. (Associated Dry Goods.)

Identification of a good value.—In an eastern grocery and meat chain with a few hundred stores—

The original reason for having any private brand of merchandise was to identify what would otherwise be sold without labels. * * * Identification of a good value is our principal reason for putting a brand upon our merchandise which can readily be identified. (Sanitary.)

Selling argument.—A large millinery chain says that its reason for the development and handling of private brands is—

Essentially to give our sales people a talking point about our merchandise being different from that of our competitors, and also as a matter of identification. (International Millinery.)

Section 4. Disadvantages of private brands.

No disadvantages.—Several chains see no particular disadvantages in the handling of private brand merchandise. A department store chain with over 30 stores, for example, states that "We have not experienced any disadvantages in the selling of our private brands as compared with standard brands." (Interstate.) One of the large variety chains says that "there are no disadvantages in our handling private brands as compared with standard brands." (Kress.) These statements are reiterated with but slight variation by another variety chain, not as large but nearly as well known (McCrory), a tobacco chain with 6 stores (Perkins), a women's ready-to-wear chain (King & Applebaum) with over 70, and a 7-store drug chain (Schlegel). In most cases, however, the attitude of the reporting chains is much more critical of private brands than would be inferred from the preceding statements.

Frequent indifference to private brands.—There are a considerable number of chains owning private brands which exhibit a lukewarm if not indifferent attitude toward them. This to some extent is no doubt due to the character of the business, most of these chains being in the variety and ready-to-wear fields where perhaps the competition of standard brand or nationally advertised articles is not so keenly felt as in more staple lines. Thus, one of the three or four largest variety chains reports—

The majority of items offered for sale by this company do not lend themselves to branding. Such brands as we have are those which will carry a trade name for the purpose of distinction and to assist trade in easy identification. (Kresge.)

This chain according to its own statement "does not go in for private brands to any extent" and an even larger chain in this line of business also says that "we have never been overanxious to develop private-brand merchandise." (Woolworth.) A third large chain in the same field closes its report with this statement:

In conclusion, please be advised that this whole question is one that does not concern us to as great a degree as compared with chain grocery stores. (Newberry.)

Similarly, an indifferent attitude is indicated by two women's ready-to-wear chains, each operating between 100 and 150 stores:

We have one private brand—silk hosiery * * *. It is made specifically for us, according to our own standards and requirements. None of our other items in the ready-to-wear department are sold under a private-brand name. (Mangel's.)

However, the question of private brands has never been a factor in our type of business, since in the women's apparel line, style and variety play an important part and we have never confined ourselves to any one particular source for the purchase of our merchandise. (Lerner.)

Even in more staple lines of merchandise, there are chains which apparently have a similar point of view. One of the largest chains in the grocery and meat business, for example, makes the following statement:

We doubt if there are any advantages in private brand merchandise as compared with standard brands provided the manufacturer of the standard branded article keeps his prices reasonably close to the price at which similar merchandise can be secured on the open market. (Safeway.)

A small grocery chain expresses the same opinion in the statement that "in all cases where standard brands are priced low enough there is no incentive for the introduction of private brands." (Busy Bee.)

"There are no advantages in private brands," and they "do not mean anything at the present time," according to one of the largest tobacco chains. (Schulte.) And a 10-store self-service grocery and meat chain says:

We do not cater to private brands. We have our private brand of coffee. We don't expect to add private labels. We prefer national advertised lines. (King's Self-Service.)

It is stated by a 28-unit drug chain that—

Private brands in our stores are practically negligible. What few we have adopted was for the reason that we had a potential market for same. (Eckerd's.)

Customer sales resistance.—Aside from those chains which see no disadvantages in private brands, most of the chains appear to be quite frank in admitting and discussing the disadvantages of private brands. An example is a California hardware chain which reports succinctly that the "public generally regards the private brands as inferior and showing a better profit to the distributor." (Imperial.) Frankness in their reports on the disadvantages of private brands seems to be particularly characteristic of a number of those who explain in detail the advantages of such brands and their reasons for handling them.

A number of chains readily concede that there is a considerable sales resistance involved in the handling of private brands. One of the three or four largest grocery and meat chains flatly states that "we consider customer resistance to little known brands as compared with customer acceptance of nationally advertised brands as the greatest disadvantage in handling private brands." (Safeway.) Likewise, one of the largest of the department store chains reports that—

> The only disadvantage in handling private brands as compared with nationally advertised brands is that it is more difficult to build up customer acceptance since, undoubtedly, the weight of advertising prejudices a large percentage of consumers in favor of the national brand merchandise. (Montgomery Ward.)

According to one of the leading variety chains—

> Standard brands usually meet with a smaller amount of sales resistence, chiefly because of advertising effort and outlay. (Kresge.)

And a drug chain with between 25 and 30 stores expresses a similar opinion:

> It has been our policy in the past to feature almost entirely the "standard brands," as due to their advertising and other sales help, we find much less sales resistance in our stores. (Eckerd's.)

Even those chains which are inclined to see no disadvantages in private brands sometimes recognize the limitation under discussion. Thus, a grocery and meat chain with something over a thousand stores and an extensive line of private brands says "there is no real disadvantage in handling private brand merchandise once it is properly introduced" (National Tea Co.) and a small department store chain with many private brand articles and a large sales volume reports that—

> There is no disadvantage when the retail distributor who introduces the private brand has established his good will sufficiently to gain rapidly consumer support for his brand. (Macy.)

Irritation of customers.—Closely connected with customer sales resistance is the "danger in having customers believe that we are forcing merchandise on them that they do not want." (Busy Bee.) That this is not peculiar to the smaller chain, however, is clearly indicated by the report of a grocery and meat chain of several thousand stores which has for many years sold a wide variety of products under private brands:

> Also, some of the owners of the so-called widely advertised standard brands have created the impression among some customers that private brands can not be equal in quality to advertised brands; and sometimes the attempt to sell a private brand may cause a customer to recall the warnings of advertisers and to fear that some inferior product is being pushed upon him. For this reason, also, it is our policy not to force the sale of our private brands, but to give the customer whatever brand he asks for. (A. & P.)

To the same effect is a report of a well-known department store chain:

Also without organized training, the sales persons may not be sufficiently well-informed about the merchandise and can not courteously give reasons for its excellence. The customers in such case may become irritated by an attempt to switch them from a brand they have read about to even a better brand they have not heard about. (Associated Dry Goods.)

Selling effort.—It is presumably because of this customer sales resistance that a grocery and meat chain reports that the "private brand requires more selling effort." (Bohack.) Moreover, one of the largest variety chains (Grant) reports, "it takes time to familiarize customers with them." A grocery chain with nearly 1,000 stores reports that—

Where the standard brands are so thoroughly advertised in newspapers, radio, and the like, there is sometimes a disadvantage in offering private brands because it takes so much of the clerk's time to explain the advantage to the consumer. (National Grocery.)

A small tobacco chain (Russell) asserts that "to keep a private brand selling takes continuous effort on the part of salesmen" and an eighty-odd store chain also in the tobacco business adds that they "require constant and consistent selling to make the volume of business worth while." (Barkalow.) A grocery and meat chain with several thousand units says that—

The selling effort is necessarily greater than on nationally advertised brands, in newer territories where (the company's) quality and service have not been fully established in consumers' minds. (Kroger.)

In contrast with these conditions in the handling of private brands, a large variety chain points out that "standard brand items generally sell themselves." (F. & W. Grand-Silver.) Another and one of the largest in the same field reports that—

We have concentrated on nationally advertised items as a demand is created through national advertising, and it is much easier to sell merchandise of that character than it is to exploit new, unknown private brands. (Woolworth.)

Still another chain which is intermediate between these two in size reports that "standard brands usually meet with a smaller amount of sales resistance, chiefly because of the advertising effort and outlay." (Kresge.) A very large women's ready-to-wear chain adds—

A cardinal principle of chain-store operation is to work for quick turnover—that involves carrying merchandise, preferably national brand or standard articles, where possible because of national reputation and frequent demand. (Mangel's.)

In this connection, a well-known department store chain makes the following interesting point:

If a store is not large enough to have a good training method, the salespeople will get a greater knowledge of a well-advertised standard brand than is taught them about similar merchandise of better quality, and therefore be able to sell the standard brand with greater facility. (Associated Dry Goods.)

Cost of development and promotion.—A third disadvantage frequently mentioned is the cost of the development and promotion work. As a large women's ready-to-wear chain puts it—

A private brand has to be put over by the strength of your own reputation and at your own cost of advertising. (Mangel's.)

Similarly, a grocery chain with over 400 stores reports that—

> The main disadvantage in handling private brands as compared with standard brands is the advertising expense which a company incurs in placing its private brands on a competitive basis with standard brands which appeal to the consumer both from the standpoint of quality and price. (Pender.)

A large variety chain cites as a disadvantage "the amount of effort and expense to properly introduce a private brand as against a highly advertised standard brand." (Newberry.) Another large chain in the same business refers to the fact that "We must do our own advertising, if any, and furnish our own display material, if any, whereas standard-brand companies usually advertise extensively and supply display material gratis." (F. & W. Grand-Silver.) And a small shoe chain complains that—

> In our opinion, an independent dealer, or chain, handling its own private brands loses the benefit of national advertising by the maufacturer. (Hurley.)

Although the foregoing may be regarded as the most important disadvantages of private brands judged from the point of view of the frequency with which they were mentioned, a considerable number of other disadvantages are mentioned by one or more chains.

Larger inventories.—Another reported disadvantage in private brands is that they may result in the chain carrying larger stocks. One of the larger department store chains asserts that—

> The disadvantages of handling private brand lines lie largely in the fact that a larger stock must be on hand at all times as we, in a sense, are our own resource for such type of merchandise. (National Department Stores.)

Another statement contrasting private with standard brands on this point is to the same effect:

> Standard brand items generally sell themselves and invariably prevent accumulation, whereas, private brand merchandise, in view of the larger mark-up and profit invites overstocking by the manager of a store. (F. & W. Grand-Silver.)

A grocery and meat chain with several hundred stores also states that private brands "cause an increase to store inventory" (Bohack), while one of the two or three largest chains in this line enumerated "the necessity for carrying larger inventories" as one of three disadvantages of private brands. (Safeway.) Larger inventories also arise through duplication, according to a small grocery chain which points out that private brands give rise to the "necessity for carrying additional stocks of merchandise as in all instances when we carry private brands, we also carry the standard brand." (Busy Bee.)

The chains are not unanimous regarding the effect of private brands on inventories. A number of the chains claim a reduction in inventories as the result of the development of private brands. According to a small department store chain with a large volume of business—

> The undue multiplication of national brands places a heavy burden upon distribution. The retailer is compelled by persistent national advertising to stock dozens of competing brands of a similar type although his business may be done on only a few items. (Macy.)

A grocery and meat chain with between 50 and 100 stores says that—

The only reason we handle private brands is on account of so many different brands of the same kind of merchandise on the market, therefore, felt it necessary in some cases to use a private brand, in order to cut down on so many different brands of the same kind of merchandise. (Mohican.)

In a large women's ready-to-wear chain operating in 34 States, it was found that—

Each State had a different hosiery favorite. Stocking several brands would involve carrying excessive inventories. Concentration on one private brand of a quality would enable us to operate with minimum inventories. (Mangel's.)

Responsibility for adjustments.—A further disadvantage of private brands, reported by a few chains, is that the chain may be held responsible for any adjustments which may be claimed by purchasers. As a small shoe chain expresses it "complaints and adjustments are not so readily referred to manufacturer as customer recognizes retailer only." (Hurley.)

A variety chain also reports that—

There is always redress for inferior merchandise to the manufacturer of a standard product whereas, if our own private brand merchandise is not as specified in sales, we must ourselves make good. (F. & W. Grand-Silver.)

A slightly different angle of this type of disadvantage is mentioned by a small grocery chain which says that on private brands there is "no protection in case of price decline such as we receive when we purchase standard brands." (Busy Bee.)

Miscellaneous.—Another disadvantage of private brands, at least in certain kinds of chains, may be inferred from the following statement of a large women's ready-to-wear chain—

Manufacturers of standard brands have a large organization focusing their attention on one commodity and naturally have many advantages in getting advance information on future colors, weaves, etc. (Mangel's.)

Another disadvantage mentioned by a small grocery chain was, "no real 'pull' power in the sale of private brands as there is no ready comparison between the prices charged by us and by our competitors." (Busy Bee.)

Section 5. Quality of chain private brands of canned vegetables and fruits.

At the time of the preparation of this report, adequate information was not available on the comparative quality of standard brand and chain-store private label merchandise. Neither is it likely that it will be possible to make such a study, both because of the amount of expense involved and the difficulties of procuring strictly comparable merchandise outside of a very limited number of lines, such as some groceries and drugs.

In connection, however, with the study of prices and margins in Des Moines, Memphis, and Detroit, the commission purchased samples of certain brands of canned fruits and canned vegetables on which costs and retail selling prices had been obtained by its agents. The goods thus purchased amounted to some 511 brand items, the brands in question being owned by manufacturers, wholesalers, chain stores, and cooperative chains.

To make the comparisons required by the price and margin study in question it was necessary that the grades of these commodities should be accurately determined and for this purpose the samples procured were submitted to the warehouse division of the Department of Agriculture for grading. The results of these tests, however, were interesting in and of themselves and the details of the analysis, together with the methods of selecting the commodities and the representativeness of the results, are scheduled for subsequent presentation. As this study involves the private brands of chain stores, however, a comparative summary of the figures is presented in this report.

Canned vegetables.—The following table shows the proportions of cans of each type of distributor falling in each grade together with the combined percentages for the two higher and the two lower grades, respectively:

TABLE 1.—*Percentage distribution, by types of brand owners, of grades of canned vegetables*

Grades of canned vegetables (except spinach and pumpkin)	Manufacturers			Distributors			All groups combined
	National advertisers	Other	Total	Wholesalers	Chains	Cooperatives	
Fancy	16.2	13.5	14.5	4.6	14.6	11.5	12.2
Extra standard	44.1	24.0	32.0	49.2	43.7	57.7	39.6
Standard	33.8	49.0	43.0	44.6	33.4	30.8	40.8
Substandard	4.4	12.5	9.3	1.6	8.3		6.8
No grade	1.5	1.0	1.2				.6
Fancy and extra standard combined	60.3	37.5	46.5	53.8	58.3	69.2	51.8
Standard and substandard combined	38.2	61.5	52.3	46.2	41.7	30.8	47.6
All grades combined	100.0	100.0	100.0	100.0	100.0	100.0	100.0
Number of cans graded	68	104	172	65	48	26	311

From this table it appears that, as regards all vegetables except spinach and pumpkin, the chains are only slightly below nationally advertising manufacturers in the proportions of their cans grading "fancy," "extra standard," and "standard," respectively. They make a slightly better showing than nonnationally advertising manufacturers in the "fancy" grade, and show a materially higher proportion for "extra standard." Compared with wholesalers, the chains show a distinctly higher proportion in "fancy" and a somewhat lower proportion in "extra standard," but combining the two grades the chains show 58.3 per cent in contrast with 53.8 per cent for wholesalers. Chains lead cooperatives slightly in the proportions graded "fancy" (14.6 and 11.5 per cent, respectively) but for the "extra standard" grade the cooperatives show so high a ratio (57.7 per cent) as to become the leader in the combined proportions of "fancy" and "extra standard" (69.2 per cent, compared with 60.3 per cent for nationally advertising manufacturers, 58.3 per cent for chains, 53.8 per cent for wholesalers, and 37.5 per cent for other manufacturers).

Canned fruits.—Table 2 shows similar data for canned fruits.

TABLE 2.—*Percentage distribution, by types of brand owners, of grades of canned fruits*

Grades of canned fruits	Manufacturers			Distributors			All groups combined
	National advertisers	Other	Total	Wholesalers	Chains	Cooperatives	
Fancy	26.4	16.8	23.9	28.7	25.9	17.2	24.6
Choice	57.8	46.1	54.8	55.0	63.0	57.8	55.9
Standard	13.4	29.2	17.5	10.0	11.1	18.7	15.1
Seconds	.8	5.6	2.0	5.0		4.7	2.9
No grade	1.6	2.3	1.8	1.3		1.6	1.5
Fancy and choice combined	84.2	62.9	78.7	83.7	88.9	75.0	80.5
Standards and seconds combined	14.2	34.8	19.5	15.0	11.1	23.4	18.0
All grades combined	100.0	100.0	100.0	100.0	100.0	100.0	100.0
Number of cans graded	254	89	343	160	54	64	621

The proportion of chain-store brands of fruits grading "fancy" (25.9 per cent) was slightly higher than the average (24.6 per cent), although the chain proportions are below both nationally advertising manufacturers (26.4 per cent) and wholesalers (28.7 per cent). In the proportion of brands grading "choice" the chains substantially exceeded the figures shown by any other group. Their proportion of brands grading "choice" and "fancy" combined (88.9 per cent) was not only above the general average (80.5 per cent) but was also higher than that of the nationally advertising manufacturers (84.2 per cent), and appreciably higher than the proportions for wholesalers (83.7 per cent), cooperative chains (75 per cent) and other manufacturers (62.9 per cent). In canned fruits, none of the chain-store private brands graded "seconds."

Section 6. Extent of ownership of private brands.

The original chain store schedules were sent out by the commission in March, 1929, and the supplementary schedules in March, 1931. Although a few of the original schedules were filled out and returned prior to June 1, 1929, and after December 31, 1930, the greater part of them were received during the intervening period. Since no date was specified in the question on the ownership of private brands, the summary of answers received applies to this period.

The greater part of the supplementary schedules were returned between the middle of March and the last of June, 1931. Answers received to the private brand question in this schedule apply to this three and one-half months' period rather than to any specific date.

Table 3 summarizes the information on the ownership of private brands contained in both the original and supplementary schedules. One thousand six hundred and sixty chains replied to this question in the original schedule. They were operating a total of 65,624 stores on December 31, 1928 and their total volume of sales in that year was $5,051,591,700. Reports on private-brand ownership in the supplementary schedule were received from 1,247 chains. These companies operated a larger number of stores (67,593), however, and had a larger volume of sales ($5,262,940,600) than the 1,660 chains reporting on the original schedule.

TABLE 3.—*Extent of private-brand ownership by all reporting chains in 1929–30 and 1931*

	All reports	Reports of chains owning private brands		Reports of chains not owning private brands	
		Number	Per cent	Number	Per cent
Chains reporting in 1929–30	1,660	412	24.8	1,248	75.2
Stores operated on Dec. 31, 1928	65,624	50,451	76.9	15,173	23.1
Sales in 1928	$5,051,591,700	$3,808,669,800	75.4	$1,242,921,900	24.6
Average sales per store	$76,978	$75,492		$81,917	
Average stores per chain	40	122		12	
Chains reporting in 1931	1,247	351	28.1	896	71.9
Stores operated on Dec. 31, 1930	67,593	54,853	81.2	12,740	18.8
Sales in 1930	$5,262,940,600	$4,248,950,100	80.7	$1,013,990,500	19.3
Average sales per store	$77,862	$77,461		$79,591	
Average stores per chain	54	156		14	

Four hundred and twelve chains reported the ownership of private brands on the original schedule as contrasted to 351 on the supplementary. The smaller number of private-brand-owning chains reporting in 1931, however, operated a larger number of stores and had a larger total volume of sales than those answering the original schedule in 1929–30. Part of this difference in total sales volume was due to the larger number of stores operated and part to a higher average sales per store for chains answering the supplementary schedule.

Although only one-fourth of the 1,660 chains which furnished brand information on the original schedule owned private brands, this number operated 77 per cent of the stores included and transacted 75 per cent of the business. Twenty-eight per cent of the 1,247 chains reporting on the supplementary schedule owned private brands. They operated over 81 per cent of the stores included and they transacted nearly 81 per cent of the total business.

From these figures it is apparent that the difference between the average size of chains owning and not owning private brands is large, the former operating on the average more than ten times as many stores as the latter, in both 1929–30 and in 1931.

Section 7. Extent of ownership of private brands, by kind of chain.

Chains.—The proportion of chains in each of 26 kinds of business which reported the ownership of one or more private brands is shown in Table 4. At least one chain in each of 24 of the 26 kinds of business listed owned private brands both in 1929–30 and in 1931. None of the $5 limit variety chains which reported on the original schedule, owned private brands, and no such brands were reported by any of the unlimited price variety chains which returned the supplementary schedule.

TABLE 4.—*Distribution of chains owning private brands in 1929–30 and 1931, by kind of chain*

Kind of chain	Brand ownership, 1929–30			Brand ownership, 1931		
	Total chains reporting	Number owning private brands	Per cent owning private brands	Total chains reporting	Number owning private brands	Per cent owning private brands
Grocery	152	64	42.1	98	43	43.9
Grocery and meat	164	74	45.1	135	55	40.7
Meat	62	4	6.5	52	4	7.7
Confectionery	36	23	63.9	29	20	69.0
Drug	171	75	43.9	174	75	43.1
Tobacco	30	13	43.3	35	20	57.1
Variety ($1 limit)	84	8	9.5	69	13	18.8
Variety ($5 limit)	28	0	0	14	1	7.1
Variety (unlimited)	13	1	7.7	5	0	0
Men's ready-to-wear	101	24	23.8	66	15	22.7
Women's ready-to-wear	99	3	3.0	87	4	4.6
Men's and women's ready-to-wear	80	5	6.3	50	5	10.0
Men's furnishings	35	6	17.1	21	2	9.5
Women's accessories	16	9	56.3	15	7	46.7
Hats and caps	25	13	52.0	17	8	47.1
Millinery	36	2	5.6	24	2	8.3
Men's shoes	16	6	37.5	12	5	41.7
Women's shoes	33	8	24.2	28	11	39.3
Men's and women's shoes	164	31	18.9	112	27	24.1
Dry goods	29	2	6.9	15	2	13.3
Dry goods and apparel	124	12	9.7	77	10	13.0
Department store	30	13	43.3	20	9	45.0
General merchandise	47	7	14.9	30	2	6.7
Furniture	30	1	3.3	23	2	8.7
Musical instruments	17	7	41.2	14	6	42.9
Hardware	38	1	2.6	25	3	12.0
Total	1,660	412	24.8	1,247	351	28.1

In 18 of the kinds of business there was an increase in the proportion of chains owning private brands during the period intervening between the filling out of the two schedules, while a decline occurred in the remaining eight groups.

In both periods the proportion of brand-owning chains in 10 groups (grocery, grocery and meat, confectionery, drug, tobacco, women's accessories, hats and caps, men's shoes, department store, and musical instruments) was above the average for all chains reporting, and in nine of these the proportion of brand-owning chains was over 40 per cent in each period, men's shoes reporting only 37.5 per cent in the earlier period. Of these, the confectionery chains ranked first in both years, over 60 per cent of such companies reporting private brands.

Seven groups, namely, meat, variety $5 limit, variety unlimited, women's ready-to-wear, men's and women's ready-to-wear, millinery, and furniture chains, were low in the proportion of chains owning private brands, none of the proportions exceeding 10 per cent in either period. In both periods less than 5 per cent of the women's ready-to-wear chains reported private brands; no variety unlimited chains in the latter period, and no variety $5 limit chains in the first period reported that they owned private brands.

Stores.—As shown by Table 3, chains owning private brands operated a much larger number of stores per chain than those not having private brands. As shown in Tables 4 and 5, the proportion of stores operated by private-brand-owning chains was higher for most kinds of business than was the corresponding proportion of chains owning such brands. From one point of view, the number of stores operated by chains owning private brands is more significant in this study than the number of brand-owning chains for the reason that, subject to some qualification, the larger the number of stores operated by chains owning private brands, the more general will be the distribution of such brands.

The number of stores operated is also important from the standpoint of the effect of chain ownership of private brands on competition between brand-owning chains and independent retailers, on the one hand, and brand-owning chains and manufacturers of standard brands, on the other. A small chain, even if it should advertise its brands aggressively, could make serious inroads only on the business of a limited number of independent merchants selling merchandise of the same kind. Its competition could not seriously affect the business of merchants operating in territories where it has no stores. In like manner a small chain owning private brands can not make serious inroads on the business of manufacturers selling competing standard brands, since the chain's brands are at best accessible only to the limited number of consumers residing in the localities where it has stores.

On the other hand, where a nationally advertised private brand is readily accessible to large numbers of consumers in every part of the country, it approaches the status of a nationally advertised "standard" brand. Furthermore, through extensive advertising and careful salesmanship some large chains have built up a demand for a private brand in the area in which they operate equal to that enjoyed by manufacturers of competing nationally advertised standard brands in the same localities.

Some private-brand merchandise, presumably, is sold in practically every store operated by chains owning private brands.[5] If this assumption is correct, private brands were sold in about 97 per cent of the chain grocery and meat stores, in from 84 to 90 per cent of the chain grocery and chain department stores, in about 86 per cent of the confectionery stores, in from 63 to 81 per cent of the chain dry goods and apparel stores, and in from 62 to 75 per cent of the dollar-limit variety stores.

---

[5] There may be exceptional cases where, because of peculiarities in the local demand, a store sells none of the private brands of the chain to which it belongs and undoubtedly there are some stores in which not all of a chain's private branded articles are sold.

Table 5.—*Distribution of stores operated on December 31, 1928 and 1930, by chains owning private brands in 1929–30 and 1931, by kind of chain*

Kind of chain	Stores operated Dec. 31, 1928			Stores operated Dec. 31, 1930		
	By all chains reporting, 1929–30	By chains owning private brands, 1929–30	Per cent operated by brand-owning chains	By all chains reporting, 1931	By chains owning private brands, 1931	Per cent operated by brand owning chains
Grocery	10, 552	8, 840	83 8	10, 566	9, 608	90. 9
Grocery and meat	32, 631	31, 361	96. 1	33, 681	32, 882	97. 6
Meat	866	107	12. 4	666	149	22. 4
Confectionery	656	561	85. 5	513	441	86. 0
Drug	1, 926	1, 024	53. 2	2, 384	1, 283	53. 8
Tobacco	3, 553	1, 600	45. 0	3, 616	1, 156	32. 0
Variety ($1 limit)	4, 286	2, 660	62. 1	5, 266	3, 926	74. 6
Variety ($5 limit)	193	0	. 0	142	53	37. 3
Variety (unlimited)	78	6	7. 7	82	0	. 0
Men's ready-to-wear	676	264	39. 1	545	172	31. 6
Women's ready-to-wear	724	131	18. 1	872	98	11. 2
Men's and women's ready-to-wear	814	64	7. 9	639	48	7. 5
Men's furnishings	221	56	25. 3	160	21	13. 1
Women's accessories	182	108	59. 3	154	90	58. 4
Hats and caps	530	340	64. 2	475	126	26. 5
Millinery	683	19	2. 8	821	305	37. 1
Men's shoes	526	317	60. 3	434	305	70. 3
Women's shoes	437	212	48. 5	467	249	53. 3
Men's and women's shoes	2, 828	972	34. 4	2, 274	1, 112	48. 9
Dry goods	108	8	7. 4	87	49	56. 3
Dry goods and apparel	1, 743	1, 093	62. 7	2, 059	1, 669	81. 1
Department store	580	489	84. 3	1, 074	972	90. 5
General merchandise	332	126	38. 0	178	16	9. 0
Furniture	162	3	1. 9	163	38	23. 3
Musical instruments	138	81	58. 7	106	71	67. 0
Hardware	199	9	4. 5	169	14	8. 3
Total	65, 624	50, 451	76. 9	67, 593	54, 853	81. 2

The consumer's chances of getting private brands in a chain hardware store are small, since chains owning private brands operated less than 9 per cent of such stores. Private brands also were relatively unimportant in the following kinds of chains: Meat, women's ready-to-wear, furniture, unlimited price variety, and men's and women's ready-to-wear.

Sales.—The relative importance of brand-owning chains in the different commodity groups also can be indicated by comparing the sales volume of brand-owning and nonbrand-owning chains.

TABLE 6.—*Distribution of 1928 and 1930 total sales of chains owning private brands in 1929–30 and 1931, by kind of chain*

Kind of chain	1928			1930		
	Total sales of all chains reporting in 1929–30	Total sales of chains owning private brands in 1929–30	Per cent of private-brand chains' sales to sales of all chains reporting	Total sales of all chains reporting in 1931	Total sales of chains owning private brands in 1931	Per cent of private-brand chains' sales to sales of all chains reporting
Grocery	$445, 484, 000	$377, 945, 100	84. 8	$455, 275, 200	$405, 704, 100	89. 1
Grocery and meat	1, 819, 671, 800	1, 742, 773, 400	95. 8	2, 018, 242, 700	1, 966, 160, 400	97. 4
Meat	48, 944, 500	9, 009, 300	18. 4	46, 233, 500	12, 866, 400	27. 8
Confectionery	57, 056, 000	38, 012, 900	66. 6	46, 682, 900	43, 920, 000	94. 1
Drug	195, 922, 800	109, 040, 800	55. 7	227, 788, 300	132, 122, 100	58. 0
Tobacco	131, 319, 700	103, 302, 700	78. 7	120, 629, 500	68, 427, 800	56. 7
Variety ($1 limit)	723, 142, 300	489, 109, 700	67. 6	788, 406, 900	687, 292, 000	87. 2
Variety ($5 limit)	8, 001, 100	0	. 0	4, 552, 400	1, 428, 000	31. 4
Variety (unlimited)	3, 516, 700	213, 100	6. 1	3, 086, 700	0	. 0
Men's ready-to-wear	113, 317, 500	59, 820, 800	52. 8	73, 267, 300	29, 600, 800	40. 4
Women's ready-to-wear	96, 022, 300	13, 103, 400	13. 6	128, 450, 700	19, 963, 900	15. 5
Men's and women's ready-to-wear	62, 977, 200	7, 244, 500	11. 5	49, 162, 200	14, 091, 700	28. 7
Men's furnishings	10, 668, 400	3, 149, 000	29. 5	6, 547, 800	1, 360, 600	20. 8
Women's accessories	8, 262, 500	5, 193, 000	62. 9	6, 645, 400	4, 429, 500	66. 7
Hats and caps	22, 950, 200	15, 038, 800	65. 5	17, 907, 000	4, 835, 600	27. 0
Millinery	31, 513, 600	1, 426, 900	4. 5	31, 256, 500	18, 752, 500	60. 0
Men's shoes	23, 773, 700	12, 829, 300	54. 0	15, 157, 800	10, 541, 000	69. 5
Women's shoes	46, 372, 900	26, 037, 100	56. 1	43, 858, 900	22, 867, 400	52. 1
Men's and women's shoes	175, 361, 800	59, 117, 600	33. 7	128, 672, 600	71, 257, 700	55. 4
Dry goods	4, 380, 300	244, 500	5. 6	2, 603, 700	1, 452, 900	55. 8
Dry goods and apparel	243, 031, 000	188, 417, 700	77. 5	242, 870, 000	213, 935, 300	88. 1
Department store	675, 635, 900	525, 243, 800	77. 7	732, 027, 500	503, 997, 600	68. 8
General merchandise	24, 748, 600	8, 118, 100	32. 8	15, 521, 700	1, 636, 200	10. 5
Furniture	43, 922, 300	192, 000	. 4	37, 542, 800	3, 744, 700	10. 0
Musical instruments	21, 395, 200	12, 891, 700	60. 3	11, 326, 200	8, 177, 500	72. 2
Hardware	14, 199, 400	1, 194, 600	8. 4	9, 224, 400	384, 400	4. 2
Total	5, 051, 591, 700	3, 808, 669, 800	75. 4	5, 262, 940, 600	4, 248, 950, 100	80. 7

Percentage figures for the proportion of stores operated and for the proportion of total sales made by brand-owning chains are shown in Tables 5 and 6, respectively. As far as the totals for all groups combined are concerned, private-brand-owning chains are slightly more important when measured by the proportion of stores which they operated than when measured by their proportion of total sales. In 1929–30 such chains operated 76.9 per cent of the stores and had 75.4 per cent of the total sales; in 1931 they operated 81.2 per cent of the stores and had 80.7 per cent of the sales.

By kinds of business, however, it appears that in 12 out of the 26 groups private brands are of greater (or equal) importance in both years when measured by sales than when measured by the number of stores operated. This is true for meat, drug, tobacco, $1 limit variety, men's ready-to-wear, men's and women's ready-to-wear, men's furnishings, women's accessories, hats and caps, millinery, dry goods and apparel, and musical instruments. Only in five groups (grocery and meat, men's shoes, dry goods, department store, and furniture) do the proportions of stores outweigh the proportions of sales in both years. In $5 limit variety and unlimited price variety chains the proportions of stores exceed those of sales in one of the two periods, these kinds of chains showing no private-brand business in the other period.

In the remaining seven groups, the proportions of sales made by private-brand-owning chains exceed the proportions of stores operated by such chains either in 1929–30 or 1931 while the reverse is true in the other year. Considered, therefore, from the point of view of the different kinds of business involved, it seems fair to conclude that the importance of private brands is somewhat greater as measured by sales than as measured by stores.

By way of summarizing the foregoing discussion, there are brought together in the following table for each of the two years the proportions of chains owning private brands and the corresponding proportions of stores operated and total sales made by them.

TABLE 7.—*Proportions of total reporting chains, their stores and sales, represented by chains owning private brands in 1929–30 and 1931, by kind of chain*

Kind of chain	Percentages of brand-owning chains to totals reported in 1929–30			Percentages of brand-owning chains to totals reported in 1931		
	Chains, 1929–30	Stores, Dec. 31, 1928	Sales, 1928	Chains, 1931	Stores, Dec. 31, 1930	Sales, 1930
Grocery	42.1	83.8	84.8	43.9	90.9	89.1
Grocery and meat	45.1	96.1	95.8	40.7	97.6	97.4
Meat	6.5	12.4	18.4	7.7	22.4	27.8
Confectionery	63.9	85.5	66.6	69.0	86.0	94.1
Drug	43.9	53.2	55.7	43.1	53.8	58.0
Tobacco	43.3	45.0	78.7	57.1	32.0	56.7
Variety ($1 limit)	9.5	62.1	67.6	18.8	74.6	87.2
Variety ($5 limit)	0	0	0	7.1	37.3	31.4
Variety (unlimited)	7.7	7.7	6.1	0	0	0
Men's ready-to-wear	23.8	39.1	52.8	22.7	31.6	40.4
Women's ready-to-wear	3.0	18.1	13.6	4.6	11.2	15.5
Men's and women's ready-to-wear	6.3	7.9	11.5	10.0	7.5	28.7
Men's furnishings	17.1	25.3	29.5	9.5	13.1	20.8
Women's accessories	56.3	59.3	62.9	46.7	58.4	66.7
Hats and caps	52.0	64.2	65.5	47.1	26.5	27.0
Millinery	5.6	2.8	4.5	8.3	37.1	60.0
Men's shoes	37.5	60.3	54.0	41.7	70.3	69.5
Women's shoes	24.2	48.5	56.1	39.3	53.3	52.1
Men's and women's shoes	18.9	34.4	33.7	24.1	48.9	55.4
Dry goods	6.9	7.4	5.6	13.3	56.3	55.8
Dry goods and apparel	9.7	62.7	77.5	13.0	81.1	88.1
Department store	43.3	84.3	77.7	45.0	90.5	68.8
General merchandise	14.9	38.0	32.8	6.7	9.0	10.5
Furniture	3.3	1.9	.4	8.7	23.3	10.0
Musical instruments	41.2	58.7	60.3	42.9	67.0	72.2
Hardware	2.6	4.5	8.4	12.0	8.3	4.2
Total	24.8	76.9	75.4	28.1	81.2	80.7

Except in nine kinds of business (tobacco, $5 and unlimited variety, men's and women's ready-to-wear, hats and caps, millinery, dry goods, furniture, and hardware) the proportions of both sales made and stores operated by brand-owning chains in each year exceed the proportions of chains. In some cases, however, the margin of excess is not great. For example, in the case of drugs, the proportions of chains owning private brands are between 40 and 45 per cent, whereas the proportions of both stores and sales lie between 53 and 58 per cent. In most of the other kinds of business the differences between the chains on the one hand and stores and sales on the other are much greater. One of the most striking instances is in dry goods and apparel. Less than 10 per cent of the chains in 1929–30 owned private brands, but this group operated nearly 63 per cent of the stores and had over 77 per cent of the sales. In 1931, 13 per cent of the chains reporting in this group owned private brands with 81 per cent of the total stores and 88 per cent of the total sales. Another rather striking difference of a similar character appears in the $1 limit variety chains, and for either stores or sales separately in a number of the other groups.

Section 8. Extent of ownership of private brands, by size of chain.

All chains combined.—Data reported by chains on the ownership of private brands have been further analyzed by classifying all chains according to the number of stores which each reported in operation on December 31, 1928, December 31, 1930, or both. From the following table, it appears that although the smaller chains are more numerous in both periods, the proportion of brand-owning chains increases with the size of the chain. For example, only 14 to 19 per cent of the chains operating from two to five stores in the two periods owned private brands although the number of reporting chains in this size group represents over 50 per cent of the total number reporting. At the other extreme, approximately 90 per cent of the chains operating over 1,000 stores each owned private brands. With the exception of the 501 to 1,000 stores group, the increase is unusually regular.

TABLE 8.—*Distribution of chains owning private brands in 1929–30 and 1931, and of their stores on December 31, 1928 and 1930, by size of chain*

Number of stores per chain	Reports on brand ownership in 1929–30					
	Total chains reporting	Stores operated Dec. 31, 1928, by all chains reporting	Chains owning private brands		Stores operated Dec. 31, 1928, by chains owning private brands	
			Number	Per cent of total reporting	Number	Per cent of total reported
2 to 5	886	2,901	126	14.2	437	15.1
6 to 10	323	2,412	69	21.4	517	21.4
11 to 25	224	3,529	84	37.5	1,319	37.4
26 to 50	99	3,481	44	44.4	1,608	46.2
51 to 100	57	4,236	33	57.9	2,480	58.5
101 to 500	53	11,679	41	77.4	9,516	81.5
501 to 1,000	8	4,831	6	75.0	3,821	79.1
1,001 and over	10	32,555	9	90.0	30,753	94.5
Total	1,660	65,624	412	24.8	50,451	76.9

Number of stores per chain	Reports on brand ownership in 1931					
	Total chains reporting	Stores operated Dec. 31, 1930, by all chains reporting	Chains owning private brands		Stores operated Dec. 31, 1930, by chains owning private brands	
			Number	Per cent of total reporting	Number	Per cent of total reported
2 to 5	634	1,947	119	18.8	353	18.1
6 to 10	240	1,841	60	25.0	488	26.5
11 to 25	175	2,864	60	34.3	982	34.3
26 to 50	86	3,205	33	38.4	1,240	38.7
51 to 100	43	3,121	23	53.5	1,639	52.5
101 to 500	48	10,167	37	77.1	8,243	81.1
501 to 1,000	12	8,871	11	91.7	8,322	93.8
1,001 and over	9	35,577	8	88.9	33,586	94.4
Total	1,247	67,593	351	28.1	54,853	81.2

Among the three larger chains which are classified as not owning private brands is the Louis K. Liggett Co.[1] To one unacquainted with the situation it might appear that the Rexall and Liggett products sold in its stores should be termed private brands. All these products are manufactured by the United Drug Co., which owns Louis K. Liggett Co. The United Drug Co., however, sells its products not only to Louis K. Liggett Co., but also to several thousand independent retail druggists, most of the merchandise being sold on an exclusive agency basis. Incidentally, a similar situation exists in several candy chains which sell their branded candy at wholesale to independent merchants in addition to retailing it through their own stores. Such candy chains also were classified as nonprivate brand chains even though they manufactured all of the candy sold in their own stores. A number of shoe and other kinds of chains in the same situation were similarly classified.

By kind of chain.—Table 9 shows the proportion of chains, by kind and size of business, which reported the ownership of private brands in 1929–30.

TABLE 9.—*Proportions of chains owning private brands in 1929–30, by kind and size of chain*

Kind of chain	Number of stores per chain							
	2 to 5	6 to 10	11 to 25	26 to 50	51 to 100	101 to 500	501 to 1,000	1,001 and over
Grocery	21.7	19.2	29.2	66.7	63.6	83.3	100.0	100.0
Grocery and meat	21.7	29.0	60.0	57.1	69.2	93.3	100.0	100.0
Meat	0	0	22.2	28.6	0	0	-------	-------
Confectionery	30.8	66.7	90.0	75.0	100.0	100.0	-------	-------
Drug	37.0	52.4	71.4	66.7	100.0	100.0	0	-------
Tobacco	25.0	42.9	50.0	0	100.0	100.0	-------	50.0
Variety ($1 limit)	5.7	0	0	0	50.0	57.1	0	100.0
Variety ($5 limit)	0	0	0	0	-------	-------	-------	-------
Variety (unlimited)	0	25.0	0	-------	-------	-------	-------	-------
Men's ready-to-wear	10.3	33.3	50.0	75.0	-------	-------	-------	-------
Women's ready-to-wear	0	0	15.4	-------	50.0	-------	-------	-------
Men's and women's ready-to-wear	4.3	6.3	12.5	11.1	0	-------	-------	-------
Men's furnishings	8.3	60.0	0	100.0	-------	-------	-------	-------
Women's accessories	42.9	100.0	66.7	50.0	-------	-------	-------	-------
Hats and caps	33.3	100.0	80.0	66.7	33.3	100.0	-------	-------
Millinery	9.1	0	11.1	0	0	0	-------	-------
Men's shoes	25.0	33.3	0	50.0	50.0	100.0	-------	-------
Women's shoes	18.8	20.0	14.3	50.0	100.0	-------	-------	-------
Men's and women's shoes	11.6	9.7	36.7	50.0	42.9	25.0	-------	-------
Dry goods	3.8	50.0	0	-------	-------	-------	-------	-------
Dry goods and apparel	4.8	17.9	25.0	0	0	-------	-------	100.0
Department store	31.6	66.7	33.3	-------	-------	100.0	-------	-------
General merchandise	7.4	20.0	25.0	-------	100.0	-------	-------	-------
Furniture	4.0	0	0	0	-------	-------	-------	-------
Musical instruments	22.2	50.0	66.7	100.0	-------	-------	-------	-------
Hardware	0	16.7	0	0	-------	-------	-------	-------
Total	14.2	21.4	37.5	44.4	57.9	77.4	75.0	90.0

In the discussion of combined figures for all chains reporting, it was pointed out that the proportion of brand-owning chains, with one exception, varied directly with the size of the group. The statement is true without exception for four commodity groups (men's ready-to-wear, women's ready-to-wear, general merchandise, and musical instruments). It is true with certain exceptions, none of which are of much significance, for five other commodity groups, as

[1] The other 2 large chains are the Union News Co. and, for 1929–30, the S. S. Kresge Co.

follows: Grocery, grocery and meat, confectionery, drug, and women's shoes. The statement does not hold true for 16 of the remaining 17 groups. None of the variety ($5 limit) chains reported the ownership of private brands.

In general, a much larger proportion of the chains which operated 51 stores or more owned private brands than of those operating less than 51 stores. Seventeen figures are 100 per cent, thus accounting for nearly one-half of the 37 percentage figures in this table reported by chains operating more than 50 stores.

For chains of less than 51 stores, however, only 4 of the 99 percentage figures are 100 per cent.

In every kind of business practically all the 100 per cent figures occur in the four size groups of 51 stores and over. Exceptions appear in the case of men's furnishings, women's accessories, hats and caps, and musical instruments. It is also true that in general in the groups of less than 51 stores, the highest proportions reported are shown by either the 11 to 25 or the 26 to 50 store groups or both. Exceptions are found in six groups; unlimited-price variety, women's accessories, hats and caps, dry goods, department store, and hardware.

It should be remembered, however, that in a number of size-group classifications only one chain reported and where the one chain sold private brands, the resulting percentage, of course, was 100.[8]

The proportion of chains in each commodity group which reported the ownership of private brands in 1931 is shown in the following table:

TABLE 10.—*Proportions of chains owning private brands in 1931, by kind and size of chain*

Kind of chain	Number of stores per chain							
	2 to 5	6 to 10	11 to 25	26 to 50	51 to 100	101 to 500	501 to 1,000	1,001 and over
Grocery	16.0	17.6	20.0	54.5	87.5	86.7	100.0	100.0
Grocery and meat	23.1	24.1	50.0	50.0	100.0	87.5	100.0	100.0
Meat	0	0	9.1	40.0	50.0	-------	-------	-------
Confectionery	72.7	33.3	71.4	100.0	100.0	100.0	-------	-------
Drug	37.5	64.7	55.6	66.7	0	100.0	0	-------
Tobacco	62.5	60.0	55.6	100.0	0	0	100.0	0
Variety ($1 limit)	8.3	12.5	12.5	0	20.0	71.4	100.0	100.0
Variety ($5 limit)	0	0	0	0	100.0	-------	-------	-------
Variety (unlimited)	0	0	0	0	-------	-------	-------	-------
Men's ready-to-wear	5.6	33.3	66.7	0	0	-------	-------	-------
Women's ready-to-wear	3.6	0	9.1	0	50.0	0	-------	-------
Men's and women's ready-to-wear	4.8	18.8	16.7	0	0	-------	-------	-------
Men's furnishings	7.7	0	20.0	0	-------	-------	-------	-------
Women's accessories	20.0	75.0	40.0	100.0	-------	-------	-------	-------
Hats and caps	50.0	100.0	100.0	25.0	33.3	0	-------	-------
Millinery	0	0	0	0	100.0	33.3	-------	-------
Men's shoes	25.0	0	0	100.0	66.7	100.0	-------	-------
Women's shoes	35.7	40.0	33.3	25.0	100.0	100.0	-------	-------
Men's and women's shoes	16.3	25.9	28.6	28.6	25.0	75.0	-------	-------
Dry goods	0	-------	100.0	100.0	-------	-------	-------	-------
Dry goods and apparel	2.1	11.8	42.9	60.0	-------	-------	-------	100.0
Department store	30.0	75.0	0	50.0	-------	100.0	100.0	-------
General merchandise	0	28.6	0	-------	-------	-------	-------	-------
Furniture	6.7	0	0	100.0	-------	-------	-------	-------
Musical instruments	14.3	50.0	100.0	-------	-------	-------	-------	-------
Hardware	11.1	25.0	0	0	-------	-------	-------	-------
Total	18.8	25.0	34.3	38.4	53.5	77.1	91.7	88.9

[8] See Appendix Tables 1 and 2, showing the number of chains reporting the ownership of private brands, by kinds of business and by size groups, for 1929–30 and 1931.

The results shown in this table are substantially similar to those presented in Table 9. A few groups show a regular progression from the smallest to the largest size of chain (meat, dry goods and apparel, and musical instruments). The same statement holds true for six additional commodity groups with certain exceptions; grocery, grocery and meat, confectionery, millinery, men's shoes, and dry goods.

In only 8 of the 26 kinds of business do any of the size groups of under 51 stores show instances of 100 per cent of the reporting chains owning private brands, there being only 10 cases of 100 per cent in the 101 specific groups for these sizes of chains. In 18 kinds of business in which there are chains with over 50 stores reported, 12, or two-thirds of them, show 100 per cent of the reporting chains owning private brands, in at least some size group of over 50 stores. In fact 100 per cent ownership of private brands is reported for 19 of the 40 specific entries for chains of more than 50 stores. Attention is again directed to the fact that in many of the 100 per cent groups both for the larger and for the smaller chains, only one chain reported.

Appendix Tables 3 and 4 show the numbers and proportions of stores operated by chains which reported the ownership of private brands in 1929–30 and 1931, respectively.

Since the analysis of data presented in this section of the report is based entirely on the size of chains reporting, these two tables agree in general with the tables showing the proportions of different kinds of chains, by size groups, owning private brands.

Section 9. Relative importance of private-brand sales.

Amounts and proportions of total sales.—Information with regard to both the total sales of private brand merchandise and the percentage of total sales represented by such merchandise was requested from chains for the years 1919, 1922, 1925, and 1928. Later the chains were also requested to furnish for the years 1929 and 1930 the percentages of private-brand sales to total sales. The returns procured are by no means as comprehensive as could be desired though this is much less true of the recent than of the earlier years. This scarcity of data for the earlier years is perhaps partly due to the fact that some (and perhaps many) of the chains reporting for the more recent years did not have private brands in the earlier years. In the second place, a number of chains kept no records of private brand sales as such and not only had no available figures in the earlier four years but claimed that they could not even estimate the proportions of such sales for any year. In other cases, estimates or reports were procured for certain years later or earlier than other years for which none were reported available. For example, the Kroger Grocery & Baking Co. furnished percentages of private-brand sales for 1925 and 1928 but was unable to supply similar information for 1929 and 1930 owing to changes in the system of keeping records initiated by the new management.[10] Similarly, information for the J. C. Penney Co. is available only for 1929 and 1930 and for Woolworth, only for the year 1928.

In computing the private-brand sales figures shown in this section, the method employed, with qualifications for A. & P. and Kroger

[10] Under the new decentralized system of organization many of the branch headquarters offices did not keep separate records of private-brand sales and were unable to make satisfactory estimates of them.

subsequently noted, has been to combine the actually reported private-brand sales with estimates of private-brand sales. The latter were obtained by applying to the total sales figures for each chain the percentages of sales made in private brands.

The following table presents the total sales and private-brand sales as thus constructed, excluding and including A. & P. and Kroger.

TABLE 11.—*Private-brand sales, and proportions of total sales, of all chains reporting amounts of private brand sales in specified years*

Year	Chains reporting amounts of private brand sales	Stores operated Dec. 31	Total sales (000 omitted)	Private brand sales	
				Amount (000 omitted)	Per cent of total sales
Excluding the Great Atlantic & Pacific Tea Co. and Kroger Grocery & Baking Co.:					
1919	26	1,467	$127,437	$23,957	18.8
1922	57	2,133	192,631	41,053	21.3
1925	95	3,986	377,333	104,381	27.7
1928	187	14,751	1,270,128	259,676	20.4
1929	255	19,754	1,815,567	514,455	28.3
1930	274	21,450	1,859,311	519,527	27.9
Including estimates for the Great Atlantic & Pacific Tea Co. and Kroger Grocery & Baking Co.:					
1925	97	20,876	933,592	226,925	24.3
1928	189	35,188	2,437,369	495,858	20.3
1929	257	40,748	3,140,821	762,455	24.3
1930	276	42,353	3,177,556	770,657	24.3

As already pointed out, the Kroger Grocery & Baking Co. reported proportions of private-brand sales for 1925 and 1928 but was unable to report for the two years, 1929 and 1930. In the case of the Great Atlantic & Pacific Tea Co., percentage estimates of sales of private brands manufactured by that company were furnished for the four years 1925, 1928, 1929, and 1930. A separate estimate for print butter was furnished for the same period. For other nonmanufactured private brands, the company gave an approximation and stated "it would appear that * * * this ratio (of such sales) has not varied materially for some years back."

On account of the huge volume of the private-brand sales of these two companies, it was deemed important to present at least approximate figures for them for all four years. In the case of the Great Atlantic & Pacific Tea Co. this involved the use of an estimated figure for nonmanufactured private brands for 1925, 1928, 1929, and 1930, using the approximation as a constant ratio. As the volume of nonmanufactured private-brand sales is relatively small as compared with the total sales of the manufactured private brands, the figures resulting from this computation can have only a minor influence in the total. In the case of Kroger as already stated, the proportion of private-brand sales was available for 1925 and 1928 but not for 1929 and 1930. For these two years, therefore, the private-brand sales were estimated by applying to the number of stores reported on December 31, 1929 and 1930, the average private-brand sales per store for the year 1928 obtained by dividing the total 1928 private-brand sales by the number of stores reported in operation on December 31, 1928. The figures of private-brand sales of the Kroger Co. for both the years 1929 and 1930, therefore, should be understood to be the estimates of the commission and not those of the Kroger Co.

Although the information for the two earliest years is very limited, there is no way of determining to what extent, particularly in 1919, this lack of data is due to the fact that many of the chains now owning private brands had no such brands. For this reason, the figures for these earlier years may be somewhat more representative than the number of returns would imply. For the later years, the figures are more comprehensive. Over 250 chains, excluding the Great Atlantic & Pacific Tea Co. and Kroger Grocery & Baking Co., furnished information on private-brand sales for both 1929 and 1930. This number, therefore, is equivalent to over 60 per cent of the 412 chains reporting ownership of private brands in 1929-30 in the original chain-store schedule and is equal to over 70 per cent of the 351 reporting such ownership in 1931 in the supplementary schedule. (Table 3.)

If figures of the Great Atlantic & Pacific Tea Co. and the Kroger Grocery & Baking Co. are included on the basis of the commission's estimates, the number of chains reported is not substantially increased but the number of stores rises by approximately 100 per cent (from 19,754 in 1929 and 21,450 in 1930 to 40,748 in 1929 and 42,353 in 1930) and represents between 75 and 80 per cent of the total stores operated on December 31, 1928, and December 31, 1930, by the 412 and 351 chains respectively (Table 3). Excluding the estimates for these two chains the reports would none the less cover nearly 40 per cent of the total stores in each year operated by all chains reporting private-brand ownership in the two periods.

Similarly, the total sales of the chains for which figures of private-brand sales are presented in this table are equal to over 70 per cent of the total sales of all chains reporting the ownership of private brands in 1929–30 and 1931. From these figures, therefore, it seems fairly safe to conclude that the private-brand sales estimates of the two more recent years are representative of the situation among the private-brand owning chains.

Because of the uncertainty of the representativeness of the figures in the earlier years, and the variations in the size of the sample, no attempt should be made to estimate from the tables in this section the possible or probable increases in the sales of private brands. Subsequently in this report by the use of identical companies and in other ways the attempt has been made to determine the trend of chain store private-brand sales. The present section, therefore, should be considered as merely a presentation of such private-brand sales data as were available on either an actual or estimated basis for the years in question.

Referring to Table 11, it would appear that the proportion of private-brand sales to total sales for all chains owning private brands is between 20 and 30 per cent.

In 1929 and 1930 the total reported private-brand sales of over 250 chains, excluding Kroger and A. & P., aggregated over half a billion dollars and represented practically 28 per cent of their total sales. The addition of estimates for these two companies raises the total to over three-quarters of a billion dollars in each year but lowers the percentage of total sales to about 24 per cent.

Considered from the standpoint of absolute volume, however, the great bulk of the private-brand sales at least in recent years has been made by the chains in a limited number of lines of business. Appendix Table 5 shows by kind of chain both the total sales and estimated private-brand sales for all chains furnishing such private-brand information. This table shows that, excluding A. & P. and Kroger, nearly four-fifths of the total private-brand sales of $520,000,000 in 1930 were made in 5 of the 26 kinds of chains—dry goods and apparel, department store, men's and women's shoes, grocery, and grocery and meat. If the two largest chains are included, the sales of these five kinds of business aggregate nearly six-sevenths of the total. Moreover, approximately one-third ($250,000,000) of the total private-brand sales of $770,000,000 in 1930 is accounted for by A. & P. and Kroger. Furthermore, most of the private-brand sales of the dry goods and apparel group are accounted for by the J. C. Penney Co., which reported that approximately 90 per cent of its sales were in private brands. For the year 1930, therefore, it is estimated that over $400,000,000 of the private-brand sales, and hence more than half of the total estimated for the 276 reporting chains, were those of three chains—the Great Atlantic & Pacific Tea Co., the Kroger Grocery & Baking Co., and the J. C. Penney Co.

The following table presents the percentage of private-brand sales to total sales for all chains reporting the data in each kind of business for specified years.[11]

TABLE 12.—*Proportions of private-brand to total sales for all chains reporting amounts of private-brand sales in specified years, by kind of chain*

Kind of chain	Year					
	1919	1922	1925	1928	1929	1930
Grocery		3.6	3.3	8.8	9.0	10.1
Grocery and meat	4.9	12.6	20.9	21.1	19.1	18.6
Meat				10.0	2.0	2.0
Confectionery	100.0	100.0	99.4	88.0	90.9	91.5
Drug	14.3	9.1	16.0	20.7	16.6	17.3
Tobacco	9.3	8.8	8.3	7.8	8.3	5.6
Variety ($1 limit)	3.2	5.8	7.4	4.0	3.6	3.7
Variety ($5 limit)					3.0	3.0
Variety (unlimited)						
Men's ready-to-wear	60.4	71.0	79.9	86.1	48.7	51.4
Women's ready-to-wear					12.9	17.5
Men's and women's ready-to-wear				100.0	17.3	17.9
Men's furnishings		50.2	37.1	35.0	79.2	74.9
Women's accessories	50.9	51.1	76.0	72.7	98.1	98.3
Hats and caps		70.0	67.9	81.0	80.3	76.5
Millinery					1.0	1.0
Men's shoes		91.7	91.9	92.7	92 6	93.4
Women's shoes	17.2	26.6	69.0	76.7	86.0	86.7
Men's and women's shoes	75.1	75.8	87.4	90.3	87.6	89.5
Dry goods					12.0	8.9
Dry goods and apparel		7.9	8.5	6.9	85.3	81.5
Department store	8.0	10.0	7.0	19.5	24.1	27.5
General merchandise			12.6	6.3	3.3	3.4
Furniture				1.0	19.3	19.3
Musical instruments	87.5	86.2	87.7	63.2	42.5	51.4
Hardware					1.0	1.0
Total	18.8	21.3	27.7	20.4	28.3	27.9
A. & P. and Kroger			22.0	20.2	18.7	19.1
Grocery and meat (including A. & P. and Kroger)			22.0	20.4	18.8	19.0
Total (including A. & P. and Kroger)			24.3	20.3	24.3	24.3

Based on the proportion of total sales made in private brands by brand-owning chains the private-brand business is apparently most important in confectionery and men's shoes and least important in hardware, unlimited variety, $5-limit variety, and millinery. Every

[11] As previously stated, the number of chains, the number of stores operated by them, the amounts of total net sales and total private-brand sales are shown in Appendix. Table 5.

year in confectionery and men's shoes, the volume of private-brand sales exceeded 90 per cent of the total sales for the chains which reported owning private brands, with a qualification for confectionery in 1928 when the proportion of such sales dropped to 88 per cent. Private-brand sales are also large relative to total sales of private-brand chains (above 50 per cent in at least five of the six years) in men's ready-to-wear, women's accessories, hats and caps, men's and women's shoes, and musical instruments. They comprise relatively low proportions of sales in dollar-limit variety, grocery, meat, and tobacco lines, in none of which is the percentage of private-brand sales more than 11 per cent of total sales of brand-owning chains in any year. The dry goods and general merchandise percentages are also comparatively low.

Grocery and meat chains, in contrast to the grocery group, show comparatively high proportions of private-brand sales, though in all years less than 25 per cent of the total.

In general, the highest percentages in private-brand business are reported in those lines of business which have relatively large proportions of sales manufactured by chains: Confectionery, shoes, men's ready-to-wear, hats and caps, women's accessories, and musical instruments.[12] Moreover, both the confectionery and shoe businesses, particularly the former, probably contain higher proportions of chains distributing exclusively private-brand merchandise than do any other kinds of business discussed in this report. The indicated decline in the proportion of musical-instrument private brands in recent years has perhaps been due to the introduction of radios in musical-instrument stores.

The proportions of private-brand sales in brand-owning drug chains are only slightly lower than those of grocery and meat chains. In both these lines the merchandise in question is composed chiefly of staple necessities.[13] These chains have a large volume of sales in staple merchandise which is made and sold by many different manufacturers and much of which is nationally advertised by these manufacturers. The size and importance of the fresh fruit and vegetable business of the grocery chains and of fresh fruit, vegetable and meat sales in grocery and meat chains tend to keep the proportions of private-brand business low in these chains. In tobacco, the low proportion of private brands is no doubt due in part to the fact that most private brands of these chains are in cigars. Cigarettes which constitute the backbone of the tobacco chain business are practically without exception nationally advertised brands as are also most of the smoking and chewing tobaccos handled. In both the drug and tobacco chains, particularly the former, the proportions of private-brand sales are lower than they would be were it not for the extensive volume of business done by the soda fountain and luncheonette departments which substantially increases the total sales volume of many of these chains.

Proportions of total sales made in private brands, by size of chain.—The following table, in which chains have been classified according to the number of stores operated, presents for specified years from 1919 to 1930 the proportions of total sales of brand-owning chains made

[12] Report of Federal Trade Commission on Chain-Store Manufacturing.
[13] Commonly referred to in marketing studies as convenience goods.

in private brands. The number of chains and amounts of both total and private-brand sales for each year will be found in Appendix Table 6.

Table 13.—*Proportions of private brand to total sales for all chains reporting amounts of private-brand sales in specified years, by size of chain*

Number of stores per chain	Year					
	1919	1922	1925	1928	1929	1930
2–5	35.2	29.7	24.7	19.3	13.4	11.3
6–10	12.4	27.8	66.3	61.7	33.9	27.9
11–25	47.5	50.4	71.0	42.2	32.5	33.9
26–50	8.7	12.3	56.1	61.5	34.6	22.1
51–100	93.0	92.6	25.0	36.9	31.2	35.9
101–500	2.0	6.6	20.5	21.6	17.1	16.6
501–1,000				21.4	21.6	22.1
1,001 and over	9.3	8.8	8.1	6.4	47.7	55.4
Total	18.8	21.3	27.7	20.4	28.3	27.9
A. & P. and Kroger			22.0	20.2	18.7	19.1
1,001 and over (including A. & P. and Kroger)			20.4	16.2	26.5	27.2
Total (including A. & P. and Kroger)			24.3	20.3	24.3	24.3

This table does not indicate any marked tendency for the proportion of private-brand sales to increase with the size of the chain based on the number of stores, particularly if the estimated sales for the Great Atlantic & Pacific Tea Co. and the Kroger Grocery & Baking Co. are included. Table 8, however, indicates a rather decided tendency (based on 1929–30 and 1931 reports) for the proportion of chains owning private brands and stores operated by them to increase with the increase in the size of the chain. The 1929 and 1930 figures in Table 13, showing the proportions of private-brand sales to total sales of brand-owning chains, seem, however, to indicate that on the whole, the smaller sizes of chains have somewhat higher proportions of private-brand sales than do the larger sizes of chains, with the exception of the very large chains of more than 1,000 stores. This would suggest the conclusion that, although size is of some significance in determining whether or not a chain develops private-brand merchandise, it has no particular effect on the proportions of sales made in private-brand merchandise. Or to put it another way, the smaller chains which own private brands seemingly are able to dispose of proportionally as much private-brand merchandise as are the larger chains.

Section 10. Trend of chain-store private-brand sales.

Character of the data.—In an effort to ascertain the trend of private-brand sales, chains were requested to furnish either the volume or proportion of such sales in each of six years, namely, 1919, 1922, 1925, 1928, 1929, and 1930. In section 9, private-brand sales of all chains which reported for any one or more of these years were included in the group totals, regardless of the number of years for which they furnished information. Thus, chains which reported their sales in private brands for a single year are included in the group totals for that year. Because of the limited number of reports for the earlier years and also because many chains did not report sales data for consecutive years, these figures do not furnish a satisfactory basis for determining the trend of private-brand sales. In the present section, therefore, only identical companies which reported for four years or for three years have been included.

Because of the limited number of companies which reported for 1919 and 1922, the discussion has been confined to two groups: (*a*) Chains reporting private-brand sales for each of four years, namely, 1925, 1928, 1929, and 1930, and (*b*) chains reporting such sales for 1928, 1929, and 1930. The chief disadvantage of this method of presentation is that identical chains which reported for four years, or even those which reported for three years, are quite limited in number. Only 77 chains (exclusive of the Great Atlantic & Pacific Tea Co. and the Kroger Grocery & Baking Co.) reported their private-brand sales for each of the three years, 1928, 1929, and 1930, and only 46 of these 77 chains reported such sales for an additional year, 1925.

The fact that the 77 chains, just mentioned, in 1930 operated nearly half (48 per cent) of the stores operated by the 274 chains which reported their private-brand sales in that year indicates their relative importance. Furthermore, the total sales of the 77 companies in 1930 amounted to nearly half (43 per cent) of the total sales made by the 274 chains. It should be noted, however, that these 77 chains represent less than 22 per cent of the 351 chains reporting the ownership of private brands early in 1931 and account for only 18 per cent of the stores being operated by these brand-owning chains on December 31, 1930. (Table 3.)

The 46 chains, reporting for each of four years, in 1930 operated more than one-fifth of the stores (20.1 per cent) operated by the 274 chains which reported their private-brand sales in that year. The total sales of the 46 chains in 1930 ($393,795,700) also represent over one-fifth (21.2 per cent) of the total sales made by the 274 chains. They, however, represent only about 13 per cent of the 351 chains which indicated that they owned private brands early in 1931 and only 8 per cent of the stores being operated by these brand-owning chains on December 31, 1930.

Attention is again directed to the fact stated in section 9, that a large proportion of the private brand-owning chains was unable even to estimate either the volume or the proportion of their private-brand sales. This fact is partially responsible for the limited representation of chains owning private brands found in the present analysis.

The private-brand sales of the two largest grocery and meat chains, the Great Atlantic & Pacific Tea Co. and the Kroger Grocery & Baking Co., have not been included in the main body of the tables appearing in this section but have been added at the bottom of certain tables because they consist largely of estimates made partly by the commission [14] and in part by the companies concerned. Segregation of these companies was desirable, moreover, because the volume of their private-brand sales is so great that their inclusion would tend to obscure in the totals, the results for the smaller chains, particularly in the grocery and meat group.

If the estimated figures for A. & P. and Kroger are combined with those of the 46 and 77 chains reporting for four years and three years,

[14] See section 9 for a detailed explanation of the methods used in estimating the private-brand sales of these two companies.

respectively, the number of stores being operated by the smaller of these groups on December 31 1930, is increased from 4,326 to 25,229 and sales from $393,000,000 to almost one and three-quarters billion dollars. The group of 48 chains on December 31, 1930 operated nearly 60 per cent of the stores being operated by the 276 chains (including A. & P. and Kroger) which reported their private-brand sales in that year (Table 11) and accounted for over half (53.9 per cent) of their total sales. It should be noted, however, that these 48 chains represent less than 14 per cent of the 351 chains, which indicated that they owned private brands early in 1931, but they account for 46 per cent of the stores being operated by these brand-owning chains on December 31, 1930.

Similarly, the number of stores operated by the larger group of 79 chains on December 31, 1930, is increased from 10,347 to 31,250 stores; that is, the group operated nearly three-fourths of the stores (73.8 per cent) operated by the 276 chains (including A. & P. and Kroger) which reported their private-brand sales in that year. The total sales of the group of 79 chains amounted to over $2,000,000,000 in 1930 or their sales were approximately 67 per cent of the total sales made by the 276 chains furnishing their private-brand sales figures in that year. Although they represent only 22½ per cent of the 351 chains which reported the ownership of private brands early in 1931, they account for 57 per cent of the stores being operated by these brand-owning chains on December 31, 1930. (Table 3.)

Comparisons used in analyzing data.—The data on private-brand sales of identical chains which reported for four years and three years, respectively, found in this section of the report, can be analyzed from two different points of view: First, from the point of view of the increase in dollars of private-brand sales from year to year either alone or in comparison with the increase in the dollar volume of total sales of these chains; and second, from the point of view of the relative increase or decrease of private-brand sales, that is, the proportion of total sales of brand-owning chains which is accounted for by private-brand sales in each year. Although the private-brand sales of a chain or group of chains may show a large increase in dollar volume over a period of three or four years, it may happen that the proportion of total sales accounted for by private brands is steadily declining.

A third method of determining the trend in the importance of private-brand sales consists of a count of the number of chains (and of their stores) which show an increase, a decrease, or no change in the percentage of their private brand sales to total sales. In this comparison are included all chains which reported the ratios of private-brand sales for both 1925 and 1928; 1925 and 1929; 1925 and 1930; 1928 and 1929; 1928 and 1930; and for both 1929 and 1930, respectively.

Increase in dollar volume of private-brand sales.—Table 14 shows the total sales and the private-brand sales both of the 46 chains which reported for four years (1925, 1928, 1929, and 1930) and of the 77 chains reporting for three years (1928, 1929, and 1930). Private-brand and total sales figures also are shown in this table for the Great Atlantic & Pacific Tea Co. and the Kroger Grocery & Baking Co.

combined—first separately and then added to those of the 46 and 77 chains—thus furnishing private-brand data for 48 and 79 chains, respectively.

TABLE 14.—*Private-brand sales, and proportions of total sales, of specified groups of identical chains reporting amounts of private-brand sales in specified years*

Year	4-year identical chains				3-year identical chains			
	Number of stores	Total sales (000 omitted)	Private brand sales (000 omitted)	Per cent of total sales made in private brands	Number of stores	Total sales (000 omitted)	Private brand sales (000 omitted)	Per cent of total sales made in private brands
Excluding the Great Atlantic & Pacific Tea Co. and the Kroger Grocery & Baking Co.	46 chains				77 chains			
1925	2,807	$265,152	$57,398	21.6				
1928	3,799	365,009	95,244	26.1	8,717	$617,481	$155,201	25.1
1929	4,112	383,919	102,152	26.6	9,573	768,634	239,482	31.2
1930	4,326	393,796	101,719	25.8	10,347	799,491	257,649	32.2
The Great Atlantic & Pacific Tea Co. and the Kroger Grocery & Baking Co. (estimated)	2 chains				2 chains			
1925	16,890	556,258	122,543	22.0				
1928	20,437	1,167,241	236,182	20.2	20,437	1,167,241	236,182	20.2
1929	20,994	1,325,254	248,000	18.7	20,994	1,325,254	248,000	18.7
1930	20,903	1,318,245	251,130	19.1	20,903	1,318,245	251,130	19.1
Including the Great Atlantic & Pacific Tea Co. and the Kroger Grocery & Baking Co.	48 chains				79 chains			
1925	19,697	821,410	179,941	21.9				
1928	24,236	1,532,250	331,426	21.6	29,154	1,784,722	391,383	21.9
1929	25,106	1,709,173	350,152	20.5	30,567	2,093,888	488,483	23.3
1930	25,229	1,712,041	352,849	20.6	31,250	2,117,736	508,779	24.0

It is obvious from the table that an enormous increase in the actual volume of private-brand sales occurred between 1925 and 1930. Private-brand sales of the 4-year group of 46 chains increased from about $57,000,000 in 1925 to nearly $102,000,000 in 1930, an increase of 77 per cent. In the larger group of 77 chains reporting for three years such sales increased from about $155,000,000 to nearly $258,000,000, an increase of approximately 66 per cent.

Including A. & P. and Kroger, private-brand sales increased from nearly $180,000,000 in 1925 to nearly $353,000,000 in 1930, or over 96 per cent. For the 3-year group private-brand sales increased from $391,000,000 in 1928 to $508,000,000 in 1930, or 30 per cent.

Table 15 presents the percentages of increase in total sales of identical brand-owning chains together with their private-brand sales, stores, and total and private-brand sales per store from 1925 to 1930 and from 1928 to 1930.

TABLE 15.—*Rates of change between specified years in stores and total and private-brand sales for specified groups of identical chains reporting amounts of private-brand sales in specified years*

Years	Number of chains in group	Number of stores	Total sales	Private-brand sales	Average sales per store	Average private-brand sales per store
Excluding the Great Atlantic & Pacific Tea Co. and the Kroger Grocery & Baking Co.						
Dec. 31—						
1925–1930	46	+54.1	+48.5	+77.2	−3.6	+15.0
1928–1930	77	+18.7	+29.5	+66.0	+9.1	+39.9
The Great Atlantic & Pacific Tea Co. and the Kroger Grocery & Baking Co.						
Dec. 31—						
1925–1930	2	+23.8	+137.0	+104.9	+91.5	+65.6
1928–1930	2	+2.3	+12.9	+6.3	+10.4	+4.0
Including the Great Atlantic & Pacific Tea Co. and the Kroger Grocery & Baking Co.						
Dec. 31—						
1925–1930	48	+28.1	+108.4	+96.1	+62.7	+53.1
1928–1930	79	+7.2	+18.7	+30.0	+10.7	+21.3

Excluding A. & P. and Kroger, from 1925 to 1930 and from 1928 to 1930, both total and per store private-brand sales increased more rapidly than total sales and average sales per store, respectively. For 79 companies, including A. & P. and Kroger, private-brand sales, both in total and per store, increased more rapidly from 1928 to 1930 than did either total sales or total stores. Although both total and per store private-brand sales increased more rapidly from 1925 to 1930 than did the number of stores, the rate of increase in private-brand sales was less than that of total sales.

Because of their size the situation in the two large grocery and meat chains is of special interest. From 1925 to 1930 the total stores operated by them increased nearly 24 per cent, while their total sales rose 137 per cent. Although private-brand sales showed a larger percentage increase than did the number of stores, this increase was much less than that of total sales. Average private-brand sales per store increased only 65 per cent as compared with over 91 per cent in the average total sales per store. From 1928 to 1930 the increase in the number of stores of these two chains combined was only 2.3 per cent. Their total sales increased nearly 13 per cent, while their private-brand sales increased only 6.3 per cent. Stated in another way, although average sales per store increased 10.4 per cent, the average private-brand sales per store increased only 4 per cent.

Relative increase in private-brand sales.—Figures showing the proportion of total sales made in private brands by all identical reporting brand-owning chains (Table 14) indicate that, on the whole, private-brand sales have increased in importance during the years studied. The trend is fairly definite for both the 3-year and the 4-year groups of chains when the figures of the Great Atlantic & Pacific Tea Co. and the Kroger Grocery & Baking Co. are excluded. The estimated private-brand sales of these two chains combined, however, have shown a decline relative to their total sales. When these two companies are included, the group of 48 four-year chains shows a slight decline in the proportion of private-brand sales between 1925 and 1929, and the larger group of 79 chains reporting for three years shows a small but steady increase. In other words, the relative decline in the estimated private-brand sales of the two largest grocery and meat chains between 1928 and 1930 has been more than counterbalanced by the large increase shown by the 77 chains. In so far as the increase in average sales per store in these two chains has resulted from the expansion of their fresh meat and produce business, the proportion of private brand to total sales would tend to decline. A second reason why their private-brand sales did not show a relative, as well as an absolute, increase is that the large number of new stores opened or acquired by them from 1925 to 1928 probably has tended to increase the sales of locally and nationally known standard brands in such new stores at a faster rate than private brands.[15] It seems reasonable to assume that it takes some little time for a chain to establish its private brands in a new locality.

Increase in dollar volume of private-brand sales, by kind of chain.—Tables 16 and 17 show in detail by kinds of business the dollar volume of private-brand sales made by the 48 and the 79 identical private-brand chains, respectively. Appendix Table 7 shows corresponding figures for the number of stores operated in each year.

TABLE 16.—*Total and private-brand sales of identical chains reporting amounts of private-brand sales for four specified years, by kind of chain*

Kind of chain	Number of chains	1925		1928	
		Total sales	Private-brand sales	Total sales	Private-brand sales
Grocery	5	$21, 340, 000	$664, 400	$28, 601, 700	$790, 700
Grocery and meat	4	5, 782, 000	393, 500	5, 000, 100	465, 900
Confectionery	6	5, 824, 300	5, 701, 600	10, 524, 800	10, 156, 800
Drug	7	27, 160, 900	4, 573, 000	49, 253, 200	12, 039, 100
Tobacco	3	73, 204, 000	6, 076, 700	73, 736, 800	5, 778, 100
Variety ($1 limit)	2	76, 374, 600	7, 201, 600	120, 745, 300	13, 424, 200
Men's ready-to-wear	2	364, 600	325, 400	1, 614, 400	1, 542, 900
Men's furnishings	1	322, 200	161, 100	299, 300	149, 600
Women's accessories	3	1, 391, 400	1, 349, 400	1, 924, 200	1, 887, 200
Hats and caps	1	105, 600	100, 300	113, 700	108, 000
Men's shoes	2	7, 238, 100	6, 604, 800	7, 648, 200	7, 050, 000
Women's shoes	3	9, 772, 400	6, 703, 800	14, 620, 800	11, 317, 500
Men's and women's shoes	4	18, 047, 500	15, 968, 300	31, 190, 300	29, 042, 400
Dry goods and apparel	1	4, 574, 300	202, 200	4, 980, 800	206, 200
Department store	1	13, 037, 300	912, 600	14, 143, 100	919, 300
Musical instruments	1	612, 900	459, 000	612, 000	367, 000
Total	46	265, 152, 100	57, 397, 700	365, 008, 700	95, 244, 900
A. & P. and Kroger	2	556, 258, 500	122, 543, 500	1, 167, 241, 300	236, 182, 000
Grocery and meat (including A. & P. and Kroger)	6	562, 040, 500	122, 937, 000	1, 172, 241, 400	236, 647, 900
Total (including A. & P. and Kroger)	48	821, 410, 600	179, 941, 200	1, 532, 250, 000	331, 426, 900

[15] The number of stores operated by the Great Atlantic & Pacific Tea Co. increased from 11,421 on Mar. 1, 1925, to 15,677 on Mar. 1, 1928, an increase of over 36 per cent. The Kroger Grocery & Baking Co. was operating 2,856 stores on Dec. 31, 1925, and 5,260 stores on Dec. 31, 1928, an increase of nearly 90 per cent.

TABLE 16.—*Total and private-brand sales of identical chains reporting amounts of private-brand sales for four specified years, by kind of chain*—Continued

Kind of chain	Number of chains	1929		1930	
		Total sales	Private-brand sales	Total sales	Private-brand sales
Grocery	5	$30,987,600	$924,400	$29,721,900	$642,300
Grocery and meat	4	5,887,600	921,700	5,817,200	927,700
Confectionery	6	11,426,000	11,091,500	10,608,200	10,389,200
Drug	7	64,710,300	17,902,600	68,253,500	19,719,900
Tobacco	3	54,228,500	4,424,800	59,883,900	3,088,400
Variety ($1 limit)	2	134,377,400	8,773,100	140,659,600	9,111,400
Men's ready-to-wear	2	1,839,000	1,769,800	1,666,900	1,616,900
Men's furnishings	1	290,800	218,100	270,700	203,000
Women's accessories	3	1,946,400	1,895,500	2,594,700	2,534,200
Hats and caps	1	93,700	84,300	63,900	57,500
Men's shoes	2	7,738,200	7,095,900	6,299,200	5,831,800
Women's shoes	3	16,327,000	13,668,900	14,778,500	12,487,700
Men's and women's shoes	4	34,947,800	32,757,200	36,390,200	34,584,700
Dry goods and apparel	1	4,608,300	230,400	4,284,200	171,400
Department store	1	14,011,500	140,100	12,046,300	120,500
Musical instruments	1	498,600	254,300	456,800	233,000
Total	46	383,918,700	102,152,600	393,795,700	101,719,600
A. & P. and Kroger	2	1,325,254,300	248,000,300	1,318,244,800	251,129,800
Grocery and meat (including A. & P. and Kroger)	6	1,331,141,900	248,922,000	1,324,062,000	252,057,500
Total (including A. & P. and Kroger)	48	1,709,173,000	350,152,900	1,712,040,500	352,849,400

As shown by the above table for the smaller group of chains, the volume of private-brand sales increased steadily between 1925 and 1930 in 4 of the 16 kinds of business reporting private-brand sales figures for four years (grocery and meat, drug, women's accessories, and men's and women's shoes). The importance of these four kinds of chains is indicated by the fact that their total combined sales in 1930 (including the Great Atlantic & Pacific Tea Co. and the Kroger Grocery & Baking Co.) constituted 83.6 per cent of the combined sales of identical brand owning chains in all of the 16 kinds of business; and their private-brand sales constituted 87.5 per cent of the total combined private-brand sales of the 16 groups.

In six additional groups of identical chains reporting for four years (grocery, confectionery, men's ready-to-wear, men's shoes, women's shoes, and dry goods and apparel), the volume of private-brand sales increased steadily between 1925 and 1929 but declined between 1929 and 1930.

Table 17 for the 79 chains reporting private-brand sales for 3 years shows that the volume of private-brand sales increased steadily between 1928 and 1930 in the same 4 important kinds of chains as in the foregoing table for 4 years and in 2 others in addition (grocery and department store). Nearly 90 per cent of the combined sales volume of the 79 chains in 1930 was made by chains in these 6 groups and their private-brand sales accounted for almost 90 per cent of the private-brand sales of the 79 chains.

TABLE 17.—*Total and private-brand sales of identical chains reporting amounts of private-brand sales for the specified years, by kind of chain*

Kind of chain	Number of chains	1928 Total sales	1928 Private-brand sales
Grocery	9	$105, 583. 500	$11, 070, 100
Grocery and meat	10	116, 849, 600	22, 188, 400
Confectionery	8	15, 128, 100	11, 240, 400
Drug	13	56, 276, 100	12, 469, 200
Tobacco	3	73, 736, 800	5, 778, 100
Variety ($1 limit)	2	120, 745, 300	13, 424, 200
Men's ready-to-wear	5	5, 431, 600	5, 360, 100
Men's furnishings	1	299, 300	149, 600
Women's accessories	3	1, 924, 200	1, 887, 200
Hats and caps	2	573, 900	319, 400
Men's shoes	3	9, 736, 700	8, 975, 900
Women's shoes	4	14, 807, 100	11, 345, 500
Men's and women's shoes	8	37, 014, 800	34, 634, 200
Dry goods and apparel	2	5, 530, 800	246, 200
Department store	3	53, 231, 300	15, 745, 900
Musical instruments	1	612, 000	367, 000
Total	77	617, 481, 100	155, 201, 400
A. & P. and Kroger	2	1, 167, 241, 300	236, 182, 000
Grocery and meat (including A. & P. and Kroger)	12	1, 284, 090, 900	258, 370, 400
Total (including A. & P. and Kroger)	79	1, 784, 722, 400	391, 383. 400

Kind of chain	Number of chains	1929 Total sales	1929 Private-brand sales	1930 Total sales	1930 Private-brand sales
Grocery	9	$114, 342, 800	$12, 795, 000	$111, 762, 600	$13, 294, 900
Grocery and meat	10	162, 329, 600	38, 810, 000	165, 731, 900	39, 792, 900
Confectionery	8	15, 762, 900	15, 421, 700	14, 724, 400	14, 496, 800
Drug	13	73, 046, 500	18, 500, 100	76, 966, 800	20, 443, 300
Tobacco	3	54, 228, 500	4, 424, 800	59, 883, 900	3, 088, 400
Variety ($1 limit)	2	134, 377, 400	8, 773, 100	140, 659, 600	9, 111, 400
Men's ready-to-wear	5	7, 002, 300	6, 781, 500	6, 100, 100	5, 927, 500
Men's furnishings	1	290, 800	218, 100	270, 700	203, 000
Women's accessories	3	1, 946, 400	1, 895, 500	2, 594, 700	2, 534, 200
Hats and caps	2	559, 800	256, 700	420, 800	193, 100
Men's shoes	3	9, 915, 000	9, 011, 500	8, 204, 300	7, 508, 300
Women's shoes	4	16, 533, 100	13, 823, 500	14, 944, 700	12, 612, 300
Men's and women's shoes	8	40, 692, 300	38, 191, 900	40, 792, 400	38, 565, 700
Dry goods and apparel	2	5, 414, 900	262, 700	5, 349, 800	224, 700
Department store	3	131, 693, 600	70, 062, 300	150, 627, 700	89, 420, 200
Musical instruments	1	498, 600	254, 300	456, 800	233, 000
Total	77	768, 634, 500	239, 482, 700	799, 491, 200	257, 649, 700
A. & P. and Kroger	2	1, 325, 254, 300	248, 000, 300	1, 318, 244, 800	251, 129, 800
Grocery and meat (including A. & P. and Kroger)	12	1, 487, 583, 900	286, 810, 300	1, 483, 976, 700	290, 922, 700
Total (including A. & P. and Kroger)	79	2, 093, 888, 800	487, 483, 000	2, 117, 736, 000	508, 779, 500

The volume of private-brand sales increased steadily between 1928 and 1929 but declined between 1929 and 1930 in six kinds of chains reporting for three years, namely, confectionery, men's ready-to-wear, men's shoes, women's shoes, dry goods and apparel, and men's furnishings. The tobacco and musical instrument groups showed a steady decline in dollar sales of private brands in both the 3-year and 4-year tables for all the years under observation.

Percentage increases (or decreases) in the number of stores and in the dollar volume of both total sales and private brand sales are shown for the 4-year and 3-year identical chains in Table 18,[16] by kinds of business.

TABLE 18.—*Rates of change between specified years in stores, and total and private brand sales, for specified groups of identical chains reporting amounts of private brand sales in specified years, by kind of chain*

Kind of chain	Number of chains	Per cent increase or decrease from 1925 to 1930 in—			Number of chains	Per cent increase or decrease from 1928 to 1930 in—		
		Number of stores	Total sales	Private-brand sales		Number of stores	Total sales	Private-brand sales
	46 companies				*77 companies*			
Grocery	5	+62.0	+39.3	−3.3	9	+3.6	+5.9	+20.1
Grocery and meat	4	+36.8	+0.6	+135.8	10	+27.5	+41.8	+79.3
Confectionery	6	+126.4	+82.1	+82.2	8	+9.3	−2.7	+29.0
Drug	7	+204.5	+151.3	+331.2	13	+62.5	+36.8	+64.0
Tobacco	3	−11.9	−18.2	−49.2	3	−10.1	−18.8	−46.5
Variety ($1 limit)	2	+132.2	+84.2	+26.5	2	+37.1	+16.5	−32.1
Men's ready-to-wear	2	+271.4	+357.2	+396.9	5	+12.5	+12.3	+10.6
Men's furnishings	1	+50.0	−16.0	+26.0	1	+50.0	−9.6	+35.7
Women's accessories	3	+300.0	+86.5	+87.8	3	+100.0	+34.8	+34.3
Hats and caps	1	0	−39.5	−42.7	2	−14.3	−26.7	−39.5
Men's shoes	2	+10.3	−13.0	−11.7	3	−5.4	−15.7	−16.4
Women's shoes	3	+84.0	+51.2	+86.3	4	+11.5	+0.9	+11.2
Men's and women's shoes	4	+123.1	+101.6	+116.6	8	+14.9	+10.2	+11.4
Dry goods and apparel	1	+50.0	−6.3	−15.2	2	+100.0	−3.3	−8.7
Department store	1	0	−7.6	−86.8	3	+139.1	+183.0	+467.9
Musical instruments	1	+33.3	−25.5	−49.2	1	0	−25.4	−36.5
Total	46	+54.1	+48.5	+77.2	77	+18.7	+29.5	+66.0
A. & P. and Kroger	2	+23.8	+137.0	+104.9	2	+2.3	+12.9	+6.3
Grocery and meat (including A. & P. and Kroger)	6	+23.8	+135.6	+105.0	12	+5.3	+15.6	+12.6
Total (including A. & P. and Kroger)	48	+28.1	+108.4	+96.1	79	+7.2	+18.7	+30.0

Eight kinds of chains show an increase in the volume of their private-brand sales in both periods—namely, grocery and meat, confectionery, drug, men's ready-to-wear, men's furnishings, women's accessories, women's shoes, and men's and women's shoes. Five kinds of business show a decline in private-brand sales in both periods: Tobacco, hats and caps, men's shoes, dry goods and apparel, and musical instruments. The private brand situation differs in the two periods for grocery, dollar-limit variety, and department store chains.

It is interesting to note that there are only four kinds of business in the 4-year group and five kinds of business in the 3-year group of identical chains in which the rate of increase in private-brand sales exceeds the rate of increase both in the number of stores and in the total sales. For the 4-year group of 46 companies (1925 to 1930), these lines were grocery and meat, drug, men's ready-to-wear, and women's shoes; and for the 3-year group of 77 companies (1928 to 1930), they were grocery, grocery and meat, confectionery, drug, and department store. In addition to those mentioned above, in the 4-year group (1925 to 1930), private-brand sales increased at a slightly greater rate than total sales in confectionery, men's furnishings, women's accessories, and men's and women's shoe chains; and in the

[16] Based on data in Tables 16 and 17 and Appendix Table 7.

3-year group (1928 to 1930) private-brand sales increased relatively more rapidly than total sales in men's furnishings, women's shoe, and men's and women's shoe chains.

Relative increase in private-brand sales, by kind of chain.—Although Table 14 indicates that in general private brands have increased in their relative importance, it should be emphasized that this upward trend is by no means common to all types of chains, as is apparent from the following table.

TABLE 19.—*Proportions of private brand to total sales of specified groups of identical chains reporting amounts of private brand sales in specified years, by kind of chain*

Kind of chain	Chains	1925	1928	1929	1930	Chains	1928	1929	1930
	46 companies					*77 companies*			
Grocery	5	3.1	2.8	3.0	2.2	9	10.5	11.2	11.9
Grocery and meat	4	6.8	9.3	15.7	15.9	10	19.0	23.9	24.0
Confectionery	6	97.9	96.5	97.1	97.9	8	74.3	97.8	98.5
Drug	7	16.8	24.4	27.7	28.9	13	22.2	25.3	26.6
Tobacco	3	8.3	7.8	8.2	5.2	3	7.8	8.2	5.2
Variety ($1 limit)	2	9.4	11.1	6.5	6.5	2	11.1	6.5	6.5
Men's ready-to-wear	2	89.2	95.6	96.2	97.0	5	98.7	96.8	97.2
Men's furnishings	1	50.0	50.0	75.0	75.0	1	50.0	75.0	75.0
Women's accessories	3	97.0	98.1	97.4	97.7	3	98.1	97.4	97.7
Hats and caps	1	95.0	95.0	90.0	90.0	2	55.6	45.9	45.9
Men's shoes	2	91.3	92.2	91.7	92.6	3	92.2	90.9	91.5
Women's shoes	3	68.6	77.4	83.7	84.5	4	76.6	83.6	84.4
Men's and women's shoes	4	88.5	93.1	93.7	95.0	8	93.6	93.9	94.5
Dry goods and apparel	1	4.4	4.1	5.0	4.0	2	4.5	4.9	4.2
Department store	1	7.0	6.5	1.0	1.0	3	29.6	53.2	59.4
Musical instruments	1	74.9	60.0	51.0	51.0	1	60.0	51.0	51.0
Total	46	21.6	26.1	26.6	25.8	77	25.1	31.2	32.2
A. & P. and Kroger	2	22.0	20.2	18.7	19.1	2	20.2	18.7	19.1
Grocery and meat (including A. & P. and Kroger)	6	21.9	20.2	18.7	19.0	12	20.1	19.3	19.6
Total (including A. & P. and Kroger)	48	21.9	21.6	20.5	20.6	79	21.9	23.3	24.0

As shown by the above table, the proportion of private-brand sales to total sales of brand-owning chains increased steadily during both the 3-year and 4-year periods in five kinds of business: Grocery and meat (excluding A. & P. and Kroger), drug, women's shoes, men's and women's shoes, and men's furnishings.[17] If figures of the Great Atlantic & Pacific Tea Co. and the Kroger Grocery & Baking Co. are included, private-brand sales of grocery and meat chains show a slight decline in relative importance, although in both comparisons the figures for 1930 perhaps indicate that this decline is being checked. The other large chains included in this group in certain years are First National, with 2,549 stores in 1930, and Grand Union, with 611 stores in 1930.

The largest chain reporting in the drug group is the Walgreen Co. (411 stores in 1930), and the Owl Drug Co. (129 stores in 1930) is next in size. Both of these chains reported private-brand sales for all four years.

The two largest men's and women's shoe chains which reported for each of the 4 years were Melville Shoe Corporation, operating 3 chains with a total of 480 stores in 1930, and the Regal Shoe Co. which had 86 stores in that year. Private brands are exceedingly important in men's and women's shoe chains, and they increased steadily in importance during the periods studied.

[17] Only one chain reporting.

The proportion of private-brand sales increased in the 3-year period in grocery, confectionery, and department stores. The slight increase in the proportion of private-brand sales in the 3-year grocery group is of little significance since the five chains reporting for four years showed an even greater proportional decline.

Private brands are particularly important in confectionery, since they accounted for over 95 per cent of the sales of reporting identical brand-owning confectionery chains shown in the table. The fact that three of the 4-year chains and four of the 3-year chains sold private brands exclusively accounts largely for the fact that the proportion of private-brand sales remained about the same from year to year. The increase in the department-store group was primarily due to the expansion of Sears, Roebuck & Co. and Montgomery Ward & Co.[18]

The trend appears to have been downward in dollar-limit variety, hats and caps, and musical instruments, all with a limited number of identical brand-owning chains reporting. While no marked trend is evident in tobacco, private-brand sales appear to have declined somewhat in importance.

Only two variety chains ($1 limit), W. T. Grant Co. and S. H. Kress Co., reported private-brand sales for each of the years studied. As shown by the table, private-brand sales were most important in these two companies in 1928, 11 per cent of their total combined net sales being made in private-label merchandise as compared with approximately 6.5 per cent in 1929 and 1930. It should be mentioned that the combined figures reflected a decline in the proportion of private-brand sales of only one of these companies; the other showed an increase in such sales in 1929 as compared with 1928. An executive of the company in explaining the decline between the years 1928 and 1930 reported:

> * * * you, of course, realize that the years 1929 and 1930 were years of very disturbed conditions in the entire merchandise field, particularly with respect to merchandise costs and retail prices.
>
> My best answer with respect to the decrease in our own private-brand sales would be the fact that steadily reducing merchandise costs made it unwise to plan ahead for large purchases to be sold under our own private brands when it was possible to buy merchandise under other brands on short-term commitments.
>
> I do not think this change resulted from a change in consumer demands brought about by aggressive advertising of certain manufacturers of standard brands, but rather to the fact that the time element made it necessary for us to buy our merchandise as closely as possible to the time of sale, and that this time element made it unwise for us to contract ahead to have merchandise made up under our own private brands when equal quality and salability could be secured either unbranded or under other brands, whether private or nationally advertised.

The tobacco group, consisting of three chains, is dominated by the United Cigar Stores Co. of America, which in 1930 operated 994 of the 1,011 stores in this group. Although for the period as a whole no trend in private-brand sales is evident, a rather marked decline occurred between 1929 and 1930. This, of course, reflects a decrease in the private-brand sales of the United Cigar Stores Co. After the Morrow management assumed control of this company in 1929, it is understood that a decision was reached to feature popular standard brands instead of concentrating on private brands, and this quite possibly accounts for the decline in the proportion of private-brand sales in 1930.

[18] Scope of the Chain-Store Inquiry, Sec. 6, p. 11.

D. A. Schulte (Inc.), a tobacco chain operating 288 stores in 1930, owns a few private brands. It is not the policy of the company to push its sales in private brands, and it is stated that such sales "do not amount to anything and have not for some time." The products sold under the company's brand names differ from year to year, and no record is kept of private-brand sales. In explaining why his company was not interested in developing its private-brand business an executive made substantially the following statement:

Private brands don't amount to anything, and therefore we haven't paid much attention to them. You have to be continually changing sizes in order to meet competition. There are more styles, brands, and sizes in cigars than anything else on the market, but when it comes to cigarettes you can count them on your fingers. There are only one or two well-known brands of cigars that are sold almost anywhere, and I would say they are Robert Burns and White Owls.

No marked trend in either direction is evident in the four remaining groups, namely, men's ready-to-wear, women's accessories, men's shoes, and dry goods and apparel.

Numerical importance of increases and decreases.—As mentioned earlier, a third method of determining the trend of private-brand sales is to count for six 2-year periods the number of identical brand-owning chains (and stores operated by them) which show increases, decreases, or no change in the percentage of their private-brand sales to total sales. Figures of 93 chains are available for both years of the 2-year period 1925 and 1928, 45 for 1925 and 1929, 46 for 1925 and 1930, 79 for 1928 and 1929, 81 for 1928 and 1930, and 261 for 1929 and 1930. The following table shows for each pair of years the number and proportion of these chains which reported increases, decreases, and no change in private-brand sales in the last as compared with the first year. The figures in this table do not include those of the Great Atlantic & Pacific Tea Co. and the Kroger Grocery & Baking Co.

TABLE 20.—*Numbers and proportions of chains and of stores operated, reporting increases, decreases, and no change in the proportion of private-brand sales between specified years*

Years	Total	Chains reporting—					
		Increase		Decrease		No change	
		Number	Per cent of total	Number	Per cent of total	Number	Per cent of total
1925–1928	93	33	35.5	20	21.5	40	43.0
1925–1929	45	17	37.7	16	35.6	12	26.7
1925–1930	46	18	39.1	17	37.0	11	23.9
1928–29	79	27	34.2	31	39.2	21	26.6
1928–1930	81	30	37.0	30	37.0	21	26.0
1929–30	261	52	19.9	22	8.4	187	71.7
		Stores operated by chains reporting					
1925–1928	5,750	2,989	52.0	2,028	35.3	733	12.7
1925–1929	3,911	854	21.8	1,195	30.6	1,862	47.6
1925–1930	4,210	1,100	26.1	2,275	54.1	835	19.8
1928–29	9,213	3,505	38.0	1,665	18.1	4,043	43.9
1928–1930	10,318	5,558	53.9	3,496	33.9	1,264	12.2
1929–30	21,055	7,183	34.1	4,180	19.9	9,692	46.0

Comparing 1925 and 1928, 1925 and 1929, 1925 and 1930, and 1929 and 1930 the proportion of identical chains reporting increases in private-brand sales exceeded the proportion showing decreases. Comparing 1928 and 1929, the proportion of those showing decreases was larger than of those showing increases, and for 1928 and 1930 both proportions were the same. In the case of the store figures, the proportion of stores operated by chains showing increases in their private-brand sales exceeded that of stores operated by chains showing decreases in each of the four periods for which the number of chains reporting (and of stores operated by them) was largest. In the other two periods, 1925 and 1929 and 1925 and 1930, the situation was reversed. It may be assumed that private brands are handled in the majority of the stores operated by private-brand-owning chains. Hence, in an analysis of the relative importance of chains showing increases versus those showing decreases the number of stores involved is probably of greater significance than is the number of chains.

Nearly three-fourths of the chains showed no change between 1929 and 1930, while between 1925 and 1928 over 40 per cent were in the no-change group. Over 40 per cent of the stores reported were operated by chains showing no change in three of the comparisons—between 1925 and 1929, between 1928 and 1929, and between 1929 and 1930.

Conclusions.—Summarizing this section, the following conclusions may be drawn regarding the general trend of the private-brand business of chain stores:

1. There has been an enormous increase in the dollar volume of chain private-brand sales since 1925, both including and excluding the Great Atlantic & Pacific Tea Co. and the Kroger Grocery & Baking Co. figures.

2. Excluding the sales of the Great Atlantic & Pacific Tea Co. and the Kroger Grocery & Baking Co., there has been for the period studied a considerable increase in the proportion of the total sales of brand-owning chains made in private-brand merchandise. Even including these two companies, there was apparently an appreciable relative increase from 1928 to 1930 for the larger of the two groups of identical companies.

3. On the basis of the count of chains showing increases, decreases, and no change in sales of private brands, together with a similar count of stores operated by them, the showing is somewhat less definite. Even in this case, however, for four out of the six pairs of years the stores operated by chains showing increases in private-brand sales [19] greatly exceeded those operated by chains for which decreases were reported.

As regards the trend in individual kinds of chains, it may be concluded:

1. By both methods of comparison, the trend of the private-brand business of brand-owning chains appears to be definitely upward in grocery and meat (excluding A. & P. and Kroger), drug, women's shoes, men's and women's shoes, and the one men's furnishings chain reporting. It is also clearly upward from 1928 to 1930 according to both methods of analysis in grocery and department store chains.

2. The trend by both methods appears clearly to be downward in dollar-limit variety and for the two hat and cap and one musical-in-

[19] Probably a better basis of estimates than the number of chains.

strument chains reporting. The trend in tobacco, although not so definite, is apparently downward.

3. No conclusive tendency appears in the case of the confectionery, men's ready-to-wear, women's accessories, men's shoes, and dry goods and apparel chains. For the first two of these groups such tendency as does appear is toward an increase while for the other three groups the opposite is true.

Section 11. Kind of merchandise under private label.

Grocery and grocery and meat.—A number of the private-brand-owning chains reported to the commission the principal lines or groups of commodities which they were merchandising under their private labels in 1928. Some of these and other private-brand-owning chains also reported to the commission the principal commodities being sold under private brands on March 30, 1929. For the purpose of showing the relative importance of the different commodities under private label, these reports have been consolidated, all duplications of commodities being eliminated when any chain reported a commodity twice. The results are presented in this section together with other data dealing with the same subject.

The following table shows for 70 grocery and grocery and meat chains operating a total of over 30,000 stores as of December 31, 1928, the number of times each principal commodity was reported in the case of all such commodities which four or more chains sold under private label. Reference to Tables 4 and 5 shows that in 1929–30 the total number of private-brand-owning grocery and grocery and meat chains reporting to the commission was only 137 and that the total number of stores operated by these chains as of December 31, 1928, was barely 40,000. The chains represented in the following table, therefore, comprise more than 50 per cent of those reporting private-brand ownership and operated fully 75 per cent of the total stores of such chains.

TABLE 21.—*Principal commodities reported sold under private label by four or more grocery and grocery and meat chains in 1928 and/or on March 30, 1929*

Commodity	Number of chains reporting	Number of stores operated Dec. 31, 1928	Commodity	Number of chains reporting	Number of stores operated Dec. 31, 1928
Coffee	52	28, 744	Ketchup	7	1, 024
Flour	29	9, 292	Canned pineapple	6	475
Tea	20	24, 757	Peanut butter	5	573
Mayonnaise	14	1, 302	Vinegar	4	375
Canned milk	13	23, 566	Salt	4	178
Butter	13	1, 458	Condiments	4	3, 060
Canned peaches	12	7, 987	Canned pears	4	211
Bread	12	24, 341	Canned tomatoes	4	287
Canned fruits	10	9, 150	Cocoa	4	1, 964
Canned corn	9	5, 793	Sirup	4	187
Canned goods	8	1, 469			
Canned peas	8	5, 935	Number of times reported	261	
Extracts	8	3, 320	Number of commodities reported	24	
Canned vegetables	7	3, 952			

Based on the number of chains reporting, coffee is the outstanding item sold under private label, no other commodity except flour being reported by even half as many chains. Tea, mayonnaise, canned milk, and butter follow in the order named. Based on the number of stores operated, however, the order of importance is coffee, tea, bread, and canned milk, all of these commodities being reported as leading private-brand items by the Great Atlantic & Pacific Tea Co., with 15,177 stores as of December 31, 1928. If this chain is excluded, these items would still constitute four of the six leading private-brand commodities based upon the number of stores through which they are distributed, the other two being flour and canned fruit which would fall in the third and fourth places respectively. The foregoing table is subject to the limitation that it is based only upon the principal commodity items actually reported.

Large grocery and grocery and meat chains.—In order to give a better idea of the wide range of commodities under private label in grocery and grocery and meat chains, there is presented in Appendix Table 8 a list of the commodities reported under private label in 1931 by seven chains, all of which distribute an extensive line of such merchandise. These seven chains are the Great Atlantic & Pacific Tea Co., the Kroger Grocery & Baking Co., the Grand Union Co., the National Tea Co., the First National Stores (Inc.), the H. C. Bohack Co. (Inc.), and the American Stores Co. As of December 31, 1930, these chains were operating slightly over 29,000 stores of which number the Great Atlantic & Pacific Tea Co. owned 15,738 stores; Kroger Grocery & Baking Co., 5,165; First National Stores (Inc.), 2,548; the American Stores Co., 2,728; the National Tea Co., 1,600; H. C. Bohack Co. (Inc.), 696; and Grand Union Co., 611. All of these chains have developed extensive lines of private label merchandise.

Eleven items (canned beans, catsup, coffee, canned corn, flour, jelly, canned peaches, canned peas, sandwich spreads, canned tomatoes, and tea) are reported by all seven of these chains so that these items may be regarded as the leading items for this group of private brand owning grocery and grocery and meat chains. Twelve additional items are reported by six chains and 16 items by five chains. Moreover, reference to Appendix Table 8 shows that more than two-thirds of the total of 154 commodities represented were reported by two or more of the seven chains in question.

The largest number of commodities reported under private label by any of these seven chains is 92 for the Kroger Grocery & Baking Co., as shown in Table 22. The Great Atlantic & Pacific Tea Co. is second with 69 commodities. Each of the seven chains, however, reported more than 40 commodities under its own label.

TABLE 22.—*Number of commodities reported sold under private brands by each of seven leading grocery and grocery and meat chains, 1931*

Chains	Number of commodities reported sold under private brands	Number of private brands under which sold	Chains	Number of commodities reported sold under private brands	Number of private brands under which sold
Kroger Grocery & Baking Co.	92	19	American Stores Co.	44	11
The Great Atlantic & Pacific Tea Co.	69	28	Number of times reported	479	
Grand Union Co.	77	19	Number of commodities reported	154	
National Tea Co.	78	16			
First National Stores	68	16			
H. C. Bohack Co.	51	6			

The number of private brands under which the commodities shown in the foregoing table were merchandised in 1931 varies from as low as 6 in the H. C. Bohack Co. to 28 for the Great Atlantic & Pacific Tea Co.

The largest number of commodities reported under a single private label by any of the seven companies under discussion is 68 for the Kroger Grocery & Baking Co.'s brand, Country Club. These 68 commodities include, coffee, crackers, extracts, carbonated beverages, canned milk, olives, spices, tea, sausage, breakfast bacon, ham, dried beef, jelly, preserves, canned vegetables, canned fruit, breakfast foods, prunes, raisins, currants, dates, eggs, flour, honey, malt sirup, maple sirup, mayonnaise, salad dressing, sandwich spreads, mince meat, noodles, peanut butter, rice, canned fish, salt, spaghetti, macaroni, and vinegar. The company's highest grade products are reported to be packed under this label while what is called standard merchandise is packed under the brands Avondale and Clifton. The brands of this and the other leading companies are shown in the following table.

TABLE 23.—*Number of commodities reported under specified private brands by seven private brand owning grocery and grocery and meat chains*

Company and brand	Number
Kroger Grocery & Baking Co.:	
Country Club	68
Sunset Gold	38
Avondale	26
Lady Alice	18
Clifton	10
Kroger	10
Valentine	8
Red Goose	7
Embassy	3
Her Grace	2
Avalon	1
Eden Park	1
French	1
Guest	1
Hollywood	1
Jewel	1
Latonia Club	1
May Garden	1
Wesco	1
The Great Atlantic & Pacific Tea Co.:	
A. & P	37
Sultana	15
Iona	11
Encore	5
Grandmother's	4
Quaker Maid	4
Rajah	4
King Haakon	3
Sunnyfield	3
Pacific	2
Peacock	2
Red Front	2
Reliable	2
Bokar	1
Blue Peter	1
Economy	1
Eight O'clock	1
Entree	1
Gipsy	1
The Great Atlantic & Pacific Tea Co.—Continued.	
Jumbo	1
Mello-Wheat	1
Nectar	1
Our Own	1
Red Circle	1
Rest Blend	1
Sunnybrook	1
Victoria	1
Whitehouse	1
Grand Union Co.:	
Okade	47
Grand Union	36
Freshpak	26
Pocono	17
Kommunity	3
Berma	2
Rialto	2
Wonder	2
Bouquet de Savon	1
Darma	1
Elkhorn	1
Five O'clock	1
Granuteco	1
Oakwood	1
Oneida	1
Red Robin	1
Rosemary	1
Rugosa	1
Tea Pot	1
National Tea Co.:	
National	42
Hazel	34
American Home	32
Sweet Girl	18
Come Again	5
Fort Dearborn	4
Crosby	2
Circle A	1
Drum Boy	1

Brand	Number
National Tea Co.—Continued.	
Morning Glory	1
National Maid	1
Our Breakfast Blend	1
Pebble Brook	1
Red Ball	1
Special National	1
Wisconsin Special	1
First National Stores:	
Finast	54
Richmond	13
Brookside	3
Doraco	3
Radio	3
Golden Rose	1
Hen Field	1
Homeland	1
J. A	1
Kybo	1
Mirabel	1
Old Homestead	1
Prize	1

Brand	Number
First National Stores—Continued.	
S. & P	1
William-Elliot	1
Vermont Maid	1
H. C. Bohack Co.:	
Bohack	50
Bocris	1
Good	1
Osogood	1
Royal	1
Special	1
American Stores Co.:	
Asco	37
Glenwood	4
Farmdale	3
Prim	2
Victor	2
Acme	1
Fireside	1
Gold Seal	1
Home-de-lite	1
No-Waste	1
Supreme	1

The Great Atlantic & Pacific Tea Co., though selling a somewhat smaller number of commodities under private label than the Kroger Grocery & Baking Co., uses a larger number of brands than the latter (28 as compared with 19). The most important private brand of this company is A. & P. which appears on 37 different commodities including preserves, jellies, spices, canned vegetables, salt, flour, canned fish, toilet paper, peroxide, smoked beef, grape juice, and naphtha soap powder. The next most important brand, Sultana, is used on some 15 classes of commodities, including salmon, macaroni, spaghetti, peanut butter, sirup, jams, jellies, canned beans, and canned vegetables. Iona is used for 11 commodities including salmon, cocoa, canned vegetables, catsup, and canned beans. Encore is used for macaroni, spaghetti, noodles, olive oil, and olives. None of the company's other labels is used on as many as five commodities. Where the brand A. & P. is used, it indicates that the commodity in question is the best grade carried by that company under private label. Where a commodity is not packed under this label, the highest quality sold by the company may be found under some other label.

This situation is explained in some detail by an executive of the company.

> Where the brand A. & P. is used, it is employed for the highest quality products which are sold by this company under private label. The A. & P. brand never appears on a product having a quality lower than the highest quality we market.
>
> In the case of those products on which the brand A. & P. does not appear, some other of our private-brand names may be on the highest quality sold by the company under its own label, and this means that it is the highest quality marketed by this or any other company.
>
> At one time the top grade of all of our private brands bore the A. & P. label. Now we have so-called family groups: A. & P., Quaker Maid, Rajah, Encore, etc., any one of which labels may be on the highest quality of a given product; Rajah, in the case of salad dressing; Quaker Maid, in the case of cocoa; Encore, in the case of spaghetti and macaroni; A. & P., in the case of canned peas; Sunnyfield, in the case of flour. The other qualities of these products are under any one of a number of labels. The Iona brand is used for products of standard grade, and the Sultana brand for an intermediate grade, just under the standard set for highest quality. In some cases there is a second intermediate grade also. Thus, in canned peas, the A. & P. label designates a very fancy pea—the very best that we can buy. Then there are Sultana, Reliable, and Iona peas, each a step further down in grade. In the case of preserves, Quaker Maid signifies the

highest quality (not only the highest quality sold by this company, but the highest quality sold by any company), and Sultana indicates the next lower grade. In sirup, A. & P. maple sirup stands for the highest quality of pure maple sirup, while Sultana sirup designates the second grade, which is not 100 per cent maple, but a blended maple and cane sirup.

In First National, Bohack, and American Stores, a single private brand is relatively much more important than in the other four chains. Each of these companies sells under its leading brand a far larger number of commodities than are sold under all of its remaining brands combined, whereas in the other four chains, the number of commodities carried under other labels greatly exceeds the number under its most important label. This is particularly true of the Bohack Co. which sells 50 commodities under the label Bohack. Of the remaining five labels of this company, four are used for the four grades of coffee, roasted and packed by the company, and Osogood is used for tea.

The leading brands of the First National Stores (Inc.) are Finast used on 54 different commodities, and Richmond used on 13, no other label appearing on more than three commodities. Each of the three original companies forming the First National Stores in 1925 [20] owned private brands. Some of these brands were dropped by the new company and others continued as First National brands. Thus, the brand name Brookside formerly owned by the John T. Connor Co. was retained for the company's dairy products, milk, butter, and eggs. Likewise, the brand Richmond of Wm. O'Keefe (Inc.) was retained for products of choice or extra standard quality. A new brand (Finast) was adopted by the new company for its best or fancy goods.

The American Stores Co. sells 37 commodities under the brand name Asco, no more than four products being sold under any one of its 10 remaining labels. This company's canned vegetables are sold under both the brands Asco and Farmdale, its sliced bacon under either Asco or Fireside, the preserves and jellies bear either the brand names Asco or Glenwood, rice is packaged under the names Asco and Prim, and coffee is sold under three labels, Asco, Victor, and Acme.

Although much smaller than either The Great Atlantic & Pacific Tea Co. or the Kroger Grocery & Baking Co., both the Grand Union and National Tea companies have about as many different commodities under private label as do either of these chains. (Table 22.) Both these chains sell an exceptionally large number of commodities under each of three or four leading brands, each company reporting over 100 articles under its three principal brands, many of which are, of course, duplicates of each other. This is a larger total number under the three leading labels than are reported by any other one of these chains except Kroger (Table 23). The three principal brands of the National Tea Co. based on the total number of articles reported under each label are National, Hazel, and American Home, under each of which the company reports more than 30 distinct commodities. According to this company, its National label is used for the extra fancy lines in canned goods and the American Home brand for its fancy lines.

The principal private brands of the Grand Union Co. are Okade, Grand Union, and Freshpak. As this is the smallest of any of these seven chains, the large number of commodities placed under each of these principal labels as well as its high total of private-brand com-

---

[20] See Report of the Federal Trade Commission on Growth and Development of Chain Stores, Sec. 8.

modities is perhaps influenced by its extensive wagon-route business, this company operating several thousand house-to-house routes.

Drug.—Information is available on the commodities under private label in 1928–29 for 29 drug chains operating five hundred-odd stores as of December 31, 1928. This number is equivalent to approximately one-third of the drug chains (and one-half of the stores operated by them) which reported the ownership of private brands to the commission in 1929–30. (Tables 4 and 5.) The following table presents a summary of all such commodities which were reported by four or more of these drug chains together with the number of times reported by each.

TABLE 24.—*Principal commodities reported sold under private label by four or more drug chains in 1928 and/or on March 30, 1929*

Commodity	Number of chains reporting	Number of stores operated Dec. 31, 1928	Commodity	Number of chains reporting	Number of stores operated Dec. 31, 1928
Cough sirup	13	89	Cod-liver oil	5	28
Corn remedy	12	69	Toilet goods	4	277
Tooth paste	10	373	Talcum	4	251
Cold tablets	8	66	Cleaning fluid	4	251
Mouth wash	6	346	Aspirin	4	337
Hair preparations	6	63	Mineral oil	4	41
Lotions	6	69			
Shampoo lotion	5	290	Number of times reported	111	
Cold cream	5	274			
Milk of magnesia	5	126	Number of commodities reported	18	
Liniment	5	124			
Headache powders	5	23			

Based upon the number of chains reporting, cough sirups, corn remedies, and tooth pastes constitute the most important private label merchandise in drug chains. From the standpoint of the number of stores, however, the first two of the three items mentioned are not of outstanding importance, the three commodities sold through the largest numbers of stores being tooth pastes, mouth washes, and aspirin, each distributed through between three and four hundred stores.

Some of the private brands of the Walgreen Co., probably the leading private-brand drug chain, are Walgreen, Amelita, Leon Navar, Kellar, Peau Doux, and J. D. The Peoples Drug Stores (Inc.) sells a number of commodities under the brand name Peoples Quality, Graham's, Barnard's, and Moret.

Dollar-limit Variety.—Five leading variety chains, S. S. Kresge Co., W. T. Grant Co., McLellan Stores (Inc.), McCrory Stores Corporation, and G. C. Murphy Co. reported the number of items under private label in 1931.

TABLE 25.—*Number of commodities reported sold under private brands by each of five leading variety chains, 1931*

Chains	Number of commodities reported sold under private brands	Number of private brands under which sold
W. T. Grant Co.	43	41
S. S. Kresge Co.	19	20
McCrory Stores Corporation	13	13
McLellan Stores (Inc.)	26	9
G. C. Murphy Co.	6	3
Number of times reported	107	
Number of commodities reported	72	

The total number of commodities reported sold under private label by these chains was 72 and the number of times reported was only 107, an average of about one and one-half commodities per chain. Only one item, hosiery, was reported by all five companies. Hair nets and sanitary napkins were both reported by four; bias tape, razor blades, safety pins, and shirts were reported by three. Seventeen additional items were reported by two chains and the balance, or two-thirds of the total, by only a single company. Appendix Table 9 presents the list of commodities and the number of chains reporting them.

A number of the commodities carried by the F. W. Woolworth Co. are identified by the Woolworth trade-mark which is "W" within a diamond. In general, the use of this mark is reserved for merchandise of the best quality. At present the trade-mark is used to some extent in almost every department for merchandise which those connected with the company refer to as "our diamond 'W' grade." For example, it is used for commodities differing as widely as school pads and hosiery. Some of the executives, in fact, do not regard it as a private brand because the public has not been educated as to the meaning of the trade-mark nor has any attempt been made to gain consumer preference for it.

Most of the private brands of the S. S. Kresge Co. appear only on a single item but many articles commonly carry two or more brands. For example, Jean, Two-in-one, and Sensation are used for the one commodity, hair nets; Chef-ette and Kook-Rite for enamelware, and Smooth Shave and Moon for razor blades. The brand Green Oak appears on six different commodities, all of which are usually classed as notions, i. e., thread, shoe laces, safety pins, elastic, hose supporters, and bias seam tape. Treasure Trove was used for both hosiery and underwear.

The W. T. Grant Co. not only reports the largest number of items under private label of any of the variety chains but also the largest number of private brands. The brand Wearite was first used on knit underwear about 1913 to tie up a definite standard of quality with prices within the limits of one price range. The brand has been applied to hosiery, ties, and other articles. The company states:—

> A very definite customer following has been built up on this brand which has come to mean Grant quality to our customers.
>
> About 1925, the brand Every-ready was applied to food-choppers, vacuum bottles, and family scales within our price range and has resulted since then in the same customer following as we have for Wearite wearing apparel lines.
>
> Jack-O-Lantern child's hose (1921) and Golden Glo furniture polish (1923) are other similar examples.
>
> Upon our entry into the radio business we used private brand Songbird radio tubes which made it possible to handle a complete line of radio tubes within our price range. Standard brand tubes, at that time, were not available within our price range.
>
> Redipak sanitary napkins were instituted when the leading manufacturers of those items appeared to have a practical monopoly of that type of business. We were able to present a quality article at a much lower retail price, and have since maintained the trade-mark because of the customer following which developed.

In the McCrory Co. 13 different commodities are sold under private label. These include stationery (Ambassador), razor blades (Commander), cutlery (Dur-edge), phonograph records and needles (Oriole), toilet preparations (Ardsley), shaving cream (Kreme Lather), tooth paste (Perledent), and notions (Sanimaid).

The McLellan Stores Co. uses the brand Macleco on several different classes of commodities including dry goods, electrical goods, furniture polish, enamelware, stationery, hosiery, shoes, golf balls, tooth brushes, blankets, shirts, and notions. Hosiery is also sold under five additional labels—Strengthtex, Little Buttercup, Roughshod, Celeste, and Lella.

In October, 1931, the G. C. Murphy Co. carried only six commodities under private label. Hair nets, bias seam tape, snap fasteners, and silk hose were sold under the brand Moderne, work shirts under the brand Forty-Niner, and candy under the label Mack Shaw.

Miscellaneous.—Outside of the three foregoing lines only a limited number of reports were received covering the commodities under private brand, owing partly to the relatively limited number of chains owning private brands which belong to these groups. Moreover, certain lines obviously are almost exclusively private brand. These include both the shoe and confectionery lines where the great bulk of the chains do from 90 to 100 per cent of their business in private-brand merchandise.

In 10 men's ready-to-wear chains operating 110 stores 3 report clothing, 2 men's clothing, and 2 men's and boys' clothing under private label. One chain each reports boys' clothing, shirts and clothing, garments, suits, overcoats, pants, shirts, and ties.

In 6 tobacco chains operating 1,149 stores, all 6 report cigars under private brand and 4 of them operating 36 stores report private brands of tobacco.

Four dry goods and apparel chains (operating 1,043 stores) one of which is the J. C. Penney Co., have private brands in one or more of the following items: Overalls, work shirts, sheeting, shirts, piece goods, hosiery, underwear, blankets, neckwear, millinery, lingerie, house dresses, gloves, women's, children's, and infants' ready-to-wear, shoes, notions, men's and boys' clothing, men's and boys' hats and caps, men's furnishings, and work clothes. Only one of these items, overalls, is reported by more than one chain.

Six department store chains, operating 260 stores, one of which is Montgomery Ward & Co., report the following lines under private brands: Men's clothing, boys' clothing, shirts, hosiery, house furnishings, rugs and draperies, furniture, hardware, stoves, radios, tires and tubes, sporting goods, toilet goods and drugs, dry goods, pickles, mayonnaise, ketchup, mustard, and shoes. Four of these chains, including Montgomery Ward, report handling shoes under private brand and two, one of which is also Montgomery Ward, hosiery. The only other items reported by any two chains are toilet goods and drugs, and men's clothing.

Eight women's accessories chains operating 68 stores report only 2 items under private brand; hosiery is reported by 6 of these chains and corsets by 2.

Section 12. Proportions of private-brand sales of specified commodities.

The proportions of private-brand sales to total sales, discussed in sections 9 and 10, do not fully measure the significance of the private-brand development of the chain store. The reason is that in many cases the chain has developed only one or at most a few of such brands with the result that the percentage of reported private-brand sales is frequently very low in comparison with the total reported sales of all commodities. For this reason, it is interesting to consider the ratio of reported private-brand sales to total sales for various commodities for which such information is available. These are presented in this section. The percentages shown in the following tables are averages of similar percentage figures reported by the chains for 1928 in response to an inquiry requesting statements or estimates of the proportions of private-brand sales in the principal commodities which were sold by them under private label.

Because of the limited number of chains reporting, the available data on this subject have been consolidated into three tables, partially ignoring the kind of business in which the chains are engaged. The first table presented is for food products, reported chiefly by grocery and grocery and meat chains. The second is composed chiefly of wearing apparel, house furnishings, and miscellaneous lines, the figures being principally from wearing apparel and department store chains; and the third table is made up mainly of drug and tobacco store lines, reported chiefly by the former type of chain.

Food products.—Table 26 presents for specified food products the average percentages of total sales of these products made in private brands for chains reporting such figures.

TABLE 26.—*Average of proportions of total sales of principal grocery products made under private brand as reported by specified numbers of chains for 1928*

Product	Number of chains	Number of stores	Average of percentages of total sales made in private brands	Product	Number of chains	Number of stores	Average of percentages of total sales made in private brands
Coffee	20	24,716	39.5	Canned tomatoes and ketchup	1	121	25.0
Candy	19	853	82.3	Cleaning articles	1	60	15.0
Flour	11	7,458	38.2	Cocoa	1	201	35.0
Butter	10	1,249	64.5	Desserts	1	105	18.0
Tea	9	18,331	44.2	Dry groceries	1	611	5.0
Canned fruits	8	9,088	45.6	Evaporated milk	1	201	20.0
Mayonnaise	8	315	48.5	Extracts	1	121	90.0
Bread	7	21,905	93.6	Extracts and spices	1	1,791	30.0
Canned goods	7	1,298	32.4	Fancy groceries	1	1,041	2.7
Canned vegetables	6	3,899	61.1	Flour and cereals	1	105	27.0
Canned fish	3	1,409	26.3	Fruit	1	88	10.0
Ammonia	2	117	51.0	General groceries	1	664	12.0
Cereals	2	5,348	7.0	Mayonnaise pickles, and olives	1	121	80.0
Canned milk	2	1,349	16.7	Milk and cream	1	1,791	100.0
Cheese	2	1,129	28.7	Oils	1	1,041	4.4
Condiments	2	2,832	54.0	Package rice	1	308	58.0
Eggs	2	278	18.3	Package salt	1	88	2.0
Jellies and preserves	2	1,794	77.5	Pancake flour	1	201	80.0
Milk	2	20,437	48.5	Peanut butter	1	190	46.5
Bakery products	1	3	10.6	Preserves	1	1,041	92.4
Baking ingredients	1	1,041	39.5	Raisins	1	190	14.3
Beverages	1	1,041	69.2	Salmon	1	15,177	50.0
Bird seed	1	190	100.0	Soap and household goods	1	105	39.0
Bottled beverages	1	1,791	70.0	Spaghetti and macaroni	1	121	40.0
Bottle goods, jars, pickles, and sirup	1	105	38.0	Spices and baking ingredients	1	105	57.0
Bread and cake	1	1,791	100.0	Sirups and spreads	1	1,041	14.9
Bread, flour, and pancake flour	1	121	20.0	Tea, coffee, and cocoa	1	105	83.0
Canned corn, peas, and tomatoes	1	5,260	57.0				

The average of the reported proportions of private-brand sales in this table ranges all the way from 2 per cent for packaged salt to 100 per cent for bird seed, bread and cake, and milk and cream. Practically every extreme case, however, either low or high, is reported by only a single chain. The average proportion of sales made in private brands is in excess of 25 per cent on 16 of the 19 commodities reported on by two or more chains. For 14 of these 19 items, the reported average is above 30 per cent and for 7 items it is above 50 per cent. Bread is above 90 per cent and candy above 80. Jellies and preserves (77.5 per cent), butter (64.5) and canned vegetables (61.1 per cent) are next in importance.

Apparel, household and miscellaneous.—Table 27 presenting similar information for wearing apparel, household, and miscellaneous products shows on the whole, much larger proportions of sales made in private brands than do the commodities under private label in the food products lines, though the size and number of chains in Table 27 are much smaller than in the food group.

TABLE 27.—*Average of proportions of total sales of principal wearing-apparel, household, and miscellaneous products made under private brand as reported by specified numbers of chains for 1928*

Product	Number of chains	Number of stores	Average of percentages of total sales made in private brands
Shoes	25	2,183	80.8
Hosiery	15	1,370	70.9
Hats	6	208	89.2
Clothing	4	65	70.0
Men's clothing	4	20	83.7
Hardware	3	676	45.2
Men's and boys' clothing	3	1,044	64.0
Notions	3	1,433	19.4
Pianos	3	16	70.0
Boys' clothing	2	12	70.0
Caps	2	52	90.0
Dry goods	2	9	20.0
Overalls	2	14	95.0
Radios and supplies	2	447	70.0
Shirts	2	13	97.5
Ties	2	13	97.5
Auto supplies	1	217	25.0
Corsets	1	3	50.0
Findings	1	3	100.0
Furniture	1	230	30.0
Garments	1	7	100.0
Gloves	1	3	100.0
Hair goods	1	229	5.0
Hosiery, underwear, sweaters, blankets, and neckwear	1	1,023	95.0
House furnishings	1	230	50.0
Mattresses	1	3	1.0
Men's and boys' hats and caps	1	1,023	95.0
Men's furnishings	1	6	25.0
Men's furnishings and work clothes	1	1,023	60.0
Millinery, piece goods, lingerie, house dresses, gloves	1	1,023	20.0
Miscellaneous musical instruments	1	8	10.0
Overcoats	1	11	87.5
Paint	1	105	100.0
Pants	1	7	100.0
Piece goods	1	1,023	35.0
Records	1	229	1.0
Rubbers	1	3	100.0
Rugs and draperies	1	230	20.0
Shirts and clothing	1	10	10.0
Shoes and accessories	1	4	100.0
Shoe dressing	1	77	100.0
Shoe polish	1	41	100.0
Slippers	1	41	100.0
Sporting goods	1	230	50.0
Stayform	1	3	100.0
Stoves	1	230	100.0
Suits	1	11	87.5
Sundry furnishings, caps	1	7	100.0
Tires and tubes	1	230	100.0
Women's, children's, and infants' ready-to-wear	1	1,023	2.0
Women's wear	1	217	10.0

Except for eight commodity lines (notions; hair goods; mattresses; miscellaneous musical instruments; records; shirts and clothing; women's, children's, and infants' ready-to-wear; and women's wear), there is not an item for which the average of the reported proportions of private-brand sales is below 20 per cent. In fact, most of the averages are 50 per cent or more, with substantial proportions in excess of 70 per cent and a number above 90 per cent, even in those classes of commodities where two or more chains reported. Of the 35 commodities for which only a single chain reported, nearly one-half of the total showed 100 per cent of private-brand sales.

Drug and tobacco.—The importance of private-brand sales of commodities sold in drug and tobacco stores is strikingly less than in food products, wearing apparel, household furnishings, and miscellaneous lines shown in the two preceding tables. In only two instances, household remedies (50 per cent) and after-shaving lotions (50 per cent) were the private-brand sales as high as 40 per cent of total sales. Cigars (39.6 per cent), tobacco (35.3 per cent) and shaving cream (35 per cent) are the only other commodities reported in which the private brand sales were not below 30 per cent. Most of the remaining articles showed less than 20 per cent private-brand sales and a large number less than 10 per cent.

TABLE 28.—*Average of proportions of total sales of principal drug and cigar store products made under private brand as reported by specified numbers of chains for 1928*

Product	Number of chains	Number of stores	Average of percentages of total sales made in private brands	Product	Number of chains	Number of stores	Average of percentages of total sales made in private brands
Cigars	5	1,136	39.6	Cough sirup	1	4	5.0
Toilet goods	5	470	3.6	Cream	1	3	2.0
Drugs	3	47	15.0	Dental cream	1	3	25.0
Tobacco	3	22	35.3	Dyspepsia tablets	1	4	1.0
Cold tablets	2	7	25.0	Hair dressing	1	3	25.0
Cough remedy	2	6	26.7	Headache wafers	1	4	15.0
Patent medicine	2	8	4.0	Household remedies	1	6	50.0
Remedies	2	236	14.0	Liver pills	1	4	10.0
Toilet goods and drugs	2	6	17.5	O. S. balm	1	6	5.0
After-shaving lotion	1	3	50.0	Pharmaceuticals	1	230	1.0
Beef, iron, and wine	1	4	5.0	Prickly heat powder	1	4	10.0
Benzothymoline, mouth wash, rheumatic, antiseptic, dentoment, cascara compound, cold cream, vanishing cream, nasal oil, talcum	1	6	22.5	Proprietary	1	6	1.0
				Proprietary medicines	1	3	5.0
				Shaving cream	1	3	35.0
				Toilet articles	1	3	20.0
Carbolic salve	1	6	5.0	Toothache, earache, and corn remedies	1	3	5.0
Cleaning fluid	1	3	5.0	Tooth paste	1	3	3.0
Corn remedy	1	4	5.0	Stationery	1	193	5.3

Proportions of private-brand sales of leading chains, by commodities.—Further light upon the importance of private brands is indicated by the proportions of sales made in private brands reported by leading chains for certain specified commodities. The following table shows for a number of important grocery and grocery and meat chains operating from over 100 to several thousand stores the proportions of private brand sales in specific commodities in 1928. Included in these figures are percentages reported for various divisions of the Safeway Co., information on this organization not being available in consolidated form.

TABLE 29.—*Reported percentages of specified commodities sold under private brand by specified grocery and grocery and meat chains, for 1928*

Commodity	Market Basket Corporation	Safeway Stores (Inc.) of California Piggly-Wiggly, southern division	National Grocery Co.	National Tea Co.	Mutual Grocery Co.
Coffee	95			12.08	78
Tea	40			10.11	
Bread			100		
Butter		34.68			
Canned goods	75	12.74			
Canned fruit				55.61	68
Canned milk	[1] 20			19.46	14
Canned vegetables				60.45	71
Canned fish				[2] 24.79	24
Candy		75.6			
Bottled beverages				[4] 69.23	
Flour	25	3.25		[8] 14.84	
Jellies and preserves				[7] 92.4	

Commodity	Safeway Stores (Inc.) of California, southern Safeway division	First National Stores (Inc.)	Skaggs Safeway Stores (Nevada corporation)	The Grand Union Co.	The Great Atlantic & Pacific Tea Co.	Kroger Grocery & Baking Co.
Coffee		90		80	89	92
Tea		90			73	
Bread	90	[5] 100			81	89
Butter	100		75			
Canned goods	70					
Canned fruit		30		5		68
Canned milk					[3] 52	
Canned vegetables		70		80		[6] 57
Canned salmon					50	
Canned fish						
Bottled beverages		70				
Flour				40		27
Jellies and preserves		80				

1 Reported for "evaporated milk" only.
2 Reported for "fish in tins."
3 Reported as "milk" but as canned milk is one of the largest private brand lines of this company, it is assumed to be canned.
4 Reported as "beverages"—assumed to be bottled.
5 Reported for "bread and cake."
6 Reported for "canned corn, peas, tomatoes."
7 Reported for "preserves."
8 Reported for "bulk flour."

This table shows a wide variation in the percentages of different commodities handled under private label, not only as between commodities, but also as between different chains. For example, for the five chains reporting flour, the range is from 3¼ per cent for Safeway (Piggly-Wiggly—southern division) to 40 per cent for Grand Union. For tea the proportion sold under private label ranges from slightly under 11 per cent for the National Tea Co. to 90 per cent in First National Stores. Private brand bread, which is usually manufactured by the chain itself, represents over 80 per cent of the bread sales in five reporting chains. In the National Grocery Co. and First National Stores all bread is sold under private label. The lowest percentage of private brand bread, it is interesting to observe, was reported by the Great Atlantic & Pacific Tea Co. Except in the National Tea Co., whose private brands represent less than 15 per cent of the total of this commodity, over 78 per cent of the coffee sales of the seven chains reporting are under private brands. Canned milk is exceptionally high only in the Great Atlantic & Pacific Tea Co., amounting to around one-half of the total milk sales, while for the remaining three reporting chains it is 20 per cent or less. Relatively large proportions of canned vegetables are also sold under private label by the reporting chains, the percentages running from 57 per cent to 80 per cent of the total. Canned goods, however, comprise less than 15 per cent of the total in the Safeway (Piggly-Wiggly—southern division) and canned fruit falls as low as 5 per cent in the Grand Union Co. Jellies and preserves although reported by only the National Tea and First National Stores are sold chiefly under private label by these two companies. About 50 per cent of the canned salmon sold by the Great Atlantic & Pacific Tea Co. is under its own private label, this company operating salmon canning factories of its own.

Reports of the proportions of various commodities sold under private label by other large chains of over 100 stores are limited in number. In the exclusive private brand chains the percentages reported are, of course, all practically 100 per cent. Thus, the Fanny Farmer candy company reported 100 per cent in candy; Sarnoff-Irving, 100 per cent in hats; Sheppard & Myers, 100 per cent in shoes; and the Melville Shoe Co. for its three chains, Thom McAn, John Ward, and Rival, 100 per cent not only in shoes but also in hosiery. In the drug chains, Walgreen in 1928 sold about 15 per cent of its dentifrices under private label, 8 per cent of remedies, and 5 per cent of toilet preparations. In the variety field, the S. H. Kress Co. reported 99 per cent of hosiery sales under private label. The remaining four commodities which were reported sold under private label were candy, stationery, notions, and toilet goods, none of which amounted to as much as 10 per cent of total sales. McCrory reported three principal commodities under private label; hardware, hair goods, and phonograph records. The proportion in each case was 1 per cent or less of total sales.

In the W. T. Grant Co., the highest proportion of private brand sales reported is 75 per cent for hardware. This company sold in 1928 over 50 per cent of its hosiery under private label, 60 per cent of its radio supplies, 25 per cent of its auto supplies, 10 per cent of its women's wear, and 5 per cent of its notions. The J. C. Penney Co. had 95 per cent of its sales under private label in hosiery, underwear, sweaters, blankets, and neckwear; 100 per cent in shoes; 95 per cent in men's and boys' hats and caps; 60 per cent in men's furnishings, and work clothes; and 50 per cent in notions. Montgomery Ward sold under private label 100 per cent of its tires and tubes and also 100 per cent of its stoves; 80 per cent of its radios; 60 per cent of its hardware; and 50 per cent of both sporting goods and house furnishings. In hosiery and shoes, however, it only sold approximately 10 per cent under private label, in furniture, only 30 per cent, and in rugs and draperies, 20 per cent.

Section 13.—Mark-up policies on private and standard brand merchandise.

As shown in section 6, out of a total of 1,247 chains 351 reported the ownership of private brands in 1931. Of these 351 brand-owning chains, 304 operating 34,016 stores, reported that their mark-up on their private brands was higher than, lower than, or the same as that on standard brands.

As is shown in Appendix Table 10, which gives the distribution by kinds of business of the 304 chains (and stores operated), one or more chains reported in every line of business except unlimited price variety.[21] Based upon the number of stores operated by the reporting chains the returns are least representative for department stores, dry goods and apparel, women's accessories, women's ready-to-wear, and confectionery. In each of these five groups and in four others (hats and caps, $1 limit variety, men's ready-to-wear, and grocery and meat) the proportion of stores operated is below the average proportion (62 per cent) of all stores operated by chains reporting private brand mark-up policy.

In estimating the representativeness of the figures certain factors must be given consideration. In the first place, it must be remembered that in several kinds of business the number of reporting chains owning private brands is small. Second, reference to individual schedules indicates that the failure of many chains to reply to this question was due to the fact that they had no established mark-up policy on private as compared with standard brands. Some of their private brands carried a higher mark-up and some a lower For example, the largest chain in the grocery and meat group, the Great Atlantic & Pacific Tea Co., indicated that it had no standard policy. Since the Great Atlantic & Pacific Tea Co. is thus excluded, barely 50 per cent of the grocery and meat stores operated by chains owning private brands are represented in these tabulations. The largest chain in the dry goods and apparel group, J. C. Penney Co., indicated that the mark-up on some of its private brands was higher and on some lower than on competing standard brands. This chain, however, sells relatively few commodities bearing standard brands. A third factor is that some of the chains in certain lines reporting ownership of private brands sell only their own brands and consequently could not furnish comparisons on private brand and standard brand merchandise. Similarly, the sample of stores of department store chains is small because two of the largest of these chains sold no competing standard brands and therefore did not reply to the question.

Giving full consideration to all of the foregoing factors it seems probable that the figures presented are substantially representative of the mark-up policies of chain-store distributors on private and standard brand merchandise.

Ninety-three chains, or about 31 per cent of the 304 chains reporting, marked up private brands more than competing standard brands. These 93 chains operated 7,157 stores or about 21 per cent of the stores operated by all chains reporting.

TABLE 30.—*Distribution of 304 chains according to their reported mark-up policy on private and standard brands, 1931, and of stores operated by them, December 31, 1930*

Compared with standard brands—	Reporting on mark-up policy		Compared with standard brands—	Reporting on mark-up policy	
	Chains	Stores operated		Chains	Stores operated
Private brands are marked up:	*Number*	*Number*	Percentage of total reporting:	*Per cent*	*Per cent*
Higher	93	7,157	Higher	30.6	21.0
Lower	18	7,441	Lower	5.9	21.9
Same	193	19,418	Same	63.5	57.1
Total	304	34,016	Total	100.0	100.0

[21] No unlimited-price variety chains reported owning private brands in 1931.

Only 18 chains, or about 6 per cent of the total reporting, sold their private brands at a lower mark-up than competing standard brands, but these chains operated slightly more stores than the group marking up their private brands higher than standard brands.

By far the largest group, both in number of chains included and number of stores operated by them, indicated that the per cent of mark-up on private and standard brands was approximately the same. One hundred ninety-three or practically two-thirds of all the chains reporting followed this policy. These chains operated more than one-half of the stores operated by all chains reporting.

Mark-up on private brands higher.—Although one or more reports were received from chains in each of 25 kinds of business, chains in only 13 kinds reported higher mark-ups on private brand than on standard brand merchandise.

About three-fourths of the total chains (operating over 90 per cent of the stores) which reported higher mark-ups on private brands, are in the grocery, grocery and meat, and drug businesses.

TABLE 31.—*Number of chains reporting "higher" mark-up on private brands than on competing standard brands, 1931, and stores operated December 31, 1930, by kind of chain*

Kind of chain	Chains		Stores	
	Number reporting "higher" mark-up	Per cent of all reporting on mark-up	Number operated by chains reporting "higher" mark-up	Per cent of total operated by all chains reporting on mark-up
Grocery	15	34.9	1,996	20.8
Grocery and meat	15	28.9	3,003	21.1
Confectionery	1	9.1	3	2.1
Drug	45	63.4	1,109	89.8
Tobacco	3	15.0	59	5.1
Variety ($1 limit)	1	8.3	157	7.7
Men's ready-to-wear	1	11.1	11	13.8
Men's furnishings	1	50.0	18	85.7
Hats and caps	1	16.7	10	15.2
Women's shoes	2	33.3	120	56.6
Department store	4	66.7	22	71.0
Furniture	1	50.0	35	92.1
Hardware	3	100.0	14	100.0
Total	93	30.6	7,157	21.0

The lines in which a higher mark-up on private brands is apparently least common as measured in terms of either chains or stores are confectionery, tobacco, dollar-limit variety, men's ready-to-wear, and hats and caps; in each of these the proportion of stores or chains represented is less than 18 per cent of the total. The policy is somewhat more prevalent in grocery and grocery and meat chains as indicated by the proportions of the total stores and particularly the total chains reporting.

The hardware chains report the highest proportion (100 per cent) of chains marking up private brands higher than standard brands. The drug group is perhaps more significant for this study, however, not only because of the high proportion of chains (63.4 per cent) and stores (89.8 per cent) involved, but also because of the large number of both (45 chains and 1,109 stores) represented in the figures. Furniture, department stores, and men's furnishings are also fairly high in the proportions of both chains and stores.

Mark-up on private brands lower.—Only eight lines of business are represented by chains marking up their private brands less than standard brands.

TABLE 32.—*Number of chains reporting "lower" mark-up on private brands than on competing standard brands, 1931, and stores operated December 31, 1930, by kind of chain*

Kind of chain	Chains		Stores	
	Number reporting "lower" mark-up	Per cent of all reporting on mark-up	Number operated by chains reporting "lower" mark-up	Per cent of total operated by all chains reporting on mark-up
Grocery	3	7.0	1,170	12.2
Grocery and meat	5	9.6	5,891	34.4
Meat	1	25.0	27	18.1
Drug	3	4.2	20	1.6
Variety ($1 limit)	2	16.7	226	11.0
Men's ready-to-wear	1	11.1	10	12.5
Women's shoes	2	33.3	82	38.7
Dry goods and apparel	1	11.1	15	6.9
Total	18	5.9	7,441	21.9

In women's shoe chains about one-third of the reporting companies, operating slightly less than 40 per cent of the stores, follow this policy. Only five, or less than 10 per cent, of the grocery and meat chains marked up their private brands less than competing standard brands, but they operated nearly 35 per cent of such stores and an average of over 1,000 stores each. This accounts primarily for the fact that so large a proportion of the total stores (21.9 per cent) belonged to chains which marked up private brands less than standard brands. Most of the other kinds of chains following this policy are relatively unimportant as measured either by the proportions of chains or the proportions of stores operated in their respective lines of business, particularly drugs, where each proportion is less than 5 per cent.

Mark-up on private brands same.—One or more chains in each of 24 kinds of business reported that their private brand and standard brand merchandise carried the same mark-up. No hardware chains belong to this group, and as previously pointed out no reports on this subject were obtained from unlimited price variety chains.

TABLE 33.—*Number of chains reporting "same" mark-up on private brands and competing standard brands, 1931, and stores operated December 31, 1930, by kind of chain*

Kind of chain	Chains		Stores	
	Number reporting "same" mark-up	Per cent of all reporting on mark-up	Number operated by chains reporting "same" mark-up	Per cent of total operated by all chains reporting on mark-up
Grocery	25	58.1	6,442	67.0
Grocery and meat	32	61.5	7,608	44.5
Meat	3	75.0	122	81.9
Confectionery	10	90.9	139	97.9
Drug	23	32.4	106	8.6
Tobacco	17	85.0	1,097	94.9
Variety ($1 limit)	9	75.0	1,662	81.3
Variety ($5 limit)	1	100.0	53	100.0
Men's ready-to-wear	7	77.8	59	73.7
Women's ready-to-wear	3	100.0	27	100.0
Men's and women's ready-to-wear	3	100.0	39	100.0
Men's furnishings	1	50.0	3	14.3
Women's accessories	3	100.0	30	100.0
Hats and caps	5	83.3	56	84.8
Millinery	2	100.0	305	100.0
Men's shoes	4	100.0	246	100.0
Women's shoes	2	33.4	10	4.7
Men's and women's shoes	24	100.0	1,074	100.0
Dry goods	2	100.0	49	100.0
Dry goods and apparel	8	88.9	202	93.1
Department store	2	33.3	9	29.0
General merchandise	2	100.0	16	100.0
Furniture	1	50.0	3	7.9
Musical instruments	4	100.0	61	100.0
Total	193	63.5	19,418	57.1

One hundred per cent of the reporting chains in 10 of the 24 kinds of business represented took the same mark-up on private and standard brands. One-half or more of the reporting chains followed this policy in every line represented excepting drugs, women's shoes, and department stores. Moreover, one-half of all the stores operated by reporting chains in 18 of the 24 groups belonged to chains using the same mark-up on both types of brands.

Section 14. Pricing policies on private and standard brand merchandise.

Two hundred forty-eight chains, or approximately 60 per cent of the 412 companies reporting on the original schedule that they owned private brands in 1929–30, answered the commission's inquiry as to their policy of pricing them—that is, whether they were priced higher than or lower than or the same as competing standard brands. (Appendix Table 11.) These 248 chains, however, operated 89 per cent of the total stores operated by the 412 chains which owned private brands.

No replies which could be classified were received from five kinds of chains ($5 limit variety, unlimited price variety, women's ready-to-wear, millinery, and hardware). No $5 limit variety chains reported ownership of private brands in 1929–30 and only one chain in either unlimited price variety or hardware. Three women's ready-to-wear chains reported the sale of private brands (Table 4) but made no statement as to their policy of pricing them.

The proportion of chains reporting on private-brand pricing policy, the proportion of stores operated by them, or both (Appendix Table 11), are relatively low in confectionery, men's ready-to-wear, women's accessories, men's shoes, men's and women's shoes, and furniture. In several instances the reason for this is probably found in the fact that many of these chains sold only their own brands and could not therefore report a comparison with standard brands. Several confectionery chains, for example, sold only their own brands of candy, and the same situation existed in a number of shoe and men's ready-to-wear chains.

More than 175 chains also reported the reasons for their pricing policies on private as compared with standard brands. The importance of these various reasons, as indicated by the number of times they are reported, is discussed in connection with the numbers and proportions of chains following each of the three policies considered in this section. The great bulk of the reasons thus assigned, however (138 out of 190), were reported by chains in three kinds of business—grocery, grocery and meat, and drug.

As shown in Table 34 only 43 chains, or 17 per cent of the 248 reporting, priced their private brands higher than competing standard brands, and these chains operated only 939 stores, or only 2 per cent of the total.

TABLE 34.—*Distribution of 248 chains according to their reported pricing policy on private and standard brands, 1929–30, and of stores operated by them December 31, 1928*

Compared with standard brands—	Reporting on pricing policy		Compared with standard brands—	Reporting on pricing policy	
	Chains	Stores operated		Chains	Stores operated
Private brands are priced—	*Number*	*Number*	Percentage of total reporting:	*Per cent*	*Per cent*
Higher	43	939	Higher	17.3	2.1
Lower	79	32,733	Lower	31.9	73.0
Same	126	11,181	Same	50.8	24.9
Total reports	248	44,853	Total	100.0	100.0

Seventy-nine chains, or almost one-third of the total, reported that their private brands were priced lower than competing standard brands, and this group operated 73 per cent of the total stores. The policy of the remaining 126 chains was to sell both private brands and standard brands at the same prices. This relatively large proportion of the reporting chains (51 per cent), however, operated only one-fourth of the stores.

The chains pricing private brands higher than standard brands averaged the smallest number of stores per chain, only 22. Those pricing private and standard brands the same were next with 89 stores per chain, while those pricing private brands lower than standard brands averaged 414 stores per chain. It is to be noted, however, that this last average reflects the influence of the grocery and grocery and meat chains with their large average number of stores per chain.

Private brands priced higher.—As indicated above, a relatively small proportion of chains price their private brands higher than their standard brands, and an even smaller proportion of stores were operated by them. It is also true that the chains reporting this pricing policy were confined to 8 of the 21 kinds of business in which one or more chains reported on this subject. Moreover, in half of these eight lines of business only one chain reported (tobacco, men's furnishings, hats and caps, and dry goods and apparel), and none of these four chains operated as many as 15 stores.

TABLE 35.—*Number of chains reporting "higher" pricing of private brands than competing standard brands, 1929–30, and stores operated December 31, 1928, by kind of chain*

Kind of chain	Chains		Stores	
	Number reporting "higher" pricing	Per cent of all reporting on pricing	Number operated by chains reporting "higher" pricing	Per cent of total operated by all chains reporting on pricing
Grocery	8	15.4	661	8.6
Grocery and meat	13	21.3	124	.4
Drug	16	32.7	108	12.3
Tobacco	1	11.1	11	.7
Men's furnishings	1	20.0	7	14.3
Hats and caps	1	14.3	12	10.5
Dry goods and apparel	1	12.5	6	.6
General merchandise	2	66.7	10	10.8
Total	43	17.3	939	2.1

In all cases the proportion of chains which report pricing private brands higher than competing standard brands is above 10 per cent. From the point of view of the importance of private brands, however, store figures are probably more significant than those of chains, as they represent the possible outlets for such private brands as are owned. Considered from this point of view it would appear that not much importance attaches to this particular policy in grocery and meat, dry goods and apparel, or tobacco chains, in each of which less than three-fourths of 1 per cent of the stores were operated by chains pricing their private brands higher than standard brands.

Reasons for pricing private brands higher.—The most frequently reported reasons for pricing private brands higher than standard-brand goods, as shown by the following table, are (1) that no retail prices for such private brands are established by competition and (2) that private brands are of higher quality [22] than standard-brand products. As regards the first reason, articles bearing a chain's private brand can not be price cut by competitors because the latter are unable to handle them.

TABLE 36.—*Reasons stated for pricing private brands higher than standard brands 1929–30*

	Number of chains reporting reason
No retail price established by competition	7
Our private brands are of higher quality	7
To offset small profit made on standard brands	6
More sales effort to sell private brands	5
To cover expenses incurred for advertising, warehousing, etc	4
Private brands of no value as "leaders"	4
To make a larger (net) profit	1
To offset small profit made on staples	1
Unclassified	2

[22] Cf. sec. 5.

Other reasons also appearing to be of major importance to chains pricing private brands higher, are: That these private brands are marked up higher to offset the small profit on standard-brand merchandise, that more sales effort is required to sell private brands, to cover expenses incurred in advertising and warehousing private brands, and that private brands have no leader value.

It is interesting to note that the quality of private-brand merchandise also appears as an argument for the use of the same pricing on private brands as on standard brands. There is also a difference of opinion with regard to the value of private brands as leaders, four chains reporting that they price private brands lower for this reason.[23]

Private brands priced lower.—Thirteen of the 21 kinds of chains reporting on the question priced their private brands lower than competing standard label merchandise. No meat, confectionery, men's and women's ready-to-wear, women's shoes, dry goods, women's accessories, furniture, or musical instrument chains belong to this group.

TABLE 37.—*Number of chains reporting "lower" pricing of private brands than competing standard brands, 1929–30, and stores operated December 31, 1928, by kind of chain*

Kind of chain	Chains		Stores	
	Number reporting "lower" pricing	Per cent of all reporting on pricing	Number operated by chains reporting "lower" pricing	Per cent of total operated by all chains reporting on pricing
Grocery	27	51.9	5,284	69.0
Grocery and meat	22	35.5	26,288	86.9
Drug	11	22.4	452	51.3
Tobacco	1	11.1	2	.1
Variety ($1 limit)	1	25.0	217	10.1
Men's ready-to-wear	4	50.0	22	45.8
Men's furnishings	2	40.0	9	18.4
Hats and caps	1	14.3	49	43.0
Men's shoes	1	33.3	56	50.5
Men's and women's shoes	2	20.0	16	10.7
Dry goods and apparel	2	25.0	9	.8
Department store	4	40.0	246	52.1
General merchandise	1	33.3	83	89.2
Total	79	31.9	32,733	73.0

This table shows that nearly one-third (31.9 per cent) of the total chains reporting priced private brands lower than standard brands, and these chains operated nearly three-fourths of the stores. The proportion of chains following this mark-up policy is less than the combined average proportion in 6 of the 13 groups. From the proportion of stores operated, it appears that nearly 87 per cent of those belonging to the grocery and meat chains are operated by chains pricing their private brands lower than standard brands. Except for the general merchandise chains this is the only 1 of the 13 kinds of business in which the number of stores operated by chains pursuing this policy is above the average for all chains. In fact only 6 of the 13 lines show as much as 50 per cent of the stores operated by chains committed to this policy—the 2 just mentioned and in addition, grocery, drug, department store, and men's shoes.

[23] Cf. Reasons for pricing private brands lower, infra. Cf. also in this connection Federal Trade Commission Report on Chain-Store Leaders and Loss Leaders, secs. 4 and 8.

Reasons for pricing private brands lower.—By far the most common reason reported for pricing private brands lower than standard brands is that the private brands cost less. This reason is reported a total of thirty-five times while no other reason is given by more than seven chains. Despite a lack of pronounced concentration among these other reasons, some of them are of considerable interest.

TABLE 38.—*Reasons stated for pricing private brands lower than standard brands, 1929–30*

	Number of chains reporting reason
Private brands cost less (net purchase cost)	35
To meet competition of standard brands	7
To increase sales in private brands and obtain repeat business	7
"Low price" is chief sales argument in selling private brands	5
To attract customers to the store "leaders"	4
More profit made even at lower price	3
Profit satisfactory at lower price	3
Established policy is to sell private brands for less	2
Unclassified	3

The fact that four of these chains price private brands lower to attract customers to the store has already been mentioned above. Other reasons are the increasing of private brand sales and the obtaining of repeat business and meeting the competition of standard brands The last-mentioned reason for pricing private brands lower than standard brands is also given by 14 chains as a reason for pricing private brands the same as standard brands by those chains reporting this policy. (Table 40.)

Private and standard brands priced the same.—With the exception of the general merchandise business, one or more chains priced private-brand goods the same as standard brands in every one of the 21 kinds of business from which reports on pricing policy were received.

These chains, therefore, are more widely distributed among the various kinds of business than are those pricing their private brands below standard brands (14 kinds of business) and especially those pricing private brands above standard brands (8 kinds of business).

TABLE 39.—*Number of chains reporting "same" pricing of private brands and standard brands, 1929–30, and stores operated December 31, 1928, by kind of chain*

Kind of chain	Chains		Stores	
	Number reporting "same" pricing	Per cent of all reporting on pricing	Number operated by chains reporting "same" pricing	Per cent of total operated by all chains reporting on pricing
Grocery	17	32.7	1,712	22.4
Grocery and meat	27	44.3	3,853	12.8
Meat	2	66.7	67	38.3
Confectionery	2	100.0	23	100.0
Drug	22	44.9	321	36.4
Tobacco	7	77.8	1,551	99.2
Variety ($1 limit)	3	75.0	1,935	89.9
Men's ready-to-wear	4	50.0	26	54.2
Men's and women's ready-to-wear	2	100.0	40	100.0
Men's furnishings	2	40.0	33	67.3
Women's accessories	3	100.0	25	100.0
Hats and caps	5	71.4	53	46.5
Men's shoes	2	66.7	55	49.5
Women's shoes	3	100.0	17	100.0
Men's and women's shoes	8	80.0	134	89.3
Dry goods	2	100.0	8	100.0
Dry goods and apparel	5	62.5	1,054	98.6
Department store	6	60.0	226	47.9
Furniture	1	100.0	3	100.0
Musical instruments	3	100.0	45	100.0
Total	126	50.8	11,181	24.9

In seven lines of business all of the chains reporting on pricing policy priced private brand and standard brand merchandise the same. In each of these kinds of business the number of chains was small, three in musical instruments, women's shoes, and women's accessories; two each in confectionery, men's and women's ready-to-wear, and dry goods; and one in furniture.

Reasons for pricing private and standard brands the same.—The reason most frequently reported for making the prices on private brands the same as those on standard brands is that such a policy provides a reasonable profit or a fair basis for profits (whatever this may mean), this answer appearing in 15 reports. Closely following (14 chains) were (1) that the quality is the same, and (2) meeting competition of standard brands.

TABLE 40.—*Reasons stated for pricing private brands the same as standard brands, 1929–30*

	Number of chains reporting
A reasonable profit secured—a fair basis for profits	15
Quality is same, therefore price should be same	14
To meet competition of standard brands	14
Quality is better but price is same	5
Margin of profit is larger than on standard brands—i. e., private brands cost less	4
Price cutting lowers prestige of private brands	3
To build up dependable customer demand	1
So customers can more easily be shifted from standard to private brands	1
Unclassified	27

Section 15. Summary of private brand mark-up and pricing policies.

A summary of the reports received on mark-up and pricing policies on private as compared with standard brands follows:

1. About 70 per cent of the chains, operating 79 per cent of the stores, employed either the same mark-up or a lower mark-up on private brands than on standard brands.

2. About 83 per cent of the reporting chains, however, operating nearly 98 per cent of the stores, sold private-brand goods at prices which were the same as, or lower than, those of standard-brand merchandise.

3. Less than 6 per cent of the reporting chains, operating about 22 per cent of the stores, took a lower mark-up on private than on standard brands, but 32 per cent of the chains, operating 73 per cent of the stores, priced their private brands lower than standard brands.

4. Although 93 chains, representing 30.6 per cent of the total reporting and operating 21 per cent of the stores, marked up private brands higher than standard brands, only 17.4 per cent of the chains operating barely 2 per cent of the stores priced their own brands higher.

Section 16. A comparison of the gross profit made on private brands with that made on competing standard brands.

As shown in section 13, only 34.9 per cent of the grocery chains and 28.9 per cent of the grocery and meat chains, operating 20.8 per cent and 21.1 per cent of the stores, respectively, reported marking up their private brands higher than competing standard brands. The balance of these types of chains reported using either the same mark-up on the two kinds of brands or a lower mark-up on private brands. In view of these reported mark-up policies it might seem logical to expect that the commodity mark-up reports of these two kinds of chains discussed in the present section would conform at least somewhat closely to the reports on mark-up policies. The fact is, however, that for the 34 commodities, as shown in Table 41, the actual gross profits on private brands were less than those on competing standard brands having the highest mark-up in only three instances, and in but four cases when compared with standard brands having the lowest mark-up. In no case is the mark-up on a private brand commodity the same as that on a standard brand. Obviously, if the gross profit percentages are higher on private brands than on competing standard brands, the rate of mark-up must have been higher.

This apparent inconsistency, in the replies of these two types of chains, between the mark-up policies and the actual mark-ups reported can scarcely be attributed to differences in the two samples, either as to number of chains, stores, or average stores per chain. Possibly the wording of the question from which the gross profit percentages were computed had some influence upon the result. The question asked the chains to give the net purchase costs and retail selling prices of the "10 principal commodities sold" under private brands. It is quite probable that the "principal" items listed were those enjoying the largest sales; and, as indicated in section 3, the factor of increased profits is an important reason for developing private brands, and chains have put in private brands of those commodities which are highly competitive for the purpose of obtaining a better gross profit on these commodities than afforded by the competing brands. In other words, the indications are that the principal private-brand commodities for which gross profits are shown were developed in no small measure for the purpose of affording a high gross profit.

For the other types of chains for which gross-profit percentages on private and competing brands are shown, the results agree quite closely with the replies of these kinds of chains as to private-brand mark-up policies. This is particularly true of drug chains, for which, next to the combined grocery and grocery and meat chain the largest number of chains reported (25). Reference to Table 31 shows that 63.4 per cent of the reporting drug chains (operating 89.8 per cent of the stores) employed a higher mark-up on private brands and, as shown in Table 44, the gross-profit percentages were in all cases larger on private brands than on the competing standard brands.

In the detailed analysis of the actual mark-up taken by individual chains on specific private brands and competing standard brands,[24] which is made in the present section, reports were received from 10 groups of chains, as follows: Grocery, grocery and meat, drug, tobacco, variety ($1 limit), men's ready-to-wear, women's accessories, women's shoes, dry goods and apparel, and department store. A relatively large number of comparative price reports was received from three types of chains, grocery, grocery and meat, and drug. The number of reports received from each of the remaining groups was small.

The scope of the data presented in this section is best illustrated by reproducing a section of a schedule which was filled out by a grocery and meat chain. All brand names and names of manufacturers have been omitted.

---

[24] Brands owned by m anufacturers usually widely known and often nationally advertised.

Private brands on March 30, 1929

Commodity, name of your brand	Name of manufacturer	Unit of size, weight, or count	Net purchase or manufacturing cost (if manufactured by you)	Retail selling price per unit
1. Blank brand,[1] bread	Our own make	1 pound	$0.0377	$0.05
2. Blank brand, canned peaches	Various manufacturers	No. 2½ can	.1600	.21
3. Blank brand, canned corn	do	No. 2 can	.1010	.15
4. Blank brand, canned peas	do	do	.1140	.17
5. Blank brand, print butter	do	1 pound	.4650	.55
6. Blank brand, coffee	Our own	do	.3327	.45
7. Blank brand, flour	Various manufacturers	1 barrel	5.6000	7.84
8. Blank brand, canned milk	do	1 pound	.0800	.09
9. Blank brand, tea	Our own	½ pound	.2209	.37
10. Blank brand, corn flakes	Various manufacturers	13 ounces	.0740	.10

[1] Actual names deleted in order to conceal identity.

Competing standard brands showing highest mark-up on March 30, 1929 [1]

Brand name	Manufacturer's name	Unit of size, weight, or count	Net purchase cost	Retail selling price per unit
1. Blank brand,[2] bread	The Blank Co.[2]	1 pound	$0.076	$0.09
2. Blank brand, canned peaches	The Blank Packing Co	No. 2½ can	.177	.23
3. Blank brand, canned corn	do	No. 2 can	.110	.15
4. Blank brand, canned peas	do	do	.128	.17
5. (No competing brand of butter carried.)				
6. Blank brand, coffee	The Blank Coffee Co	1 pound	.450	.49
7. Blank brand, flour	The Blank Flour Milling Co	1 barrel	7.800	10.00
8. Blank brand, canned milk	Various manufacturers	1 pound	.087	.10
9. Blank brand, tea	Blank Tea Co	½ pound	.360	.49
10. Blank brand, corn flakes	Blank Corn Flakes Co	8 ounces	.0688	.08⅓

[1] For competing standard brands showing lowest mark-up on Mar. 30, 1929, company states: "No second competitive brand of different mark-up."
[2] Actual names deleted in order to conceal identity.

In the original schedule each chain was asked to give the net purchase or manufacturing cost and the retail selling price per unit on March 30, 1929, of the 10 principal commodities which it sold under its private brands and the net purchase cost and the retail selling price of the competing standard brands (*a*) carrying the highest and (*b*) the lowest mark-up. A number of chains, however, reported only one standard brand of certain commodities sold in direct competition with their own private brand. In most instances, the one competing standard-brand was reported under "standard brands showing the highest mark-up." The result is that the number of reports under standard-brand commodities having the highest mark-up, and, more particularly, under standard-brand commodities having the lowest mark-up often do not agree with the number of private-brand commodities reported. Since this section is based solely on gross profit percentages, standard brands which were not of exactly the same size as the private brands with which they competed are included in all the tabulations. Gross profit or gross margin percentages shown in this section are based upon the selling price.

From the information appearing on the schedule the gross profit or margin taken on each brand reported was first computed in cents and then as a percentage of the selling price as is shown for ginger ale in the following work sheet. Only group totals for each commodity are shown in the tables included in this section. Percentages in the total line in the illustration are used in Table 41.

Commodity	Unit	Private brands			Competing standard brands having highest mark-up			Competing standard brands having lowest mark-up		
		Manufacturing cost	Retail selling price	Mark-up	Purchase cost	Retail selling price	Mark-up	Purchase cost	Retail selling price	Mark-up
	Ounce			Per cent			Per cent			Per cent
Ginger ale	12	$0.083	$0.125	33.6	$0.131	$0.180	27.2	$0.110	$0.125	12.0
Do	12	.095	.140	32.1	.132	.180	26.7			
Do	12	.053	.090	41.1	.135	.180	25.0	.118	.160	26.3
Total	36	.231	.355	34.9	.398	.540	26.3	.228	.285	20.0

The discussion of the gross profit on private and standard brands is presented on two different bases. In the first comparison are shown all of the average mark-ups on both private and standard brands of specific commodities. Because several of the chains did not report both a competing standard brand having the highest mark-up and a competing standard brand having the lowest mark-up for a given commodity, there is the somewhat incongruous result in the tables that the average price of the standard brand commodity showing the lowest mark-up is frequently higher than that of the standard brand showing the highest mark-up. No great importance attaches to this fact, because the chief significance of these tabulations of gross profits lies in the relationship of the standard-brand gross profits to the private-brand gross profits rather than in any comparison of the two sets of standard-brand data. However, a second analysis has been made which considers only the gross profits for those chains which reported for each commodity the cost and selling price of the private-brand item and the cost and selling price of both the competing standard-brand item having the highest mark-up and the one having the lowest mark-up.

Fifty-nine grocery and grocery and meat chains.—Thirty-one grocery and 28 grocery and meat chains furnished information from which their gross profit on private and competing standard-brand merchandise could be computed. These 59 chains operated 13,955 stores on December 31, 1928. The Great Atlantic & Pacific Tea Co. and the American Stores Co. were the principal large chains which failed to furnish data on this subject. Three reporting chains were operating more than 1,000 stores each on December 31, 1928, the largest being the Kroger Grocery & Baking Co., with 5,260 stores. First National Stores (Inc.) had 1,791 stores and National Tea Co. had 1,041 stores. The next largest chain was Safeway Stores (Inc.), of California (Southern Safeway division), with 664 stores.[a] Only one other chain, the Grand Union Co., operated more than 500 stores (this company had 611 stores).

Three chains operated between 300 and 500 stores. These were the Sanitary Grocery Co. (Inc.), S. M. Flickinger (Inc.), and Mutual Grocery Co. Fourteen chains had from 100 to 300 stores. These

[a] The number of "stores and markets" reported in the original schedule. Not counting meat departments separately, however, this chain is shown in Growth and Development of Chain Stores as having 494 stores on Dec. 31, 1928.

were Consumers' Sanitary Coffee & Butter Stores; Sheffield Farms (Inc.); Hill Grocery Co.; H. G. Hill Co.; the Market Basket Corporation; Safeway Stores (Inc.), of California (Piggly-Wiggly, southern division); Skaggs Safeway Stores (Inc.) (central division); Red Owl Stores (Inc.); J. W. Crook Stores; Gristede Bros. (Inc.); Great Eastern Stores; The Nicholson, Thackray Co.; Continental Grocery Corporation (Ltd.); and Larkin Co. (Inc.). Six of the remaining 37 chains operated more than 50 stores. Eleven of them operated from 25 to 49 stores and 20 had less than 25 stores.

Some of the chains reported on only 1 commodity and several reported on as many as 10. Reports were received on a total of 249 private brands and 294 competing standard brands. A few chains reported on more than one private brand of a single commodity. For example, a chain which was operating 297 stores in 1928 reported on two private brands of coffee.

Table 41 shows for these two types of chains combined for specified commodities percentages of gross profit made on (*a*) private brands (*b*) competing standard brands having the highest mark-up, and (*c*) competing standard brands having the lowest mark-up.

TABLE 41.—*Gross profit on all private and competing standard brand commodities reported by 59 grocery and grocery and meat chains, March 30, 1929* [1]

Commodity	Per cent of gross profit based on retail selling price						Points per cent by which gross profit on private brands is higher (+) or lower (−) than on competing standard brands	
	Private brands		Competing standard brands having highest mark-up		Competing standard brands having lowest mark-up			
	Number of price quotations	Per cent	Number of price quotations	Per cent	Number of price quotations	Per cent	Standard brands having highest mark-up	Standard brands having lowest mark-up
Beverages and beverage bases:								
Coffee	45	23.5	42	16.9	15	13.2	+6.6	+10.3
Tea	16	27.9	16	24.2	5	24.1	+3.7	+3.8
Cocoa	5	33.0	5	19.3	1	19.0	+13.7	+14.0
Ginger ale	3	34.9	3	26.3	2	20.0	+8.6	+14.9
Malt sirup	3	27.25	3	27.31	1	31.63	−.06	−4.38
Grape juice	1	24.0	1	26.7			−2.7	
Cereal products:								
Pastry flour	23	18.4	22	15.1	6	17.0	+3.3	+1.4
Breakfast cereals	8	33.7	8	15.5			+18.2	
Bread	6	15.6	6	15.2	1	22.5	+.4	−6.9
Cornstarch	1	40.4	1	32.7			+7.7	
Pancake flour	1	49.5	1	16.6			+32.9	
Macaroni	1	25.7	1	23.1			+2.6	
Canned goods:								
Vegetables	29	28.1	27	26.7	6	20.9	+1.4	+7.2
Fruits	29	27.3	25	24.3	5	22.4	+3.0	+4.9
Milk	12	15.5	10	14.7	4	14.9	+.8	+.6
Chicken	2	21.4	2	18.8			+2.6	
Soup	1	25.4	1	19.0			+6.5	
Relishes, condiments, spreads:								
Mayonnaise	16	23.5	16	24.4	2	24.8	−.9	−1.3
Ketchup	7	36.1	6	19.5	2	8.7	+16.6	+27.4
Extracts	5	46.3	5	32.2	2	28.7	+14.1	+17.6
Peanut butter	4	31.9	4	24.9	2	23.2	+7.0	+8.7
Vinegar	4	38.8	4	29.8	1	32.4	+9.0	+6.4
Salt	3	46.4	2	27.0	1	54.3	+19.4	−7.9
Jam	1	32.0	1	29.6			+2.4	
Mustard	1	54.5	1	19.2			+35.3	

[1] The units of size, weight, count, or measure often were not identical in the comparisons made in the table.

TABLE 41.—*Gross profit on all private and competing standard brand commodities reported by 59 grocery and grocery and meat chains, March 30, 1929*—Con.

Commodity	Per cent of gross profit based on retail selling price						Points per cent by which gross profit on private brands is higher (+) or lower (−) than on competing standard brands	
	Private brands		Competing standard brands having highest mark-up		Competing standard brands having lowest mark-up			
	Number of price quotations	Per cent	Number of price quotations	Per cent	Number of price quotations	Per cent	Standard brands having highest mark-up	Standard brands having lowest mark-up
Other commodities:								
Print butter	8	12.0	8	11.5	2	11.8	+0.5	+0.2
Soaps and cleansers	3	36.0	3	18.4			+17.6	
Baking powder	2	40.8	2	22.1	1	15.5	+18.7	+25.3
Gelatin, flavored	2	25.1	2	19.6			+5.5	
Sirup	2	23.7	2	20.9			+2.8	
Mincemeat	1	26.4	1	20.7			+5.7	
Oleomargarine	2	26.1			2	16.4		+9.7
Raisins	1	25.7	1	21.2			+4.5	
Eggs	1	13.1	1	12.8			+.3	
Total (34 commodities)	249	23.1	233	19.0	61	17.8	+4.1	+5.3

The average per cent of gross profit based on retail selling prices was 23.1 per cent on private brand articles as compared with 19.0 per cent on competing standard brands having the highest mark-up and 17.8 per cent on competing standard brands having the lowest mark-up, the excess being from 4.1 to 5.3 points per cent for the private brands. For only three commodities (grape juice, malt, and mayonnaise) were the gross-profit percentages on private brands lower than on competing standard brands having the highest mark-up and in only four cases (malt, bread, salt, and mayonnaise) were they lower than those on the standard brands having the lowest mark-up. Six of the 34 private-brand commodities listed were sold at a gross profit of over 40 per cent: Mustard (54.5 per cent), pancake flour (49.5 per cent), extracts (46.3 per cent), salt (46.4 per cent), baking powder (40.8 per cent), and cornstarch (40.4 per cent). Only one of the competing standard-brand commodities, salt (54.3 per cent), carried a gross profit as high as 40 per cent. Only five (bread, pastry flour, canned milk, print butter, and eggs) of the 34 private-brand commodities, or 14.7 per cent of the total, carried a gross profit of less than 20 per cent as compared with 15 of the competing standard-brand commodities, or over 40 per cent of the total. In other words, although the table shows that the average gross profit on private brands is higher than on competing standard brands by only some four to five points per cent, the margin on private brands of individual commodities is frequently much wider than this figure and a much larger proportion of the private than of the standard-brand commodities is found in the higher ranges of gross profit.

According to the commission's preliminary figures, the percentage of gross profit to sales in 1929 for 177 grocery and grocery and meat chains operating over 42,000 stores was 18.7, and the percentage of operating expenses to sales was 16.1. The gross profits of these chains selling grocery products furnish an interesting comparison with the gross-profit margins on the different private and standard brand items on which reports were received.

In making such comparisons, however, it should be recognized that the figures given above for the 177 chains are average figures and as such they reflect the performance of all chains reporting—the inefficient as well as the ably managed chains are included. Moreover, the cost of handling different types and brands of merchandise varies. Well-known standard brands for which a dependable consumer demand has been built up through years of national advertising, require less sales effort to sell than unknown and unadvertised brands. Total operating expense figures from which the average percentage mentioned is derived, of course, include both the cost of selling the "hard-to-sell" articles and those which require little or no sales effort. Hence, one is not warranted in assuming that a chain which was selling a private brand or a standard brand on March 30, 1929, at a gross profit of less than 16.1 per cent of the selling price was necessarily making no net profit. Despite these qualifications the figures given offer some basis for judging the profitableness or unprofitableness of the brands sold.

For this purpose, Table 42 shows the gross profits on the 249 private brand items and the 294 competing standard brand items on which reports were received, distributed by ranges of 10 per cent.

TABLE 42.—*Distribution of percentages of gross profit made on private and competing standard brand items in grocery and grocery and meat chains on March 30, 1929*

Gross profit reported (per cent)	Private brand items			Competing standard brand items		
	Number	Per cent of total	Per cent cumulated	Number	Per cent of total	Per cent cumulated
Less than 10	9	3.6	3.6	21	7.1	7.1
10 to 15	21	8.4	12.0	56	19.1	26.2
15 to 16.1	7	2.8	14.8	19	6.5	32.7
16.1 to 20 [1]	28	11.3	26.1	56	19.1	51.8
20 to 25	50	20.1	46.2	58	19.7	71.5
25 to 30	51	20.5	66.7	45	15.3	86.8
30 to 35	34	13.7	80.4	23	7.8	94.6
35 to 40	24	9.6	90.0	12	4.1	98.7
40 to 45	13	5.2	95.2	3	1.0	99.7
45 to 50	6	2.4	97.6	0	----------	99.7
50 and over	6	2.4	100.0	1	0.3	100.0
Total	249	100.0	----------	294	100.0	----------

[1] The cost of doing business in 1929 in the 177 grocery and grocery and meat chains which reported their operating expenses to the commission in detail was 16.1 per cent of their total net sales (preliminary figures).

It will be seen from the table that the percentage of gross profit made on 37 of the 249 private brands was less than 16.1 per cent, the average cost of doing business in chains dealing in grocery products. By way of contrast, the gross profit made on 96 of the 294 standard brands on which reports were received was less than 16.1 per cent. Expressed in another way, only 14.8 per cent of the private brands reported were being sold on March 30, 1929, at less than the average cost of doing business as contrasted to 32.7 per cent of the standard brands.[25]

[25] It does not necessarily follow that a net loss was realized by reporting chains on sales of all 37 private and 96 standard brand items, on which the gross profit was less than 16.1 per cent. The cost of doing business in several of the reporting chains may have been well below the average for the 177 chains. See text above.

The gross profit was 20 per cent, or more, on 73.9 per cent of the private brands, as compared with only 48.2 per cent of the standard brands. Only 46.2 per cent of the private brands were sold with a gross margin of less than 25 per cent as compared with 71.5 per cent of the standard brands. At the other extreme, a gross profit of 40 per cent or more was made on 10 per cent of the private brands but on only 1.3 per cent of the standard brands.

The 37 private brand items sold at a gross profit of less than 16.1 per cent, the average cost of doing business in grocery and grocery and meat chains in 1929, included 6 brands of coffee, 1 brand of tea, 3 brands of bread, 7 brands of pastry flour, 6 brands of canned milk, 2 brands of canned vegetables, 1 brand of canned fruits, 7 brands of print butter, 2 brands of mayonnaise, 1 brand of eggs, and 1 brand of flavored gelatin.

Fifteen chains sold Maxwell House coffee (0.0 to 15.9 per cent) and eight chains sold Hills Bros. coffee (9.3 to 14.5 per cent) at a gross profit of less than 16.1 per cent. Each of the following brands was sold at a gross profit of less than 16.1 per cent by one chain: Chase & Sanborn (14.4 per cent), Autocrat (15.1 per cent), Yuban (12 per cent), Beechnut (13.2 per cent), Webb's (12.7 per cent), Royal Cup (15.6 per cent), Illini (11.6 per cent), Manru (13.5 per cent), Royal Blend (10.4 per cent), White House (12.5 per cent), and Orienta (10 per cent).

Four chains sold Gold Medal flour at a gross profit of less than 16.1 per cent and each of the following brands was sold for a gross profit of less than this amount by one chain: A 1 (13.4 per cent), Hecker's (6.1 per cent), Drifted Snow (13.2 per cent), Occident (11.1 per cent), Hungarian (8.3 per cent), Pillsbury's (13.4 per cent), Globe (9.1 per cent), and Ballard's (5 per cent).

The standard brands of canned milk which were sold at a gross profit of less than 16.1 per cent included: Pet (four chains, 12.5 to 16 per cent), Borden's (two chains, 10 and 10.9 per cent), Gold Cross (10.8 per cent), Lion (11 per cent), Sealect (14.9 per cent), and Carnation (12.5 per cent).

The gross profit on eight standard brands of print butter was below 16.1 per cent; namely: Modesto (three chains, 8.8 to 11.1 per cent), Brookfield (15.4 per cent), Armour (15.9 per cent), American Creamery (12.7 per cent), Meadow Gold (5.6 per cent), Challenge (11.3 per cent), Swift (15.6 per cent), and A. B. C. (11.8 per cent). The brands of ketchup on which the gross profit was small were Heinz (two chains, 12.7 and 14.9 per cent) and Blue Label (one chain, 3.3 per cent). Three chains sold Baker's Cocoa (14.3 to 15.0 per cent) and two chains sold Quaker Oats (13.9 and 16.0 per cent) at a gross profit of less than 16.1 per cent. Kellogg's Corn Flakes (13.1 per cent) and Comet Rice (0.0 per cent) were also sold at a gross profit which was below the average cost of doing business for all chains selling grocery products which reported to the commission in 1929.

The largest number of reports received from grocery and grocery and meat chains was on coffee and canned vegetables.

Coffee.—Forty-two chains reported mark-up figures on 45 private brands of coffee. The gross profit taken by the 42 chains ranged from 6 per cent to 40 per cent. The gross profit on about one-third, or 15 private brands, was less than 20 per cent; the gross profit on 12 brands was from 20 per cent to 25 per cent; the gross profit on

10 brands ranged from 25 per cent to 30 per cent; and eight chains reported a gross profit of 30 per cent or more.

Fifty-seven reports were received on standard brands of coffee which competed with the private brands discussed above. The following 20 different standard brands were named: Beechnut, Hills Bros., La Touraine, Maxwell House, Chase & Sanborn, Autocrat, Yuban, White House, Webb's, Seal, Royal Cup, Tenmore, Illini, Club House, Home, Manru, Royal Blend, Astor, Orienta, and Golden Gate. The gross margin taken on these brands ranged from 0.0 per cent to 39.7 per cent. Forty-seven or over four-fifths of the standard brands were sold at a gross profit of less than 20 per cent and 28 of them, at less than 15 per cent. A gross profit of less than 10 per cent was reported on six of the standard brands.

It was mentioned that the commission, in its preliminary analysis of expenses and profits in grocery and grocery and meat chains in 1929, found that 16.1 per cent of sales was required to cover the costs of doing business in the average chain. On 34 of the 57 (59.6 per cent) standard brand items of coffee, the gross profit taken was less than 16.1 per cent of sales. By way of contrast, the gross profit taken on only six of the 45 private brands (13.3 per cent) was less than this figure, the gross profit on these brands being 15.6 per cent, 14.3 per cent, 14.3 per cent, 13.9 per cent, 11.4 per cent, and 6.0 per cent, respectively. These figures should be considered in connection with the commission's report on Chain-Store Leaders and Loss Leaders.

All six chains which took a gross profit of less than 16.1 per cent on their private brands also took a low gross profit on the competing standard brands. For example, the chain which reported a gross profit of 15.6 per cent on its private brand took a gross profit of 10 per cent on the competing standard brand; and the chain which reported a gross profit of 6 per cent on its private brand took a gross profit of 18.1 per cent and 0.0 per cent, respectively, on the two competing standard brands sold in its stores.

Gross-profit percentages reported by different chains on the same standard brand of coffee differed widely. For example, gross profit figures reported by 21 chains on one well-known standard brand were as follows: 23.4 per cent, 20.4 per cent, 19.8 per cent, 16.4 per cent, 16.3 per cent (two reports), 15.1 per cent (four reports), 14.5 per cent, 14.3 per cent, 14 per cent, 13.7 per cent (two reports), 13.5 per cent, 11.1 per cent, 8.2 per cent (two reports), and 0.0 per cent (two reports), respectively.

Canned vegetables.—Cost and retail selling prices were reported on 29 private brands of canned vegetables. The following vegetables were included: Asparagus, pork and beans, corn, peas, cut green beans, red beans, beets, spinach, and tomatoes. The highest gross margin reported was 41.6 per cent on canned peas. In contrast one chain reported a loss of 0.6 per cent on canned tomatoes. The gross margin reported on two private brands of canned vegetables was between 15 and 20 per cent; 20 to 25 per cent on 6 private brands; 25 to 30 per cent on 9 private brands; and 30 per cent or over on 11 private brands.

Thirty-three reports were received on standard brands of canned vegetables which competed with the private brands discussed above. Sixteen different standard brands were named as follows: Miss Lou, Heinz, Van Camp's, Del Monte, Peter Rabbit, Hatchet, Standard, Vine Valley, Libby's, Campbell's, Silver's Co., Packer's, Home, Joan of Arc, Logan, and Snider's. Seven of the standard brands were sold at a gross profit of less than 20 per cent; 8 were sold at a gross profit between 20 and 25 per cent; 8 between 25 and 30 per cent; and 10 were sold at a gross profit of 30 per cent or more. The lowest gross profit reported on a standard brand was 3.6 per cent. The highest gross profit reported was 37.5 per cent on a little-known standard brand of tomatoes.

Comparison with the cost of doing business figures in grocery and grocery and meat chains in 1929 (16.1 per cent), indicates that six of the standard and two of the private brands of canned vegetables on which reports were received were being sold below this figure on March 30, 1929.

These six standard brands of canned vegetables are as follows: Peas, 6.7 per cent; red beans, 3.6 and 13.6 per cent; corn, 12.8 per cent; beets, 15.4 per cent; and pork and beans, 16 per cent.

The gross profit reported on the same standard brand of different canned vegetables varied rather widely. For example, percentage of gross margin figures for one well-known and widely advertised standard brand were as follows: 15.4, 21.8, 22.7, 24.7, 26.7, 27.5, 30.0, 33.3, and 37.4 per cent.

Extracts and salt.—Extracts and salt are presented as examples of branded commodities having a high mark-up.

Five chains reported mark-up figures on extracts. The gross profit taken on the private brands was as follows: 20.0, 46.6, 46.8, 50.0, and 54.8 per cent, respectively.

Seven reports were received on the following competing standard brands: Baker's, Burnett's, Price's, and Schilling's. The gross profit taken was: 25.8, 28.5, 29.6, 30.7, 31.7, 34.2, and 36.4 per cent, respectively.

Based on the average cost of doing business in grocery chains in 1929 (16.1 per cent) it would appear that a substantial net profit was being realized on all private and standard brands on which reports were received.

Three chains reported mark-up figures on salt. The first chain took a profit of 39 per cent on its private brand and 30 per cent on the competing standard brand which it sold. The second chain reported a mark-up of 60 per cent on its private brand and 54.3 per cent on the competing standard brand. The gross profit taken by the third chain on its private brand was 37.5 per cent as contrasted to 24.3 per cent for the competing standard brand. Two of the reports on standard brands were on Shaker salt and one on Morton's.

Butter and canned milk are discussed below as examples of branded commodities on which the mark-up was relatively low.

Print butter.—Reports were received on eight private brands and eight standard brands of print butter the latter including Brookfield,

Armour, Meadow Gold, Challenge, and Swift. The gross profits taken on the private and competing standard brands were as follows:

	Private brands	Standard brands		Private brands	Standard brands
	Per cent	*Per cent*		*Per cent*	*Per cent*
Chain 1	16.3	15.6 15.9	Chain 5	11.5	12.7
Chain 2	15.6	15.4	Chain 6	9.8	11.8
Chain 3	14.3	5.6	Chain 7	9.4	11.1
Chain 4	12.0	8.8 8.8	Chain 8	8.8	11.3

Unless the costs of handling butter by these eight chains is considerably lower than is their general average cost of doing business, it appears that several of them were realizing little or no net profit on their butter sales, either of private brands or of standard brands based upon the average cost of doing business (16.1 per cent) in 1929.

Canned milk.—Eleven grocery and grocery and meat chains reported cost and selling price figures on their private brands of canned milk, one chain reporting on two different private brands. The gross profit taken on the 12 brands was as follows: 10.1, 11.1, 12.1, 13.3, 14.2, 15, 16.6, 16.7, 17.5, 18, 20, and 22 per cent.

Fourteen reports were received on competing standard brands. The names of seven were: Gold Cross, Dairylea, Lion, Pet, Carnation, Borden, and Sealect. The gross profit taken on these brands on March 30, 1929 was as follows: 10, 10.8, 10.9, 11, 12.5(2), 13 (2), 14.9, 15, 16, 18.2, 22.9, and 24.5 per cent. Hence, in only three instances was the reported gross profit on standard brands more than 16.1 per cent of the selling price, the average operating expense for 1929. By way of contrast, the gross profit taken on private brands was more than this figure for 6 of the 12 private brands.

The total combined gross profit made on the 12 private brands was 15.5 per cent of their total selling price as contrasted to 14.7 per cent and 14.9 per cent for the two types of competing standard brands.

Sixteen grocery and grocery and meat chains.—As previously pointed out not all chains reporting the gross profit on private brands reported the gross profit on both the competing standard brand commodities. Returns from the chains which reported for each commodity data on (*a*) the private brand, (*b*) the competing standard brand having the highest mark-up, and (*c*) the competing standard brand having the lowest mark-up are shown in the following table. Unless a chain reported on a private brand and both types of standard brands it was not included.

TABLE 43.—*Gross profit on 15 private and competing standard brand commodities reported by 16 grocery and grocery and meat chains, March 30, 1929* [1]

Commodity	Per cent of gross profit based on retail selling price				Points per cent by which gross profit on private brands is higher (+) or lower (—) than on competing standard brands	
	Number of price quotations	Private brands	Competing standard brands having highest mark-up	Competing standard brands having lowest mark-up	Standard brands having highest mark-up	Standard brands having lowest mark-up
		Per cent	*Per cent*	*Per cent*		
Coffee	11	21.6	22.0	13.4	−0.4	+8.2
Cocoa	1	33.4	31.7	18.8	+1.7	+14.6
Ginger ale	2	36.4	26.0	20.0	+10.4	+16.4
Tea	4	35.3	32.2	24.3	+3.1	+11.0
Malt	1	38.4	35.7	31.6	+2.7	+6.8
Flour	4	22.6	27.2	12.2	−4.6	+10.4
Canned milk	2	16.7	20.3	15.5	−3.6	+1.2
Canned vegetables	4	31.8	30.5	21.9	+1.3	+9.9
Canned fruits	1	32.11	32.14	23.63	−0.03	+8.48
Extracts	2	50.5	35.4	28.8	+15.1	+21.7
Mayonnaise	2	42.9	31.0	24.8	+11.9	+18.1
Ketchup	1	30.5	12.7	−3.3	+17.8	+33.8
Peanut butter	2	30.5	26.7	23.2	+3.8	+7.3
Vinegar	1	43.3	38.5	32.3	+4.8	+11.0
Baking powder	1	37.5	20.0	15.5	+17.5	+22.0
Total (15 commodities)	39	28.1	27.2	17.5	+0.9	+10.6

[1] The units of size, weight, count, or measure often were not identical in the comparison made in this table.

Including only commodities on which all three sets of mark-up figures were reported increases the private brand gross profit from 23.1 per cent for the 59 chains (Table 41) to 28.1 per cent for the 16 chains. It increases even more the gross profit on the standard brands showing the highest mark-up which advances from 19 per cent for the 59 chains to 27.2 per cent for the 16 chains. On the other hand, the gross profit percentage on the competing standard brands carrying the lowest mark-up remains approximately the same for the 59 and the 16 chains.

The higher averages shown in Table 43 for the 39 private brand items and competing standard brand items carrying the highest mark-up as compared with those in the table for the 249 items are apparently due to the inclusion in the latter of a large number of reports on items on which the average gross profit margins were lower than those in the present table; such as flour, canned milk, canned fruits and vegetables, tea, and bread, the last of which is not reported in Table 43 at all. Other items which were included in the first table do not appear in the present table, as for example, print butter.

In contrast to Table 41, the average gross profit taken on the 39 competing standard brand items having the highest mark-up (27.2 per cent) closely approaches that taken on private brands (28.1 per cent) whereas the gross profit of the 39 standard brand items having the lowest mark-up (17.5 per cent) remains about the same as in Table 41 for 61 items (17.8 per cent). The per cent of gross profit on those standard brand items marked up the least is, therefore, 9.7 points per cent less than the standard brands which are marked up the highest in Table 43. This spread is much wider than that shown for the 59 chains in Table 41 where the gross profit on those standard brands showing the highest mark-up is 19 per cent and on those showing the lowest, 17.8 per cent.

The private brand gross profit mark-up on all but four of the commodities averages higher than that carried by the standard brand with the highest mark-up margin, the four being coffee, flour, canned milk, and canned fruits. These four, however, represent almost 50 per cent of the 39 reports.

Five of the 11 coffee reports showed a lower gross profit percentage for the private brand than for the standard brand having the largest mark-up. The gross margin taken by one chain on its private brand of coffee was only 6 per cent as compared with 18 per cent for the standard brand. Another reported a gross profit of slightly more than 22 per cent on the private brand and very little under 40 per cent for the competing standard brand showing the highest mark-up. So far as individual reports are concerned both the lowest and the highest gross margins were reported on private brands while the second highest gross margin was on a standard brand item.

In the case of flour one chain reported a gross profit of approximately 11 per cent on its private brand but over 42 per cent on the competing standard brand having the highest mark-up. In only 2 out of 18 instances for these 4 commodities, however, was the private brand gross profit percentage lower than that on the competing standard brand having the lowest mark-up. One was a coffee item and the other was canned milk.

Twenty-five drug chains.—Twenty-five drug chains, operating 495 stores, December 31, 1928, furnished cost and selling prices as of March 30, 1929 on (*a*) their private brands, (*b*) competing standard brands having the highest mark-up, and (*c*) competing standard brands having the lowest mark-up. The Walgreen Co. operating 230 stores is the largest included.[26] Peoples Drug Stores is next in size with 82 stores and Mykrantz & Sons Co. is third with 27 stores. Each of the following chains operated from 10 to 25 stores: Standard Drug Co., Harvey & Carey, (Inc.), the Muir Co., Schettler Drug Co., and John H. Wood Co. Six chains operated from 5 to 10 stores. Each of the remaining chains operated less than 10 stores, 7 of them operating only 2 or 3 stores each.

A summary of the reports received is presented in Table 44, which includes gross margin data on 120 drug and miscellaneous products and 47 toilet items.

---

[26] As previously explained, Louis K. Liggett Co. was not considered as having any private brands of its own (Sec. 8).

TABLE 44.—*Gross profit on all private and competing standard-brand commodities reported by 25 drug chains, March 30, 1929* [1]

Commodity	Per cent of gross profit based on retail selling price						Points per cent by which gross profit on private brands is higher (+) or lower (−) than on competing standard brands	
	Private brands		Competing standard brands having highest mark-up		Competing standard brands having lowest mark-up			
	Number of price quotations	Per cent	Number of price quotations	Per cent	Number of price quotations	Per cent	Standard brands having highest mark-up	Standard brands having lowest mark-up
DRUG AND MISCELLANEOUS PRODUCTS								
Cough sirups	16	64.6	16	34.2	6	30.3	+30.4	+34.3
Corn remedies	11	60.7	11	33.8	4	20.5	+26.9	+40.2
Cold tablets	8	64.6	7	33.4	6	19.2	+31.2	+45.4
Cod-liver oil	7	57.0	6	33.3	2	24.9	+23.7	+32.1
Ointments	7	60.5	6	35.6	3	24.6	+24.9	+35.9
Mineral oil	6	61.1	6	31.6	3	7.7	+29.5	+53.4
Mouth washes	6	65.9	5	18.9	3	12.9	+47.0	+53.0
Headache remedies	5	57.1	5	30.9	1	32.0	+26.2	+25.1
Liniments	5	71.5	4	34.5	3	20.2	+37.0	+51.3
Medicinal tonics	5	62.5	5	34.8	2	31.7	+27.7	+30.8
Milk of magnesia	5	46.7	4	33.8	3	6.3	+12.9	+40.4
Aspirin tablets	4	71.3	4	40.1	2	12.2	+31.2	+59.1
Cleaning fluids	4	53.2	4	35.0	2	22.6	+18.2	+30.6
Kidney pills and tablets	4	68.0	3	38.0	2	13.6	+30.0	+54.4
Laxatives	4	70.5	4	38.8	3	29.7	+31.7	+40.8
Liver pills	3	63.3	3	26.5	2	17.9	+36.8	+45.4
Nerve remedies	3	62.7	3	31.4	1	35.0	+31.3	+27.7
Bicarbonate of soda preparations	2	59.1	2	44.3	2	30.4	+14.8	+28.7
Dyspepsia tablets	2	60.0	2	33.9	1	20.0	+26.1	+40.0
Throat tablets	2	59.0	2	38.1	1	41.7	+20.9	+17.3
Insecticides	2	57.0	2	40.9	2	36.6	+16.1	+20.4
Antiseptic powder	1	50.0			1	29.4		+20.6
Cascara tablets	1	70.0	1	40.0			+30.0	
Castor oil	1	44.4	1	34.0			+10.4	
Eye remedies	1	80.0	1	34.8	1	32.6	+45.2	+47.4
Floor wax	1	46.0	1	24.0			+22.0	
Kidney remedies	1	67.6	1	31.2			+36.4	
Rheumatic pills	1	60.0	1	23.2			+36.8	
Rubbing alcohol	1	65.3	1	49.2	1	23.7	+16.1	+41.6
Sore throat remedy	1	60.0	1	37.5			+22.5	
Total (30 commodities)	120	62.0	112	33.6	57	23.3	+28.4	+38.7
TOILET ARTICLES								
Hair preparations	11	65.4	9	39.0	7	19.2	+26.4	+46.2
Tooth pastes and powders	10	59.1	10	34.6	6	14.7	+24.5	+44.4
Face creams	7	60.3	7	38.6	6	18.7	+21.7	+41.6
Face lotions	7	63.7	7	39.0	3	36.2	+24.7	+27.5
Talcum powders	4	59.4	4	42.3	3	19.7	+17.1	+39.7
Deodorants	3	76.3	3	43.0	3	24.7	+33.3	+51.6
Face powders	2	69.0	2	47.0	2	20.3	+22.0	+48.7
Shaving creams	2	53.1	2	39.2	2	28.1	+13.9	+25.0
Soap	1	72.4	1	13.5	1	−3.8	+58.9	+76.2
Total (9 commodities)	47	63.2	45	38.9	33	21.9	+24.3	+41.3

[1] The units of size, weight, count, or measure often were not identical in the comparisons made in this table.

The average per cent of gross profit based upon the selling price was 62 per cent for the 120 drug and miscellaneous private brand items, 33.6 per cent for the 112 competing standard brand items bearing the highest mark-up, and 23.3 per cent for the 57 bearing the lowest mark-up. The figures for toilet goods are roughly the same—63.2 per cent, 38.9 per cent, and 21.9 per cent, respectively. In other words, for both general types of drug-store items classified in the preceding table, the average gross profit taken on private brands is roughly twice that taken on standard brands showing the highest mark-up and three times the figure for those having the lowest mark-up. This statement also holds true for many of the 39 different commodities.

Only three private brand commodities (castor oil, milk of magnesia, and floor wax) average a gross margin of less than 50 per cent. For competing standard brands having the highest mark-up, however, not a single commodity bears a gross profit as high as 50 per cent and only two (rubbing alcohol with 49.2 per cent and face powders with 47.0 per cent) are as high as the lowest gross margin reported for private brands, castor oil (44.4 per cent).

The highest gross profit for standard brand commodities bearing the lowest mark-up is for throat tablets (41.7 per cent), but eight others carry a gross profit of 30 per cent or more. From these figures it is clear that the difference between the gross profit made on private brands and on standard brands is considerably greater in drug chains than in grocery and grocery and meat chains (Table 41).

According to the commission's preliminary figures, the percentage of gross profit to sales in 1929 of 118 drug chains operating nearly 1,900 stores was 36.9 per cent and the percentage of operating expenses to sales was 33.3. As explained in a preceding subsection, these figures can be used as a rough measure of the profitableness of the different private and standard brand commodities reported by the 25 drug chains. For this purpose Table 45 shows the gross profit on the 167 private brand items and 247 competing standard brand items for which reports were received, distributed by ranges of 5 per cent.[27]

TABLE 45.—*Distribution of percentages of gross profit made on private and competing standard brand items in drug chains on March 30, 1929*

Per cent of gross profit	Private brand items			Competing standard brand items		
	Number	Per cent of total	Per cent cumulated	Number	Per cent of total	Per cent cumulated
Less than 25	1	0.6	0.6	80	32.4	32.4
25 to 30	0		.6	23	9.3	41.7
30 to 33.3 [1]	0		.6	31	12.6	54.3
33.3 to 35	0		.6	32	13.0	67.3
35 to 40	0		.6	24	9.7	77.0
40 to 45	10	6.0	6.6	36	14.6	91.6
45 to 50	9	5.4	12.0	8	3.2	94.8
50 to 55	23	13.8	25.8	9	3.6	98.4
55 to 60	18	10.8	36.6	3	1.2	99.6
60 to 65	35	20.9	57.5	1	.4	100.0
65 and over	71	42.5	100.0	0		100.0
Total	167	100.0		247	100.0	

[1] The cost of doing business in 1929 in the 118 drug chains which reported their operating expenses to the commission in detail was 33.3 per cent of their total net sales (preliminary figures).

The percentage of gross profit made on only one of the 167 private brand items (milk of magnesia, 24 per cent) was less than 33.3 per cent, the average cost of doing business in drug chains in 1929. In contrast, the gross profit made on over half of the 247 standard

[27] This table includes reports for drug, miscellaneous, and toilet items showing both the highest and lowest mark-up.

brands on which reports were received was less than 33.3 per cent. Stating this in another way, only about one-half of 1 per cent of the private brands, as contrasted to 54.3 per cent of the standard brands, were being sold on March 30, 1929, at less than the average cost of doing business in drug chains.[28]

The gross profit was 40 per cent or more on 99.4 per cent of the private brand articles, as contrasted with 23 per cent for the standard labeled goods. The difference is even more marked for items sold at a gross profit of 50 per cent or more (88 per cent of the private and only 5.2 per cent of the standard brand articles). Finally, the gross profit was 65 per cent or more for 42.5 per cent of the privately branded items, while the highest mark-up reported for any standard brand was 60.9 per cent.

Among the standard brands on which a gross profit of less than 33.3 per cent (the average cost of doing business for drug chains in 1929) was obtained,[29] were the following: Freezone (13 to 31.3 per cent), Blue Jay (31 per cent), and Gets-It (8.7 to 32.8 per cent) corn remedies; Creomulsion (32.3 per cent), Rem (20 to 30.6 per cent), Ayer's Cherry Pectoral (23.6 to 30 per cent), Pine Balsam (28 per cent), Piso's (20.8 per cent) and Pertussin (26.5 per cent) cough sirups; Scott's Emulsion of Cod Liver Oil (4.4 to 18.1 per cent); Squibb's (20.3 to 24.7 per cent), Olgar Compound (30.9 per cent), Agarol (1.2 per cent), and Nujol (9.5 to 17.8 per cent) mineral oils; Phillips (3.1 to 26.1 per cent) and Squibb's (19.1 per cent) milk of magnesia; Mike Martin's (28.6 per cent), Omega Oil (29.6 per cent), Sloan's (31 per cent) and Warner's (0.0 per cent) liniments; Listerine (0.0 to 20.9 per cent), Astringosol (29.8 per cent), Lavoris (24.1 per cent) and Glyco Thymoline (19.1 per cent) mouth washes; Carter's (20 to 26.3 per cent) and Beecham's (10 to 26.1 per cent) liver pills; Bayer's Aspirin (1.4 to 18.2 per cent); Doan's Kidney Pills (5.7 to 21.1 per cent); Grove's Bromo Quinine (5.6 to 28 per cent), Hill's Cascara Quinine (21.1 per cent), Edward's Tablets (20 per cent) and Pape's Cold Compound (13.8 per cent) all cold medicines; Pepsodent (3.5 to 30.2 per cent), Listerine (15.4 per cent), Squibb's (31.4 per cent), and Colgate's (32 per cent) tooth pastes; Hind's Honey and Almond Cream (16.7 to 32 per cent) and Frostilla (32 per cent) face lotions; Pompeian (32.7 per cent), Three Flowers (27.5 per cent) and Coty's (13.9 per cent) face powders; Mavis (10.5 to 15.8 per cent) and Three Flowers (30.4 per cent) talcum powders; Palmolive (31 per cent) and William's (25.7 per cent) shaving creams; and Cashmere Bouquet (13.5 per cent) and Woodbury's (3.8 per cent) soaps.

Cough sirup.—A large number of reports was received on cough sirup and tooth pastes and powders.

Mark-up figures were reported on 16 private brands of cough sirup. The gross profit reported ranged from 47.7 per cent to 79.6 per cent. The gross profit on only three private brands was less than 60 per cent; the gross profit on seven brands was from 60 per cent to 70 per cent; and on six brands it was from 70 to 80 per cent.

On standard brands of cough sirup, 22 reports were received. The following 10 different standard brands were named: Creomul-

[28] It does not necessarily follow that a net loss was realized by reporting chains on sales of all brands on which the gross profit was less than 33.3 per cent. See text p. 74.

[29] See text page 74.

sion, Rem, Stearn's Pine Tar Balsam, Ayer's Cherry Pectoral, Bell's Pine Tar and Honey, Pertussin, Chamberlain's Pine Balsam, Piso's, and Foley's Honey and Tar. The gross profit taken on these brands ranged from 20 to 47.2 per cent. In 7 of the 22 instances, standard brands were sold at a gross profit of less than 30 per cent. The gross profit on nine private brands ranged from 30 per cent to 35 per cent; on two it ranged from 35 per cent to 40 per cent; while the gross profit on four brands was 40 per cent or more.

The gross profit made on all of the private brands was in excess of 33.3 per cent, the average cost of doing business in 1929 in the 118 drug chains which reported expense figures. By way of contrast, the gross profit reported on 10 or nearly half of the standard brands sold was less than 33.3 per cent of their selling prices.

Gross profit percentages reported by different chains on the same standard brand of cough sirup differed widely. For example, those reported by seven different chains on one well-known standard brand (Rem) were as follows: 20, 24, 30.6, 33.3 (two reports), 36.8, and 37.5 per cent. Gross profit figures reported by four chains on a second well advertised standard brand (Ayer's Cherry Pectoral) were 23.6, 26.3, 30, and 33.3 per cent, respectively.

Tooth pastes and powders.—Reports were received on 10 private brands of tooth pastes and powders. The gross profit taken ranged from 50 to 69.2 per cent. The combined gross profit taken on the 10 private brands was 59.1 per cent of their total selling price.

Sixteen reports were received on standard brands of tooth pastes, five different brands being named (Listerine, Squibb's, Pepsodent, Colgate's, and Orphos). The gross profit taken in these cases ranged from 3.5 per cent to 40 per cent; on two it was from 10 to 20 per cent, on one 20 to 30 per cent, and on 11, 30 to 40 per cent. The gross profit in the two remaining cases was 6.1 and 3.5 per cent, respectively. Gross profit percentages reported on one well-known and widely advertised standard brand were as follows: 3.5, 6.1, 11.4, 28.2, and 30.2 per cent, respectively, all being under 33.3 per cent. Three chains reported gross profit percentages of 32 per cent, 34 per cent, and 40 per cent on a second well-known brand.

Aspirin tablets.—Aspirin tablets and deodorants are discussed below as examples of drug products having a high average mark-up.

Reports were received on four private brands of aspirin. The gross profit taken ranged from 66.7 to 73.7 per cent. By way of contrast, the gross profit taken on the competing standard brands (Bayer's, Squibb's, and Anacin) ranged from 1.4 to 60.9 per cent.

The gross profit realized by the first chain on its private and competing standard brand was 69.3 per cent and 42.4 per cent, respectively. Likewise, percentages reported by a second chain were 73.7 and 18.2 per cent. Another reported 72.9, 60.9 and 1.4 per cent on its private and competing standard brands, respectively. The last chain reported a gross profit of 66.7 per cent on its private brand as contrasted to 50 per cent and 44 per cent on two competing standard brands.

Percentages of gross profit reported by four chains on one well-known standard brand of aspirin (Bayer's) varied widely. They were: 1.4, 18.2, 42.4 and 50 per cent. It would appear likely that two of the chains were selling this brand at a net loss.

Deodorants.—Three chains reported cost figures on their private brands of deodorants and the prices at which they were being sold on March 30, 1929. The gross profit reported by the first chain on its private brand was 87.8 per cent as contrasted to 44.9 per cent and 31.1 per cent taken on two competing standard brands. The second chain reported a gross profit of 69.6 per cent on its private brands as contrasted to 39.2 and 26.9 per cent on the two competing standard brands. The gross profit taken by the third chain on its private brand was 60 per cent as contrasted to 42.9 per cent and 7.5 per cent for the two competing standard brands. The names of the standard brands on which reports were received were as follows: Odo-ro-no, Dew, Neet, and Mum.

Cod-liver oil preparations.—Cod-liver oil and talcum powder are discussed below as examples of branded commodities on which the average mark-up was relatively low. Seven drug chains reported mark-up figures on their private brands of cod-liver oil. The gross profit taken ranged from 50 to 72.3 per cent. The gross profit on five of the seven brands was from 50 per cent to 60 per cent; and the gross profit on the two remaining brands was 60 per cent and 72.3 per cent, respectively.

Eight reports were received on well-known standard brands of this product (including Squibb's, Wampole's, and Scott's Emulsion). The gross profit taken on these brands ranged from 4.4 per cent to 40.2 per cent. Two of the eight standard brands were sold at a gross profit of less than 20 per cent; four from 30 to 40 per cent; while the gross profits on the two remaining brands were 40 and 40.2 per cent, respectively.

The gross profit on three standard brands was less than 33.3 per cent of sales, the average cost of doing business in drug chains in 1929. By way of contrast, the gross profit taken on all private brands was considerably in excess of this figure.

Gross margin figures were made available by three chains on the same well-known standard brand of cod-liver oil. They were as follows: 4.4 per cent, 18.1, and 36.7 per cent.

Talcum powder.—Reports were received on four private brands of talcum powder. The gross profit on these brands ranged from 45.5 per cent to 60 per cent, being exactly 60 per cent in two instances. The total gross profit on the four brands was 59.4 per cent of their total selling price.

Seven reports were received on five standard brands of talcum powder (Armand's, Mennen's, Cappi, Mavis, and Three Flowers). The gross profit made on these brands ranged from 10.5 per cent to 50 per cent. Arranged in the order of increasing size, percentages of gross profit reported on the standard brands were as follows: 10.5, 15.8, 30.4, 34.8, 36, 48, and 50 per cent.

Two chains, which sold the same standard brand, realized a gross profit on such sales of only 10.5 per cent and 15.8 per cent, respectively. While the percentage of total operating expenses to total net sales in these two chains is not known, it would appear probable that both incurred a substantial net loss on sales of this particular brand.[30]

Thirteen drug chains.—As previously pointed out not all chains reported the gross profit on both types of competing standard brands

---

[30] See footnote 28, p. 83.

of commodities. Returns from the chains which reported for each commodity data on (*a*) the private brand, (*b*) the competing standard brand having the highest mark-up, and (*c*) the competing standard brand having the lowest mark-up are shown in the following table. Unless a chain reported on the private brand and both types of standard brands, it was not included.

The average per cent of gross profit on private brands of drug and miscellaneous items reported by the 13 drug chains included in the table was 65.8 per cent. This figure exceeded, by 26.4 points per cent, the gross profit on the standard brand items having the highest mark-up and by 41.7 points per cent, that on the standard brands having the lowest mark-up. Approximately the same gross profits and differences between private and standard brand items are found on toilet articles. For every one of the 32 commodities, the percentage of gross profit on the private brand was higher than that on either of the two competing standard brands.

TABLE 46.—*Gross profit on 23 drug and miscellaneous and 9 toilet private and competing standard brand commodities reported by 13 drug chains, March 30, 1929* [1]

Commodity	Per cent of gross profit based on retail selling price				Points per cent by which gross profit on private brands is higher (+) or lower (−) than on competing standard brands	
	Number of price quotations	Private brands	Competing standard brands having highest mark-up	Competing standard brands having lowest mark-up	Standard brands having highest mark-up	Standard brands having lowest mark-up
DRUG AND MISCELLANEOUS PRODUCTS		*Per cent*	*Per cent*	*Per cent*		
Cough sirups	6	67.6	40.0	30.3	+27.6	+37.3
Cold tablets	5	69.9	35.3	20.5	+34.6	+49.4
Corn remedies	4	68.5	37.1	20.5	+31.4	+48.0
Laxatives	3	70.5	38.8	29.7	+31.7	+40.8
Mineral oil	3	68.6	36.3	7.7	+32.3	+60.9
Aspirin tablets	2	71.4	58.4	12.2	+13.0	+59.2
Bicarbonate of soda preparations	2	59.1	44.3	30.4	+14.8	+28.7
Cleaning fluids	2	53.7	34.5	22.6	+19.2	+31.1
Liniments	2	82.5	28.9	15.7	+53.6	+66.8
Medicinal tonics	2	64.2	49.1	31.7	+15.1	+32.5
Milk of magnesia	2	50.7	30.8	6.2	+19.9	+44.5
Mouth washes	2	65.8	18.8	12.8	+47.0	+53.0
Ointments	2	69.1	42.5	29.4	+26.6	+39.7
Cod-liver oil	1	60.0	40.0	36.7	+20.0	+23.3
Dyspepsia tablets	1	48.9	30.8	20.0	+18.1	+28.9
Eye remedies	1	80.0	34.8	32.6	+45.2	+47.4
Headache remedies	1	64.0	40.0	32.0	+24.0	+32.0
Insecticides	1	55.7	46.7	33.3	+9.0	+22.4
Kidney pills	1	75.0	38.2	21.1	+36.8	+53.9
Liver pills	1	64.0	20.0	10.0	+44.0	+54.0
Nerve remedies	1	50.0	40.0	35.0	+10.0	+15.0
Rubbing alcohol	1	65.3	49.2	23.7	+16.1	+41.6
Throat tablets	1	68.0	43.5	41.7	+24.5	+26.3
Total (23 commodities)	47	65.8	39.4	24.1	+26.4	+41.7
TOILET ARTICLES						
Face creams	6	62.6	39.2	18.7	+23.4	+43.9
Tooth pastes and powders	6	60.6	36.1	14.7	+24.5	+45.9
Hair preparations	5	72.2	43.9	23.2	+28.3	+49.0
Deodorants	3	76.3	43.0	24.7	+33.3	+51.6
Face lotions	3	66.4	50.3	36.2	+16.1	+30.2
Talcum powders	3	59.3	44.5	19.7	+14.8	+39.6
Face powders	2	69.0	47.0	20.3	+22.0	+48.7
Shaving cream	2	53.1	39.2	28.1	+13.9	+25.0
Soap	1	72.4	13.5	−3.8	+58.9	+76.2
Total (9 commodities)	31	65.6	41.7	23.1	+23.9	+42.5

[1] The units of size, weight, count, or measure often were not identical in the comparisons made in this table.

Table 46 shows that high percentages of gross profits on private brands were quite general throughout the list of commodities, the lowest being 48.9 per cent on dyspepsia tablets. This percentage was exceeded by that on only four competing standard-brand items—aspirin tablets, 58.4 per cent; face lotions, 50.3 per cent; rubbing alcohol, 49.2 per cent; and medicinal tonics, 49.1 per cent. The smallest percentage of gross profit reported on private brands of toilet articles was 53.1 per cent on shaving cream, whereas the largest gross profit on any standard brand toilet articles was 50.3 per cent reported for face lotions.

Significance of grocery and drug gross profits.—Before continuing with the discussion of the more limited gross profit data obtained from other kinds of chains, certain points developed in the preceding pages of this section on gross margins of drug and grocery items deserve summarization and some expansion.

1. Both private and standard brands of drug chains are marked up from one and one-third to three times as much, on the average, as those reported by grocery and grocery and meat chains. In any comparison of this sort, however, consideration should be given both to the difference in average gross profits, 36.9 per cent for drug and 18.5 per cent for grocery chains, and to average costs of doing business, 33.3 per cent for drug and 16.1 per cent for grocery chains.

2. The difference in mark-up between private brands and competing standard brands is materially greater in the case of drug chains than in grocery and grocery and meat chains.

3. Finally, the standard-brand items of drugs are sold much more commonly below the average cost of doing business for drug chains than standard-brand items of groceries are sold below the average cost of doing business for grocery and grocery and meat chains.

Over 30 per cent of the grocery standard-brand items included in the comparisons were sold at a gross profit which was less than 16.1 per cent, the average cost of doing business in grocery and grocery and meat chains, 1929, as compared with only half that proportion of private brands (14.8 per cent). In drugs, over 50 per cent of the standard-brand items reported in this connection were sold at less than the average cost of doing business in 118 drug chains as compared with less than 1 per cent of the private brands.

These gross profits on grocery and drug store items tend to support the figures in the commission's report on Leaders and Loss Leaders which indicated that considerable quantities of goods were sold by chains in these two kinds of business at prices which yielded no net profit to the chain and which frequently showed a loss if the cost of doing business was considered. They also tend to confirm the conclusion of that same report which showed that private-brand items of these kinds of chains were seldom used for leader merchandising as compared with standard-brand items.

It is obvious, therefore, that if a chain sells its private-brand items at a sufficiently high profit and in sufficient volume, its standard-brand goods can be sold in large quantities either without net profit or at a loss, thereby creating an impression (as has so often been claimed) of low prices. Although the private-brand goods carry a much higher gross profit and probably net profit than competing standard-brand goods, the following section shows that prices at which they are sold are commonly below those of competing standard-brand products. This statement is particularly interesting in the light of recent studies of prices charged in chain and independent grocery stores, which have been made in the following cities: New York and environs; Durham, N. C.; Lexington, Ky.; Chicago, Champaign-Urbana, Ill.; and five New York State towns. With one exception, these studies show that prices charged on identical standard brands (or comparable merchandise) by chain stores are from 8 to slightly more than 14 per cent lower than prices charged by independents.[31]

Tobacco chains.—Four tobacco chains furnished gross-profit figures on private brands and competing standard brands. The largest chain, United Cigar Stores of America, which was operating more than 1,000 stores in 1928, reported on seven private brands of cigars. A second chain, which was operating 14 stores in 1928, reported on two private brands of cigars and one brand of smoking tobacco. The third chain, which was operating 11 stores in 1928, reported on one private brand of cigars and one private brand of smoking tobacco, while the fourth chain, which had two stores in 1928, reported on one private brand of cigars.

As shown in Table 47, the total combined gross profit taken on the 11 private brands of cigars was 31.5 per cent of their total selling price as contrasted to 32.5 per cent for the 11 competing standard brands having the highest mark-up and 29.4 per cent for the three competing standard brands having the lowest mark-up.

[31] A Study in Retail Grocery Prices, by R. S. Alexander. Journal of Commerce, Feb. 9, ff., 1929. According to one method of handling the statistical material, this study showed that independents were underselling chains by about 4.6 per cent. According to another method, the chains were underselling independents by about 2.6 per cent. Prices in Chain and Independent Grocery Stores in Durham, N. C., by Malcolm D. Taylor.—Harvard Business Review, July, 1930. As shown by this study, chain-store prices on 60 branded articles averaged 13.8 per cent lower than the prices charged in independent stores. Chain Store Price Survey in Lexington, Ky., by E. Z. Palmer. Journal of Commerce, July 19, 1930. This study showed that chain prices averaged 14.3 per cent lower than prices in independent stores. A Study of the Prices of Chain and Independent Grocers in Chicago, by J. L. Palmer and Einar Bjorklund, Chicago University Press. This study showed a difference of 9 to 10 per cent in favor of the chains when compared with nonservice independents and 11 to 12 per cent when compared with service independents. Prices and Services of Chain and Independent Stores in Champaign-Urbana, Ill., by P. D. Converse. Bulletin of National Association of Teachers of Marketing and Advertising, October, 1931. The average prices of all chains were 8.4 per cent less than the average prices of all independents. A report on chain, voluntary chain, and independent store prices in five New York State towns, by C. F. Phillips. Reported in Chain Store Progress, by R. W. Lyons, May, 1931. According to this study, in these five small towns, the chains were underselling the unorganized independents 10.7 per cent and the cooperative chain stores 9.2 per cent. A Comparison of Independent and Chain Store Prices, by Dorothy Dowe. Journal of Business, April, 1932. This study showed that the chains had a price advantage of 8.5 per cent over independents.

TABLE 47.—*Gross profit on all private and competing standard brand commodities reported by four miscellaneous kinds of chains, March 30, 1929* [1]

Commodity	Per cent of gross profit based on retail selling price						Points per cent by which gross profit on private brands is higher (+) or lower (−) than on competing standard brands	
	Private brands		Competing standard brands having highest mark-up		Competing standard brands having lowest mark-up			
	Number of price quotations	Per cent	Number of price quotations	Per cent	Number of price quotations	Per cent	Standard brands having highest mark-up	Standard brands having lowest mark-up
Tobacco chains:								
1. Cigars	11	31.5	11	32.5	3	29.4	−1.0	+2.1
2. Smoking tobacco	2	32.7	2	29.5	1	30.2	+3.2	+2.5
Variety ($1 limit) chains:								
1. Toilet soap	1	31.8	1	23.8	---	---	+8.0	---
2. Sanitary napkins	1	34.4	1	37.5	---	---	−3.1	---
Dry goods and apparel chains:								
1. Work shirts	2	28.3	2	17.5	1	20.3	+10.8	+8.0
2. Sheeting	1	23.5	1	33.7	---	---	−10.2	---
3. Overalls	1	7.8	1	20.2	---	---	−12.4	---
Department-store chains:								
1. Dress shirts	1	35.4	---	---	1	33.7	---	+1.7
2. Dress shoes	1	38.67	1	38.64	---	---	+.03	---
3. Men's clothing	1	26.7	1	26.7	---	---	---	---

[1] The units of size, weight, count, or measure often were not identical in the comparisons made in this table.

The range of gross profit for the 11 private brands was from 25 to 36.4 per cent while for 14 competing standard brands it was 8.8 to 38.3 per cent. Three of the 11 private brands and 3 of the 14 competing standard brands were sold at less than 29.3 per cent, the average gross profit reported by 26 tobacco chains, operating 1,658 stores in 1929 and with sales of $107,800,000. The average operating expense of these 26 chains was 29 per cent.[32]

The percentage of gross profit on six private brands was less than the percentage of gross profit on the standard brand which competed with them. In one instance the percentage of gross profit on both private and standard brands was the same. Four private brands were sold at a higher percentage of gross profit than the competing standard brands.

Only two tobacco chains reported mark-up figures on their private brands of smoking tobacco. The first chain reported a gross profit of 17.8 per cent on both the private-brand and a competing standard-brand item. The gross profit taken by the second chain was 33.6 per cent on its own brand as compared with 30.2 per cent for the competing standard brand having the highest and that having the lowest mark-up. The gross profit taken on the two private brands of tobacco was 32.7 per cent of the selling price, as contrasted to 29.5 per cent and 30.2 per cent on the two types of competing standard brands.

Variety ($1 limit) chains.—Only one dollar-limit variety chain (operating over 100 stores on December 31, 1928), reported mark-up figures. It furnished comparative prices on its private

[32] Preliminary figures.

and competing standard brands of toilet soap and napkins. The gross profit taken on the toilet soap which bore its private brand was 31.8 per cent as contrasted to 23.8 per cent for a well-known standard brand. The private brand, which cost 3.4 cents, was sold at 5 cents a cake. The competing standard brand, which cost 6.4 cents, was sold at 8⅓ cents a cake (three cakes for a quarter).

The gross profit taken by this chain on its private brand of napkins was 34.4 per cent as contrasted to 37.5 per cent for a competing standard brand.

Dry goods and apparel chains.—Two dry goods and apparel chains reported mark-up figures. The first chain reported on work shirts; the second on work shirts, sheeting, and overalls. Both chains were operating six stores in 1928. The gross profit on the two private brands of work shirts was 28.3 per cent and on the two standard brands having the highest mark-up, 17.5 per cent. The standard brand having the lowest mark-up reported by one of the chains cost 63 cents and sold at 79 cents, with a gross profit of 20.3 per cent.

Both brands of sheeting were sold at 49 cents a yard. The cost of the private brand was 37½ cents a yard, and the cost of the standard brand was 32½ cents a yard. Hence the gross profit on the private brand was 23.5 per cent of its selling price as contrasted to a gross profit of 33.7 per cent for the standard brand.

The private brand of overalls cost $1.19 and was sold for $1.29, or at a gross profit of only 7.8 per cent. The standard brand, which cost $1.58, was sold for $1.98 with a gross profit of 20.2 per cent of the selling price.

Department store chains.—Reports were received from two department store chains. The first chain reported on dress shirts and dress shoes. The second chain reported on men's clothing. The first chain was operating three stores and the second, 18 stores, in 1928. The first reported that the cost of both brands of dress shirts was the same, namely, $1.29. The private brand was sold at $2 and the competing standard brand was sold at $1.95, or the gross profit on the private brand was 35.4 per cent of its selling price, and the gross profit on the standard brand was 33.7 per cent. Its private brand of dress shoes, which was sold at $7.50, cost $4.60 a pair. In other words, the gross profit realized was 38.7 per cent. The well-known standard brand of shoes, which it sold at $11 a pair, cost $6.75 a pair. That is, the gross profit was 38.6 per cent of the selling price.

Both brands of clothing were sold by the second chain at $22.50 a suit. The cost of both brands was $16.50 a suit, the gross profit on both brands being 26.7 per cent of the selling price. The standard brand was a well-known nationally advertised brand.

Men's ready-to-wear chains.—Mark-up figures were received from only one men's ready-to-wear chain. It reported on its private brand of shirts, which was sold in competition with a well-known nationally advertised standard brand. The cost of its private brand was $1.21 as contrasted to $1.25 for the competing standard brand. Both brands were being sold on March 30, 1929 at $1.95, the gross profit on the private brand being 38 per cent as contrasted to 35.9 per cent for the competing standard brand.

Women's accessories chains.—One women's accessories chain reported mark-up figures on its private brand of hosiery. The private brand of hosiery, which cost 83 cents a pair, was being sold at $1.25 on March 30, 1929, or the gross profit was 33.6 per cent of the selling price. The cost of a well-known competing standard brand, which was being sold for $1.85 a pair, was $1.18¾, or the gross profit was 35.8 per cent of the selling price.

Women's shoe chains.—Only one report was received from a chain selling women's shoes. The cost of its private brand was $6.25 a pair as contrasted to $6.60 a pair for the competing standard brand. Both brands were being sold on March 30, 1929, at $10.50 a pair. Hence, the gross profit on the private brand amounted to 40.5 per cent of its selling price and the gross profit on the standard brand was 37.1 per cent.

Section 17. Prices of private brands compared with those of competing standard brands having highest mark-up.

On the original schedule, as reported in section 16, each chain was requested to give for March 30, 1929, its net purchase cost and retail selling price on each of the 10 principal commodities sold under its private brands and its net purchase cost and retail selling prices on two groups of competing standard brands; first, those which carried the highest mark-up and second, those which carried the lowest mark-up. It must be kept in mind that although the mark-up on a private brand may have been higher than that on competing standard brands, as pointed out in the preceding section, this policy does not necessarily result in the private brand being priced higher than the competing standard brand.

In comparing a private and competing standard brand, price comparisons have been made only between brands of identical weight, size, count, or measure. As shown on page 70, information given on the tenth commodity, corn flakes, could not be used because the private brand contained 13 ounces as contrasted with 8 ounces for the standard brand. Because of this need for identical weight, size, count, or measure, moreover, some of the reports for certain chains could not be used. Price information shown in this and the following section was received from 58 grocery and grocery and meat chains, operating 13,938 stores; 19 drug chains, operating 245 stores; 4 tobacco chains, operating 1,138 stores; and chains in 8 other miscellaneous groups. A comparison of prices of private brands with competing standard brands which had the highest mark-up is shown in the present section. A similar comparison of private brands with competing standard brands which had the lowest mark-up is made in the following section.

Twenty-two of the 58 reporting grocery and grocery and meat chains were operating 100 or more stores on December 31, 1928. The largest reporting chain was the Kroger Grocery & Baking Co., which had 5,260 stores. First National Stores (Inc.) was second with 1,791 stores and the National Tea Co. was third with 1,041 stores. These were the only chains operating more than 1,000 stores. Two chains had between 500 and 1,000 stores, namely: Safeway Stores (Inc.) of California (southern Safeway division)[b] and the Grand Union Co. Three chains had between 300 and 500 stores. These

[b] See note a, p. 71.

were the Sanitary Grocery Co., S. M. Flickinger (Inc.), and Mutual Grocery Co. The following chains had between 100 and 300 stores: H. G. Hill Co.; Skaggs Safeway Corporation (Nevada corporation); Red Owl Stores (Inc.); F. W. Crook Stores; Consumers' Sanitary Coffee and Butter Stores; Sheffield Farms (Inc.); Hill Grocery Co.; the Market Basket Corporation; Safeway Stores (Inc.) of California (Piggly-Wiggly southern division); Gristede Bros. (Inc.); Great Eastern Stores; The Nicholson, Thackray Co.; Continental Grocery Corporation (Ltd.); and Larkin Co. (Inc.). Of the remaining chains, 6 had more than 50 stores, 11 operated from 25 to 50 stores, and 19 had less than 25 stores.

Only two of the 19 reporting drug chains were operating 25 stores or more on December 31, 1928. The largest chain was Peoples' Drug Stores (Inc.) with 82 stores and Mykrantz & Sons Drug Co. was second with 27 stores. Five chains had from 10 to 25 stores, namely: Standard Drug Co.; Harvey & Carey (Inc.); the Muir Co.; the Schettler Drug Co.; and John H. Wood Co. The following five chains had from 5 to 10 stores: Vernon Drug Co. (Inc.); Red Cross Drug Co.; A. R. Reno & Co.; Schwarz Druggists (Inc.); and Stanley Drug Co. Each of the remaining chains operated less than 5 stores.

The largest tobacco chain which reported was the United Cigar Stores of America with over 1,000 stores. Moss & Lowenhaupt Cigar Co. was second with 15 stores; R. Russell & Co. (Inc.) was third with 11 stores; and Post Cigar Co. was fourth with 2 stores.

A limited number of chains in other lines of business furnished comparative price data on private and standard brands. S. H. Kress & Co., a variety $1 limit chain, was operating 193 stores on December 31, 1928. A men's ready-to-wear chain, Stumpfs (Inc.), was operating 6 stores. Terminal Hosiery Shops (Inc.), a women's accessories chain, was operating 9 stores. Applebaum-Mautner Co., a women's shoe chain, operated 4 stores. Gorin's, and L. T. Hill Co., two dry goods and apparel chains, each operated 6 stores. Two department store chains furnished information, Ed. Schuster & Co. (Inc.), which was operating 3 stores, and C. C. Anderson Co., which was operating 18 stores.

Grocery and grocery and meat.—In the comparison between the selling prices of private brands and competing standard brands which had the highest mark-up, a total of 212 usable comparative price reports on 44 different commodities was received from grocery and grocery and meat chains as shown in Table 48. In order to avoid possible misinterpretation of data appearing in this and the succeeding section, it should be pointed out that several chains returned quotations on the same standard brand of a single commodity. For example, Del Monte was named by several chains as a competitive brand of various kinds of canned fruits; Gold Medal was given as a competitive brand of flour by several chains; and Borden's Milk was given as a competitive brand of canned milk by several chains.

TABLE 48.—*Comparative prices of private and competing standard brand commodities (showing highest mark-up) of the same size, sold by grocery and grocery and meat chains, March 30, 1929*

Commodity	Number of reports	Total of sizes or weights included	Total retail selling price		Selling price on private brand is higher (+) or lower (−)	
			Private brands	Competing standard brands	Amount	Per cent
Beverages and beverage bases:						
Coffee	44	44 pounds	$19.07	$22.92	−3.85	−16.8
Tea	15	9½ pounds	7.07	9.05	−1.98	−21.9
Cocoa	5	3 pounds	.81	1.14	−.33	−29.0
Ginger ale	3	36 ounces	.355	.54	−.185	−34.3
Malt sirup	2	5 pounds	.86	1.10	−.24	−21.8
Grape juice	1	1 pint	.25	.30	−.05	−16.7
Cereal products:						
Flour	21	876¼ pounds	36.85	40.52	−3.67	−9.1
Bread	7	8 pounds 9 ounces	.61	.769	−.159	−20.7
Rolled oats	2	38 ounces	.183	.20	−.017	−8.5
Corn flakes	1	8 ounces	.075	.08	−.005	−6.3
Cornstarch	1	1 pound	.10	.10		
Farina	1	1 package	.23	.24	−.1	−4.2
Macaroni	1	14 ounces	.13	.13		
Canned goods:						
Vegetables—						
Corn	7	7 cans	1.21	1.20	+.01	+0.8
Peas	6	6 cans	1.045	1.13	−.085	−7.5
Tomatoes	3	3 cans	.53	.50	+.03	+6.0
Asparagus	1	1 pound	.33	.35	−.02	−5.7
Green beans	1	1 can	.10	.15	−.05	−33.3
Red beans	1	do	.09	.14	−.05	−35.7
Pork and beans	1	do	.09	.09		
Beets	1	do	.15	.26	−.11	−42.3
Spinach	1	do	.16	.17	−.01	−5.9
Fruit—						
Peaches	11	11 cans	2.70	2.75	−.05	−1.8
Pineapple	6	6 cans	1.43	1.55	−.12	−7.7
Pears	3	3 cans	.86	.92	−.06	−6.5
Apricots	2	2 cans	.48	.52	−.04	−7.7
Cherries	2	do	.60	.63	−.03	−4.8
Chicken	2	18 ounces	1.60	1.60		
Milk	10	10 pounds	.933	.993	−.06	−6.0
Soup	1	10½ ounces	.09	.095	−.005	−5.3
Relishes, condiments, spreads:						
Mayonnaise	15	192 ounces	4.57	5.28	−.71	−13.5
Ketchup	4	56 ounces	.88	.97	−.09	−9.3
Vinegar	4	6 pints	.745	.89	−.145	−16.3
Flavoring extracts	3	6 ounces	.71	.93	−.22	−23.7
Peanut butter	3	3 pounds	.69	.83	−.14	−16.9
Salt	2	56 ounces	.20	.21	−.01	−4.8
Jam	1	15 ounces	.25	.27	−.02	−7.4
Mustard	1	8 ounces	.12	.13	−.01	−7.7
Other commodities:						
Butter	8	8 pounds	3.78	4.06	−.28	−6.9
Baking powder	2	2 pounds	.45	.63	−.18	−28.6
Gelatine, flavored	2	2 packages	.152	.158	−.006	−3.8
Sirup	2	3 pounds	.23	.24	−.01	−4.2
Raisins	1	15 ounces	.07	.08	−.01	−12.5
Eggs	1	1 dozen	.38	.39	−.01	−2.6
Total (44 commodities)	212		92.218	105.205	−12.987	−12.3

If a hypothetical customer on March 30, 1929, had purchased all 424 commodities (212 private brands and 212 standard brands) from the grocery and grocery and meat chains reporting, his private brands would have cost him $92.22 and his standard brands would have cost $105.21. In other words, the private brands were lower than the competing standard brands by $12.99. Expressed in the form of a percentage, the private brands sold for 12.3 per cent less than the standard brands.

In only 2 cases out of 44, canned corn and canned tomatoes, was the average price of the private brand item higher than that of the competing standard brand.

142189—S. Doc. 142, 72-2——8

The selling price on 38 commodities packed under private brands was lower than on the competing standard brand merchandise. The widest price differences of the private under the standard brand merchandise are in canned vegetables: Beets (42.3 per cent) and red beans (35.7 per cent). These are followed closely by ginger ale (34.3 per cent), green beans (33.3 per cent), cocoa (29 per cent), and baking powder (28.6 per cent). An interesting difference appears between canned vegetables and canned fruits in that private brands of fruits are priced, on the average, only slightly below those of standard brands, whereas the private brands of the three canned vegetables referred to above are among the items which show the greatest average price differences, private brands being the lower.

The saving on private brands was 20 per cent or more for the following 10 commodities: Cocoa, ginger ale, tea, malt, bread, canned green beans, canned red beans, canned beets, flavoring extracts, and baking powder. The saving on private brands was less than 10 per cent on 22 commodities as follows: Corn flakes, rolled oats, farina, flour, canned milk, canned asparagus, canned peas, canned spinach, canned apricots, canned cherries, canned peaches, canned pears, canned pineapple, butter, salt, mustard, ketchup, jam, sirup, soup, flavored gelatine, and eggs. Prices were the same on the competing brands of four commodities covered by reports: Canned chicken, canned pork and beans, corn starch, and macaroni.

Individual variations.—Of 212 comparative price quotations, there were 173 in which the private brand was sold at a lower price than the standard brand item, 33 in which both were sold at the same price, and 6 in which the private brand was sold at a higher price than the standard brand. Most of the instances in which the private brand was sold at a higher price than the standard brand are lost in the averages. The exceptions are canned corn and canned tomatoes. The 6 private brands of commodities which were sold at a higher price were: Coffee (2 brands), canned tomatoes (2), canned corn and canned peaches (1 each). Both private brands of coffee were 2 cents higher than the competing standard brands; the private brands of canned tomatoes were 1 and 2 cents higher, respectively; the private brand of canned corn was 3 cents higher; and the private brand of canned peaches, 8 cents more.

A large number of reports was received on coffee, flour, and mayonnaise. The average pound of coffee packed under a private label sold for 43 cents as compared with 52 cents for the competing standard brand, a difference of 16.8 per cent in favor of the private brand. One chain sold its own brand at 29 cents or 34 cents (54 per cent) a pound less than the competing standard brand. This was the largest difference reported for coffee.[33]

One chain sold its private brand of flour for 33.6 per cent less than the competing standard brand; another sold its private brand for only 0.95 per cent less. These represent the extreme cases. On the average, flour packed under a private brand sold for 9.1 per cent less than flour under a standard brand.

From Table 48, it will be seen that the private brands of mayonnaise reported were selling for 13.5 per cent less than the competing

---

[33] The two brands of coffee may not have been of comparable quality or the chain may have had a special sale on its own brand on Mar. 30, 1929.

standard brands. The prices reported on competing brands of mayonnaise are shown in the following tabular statement:

Unit	Retail selling price		Private brand is lower by—		Unit	Retail selling price		Private brand is lower by—	
	Private brand	Standard brand	Am't	Per cent		Private brand	Standard brand	Am't	Per cent
32 ounces	$0.69	$0.85	$0.16	18.8	8 ounces	$0.21	$0.25	$0.04	16.0
Do	.69	.74	.05	6.8	Do	.21	.25	.04	16.0
16 ounces	.39	.45	.06	13.3	Do	.21	.25	.04	16.0
Do	.39	.43	.04	9.3	Do	.20	.23	.03	13.0
Do	.36	.39	.03	7.7	Do	.19	.21	.02	9.5
8 ounces	.23	.25	.02	8.0	Do	.19	.23	.04	17.4
Do	.22	.25	.03	12.0	Do	.18	.25	.07	28.0
Do	.21	.25	.04	16.0					

The quantity sold in a container appears to have little influence upon the per cent of difference between the selling price of private and standard brands of mayonnaise. There is a wide variation in the spreads between the prices for private and standard brands in all of the three sizes reported. For the 32-ounce size the range is from 6.8 to 18.8 per cent, while for the 8-ounce size it is 8 to 28 per cent.

In addition to canned beets, red and green beans, ginger ale, and cocoa are examples of commodities for which the price differential between private and standard brand merchandise is wide. The average price of ginger ale is 34 per cent lower when packed under a private label, being 50, 30.6, and 22.2 per cent lower, respectively, for the three private brands, according to the individual reports.

Among the five reports on cocoa, one private brand was 52.5 per cent lower than the competing standard brand having the highest mark-up. At the other extreme, one was only 10 per cent lower. The average price for all five private brands was 29 per cent lower than for the competing standard brands.

Flavored gelatine and canned peaches are examples of products for which price differences between private and standard brands are not great. Two chains reported on flavored gelatine. One reported no difference at all while the other indicated that the private brand was lower by 8 per cent. Prices were reported on canned peaches by 11 chains. In all but one report the private brand was sold at the same or a lower price than the competing standard brand. The average price of all private brands of peaches reported was only 1.8 per cent less than that of competing standard brands. (Table 48.) Below are the prices shown by the 11 reports.

Retail selling price		Private brand is lower by—	
Private brand [1]	Standard brand [1]	Amount	Per cent
$0.35	$0.27	[2] $0.08	[2] 29.6
.29	.29	.00	0.0
.27	.28	.01	3.6
.25	.27	.02	7.4
.25	.25	.00	0.0
.24	.25	.01	4.0
.23	.25	.02	8.0
.22	.24	.02	8.3
.21	.23	.02	8.7
.21	.21	.00	0.0
.18	.21	.03	14.3

[1] All reports are for No. 2½ can.

[2] Private brand is higher.

Drug chains.—Comparative prices were received from drug chains on private and standard brands of 37 drug, 4 miscellaneous, and 12 toilet articles. Data on these products are shown in Table 49.

TABLE 49.—*Comparative prices of private and competing standard brand commodities (showing highest mark-up) of the same size, sold by drug chains, March 30, 1929*

Commodity	Number of reports	Total of sizes or weights included	Total retail selling price		Selling price on private brand is higher (+) or lower (−)	
			Private brands	Competing standard brands	Amount	Per cent
DRUG AND MISCELLANEOUS ARTICLES						
Mineral oil	5	80 ounces	$3.42	$4.56	−1.14	−25.0
Cod-liver oil	4	52 ounces	3.39	3.69	−.30	−8.1
Cold tablets	4	98 tablets	.98	.93	+.05	+5.4
Corn remedies	4	1¼ ounce	1.00	1.30	−.30	−23.1
Ointments	4	7 ounces	2.00	2.47	−.47	−19.0
Aspirin tablets	3	300 tablets	1.81	2.82	−1.01	−35.8
Cough sirups	3	16 ounces	1.84	2.28	−.44	−19.3
Insecticides	2	24 ounces	1.28	1.59	−.31	−19.5
Nerve remedies	2	16 ounces	1.98	1.69	+.29	+17.2
Bicarbonate of soda	1	4 ounces	.43	.75	−.32	−42.7
Cascara	1	100 tablets	.29	.40	−.11	−27.5
Cleaning fluid	1	8 ounces	.30	.35	−.05	−14.3
Floor wax	1	1 pound	.50	.75	−.25	−33.3
Kidney remedies	1	12 ounces	1.39	1.09	+.30	+27.5
Laxative	1	24 tablets	.25	.24	+.01	+4.2
Medicinal tonics	1	12 ounces	1.19	.98	+.21	+21.4
Milk of magnesia	1	8 ounces	.25	.50	−.25	−50.0
Rheumatic pills	1	100 pills	1.00	1.25	−.25	−20.0
Rubbing alcohol	1	16 ounces	.49	.59	−.10	−16.9
Total (19 commodities)	41		23.79	28.23	−4.44	−15.7
TOILET ARTICLES						
Cold cream	2	19 ounces	1.04	3.10	−2.06	−66.5
Lotions	2	9 ounces	.84	.99	−.15	−15.2
Tooth paste	2	4 ounces	.89	.78	+.11	+14.1
Deodorant	1	1 ounce	.49	.49		
Face powder	1	3 ounces	.50	.49	+.01	+2.0
Brilliantine	1	2 ounces	.50	.50		
Shampoo	1	6 ounces	.49	.35	+.14	+40.0
Soap	1	1 cake	.19	.197	−.007	−3.6
Vanishing cream	1	4 ounces	.50	.50		
Total (9 commodities)	12		5.44	7.397	−1.957	−26.5

If a hypothetical customer had purchased all 82 drug products (41 private-brand items and 41 standard-brand items) on March 30, 1929, from the chains reporting, the private brands would have cost $23.79 and the standard brands $28.23. In other words, the private brands were lower by $4.44 or 15.7 per cent.

Of the 28 commodities on which reports were received as shown in the table, the private brands were lower than or the same as the standard brands on 20 and higher on 8. Private brands of 19 drug and miscellaneous commodities were higher in five instances, and they were also higher on three of the nine toilet articles.

The range of the percentages in those cases in which standard brands are lower is from 2 per cent for face powder, to 40 per cent for shampoos. The range is somewhat narrower than the differences in favor of the private brands (3.6 per cent for soap to 66.5 per cent for cold cream). The two extremes in both cases, it will be noted, are in toilet articles. The same general statement holds true, however, for drug and miscellaneous items. The range for the products for which private-brand prices were lower than standard-brand prices is from 8.1 per cent on cod-liver oil to 50 per cent on milk of magnesia. For those products for which standard-brand prices are lower, the range is from 4.2 to 27.5 per cent, for laxative tablets and kidney remedies, respectively. Except for cod-liver oil, the 13 private-brand drug and miscellaneous commodities which are priced lower than standard brands are less by at least 14 per cent.

Commodity variations of drug and miscellaneous articles.—Ten of the 41 private brands of drug and miscellaneous products were sold at higher prices than competing standard brands, 28 were sold at lower prices, and in three cases, both were the same price.[34] The 10 private brands which were sold at higher prices were: Two brands of cold tablets, a kidney remedy, a medicinal tonic, a nerve remedy, a cough sirup, an ointment, a cod-liver oil preparation, a laxative, and one insecticide.

Among the drug commodities reported most frequently are mineral oil, cod-liver oil, cold tablets, corn remedies, and ointments. Prices were reported on mineral oil in 16-ounce bottles by five chains. The customer who purchased five bottles of the private-brand and five of the competing standard-brand goods would have bought the former for 25 per cent less than the latter.

Four price quotations were received on cod-liver oil. The largest difference reported was 40 cents (40 per cent), the private brand being lower by that amount. One chain sold both brands at the same price; another sold the private brand for 21 cents (21 per cent) less than the competing standard brand; and the fourth sold the private brand for 31 cents (44.9 per cent) more than the standard brand. A customer who purchased on March 30, 1929, a private and a standard brand of cod-liver oil from each of the four chains reported would have paid 30 cents (8.1 per cent) less in total for the private brands than for the standard brands.

All private brands of corn remedies for which price quotations were received were sold lower than the competing standard brands. The four private brands were sold for 25 cents each and the competing standard brands were sold for 30, 32, 33, and 35 cents, respectively. In other words, the private brands listed cost $1 on March 30, 1929, as contrasted to $1.30 for the standard brands, or the private brands were approximately 23 per cent lower.

Milk of magnesia, bicarbonate of soda, and aspirin tablets are drug products for which the standard-brand price is much higher than that for the private brand. One chain reported that its private brand of milk of magnesia was priced at 25 cents or one-half the price of the competing standard brand. The private brand of bicarbonate of soda reported by one chain was sold 42.7 per cent less than the 75-cent price of the competing standard brand. Although

[34] In order to avoid any misinterpretation of the data it should be noted that price quotations were not received on 41 different standard brands since several chains reported price quotations on the same standard brand.

three chains reported data on aspirin tablets, their private brands averaged 35.8 per cent less than the competing standard brands.

The two drug products showing the narrowest price differences are laxatives and cold tablets. On both of these products, the average private-brand prices were higher than those of the competing standard brands by 4.2 per cent for the former and 5.4 per cent for the latter.

Commodity variations of toilet articles.—Comparative prices received from drug chains on 9 toilet articles are shown in Table 49. Of the 12 reports, on these 9 commodities, the private brands were lower on 5 and higher on 4, while the prices were the same on the remaining 3. A customer who purchased on March 30, 1929, all of the toilet preparations on which quotations were received would have paid $5.44 for the private brands and $7.40 for the competing standard brands, or 26.5 per cent less for the former.

Drug and grocery variations.—Comparing the figures of drug chains in Table 49 with those shown in Table 48 for grocery products, it will be noted that the private brands of toilet goods, and also drug and miscellaneous items, are priced relatively lower with reference to competing standard brands than in the case of grocery products. The private brands of grocery items are sold, on the average, at slightly less than 13 per cent below the prices of standard brands; drug and miscellaneous private brand items at 15.7 per cent below; and toilet articles at 26.5 per cent below.

Moreover, average private-brand prices reported by drug chains are more often above their competing standard-brand prices on commodities having the highest mark-up than is the case with grocery products, and they also exceed the competing standard-brand prices by greater percentages. In the grocery table, the average prices on the private brands of only 2 of the 44 commodities, or 4.5 per cent, exceed those of the standard-brand commodities. In drug-store merchandise, on the other hand, the average prices on 8 of the 28 commodities, or 28.6 per cent, are higher for the private brand. Prices of the two private brands of grocery articles mentioned are higher than prices of competing standard brands by only 6 and 0.8 per cent. For drug chains the differences range from 2 per cent for face powder to as high as 27.5 per cent on one report for kidney remedies and 40 per cent for one on shampoos.

Miscellaneous kinds of chains.—Quotations on 11 competing brands of cigars were received from 4 tobacco chains which operated 1,138 stores in 1928. Eight of the 11 competing brands sold at exactly the same price, 2 private brands were slightly lower, and 1 private brand was slightly higher. A customer who had purchased the 22 cigars on which prices were quoted (11 private brands and 11 standard brands) would have paid about 2 cents less for his private brands than for his standard brands.

Two quotations were received on smoking tobacco. The first chain, operating 11 stores, sold both brands at the same price. The second chain, operating 14 stores, sold its private brand for 11 per cent more than the competing standard brand.

Quotations were received from two dry goods and wearing-apparel chains on four commodities—work shirts, sheeting, overalls, and shirts. A small chain which was operating six stores in 1928 reported prices on the first three commodities. The report on shirts was received from a second chain of approximately the same size. No differences in prices were reported between private and standard brands of work shirts sold at 98 cents and between competing brands of sheeting, sold at 49 cents a yard. The private brand of overalls was lower in price than the competing standard brand by nearly 35 per cent. The private brand of shirts sold for $1 as contrasted to 88 cents for the standard brand, or the private brand was higher by 13.6 per cent.

Two department store chains furnished price quotations. The first chain reported that its private brand of shoes sold at $7.50 as compared to $11 for the standard brand. In other words, the private brand was nearly 32 per cent lower. Both brands of shoes featured a special type of arch support. The second chain reported that its private brand of men's clothing was sold at the same price as the competing standard brand. Both were being sold on March 30, 1929, for $22.50 a suit. This chain operated 18 stores and the standard brand is a well-known, nationally advertised brand.

Reports were received from one variety ($1 limit) chain on two commodities—soap and napkins. The private brand of soap sold for 5 cents, while the competing standard brand sold for 10 cents. The private brand of napkins was approximately 24 per cent lower than the standard brand.

One men's clothing chain reported on one commodity, namely, shirts. Both its private brand and the competing standard brand were sold at the same price ($1.95) on March 30, 1929. The standard brand is a well-known, nationally advertised brand.

One women's accessories chain reported on hosiery. Its private brand was sold on March 30, 1929, for $1.25 and the competing standard brand was sold for $1.85. In other words, the private brand was lower by 32.4 per cent.

One women's shoe chain reported that its private brand of shoes and the competing standard brand were both being sold at $10.50 a pair on March 30, 1929. The standard brand is a well-known shoe of the orthopedic type.

Section 18. Prices of private brands compared with those of competing standard brands having lowest mark-up.

Comparative data on prices of private-brand items and competing standard-brand commodities having the lowest mark-up were collected in the manner explained in the opening paragraphs of the preceding section. Fewer reports were received, however.

Grocery and grocery and meat chains.—A total of 59 comparative price quotations was received from grocery and grocery and meat chains on 26 different commodities.[35] Comparative prices for each of the commodities reported are shown in Table 50.

---

[35] It should be remembered that in the case of a few commodities different chains reported the same standard brand commodity. Obviously, different chains could not report the same private brand.

TABLE 50.—*Comparative prices of private and competing standard-brand commodities (showing lowest mark-up) of the same size, sold by grocery and grocery and meat chains, March 30, 1929*

Commodity	Number of reports	Total of sizes or weights included	Total retail selling price		Selling price on private brand is higher (+) or lower (−)	
			Private brands	Competing standard brands	Amount	Per cent
Beverages and beverage bases:						
Coffee	15	15 pounds	$6.59	$7.45	−$0.86	−11.5
Tea	5	4 pounds	2.68	3.00	−.32	−10.7
Cocoa	1	One-half pound	.18	.20	−.02	−10.0
Ginger ale	1	12 ounces	.125	.125		
Malt sirup	1	1 can	.45	.49	−.04	−8.2
Cereal products:						
Flour	6	290¼ pounds	12.23	13.29	−1.06	−8.0
Bread	1	1½ pounds	.10	.129	−.029	−22.5
Canned goods:						
Vegetables—						
Corn	3	3 cans	.41	.425	−.015	−3.5
Peas	1	1 can	.11	.12	−.01	−8.3
Asparagus	1	do	.33	.29	+.04	+13.8
Red beans	1	do	.09	.083	+.007	+8.4
Fruit—						
Peaches	1	do	.27	.21	+.06	+28.6
Pineapple	1	do	.27	.24	+.03	+12.5
Pears	1	do	.35	.31	+.04	+12.9
Apricots	1	do	.35	.29	+.06	+20.7
Cherries	1	do	.39	.35	+.04	+11.4
Milk	3	3 cans	.292	.31	−.018	−5.8
Relishes, condiments, spreads:						
Mayonnaise	3	32 ounces	.78	.90	−.12	−13.3
Ketchup	2	28 ounces	.38	.44	−.06	−13.6
Vinegar	1	1 quart	.25	.25		
Vanilla extract	2	4 ounces	.46	.60	−.14	−23.3
Peanut butter	1	1 pound	.25	.31	−.06	−19.4
Salt	1	do	.12	.07	+.05	+71.4
Other commodities:						
Butter	2	2 pounds	.93	1.02	−.09	−8.8
Baking powder	1	16 ounces	.20	.29	−.09	−31.0
Oleomargarine	2	2 pounds	.46	.55	−.09	−16.4
Total (26 commodities)	59		29.047	31.742	−2.695	−8.5

If a hypothetical customer on March 30, 1929, had purchased all 118 commodities (59 private brands and 59 standard brands) from the chains furnishing price information, his private brands would have cost him $29.05 and his standard brands would have cost him $31.74. In other words, the private brands were lower than the competing standard brands by $2.69, or 8.5 per cent.

Of the 26 commodities reported on, the private-brand items, on the average, were sold at lower prices than the standard-brand items in 16 cases. On eight other commodities, the prices on the private brands were higher than on the standard brands; while on two commodities, prices were the same. In the 16 instances where private brands sold for less than standard brands the amount by which the average private brand was lower ranged from 3.5 per cent on canned corn to 31 per cent on baking powder; aside from baking powder, vanilla extract, and bread, all these differences in favor of private brands are less than 20 per cent and most of them are below 15 per cent.

The lowest differential in favor of the standard brand was on canned red beans, where the private brand was 8.4 per cent higher than the standard brand. On the other seven commodities, the private brand was more than 10 per cent higher than the standard brand. The most striking instance was salt, the private brand being sold at 12 cents, or 71.4 per cent more than the standard brand at 7 cents. Canned apricots and canned peaches are the only other items on which the private brand was priced at more than 20 per cent higher than the competing standard brand.

Private brands of the following commodities were sold at the same prices as the standard brands—vinegar, at 25 cents a quart, and ginger ale, at 12½ cents for a bottle of 12 ounces.

Commodity variations.—In 12 of the 59 individual price comparisons, the private brands were sold at higher prices than the standard brands with which they competed; in 44 cases, lower; and in three instances, both were sold at the same price.

Following are summary statements presented as typical of various products, either because of the large number of reports or because the price differential percentage between private and standare brands is large or small.

Fifteen chains reported comparative prices on coffee, all quotations on a 1-pound basis. In 12 of the 15 instances, the private brand was sold for less than the competing standard brand. The largest price difference, 17 cents, represented only 27.4 per cent of the higher price charged for the standard brand, whereas in another case, a difference of 14 cents, represented 32.6 per cent of the standard-brand price. At the other extreme, a differential of 1 cent (1.8 per cent) in favor of the standard brand, the price of which was lower, represented the smallest difference reported on coffee. The average pound of coffee packed under a private label sold for approximately 44 cents as contrasted to about 50 cents for the average competing standard brand; that is, the private brand price of coffee was lower by 11.5 per cent.

Six chains reported prices on flour in containers ranging in weight from 10 to 196 pounds. The greatest percentage difference was 24.2 on a 24-pound sack, the standard brand of which sold at 99 cents as compared with 75 cents for the brand owned by the chain. The smallest difference was only 3.9 per cent, the private brand being the lower. A hypothetical customer who had purchased, March 30, 1929, all the flour on which comparative quotations were received, would have saved about $1.06 on the private brands, or 8 per cent of the standard-brand price.

As already stated, the highest price difference for any one product was reported by a chain on salt, this difference being in favor of the standard brand. The widest difference in favor of the private brand (private brand lower) is 31 per cent for baking powder. Vanilla extract also shows a large difference (23.3 per cent on the basis of two reports) in favor of the private brand. Among those showing a small difference are canned corn and canned milk.

While differences are not so great as in the previous comparison of private brands and standard brands showing the highest mark-up (Table 48), the competing standard brands showing the lowest mark-up are none-the-less substantially higher than the prices of private brands.

In the comparison of private brands with competing standard brands showing the highest mark-up there are only two commodities out of the 44, or 4.5 per cent, where the private brand is higher than the standard brand (Table 48). In the present case, when the private brands are compared with competing standard brands showing the lowest mark-up, however, eight of the 26 commodities, or over 30 per cent, are priced higher. In the former comparison, there are 212 individual reports and in the latter, 59. Of the 212, only 6, or slightly less than 3 per cent, showed the private brands priced higher, and of the 59, a total of 12, or something over 20 per cent indicated that the private brand was priced higher.

Drug chains.—Twenty-three comparative prices were received from drug chains on 10 drug and miscellaneous products and 7 toilet preparations. Comparative prices for each of the commodities on which quotations were received are shown below.

TABLE 51.—*Comparative prices of private and competing standard-brand commodities (showing lowest mark-up) of the same size, sold by drug chains, March 30, 1929*

Commodity	Number of reports	Total of sizes or weights included	Total retail selling price		Selling price on private brands is higher (+) or lower (−)	
			Private brands	Competing standard brands	Amount	Per cent
DRUG AND MISCELLANEOUS ARTICLES						
Cold tablets	3	74 tablets	$0.73	$0.67	+$0.06	+9.0
Insecticides	2	24 ounces	1.28	1.34	−.06	−4.5
Oils	2	20 ounces	2.00	2.20	−.20	−9.1
Ointments	2	4 ounces	1.00	.98	+.02	+2.0
Aspirin	1	100 tablets	.49	.73	−.24	−32.9
Bicarbonate of soda preparation	1	2 ounces	.50	.43	+.07	+16.3
Blood tonic	1	12 ounces	.85	.98	−.13	−13.3
Hinkle's pills	1	100 pills	.25	.25		
Nerve remedy	1	8 ounces	1.00	1.00		
Rubbing alcohol	1	16 ounces	.49	.59	−.10	−17.0
Total (10 commodities)	15		8.59	9.17	−.58	−6.3
TOILET ARTICLES						
Lotions	2	10 ounces	.92	1.84	−.92	−50.0
Deodorant	1	1 ounce	.25	.20	+.05	+25.0
Depilatory	1	do	.49	.45	+.04	+8.9
Shampoo	1	6 ounces	.49	.60	−.11	−18.3
Soap	1	1 cake	.19	.157	+.033	+21.0
Tooth paste	1	3 ounces	.39	.39		
Tonic	1	8 ounces	.95	1.39	−.44	−31.7
Total (7 commodities)	8		3.68	5.027	−1.347	−26.8

Nine of the 23 individual reports indicated that private-brand items were sold higher than competing standard brands, 11 indicated that they were sold at a lower price, and 3 at the same price.

If a hypothetical customer on March 30, 1929, had purchased the 30 drug and miscellaneous products (15 private brands and 15 competing standard brands) from the chains reporting, his private brands would have cost him $8.59 and his standard brands would have cost $9.17. In other words, the private brands were lower by 58 cents, or 6.3 per cent. This percentage compares with 15.7 per cent, the differential between private brands and the competing standard brands having the highest mark-up. (Table 49.)

Commodity variations.—Of the 17 commodities, private-brand items were sold at a higher price than the competing standard brands in 6 cases and at a lower price in 8 cases. In three cases both were sold at the same price. A wide range of differences (4.5 per cent for insecticides to 50 per cent on lotions) is shown by the commodities where the standard brand is priced higher. The range for the commodities where the private brand is priced higher, though less, is rather wide, 2 per cent for ointments to 25 per cent for a deodorant.

There were only five commodities for which more than one report was received, namely, ointments, oils, cold tablets, insecticides, and lotions. Two quotations were received on ointments from a chain which was operating 24 stores in 1928. Both of its private brands were sold at 50 cents, or 1 cent more than for competing standard brands of the same size.

Quotations were received from two chains on cod-liver oil preparations. The first chain sold a 12-ounce bottle of both brands at $1, the second sold an 8-ounce bottle at $1 for the private brand and $1.20 for the competing standard brand. A customer who purchased all the cod-liver-oil preparations on which quotations were received would have saved about 9 per cent on his purchases of private brands.

Three chains furnished price information on cold tablets. The first chain sold its private brand (24 tablets to a box) at 25 cents as contrasted to 19 cents for the standard brand of the same size, a difference of about 31.5 per cent. The second chain sold its private brand (30 tablets to a box) for 23 cents as contrasted to 18 cents for a well-known standard brand of the same size. The private brand of the third chain (20 tablets to a box) was sold at 25 cents as contrasted to 30 cents for the competing standard brand.

Quotations on insecticides were received from two chains. The first chain sold its own brand at 79 cents as contrasted with 75 cents for the competing standard brand. The second chain sold its own brand at 49 cents as contrasted to 59 cents for the competing standard brand.

Comparative prices were received from drug chains on eight toilet articles. A hypothetical customer who had purchased on March 30, 1929, all of the toilet preparations on which quotations were received, would have paid $3.68 for his private brands and $5.03 for his standard brands. In other words, the saving on the private brands would have been $1.35, or 26.8 per cent. The largest saving recorded was on a lotion, the private brand being 50 per cent lower than the competing standard brands. No more than one report on any other toilet article was received from drug chains.

Miscellaneous groups.—Quotations were received on three competing brands of cigars from two small chains, one operating 2 stores and the other operating 14 stores. The same price was charged for competing brands (private and standard) by each of the chains.

One quotation on smoking tobacco was received from the chain which operated 14 stores. Its 16-ounce can, bearing its own private brand, sold for $2.50 on March 30, 1929, in contrast to $2.25 for a well-known competing standard brand. In other words, the private brand was sold for about 11 per cent more than the standard brand.

Only one quotation was received from dry-goods and wearing-apparel chains. This was from a chain which was operating six stores. It sold its private brand of work shirts at $1 as contrasted to 79 cents for the competing standard brand, or about 26½ per cent more.

One quotation on dress shirts was received from a department-store chain which was operating three stores. It sold its private brand of dress shirts at $2 as contrasted to $1.95 for a well-known, nationally advertised, standard brand, or at about 2½ per cent more than the competing standard brand.

Section 19. National advertising of private brands.

Three hundred seventy-three, or 91 per cent of the 412 private-brand-owning chains, answered the question: "Are any of your private brands nationally advertised?" which appeared on the original schedule. These 373 chains operated 49,382, or nearly 98 per cent of the total stores of brand-owning chains and were distributed over 23 kinds of business as shown in Appendix Table 12.[36] The returns were least satisfactory, both from the standpoint of the number of chains reporting and the proportion of stores which they operated, in confectionery, meat, and millinery chains.

TABLE 52.—*Numbers and proportions of chains reporting on national advertising of private brands, 1929–30, and of stores operated by them, December 31, 1928*

	Reporting on advertising policy			Reporting on advertising policy	
	Chains	Stores operated		Chains	Stores operated
	Number	*Number*	Percentages of total reporting:	*Per cent*	*Per cent*
Private brands advertised nationally	34	18,176	Advertised nationally	9.1	36.8
Private brands not advertised nationally	339	31,206	Not advertised nationally	90.9	63.2
Total reporting	373	49,382	Total	100.0	100.0

As shown by Table 52 above, 34 chains, or about 9 per cent of all the chain systems which reported on this question, indicated that they advertised their private brands nationally. This relatively small number of chains, however, operated nearly 37 per cent of the stores. The nationally advertised private brands of these 34 chains were sold, presumably, in the majority of the 18,176 stores operated by them in 1928. These chains, however, were confined to 13 of the 23 kinds of business, as shown by Table 53.

[36] $5 limit variety chains sold no private brands. No replies to the inquiry on national advertising were received from two groups, hardware and variety—unlimited. It should be mentioned, however, that the sale of private brands was reported in only one small hardware chain which operated nine stores, and in one variety—unlimited chain of six stores.

TABLE 53.—*Numbers and proportions of chains advertising their private brands nationally, 1929–30, and of stores operated by them, December 31, 1928, by kind of chain*

Kind of chain	Chains advertising private brands nationally		Stores operated by chains advertising private brands nationally	
	Number	Per cent of total reporting	Number	Per cent of total reporting
Grocery and meat	2	2.8	15,517	49.6
Confectionery	2	12.5	181	41.6
Drug	3	4.2	108	10.6
Men's ready-to-wear	3	15.0	21	9.9
Men's and women's ready-to-wear	3	60.0	43	67.2
Men's furnishings	1	16.7	7	12.5
Women's accessories	2	22.2	12	11.1
Men's shoes	1	20.0	112	35.9
Women's shoes	5	62.5	163	76.9
Men's and women's shoes	7	26.9	553	64.5
Dry goods and apparel	1	9.1	1,023	93.9
Department store	2	20.0	422	89.6
Musical instruments	2	33.3	14	20.9
Total	34	9.1	18,176	36.8

A study of the table discloses that from the standpoint of the number of stores operated by chains, which did national advertising, the five most important types were grocery and meat, dry goods and apparel, men's and women's shoes, department stores, and confectionery. Nearly 90 per cent of the stores are found in the grocery and meat and dry goods and apparel fields. Most of those in the former belong to the Great Atlantic & Pacific Tea Co., and all those in the latter to J. C. Penney Co.

From the point of view of the number of chains of each type, advertising some or all of their private brands, the order of importance differs from that given above. Seven chains selling both men's and women's shoes advertised their private brands nationally. Five chains selling their own brands of women's shoes engaged in national advertising. Then follow three kinds of chains in each of which one finds three organizations advertising their private brands nationally.

From the standpoint of the relative number of chains in each group which advertised their brands nationally during the period under consideration the women's shoe group makes the best showing, since 62.5 per cent of these chains reporting on this question advertised their private brands nationally. Following, in the order of their importance, would come men's and women's ready-to-wear, musical instruments, men's and women's shoes and women's accessories.

A fourth method of analysis involves a comparison of the relative number of stores operated by chains in each group in most of which, presumably, advertised private brands are sold. For example, in five groups (dry goods and apparel, department store, women's shoes, men's and women's ready-to-wear, and men's and women's shoes) 50 per cent or more of the stores belonging to all chains reporting on their advertising policy were operated by chains which did national advertising.

Nearly 50 per cent of the stores (49.6 per cent) operated by all reporting grocery and meat chains belonged to the two chains which did national advertising. Nearly 42 per cent of the stores operated by reporting confectionery chains belonged to the two chains which advertised their private brands nationally. Use of these relative figures is open to a criticism common to any general use of percentage figures in analyzing data of this nature. For example, nearly 94 per cent of the stores included in the dry goods and apparel group were operated by the one chain which advertised its private brands nationally, the 10 chains not advertising their brands nationally being small. (Appendix Table 12.) Discontinuance of advertising by this one chain, therefore, would decrease the percentage for the group to zero.

The first comparison by number of stores operated, in most of which stores, presumably, advertised private brands were sold, is probably the most significant one. A small chain, even though it should advertise its brands nationally, could not make serious inroads on the business of independent merchants selling merchandise of the same kind. Unless a mail-order business is carried on in connection with its chain-store activities, the areas in which the small chain competes with independents are limited to the few cities or towns in which it has stores. Its competition can not seriously affect the business of merchants operating in localities where it has no stores. In like manner, a small chain which might advertise its private brands nationally could not make serious inroads on the business of manufacturers selling competing standard brands, since the chain's brands are at best accessible only to consumers residing in the localities where it has stores.

On the other hand, where a chain's nationally advertised private brand is readily accessible to large numbers of consumers in every part of the country, it approaches the status of a nationally advertised "standard" brand.

The Great Atlantic & Pacific Tea Co., for example, reported the following, in reply to the question concerning the advertising of its private brands nationally:

> The following private brands occasionally appear in our newspaper advertising in all territories and might be considered as nationally advertised: Grandmother's Tea, Bokar Coffee, Red Circle Coffee, Eight O'clock Coffee, Whitehouse Milk, and Grandmother's Bread.

The J. C. Penney Co., the only chain in the dry goods and apparel field to report national advertising of private brands, stated that approximately 30 of its private brands have been so advertised. With a few exceptions, it does not carry standard brands which compete directly with advertised merchandise bearing its own brand names. The advertised commodities which are sold under private brand names include play suits, cotton piece goods, shirting, muslin, sheeting, toilet articles, razor blades, shaving articles, hosiery, straw and felt hats, caps, work suits and overalls, work shirts, and union suits.

The two department stores which were advertising their private brands nationally are Montgomery Ward & Co. and Sears, Roebuck & Co. The company first mentioned operated 230 department stores in 1928 and the latter company had 192. In the period under consideration, "national advertising" in both chains was reported to be chiefly confined to newspapers.

The seven chains which reported that they advertised private brands of both men's and women's shoes nationally include Shoecraft, Chisholm, Hurley, Emerson, Beacon, Regal, and Melville.

Section 20. Policy of chains in respect to future development of private brands.

The letter sent to chains in the spring of 1932 asking for information on private brands contained questions as to the future policy of the chains in respect to such brands. It was desired to know if the chains favored expanding or curtailing their private brands or if they expected the present ratios of private brands to standard brands to be maintained.

Many of the statements with regard to future policy reiterated in whole or in part either the reasons given by the chains for the development of their private brands or their statements as to the advantages or disadvantages of such brands. (Secs. 3 and 4.)

Eighty-seven companies answered these questions, but several of the replies were not classifiable. The remaining answers, however, furnished a limited amount of information concerning the general policies of these companies in respect to the future development of their private brands. It was to be expected, perhaps, that many of the answers would be vague and the replies of several chains indicated that the present business situation influenced their reports.

Only three chains definitely favored curtailing their private brands, while 21 companies were inclined to favor expansion and 27 expected the ratio between their private brands and standard brands to remain the same. The tendency, therefore, will be for a majority of these chains to increase their private brands rather than to decrease them, always provided the situation warrants it. This last qualification is an important one as appears from the following statement of one of the largest grocery and meat chains:

> This question can not be answered from the standpoint of what our company favors; it does not depend upon what we wish, but upon what the public wishes. If the public, either as a result of reason or whim or chance, favors the private brands they will increase, while if it favors the so-called standard brands the latter will increase. We, as purveyors of food to the public, do not attempt to, and possibly could not, stem the running of the tide. As we have said, we give the public what it wants.
>
> Furthermore, if we are able to sell the so-called standard brands to our customers at a price which we feel gives them proper value at a reasonable profit to ourselves, there is no incentive to us to expand our private brands. However, if so-called standard brands do not meet this requirement, and we can give the customer greater value, then there is an incentive to us to pursue that course.
>
> The figures which we have heretofore given to you indicate a rather slow but steady recession in the percentage of our sales represented by private brands. That is what the figures show for the last few years; what the future has in store, we can not tell, for it rests largely with the public. Even our own policy, as we have pointed out, is dependent upon the acts of others and conditions not of our own creation.

An eastern grocery and meat chain was likewise somewhat indefinite in its reply.

> This company has never placed an item under its private brand for the sole purpose of competing with an advertised product. Unless there has been some reason whereby we could offer the trade a better value, such brands have never

been established. It is generally conceded that nationally advertised products carry a considerable overhead charge for direct advertising and also for sales promotion and introduction of the advertised brand. Hardly anything, except special formula items, is such that it can not readily be duplicated in bulk.

Reasons for curtailing private brands.—As previously stated, only three chains contemplated or favored curtailing their private brands. One of these was a grocery chain which stated that it would discontinue its private brands if the manufacturers of standard brands would "permit of more generous profits on resale." This company amplified its statement by giving the following reasons for not favoring private brands:

In conclusion, we believe that the manufacturers in a great many instances make special allowances and rebates of one kind or another to large purchasers which enables those purchasers to sell the advertised brands at very low prices; sometimes at cost and sometimes a little above cost, but not sufficient to cover their overhead expenses. Smaller merchants are, therefore, forced to try to get extra profits by the sale of private brands. In addition to that, the manufacturers of standard brands in a great many instances charge much too much for their products, making it tempting for their competitors to offer substitute lines for greatly reduced prices. In all cases where standard brands are priced low enough there is no incentive for the introduction of private brands.

A grocery and meat chain of over 2,000 stores qualified its statement that it favored reducing private brands by adding "at that time." It explained its position as follows:

Under present conditions we believe that more advantageous results will be obtained by handling a preponderance of standard brands, but in keeping alive our private label so that if conditions change we will be in position to expand our private brands.

A third company which favored curtailing private brands (a women's ready-to-wear chain) also limited its statement of policy to "the present time." Its reason for favoring a reduction of private brands was:

During the period of good business concentration on a private brand hose enabled us to get maximum business with a minimum inventory, particularly when we knew the standard of our hose was at the highest and they could be sold with an unlimited guaranty at a minimum price. But, during a period of sales resistance in order to stimulate business or to get the maximum out of each section of the country, we may find it necessary to carry a little larger inventory by taking on two or more standard brands.

Reasons for maintaining present ratios.—Replies from 27 chains were to the effect that they expected present ratios between their private brands and standard brands to be maintained. Perhaps one of the most interesting presentations of the policy regarding private brands is that of an important eastern grocery and meat chain:

Our company does not favor the expansion of its private brands except to identify merchandise which is now being sold by us, in bulk, without identification. We have no thought of reducing the limited number of private brands we now have established. We, therefore, do not anticipate changing the ratio of private brands with respect to standard brands.

* * * * * *

Of late, with radically lower markets on raw materials, nationally advertised goods have failed to show any appreciable declines in list prices, with the consequent result that many items can be purchased under other labels at much lower prices.

Please bear in mind that this company has established no private brands whatever to compete directly on the same basis, or same price basis, of so-called standard brands.

A second grocery and meat chain also expects ratios between the two kinds of brands to remain the same:

This company feels that there is a definite place for both nationally advertised brands of merchandise and for privately labeled merchandise. We feel that the healthy condition of distribution is the maintenance of a competitive balance between the two.

A straight grocery chain replied that it was "of the opinion that we have reached the point of diminishing returns in so far as further expansion of our private brands is concerned."

A grocery and meat chain operating between 50 and 100 stores stated "we are not increasing our private brands to any extent, and much prefer to handle the regular standard brands of foods."

A medium-sized tobacco chain stated:

Our company does not anticipate any extensive expansion of our private brands nor do we anticipate any reduction in our private brands and we assume that we will be able to maintain the present ratio of private brands with respect to standard brands.

Our reasons for not anticipating any expansion of private brands is primarily based on our desire to hold down inventories.

Two variety dollar-limit chains expect the present ratio between private brand and standard brand to be maintained. One company stated:

While we favor the expansion of private brands where possible, the probabilities are that the present ratio of private brands with respect to standard brands will not change, due to the fact that highly advertised standard brands are prefered by the public.

The other chain commented as follows:

Present ratios of private brands with respect to standard brands will probably be maintained.

We are not primarily interested in developing brands, our chief concern is to give maximum value in the belief that public appreciation will result in an increase of our business.

Its small size is given by a grocery and meat chain operating 15 stores on December 31, 1930, as a reason for not expanding private brand business.

We do not contemplate expanding our private brands in view of the fact that our outlet for distribution is limited to such an extent that it would not be advantageous to us to expend a considerable amount of money for private labels.

One relatively large millinery chain, though giving no reasons, replied, "This company will probably continue its present ratio of private brands as at present."

Reasons for expanding private brands.—The principal reasons given by chains for favoring the expansion of their private brand business were, first, the ability of the chain to develop good will through the use of private brands and, second, the higher profit which is earned on private brands as compared with competing standard brands.

A department store chain said:

We are opposed in principle to the advertising and promotion of nationally known brands by the retailer because such policies tend to give the national brand increased consumer prestige and place control of an increasing amount of retail business in the hands of a limited number of powerful national advertisers. We rarely advertise a national brand because we prefer to use our money to establish our own good will and not to build up good will for the manufacturer.

A very small drug chain stated:

It is our intention to increase the number of private-brand preparations, for we find that sales effort on our own preparations builds a clientele for ourselves exclusively instead of aiding the popularity of some one else's product.

Similarly, a large dollar-limit variety chain stated that its reasons for increasing private brands were:

To identify in customers' minds definite standards of price and quality with such private branded items to facilitate our sales promotion of merchandise, and to build up the institutional good will of the company.

A second chain of this kind also mentioned good will and further stated that private brands prevented certain competitors from offering merchandise of inferior quality under the same or a similar label.

A large chain of women's clothing stores reported:

Our company favors the continued development of its private brands because we have spent a considerable amount of money advertising it, and in selling women's wear style merchandise we feel that it has a definite value when the standard of quality is maintained.

Our reason * * * is the fact that in selling women's style merchandise we believe a private brand has a definite value because there are very few established manufacturers' standard brands known by consumers as such.

A grocery and meat chain with over 500 stores summarized very succinctly the reasons for favoring a conservative policy of expanding its private brands. "Our past experience," it says, "proves that the public approve of private-brand merchandise."

Those chains which claim that they are expanding their line of private brands because of their ability to earn greater profits also consciously or unconsciously assume that these private brands gain the good will of a certain proportion of the buying public. A grocery chain, for example, says: "We do not favor the expansion of our private brands but are compelled to do so." Its reason, stated in great detail, was that private brands are necessary to maintain reasonable margins of profit. This chain concluded, "Our action as to reduction or expansion of private brands depends largely on the consideration and protection that the manufacturer gives to the distributor in preventing a demoralized price basis on his merchandise."

This same idea is developed by a department store chain as follows:

We have found from long experience that the manufacturer of standard brands has very often made unreasonable demands of us, especially if the product has become sufficiently advertised.

Ability to maintain the margins on private brands and escape price cutting is also advanced by a drug chain as the reason for expanding private brands. A second drug organization also mentions the difficulty of making a profit on standard brands and further states that the building up of good will was an added reason for such a policy.

One of the large drug chains indicates that it expects to expand its private brands because of added profit they will bring when it states,

"We shall continue to expand our own line of merchandise in proportion to the ability of our chemists to come out with new ideas."

Two department store chains go into the question of their profits a little more fully. One, a small chain of large stores, reported:

> Our company most decidedly favors expansion of private brands due to the better service it can give its customers and the better profit it can obtain from them and the added good will built up by good service.
>
> In conclusion * * * we think our attitude toward standard brands is a sound, businesslike attitude, uninfluenced by prejudice. We believe that to be successful we must make a fair profit, and to achieve that, we must please our customers.
>
> From long experience we have found that the best way to do that is to give them honest, prompt, courteous, and complete service.

The second chain which operates a large number of medium sized stores reported as follows:

> Our company does favor the expansion of private-brand merchandise rather than its reduction, whenever the merchandise lends itself to this type of exploitation. However, it is difficult to state whether the present ratios will be maintained or not. Circumstances may warrant a complete change of attitude on the part of ourselves or other distributors.
>
> We have no particular grievances or dislike for distributing national brands. We * * * carry them in our stores. It is obvious, however, that restricted retail selling prices are the chief factor against the expansion of nationally advertised items.

A few chains emphasize quality alone as a factor in determining their policy of further expanding private brands. One grocery chain has the following to say on the point:

> This company does not contemplate any particular expansion of private brands; only where we discover that a noncompetitive trade can be built up on a superior line of goods at fair profit.

A men's and women's shoe chain believes that good will obtained from its own private brands, the quality of which it controls, is a primary reason for the contemplated expansion of its line of private-brand merchandise.

A department store chain feels that as it grows larger it will expand its line of private brands because of its ability to manufacture in economical quantities. Its statement follows:

> Manufacturing methods require a minimum amount of business in most lines to justify the development of a private brand. As our facilities for distribution increase, various lines or items of merchandise will come into the minimum volume requirement and can then be developed. * * *

APPENDIXES

APPENDIXES

Appendix I

KIND OF CHAIN CLASSIFICATION

In preparing some of the tables in this series of reports it was found that the commodity-group designations tended to be so long as to use much valuable space in the table stubs. It was decided, therefore, to abbreviate some of the groups in order to shorten the table stubs. In parallel columns below are shown the commodity-group designations fully written out, together with the comparable abbreviations generally used. The complete description of each of the 26 commodity groups will be found in the report, Scope of the Chain-Store Inquiry.

AS GENERALLY USED IN TABLES THROUGHOUT THE CHAIN-STORE REPORTS.	EXPLANATION
Grocery	Grocery.
Gro. & meat	Grocery and meat.
Meat	Meat.
Confectionery	Confectionery.
Drug	Drug.
Tobacco	Tobacco.
Var. ($1 limit)	Variety ($1 limit).
Var. ($5 limit)	Variety ($5 limit).[1]
Var. (unlimited)	Variety (unlimited).[2]
M. r'dy-to-wear	Men's ready-to-wear.
W. r'dy-to-wear	Women's ready-to-wear.
M. & W. r'dy-to-wear	Men's and women's ready-to-wear.
M. furnishings	Men's furnishings.
W. accessories	Women's accessories.
Hats & caps	Hats and caps.
Millinery	Millinery.
M. shoes	Men's shoes.
W. shoes	Women's shoes.
M. & W. shoes	Men's and women's shoes.
Dry goods	Dry goods.
D. G. & apparel	Dry goods and apparel.
Dept. store	Department store.
Gen'l mdse	General merchandise.
Furniture	Furniture.
Mus. inst'm'ts	Musical instruments.
Hardware	Hardware.

[1] Does not include variety chains with $1 limit.
[2] Does not include variety chains with $1 limit or $5 limit.

APPENDIX II

APPENDIX TABLES

TABLE 1.—*Number of reporting chains owning private brands in 1929–30, by kind and size of chain*

Kind of chain	Number of stores per chain							
	2 to 5	6 to 10	11 to 25	26 to 50	51 to 100	101 to 500	501 to 1,000	1,001 and over
Grocery	10	5	7	14	7	15	4	2
Grocery and meat	13	9	15	8	9	14	2	4
Meat	0	0	2	2	0	0	------	------
Confectionery	4	4	9	3	2	1	------	------
Drug	47	11	10	2	4	1	0	------
Tobacco	2	3	5	0	1	1	------	1
Variety ($1 limit)	2	0	0	0	1	4	0	1
Variety ($5 limit)	0	0	0	0	------	------	------	------
Variety (unlimited)	0	1	0	------	------	------	------	------
Men's ready-to-wear	6	9	6	3	------	------	------	------
Women's ready-to-wear	0	0	2	------	1	------	------	------
Men's and women's ready-to-wear	2	1	1	1	0	------	------	------
Men's furnishings	2	3	0	1	------	------	------	------
Women's accessories	3	1	4	1	------	------	------	------
Hats and caps	4	1	4	2	1	1	------	------
Millinery	1	0	1	0	0	0	------	------
Men's shoes	1	1	0	1	2	1	------	------
Women's shoes	3	1	1	2	1	------	------	------
Men's and women's shoes	10	3	11	3	3	1	------	------
Dry goods	1	1	0	------	------	------	------	------
Dry goods and apparel	4	5	2	0	0	------	------	1
Department store	6	4	1	------	------	2	------	------
General merchandise	2	3	1	------	1	------	------	------
Furniture	1	0	0	0	------	------	------	------
Musical instruments	2	2	2	1	------	------	------	------
Hardware	0	1	0	0	------	------	------	------
Total	126	69	84	44	33	41	6	9

TABLE 2.—*Number of reporting chains owning private brands in 1931, by kind and size of chain*

Kind of chain	Number of stores per chain							
	2 to 5	6 to 10	11 to 25	26 to 50	51 to 100	101 to 500	501 to 1,000	1,001 and over
Grocery	4	3	3	6	7	13	6	1
Grocery and meat	12	7	12	5	5	7	2	5
Meat	0	0	1	2	1	------	------	------
Confectionery	8	2	5	3	1	1	------	------
Drug	51	11	5	4	0	4	0	------
Tobacco	10	3	5	1	0	0	1	0
Variety ($1 limit)	2	2	1	------	1	5	1	1
Variety ($5 limit)	0	0	0	------	1	------	------	------
Variety (unlimited)	0	0	0	------	------	------	------	------
Men's ready-to-wear	2	5	8	------	0	------	------	------
Women's ready-to-wear	2	0	1	------	1	0	------	------
Men's and women's ready-to-wear	1	3	1	------	0	------	------	------
Men's furnishings	1	0	1	------	------	------	------	------
Women's accessories	1	3	2	1	------	------	------	------
Hats and caps	3	2	1	1	1	0	------	------
Millinery	0	0	0	------	1	1	------	------
Men's shoes	1	0	0	1	2	1	------	------
Women's shoes	5	2	1	1	1	1	------	------
Men's and women's shoes	8	7	6	2	1	3	------	------
Dry goods	0	------	1	1	------	------	------	------
Dry goods and apparel	1	2	3	3	------	------	------	1
Department store	3	3	0	1	------	1	1	------
General merchandise	0	2	0	------	------	------	------	------
Furniture	1	------	0	1	------	------	------	------
Musical instruments	1	2	3	------	------	------	------	------
Hardware	2	1	0	0	------	------	------	------
Total	119	60	60	33	23	37	11	8

TABLE 3.—*Distribution of stores operated on December 31, 1928, by chains owning private brands in 1929–30, by kind and size of chain*

Kind of chain	Number of stores per chain							
	2 to 5	6 to 10	11 to 25	26 to 50	51 to 100	101 to 500	501 to 1,000	1,001 and over
NUMBER OF STORES								
Grocery	32	34	128	487	459	3, 032	2, 546	2, 122
Grocery and meat	55	73	256	316	692	3, 920	1, 275	24, 774
Meat	0	0	29	78	0	0	---	---
Confectionery	18	33	126	134	130	120	---	---
Drug	152	76	175	62	329	230	0	---
Tobacco	4	26	68	0	89	302	---	1, 111
Variety ($1 limit)	7	0	0	0	81	849	0	1, 723
Variety ($5 limit)	0	0	0	0	---	---	---	---
Variety (unlimited)	0	6	0	---	---	---	---	---
Men's ready-to-wear	25	66	82	91	---	---	---	---
Women's ready-to-wear	0	0	33	---	98	---	---	---
Men's and women's ready-to-wear	6	10	18	30	0	---	---	---
Men's furnishings	7	21	0	28	---	---	---	---
Women's accessories	11	7	54	36	---	---	---	---
Hats and caps	12	10	69	77	53	119	---	---
Millinery	4	0	15	0	0	0	---	---
Men's shoes	5	7	0	48	145	112	---	---
Women's shoes	11	9	23	74	95	---	---	---
Men's and women's shoes	34	21	161	120	226	410	---	---
Dry goods	2	6	0	---	---	---	---	---
Dry goods and apparel	13	35	22	0	0	---	---	1, 023
Department store	22	27	18	---	---	422	---	---
General merchandise	6	23	14	---	83	---	---	---
Furniture	3	0	0	0	---	---	---	---
Musical instruments	8	18	28	27	---	---	---	---
Hardware	0	9	0	0	---	---	---	---
Total	437	517	1, 319	1, 608	2, 480	9, 516	3, 821	30, 753
PROPORTIONS								
Grocery	21. 6	18. 3	30. 3	67. 4	62. 4	82. 6	100. 0	100. 0
Grocery and meat	25. 9	30. 7	61. 5	62. 0	64. 3	94. 9	100. 0	100. 0
Meat	0. 0	0. 0	20. 0	31. 1	0. 0	0. 0	---	---
Confectionery	36. 0	70. 2	85. 1	83. 2	100. 0	100. 0	---	---
Drug	38. 9	49. 7	75. 8	70. 5	100. 0	100. 0	0. 0	---
Tobacco	16. 7	45. 6	48. 9	0. 0	100. 0	100. 0	---	38. 1
Variety ($1 limit)	6. 1	0. 0	0. 0	0. 0	55. 5	68. 4	0. 0	100. 0
Variety ($5 limit)	0. 0	0. 0	0. 0	0. 0	---	---	---	---
Variety (unlimited)	0. 0	22. 2	0. 0	---	---	---	---	---
Men's ready-to-wear	14. 3	31. 7	49. 4	71. 7	---	---	---	---
Women's ready-to-wear	0. 0	0. 0	16. 8	---	57. 3	---	---	---
Men's and women's ready-to-wear	3. 8	8. 1	14. 0	8. 7	0. 0	---	---	---
Men's furnishings	9. 0	56. 8	0. 0	100. 0	---	---	---	---
Women's accessories	45. 8	100. 0	62. 1	56. 3	---	---	---	---
Hats and caps	30. 8	100. 0	82. 1	73. 3	30. 6	100. 0	---	---
Millinery	11. 1	0. 0	10. 3	0. 0	0. 0	0. 0	---	---
Men's shoes	33. 3	29. 2	0. 0	60. 8	54. 9	100. 0	---	---
Women's shoes	20. 8	25. 7	20. 7	51. 7	100. 0	---	---	---
Men's and women's shoes	11. 7	9. 2	34. 9	54. 8	38. 8	39. 2	---	---
Dry goods	2. 4	40. 0	0. 0	---	---	---	---	---
Dry goods and apparel	4. 7	17. 2	17. 1	0. 0	0. 0	---	---	100. 0
Department store	31. 9	65. 9	37. 5	---	---	100. 0	---	---
General merchandise	7. 1	20. 7	26. 4	---	100. 0	---	---	---
Furniture	3. 4	0. 0	0. 0	0. 0	---	---	---	---
Musical instruments	23. 5	56. 3	62. 2	100. 0	---	---	---	---
Hardware	0. 0	20. 9	0. 0	0. 0	---	---	---	---
Total	15. 1	21. 4	37. 4	46. 2	58. 5	81. 5	79. 1	94. 5

TABLE 4.—*Distribution of stores operated on December 31, 1930, by chains owning private brands in 1931, by kind and size of chain*

Kind of chain	Number of stores per chain							
	2 to 5	6 to 10	11 to 25	26 to 50	51 to 100	101 to 500	501 to 1,000	1,001 and over
NUMBER OF STORES								
Grocery	15	26	54	229	537	2,577	4,788	1,382
Grocery and meat	39	59	209	188	361	1,853	1,302	28,871
Meat	0	0	13	74	62	-------	-------	-------
Confectionery	27	17	82	118	54	143	-------	-------
Drug	135	84	80	134	0	850	0	-------
Tobacco	23	25	69	45	0	0	994	0
Variety ($1 limit)	6	18	14	0	91	1,238	678	1,881
Variety ($5 limit)	0	0	0	0	53	-------	-------	-------
Variety (unlimited)	0	0	0	0	-------	-------	-------	-------
Men's ready-to-wear	8	44	120	0	0	-------	-------	-------
Women's ready-to-wear	4	0	23	0	71	0	-------	-------
Men's and women's ready-to-wear	3	24	21	0	0	-------	-------	-------
Men's furnishings	3	0	18	0	-------	-------	-------	-------
Women's accessories	5	27	29	29	-------	-------	-------	-------
Hats and caps	11	19	19	26	51	0	-------	-------
Millinery	0	0	0	0	81	224	-------	-------
Men's shoes	3	0	0	44	141	117	-------	-------
Women's shoes	22	16	14	31	51	115	-------	-------
Men's and women's shoes	24	56	93	74	86	779	-------	-------
Dry goods	0	-------	15	34	-------	-------	-------	-------
Dry goods and apparel	3	15	54	145	-------	-------	-------	1,452
Department store	10	21	0	34	-------	347	560	-------
General merchandise	0	16	0	-------	-------	-------	-------	-------
Furniture	3	0	0	35	-------	-------	-------	-------
Musical instruments	4	12	55	-------	-------	-------	-------	-------
Hardware	5	9	0	0	-------	-------	-------	-------
Total	353	488	982	1,240	1,639	8,243	8,322	33,586
PROPORTIONS								
Grocery	19.0	20.6	21.9	52.8	88.0	88.9	100.0	100.0
Grocery and meat	24.5	26.3	53.5	51.9	100.0	92.1	100.0	100.0
Meat	0.0	0.0	7.6	41.3	40.5	-------	-------	-------
Confectionery	71.1	33.3	75.2	100.0	100.0	100.0	-------	-------
Drug	37.0	63.6	55.2	63.8	0.0	100.0	0.0	-------
Tobacco	54.8	62.5	51.5	100.0	0.0	0.0	100.0	0.0
Variety ($1 limit)	9.2	14.8	11.8	0.0	22.7	71.2	100.0	100.0
Variety ($5 limit)	0.0	0.0	0.0	0.0	100.0	-------	-------	-------
Variety (unlimited)	0.0	0.0	0.0	0.0	-------	-------	-------	-------
Men's ready-to-wear	7.8	36.1	60.9	0.0	0.0	-------	-------	-------
Women's ready-to-wear	2.3	0.0	11.8	0.0	43.3	0.0	-------	-------
Men's and women's ready-to-wear	4.7	18.3	19.3	0.0	0.0	-------	-------	-------
Men's furnishings	7.5	0.0	25.4	0.0	-------	-------	-------	-------
Women's accessories	29.4	79.4	39.2	100.0	-------	-------	-------	-------
Hats and caps	61.1	100.0	100.0	19.1	30.7	0.0	-------	-------
Millinery	0.0	0.0	0.0	0.0	100.0	47.0	-------	-------
Men's shoes	25.0	0.0	0.0	100.0	62.9	100.0	-------	-------
Women's shoes	41.5	40.0	26.9	19.9	100.0	100.0	-------	-------
Men's and women's shoes	15.0	26.5	26.8	27.3	24.9	83.0	-------	-------
Dry goods	0.0	-------	100.0	100.0	-------	-------	-------	-------
Dry goods and apparel	1.9	12.1	45.8	69.0	-------	-------	-------	100.0
Department store	26.3	77.8	0.0	55.7	-------	100.0	100.0	-------
General merchandise	0.0	29.6	0.0	-------	-------	-------	-------	-------
Furniture	6.3	0.0	0.0	100.0	-------	-------	-------	-------
Musical instruments	15.4	48.0	100.0	-------	-------	-------	-------	-------
Hardware	9.4	31.0	0.0	0.0	-------	-------	-------	-------
Total	18.1	26.5	34.3	38.7	52.5	81.1	93.8	94.4

TABLE 5.—*Numbers of chains and stores, and amounts of private-brand and total sales, for all chains reporting amounts of private-brand sales in specified years, by kind of chain*

Kind of chain	1919				1922				1925			
	Number of chains	Number of stores	Total net sales	Private-brand sales	Number of chains	Number of stores	Total net sales	Private-brand sales	Number of chains	Number of stores	Total net sales	Private-brand sales
Grocery					4	57	$3,457,000	$125,000	10	686	$30,200,000	$1,000,000
Grocery and meat	2	58	$3,773,000	$184,000	5	193	10,760,000	1,352,000	9	544	26,068,000	5,445,000
Confectionery	3	18	1,672,000	1,672,000	7	65	3,974,000	3,974,000	13	279	19,399,000	19,276,000
Drug	5	43	8,090,000	1,157,000	11	75	13,162,000	1,196,000	15	230	29,290,000	4,693,000
Tobacco	2	1,034	62,311,000	5,812,000	2	1,219	72,988,000	6,413,000	3	1,147	73,204,000	6,077,000
Variety ($1 limit)	2	181	19,429,000	627,000	2	211	32,506,000	1,881,000	3	425	105,968,000	7,794,000
Men's ready-to-wear	3	26	11,104,000	6,708,000	5	43	13,320,000	9,460,000	9	84	29,237,000	23,368,000
Men's furnishings					1	2	323,000	162,000	2	5	469,000	174,000
Women's accessories	1	3	55,000	28,000	1	3	45,000	23,000	6	26	2,030,000	1,543,000
Hats and caps					2	5	227,000	159,000	2	5	265,000	180,000
Men's shoes					3	107	6,851,000	6,282,000	3	150	7,946,000	7,305,000
Women's shoes	1	21	4,690,000	805,000	2	32	4,068,000	1,084,000	4	57	9,973,000	6,884,000
Men's and women's shoes	4	73	6,939,000	5,212,000	5	80	7,458,000	5,653,000	9	313	20,442,000	17,870,000
Dry goods and apparel					3	15	7,591,000	599,000	3	22	7,764,000	661,000
Department store	1	3	8,113,000	649,000	2	19	14,461,000	1,449,000	1	3	13,037,000	913,000
General merchandise									1	3	788,000	99,000
Musical instruments	2	7	1,261,000	1,103,000	2	7	1,440,000	1,241,000	2	7	1,253,000	1,099,000
Total	26	1,467	127,437,000	23,957,000	57	2,133	192,631,000	41,053,000	95	3,986	377,333,000	104,381,000
A. & P. and Kroger									2	16,890	556,259,000	122,544,000
Grocery and meat, (including A. & P. and Kroger)									11	17,434	582,327,000	127,989,000
Total (including A. & P. and Kroger)									97	20,876	933,592,000	226,925,000
	1928				**1929**				**1930**			
Grocery	30	3,693	$164,637,000	$14,551,000	27	7,384	$309,096,000	$27,902,000	31	7,649	$318,188,000	$32,230,000
Grocery and meat	24	4,471	195,680,000	41,192,000	30	4,129	233,247,000	44,663,000	35	4,855	244,960,000	45,610,000
Meat	1	50	5,589,000	559,000	3	78	6,650,000	131,000	3	87	6,734,000	134,000
Confectionery	20	527	33,409,000	29,385,000	16	272	18,445,000	16,763,000	16	292	17,369,000	15,885,000
Drug	27	504	62,518,000	12,923,000	54	1,041	117,507,000	19,486,000	56	1,202	125,742,000	21,816,000
Tobacco	3	1,124	73,737,000	5,778,000	15	1,145	59,190,000	4,908,000	16	1,112	66,358,000	3,721,000
Variety ($1 limit)	5	2,572	469,882,000	18,770,000	8	1,147	297,477,000	10,608,000	9	1,369	300,302,000	11,248,000
Variety ($5 limit)					1	51	1,554,000	47,000	1	53	1,428,000	43,000
Variety (unlimited)												

TABLE 5.—*Numbers of chains and stores, and amounts of private-brand and total sales, for all chains reporting amounts of private-brand sales in specified years, by kind of chain*—Continued

Kind of chain	1928				1929				1930			
	Number of chains	Number of stores	Total net sales	Private-brand sales	Number of chains	Number of stores	Total net sales	Private-brand sales	Number of chains	Number of stores	Total net sales	Private-brand sales
Men's ready-to-wear	15	195	$45,675,000	$39,336,000	14	152	$31,162,000	$15,190,000	14	161	$28,527,000	$14,674,000
Women's ready-to-wear					3	56	15,754,000	2,035,000	4	98	19,964,000	3,498,000
Men's and women's ready-to-wear	1	3	83,000	83,000	5	45	15,147,000	2,628,000	5	48	14,092,000	2,519,000
Men's furnishings	3	16	797,000	279,000	2	21	1,791,000	1,418,000	2	21	1,361,000	1,020,000
Women's accessories	7	59	3,658,000	2,659,000	5	41	2,725,000	2,674,000	6	75	3,793,000	3,728,000
Hats and caps	6	108	4,833,000	3,916,000	7	115	4,943,000	3,968,000	7	107	4,051,000	3,099,000
Millinery					1	209	12,073,000	121,000	1	224	13,219,000	132,000
Men's shoes	5	269	10,638,000	9,861,000	5	297	12,285,000	11,379,000	5	305	10,541,000	9,841,000
Women's shoes	5	90	14,933,000	11,459,000	10	134	21,059,000	18,105,000	10	134	18,831,000	16,320,000
Men's and women's shoes	17	739	47,724,000	43,073,000	23	894	60,558,000	53,054,000	23	899	58,249,000	52,121,000
Dry goods					1	13	208,000	25,000	2	49	1,453,000	130,000
Dry goods and apparel	5	35	9,190,000	636,000	8	1,549	222,200,000	189,443,000	10	1,669	213,935,000	174,402,000
Department store	7	266	124,323,000	24,274,000	7	876	360,424,000	86,758,000	7	932	380,511,000	104,550,000
General merchandise	2	11	1,269,000	80,000	2	16	1,746,000	58,000	2	16	1,636,000	55,000
Furniture	1	3	192,000	2,000	2	38	5,053,000	974,000	2	38	3,745,000	723,000
Musical instruments	3	16	1,361,000	860,000	4	42	4,971,000	2,114,000	4	41	3,938,000	2,024,000
Hardware					2	9	302,000	3,000	3	14	384,000	4,000
Total	187	14,751	1,270,128,000	259,676,000	255	19,754	1,815,567,000	514,455,000	274	21,450	1,859,311,000	519,527,000
A. & P. and Kroger	2	20,437	1,167,241,000	236,182,000	2	20,994	1,325,254,000	248,000,000	2	20,903	1,318,245,000	251,130,000
Grocery and meat (including A. & P. and Kroger)	26	24,908	1,362,921,000	277,374,000	32	25,123	1,558,501,000	292,663,000	37	25,758	1,563,205,000	296,740,000
Total (including A. & P. and Kroger)	189	35,188	2,437,369,000	495,858,000	257	40,748	3,140,821,000	762,455,000	276	42,353	3,177,556,000	770,657,000

TABLE 6.—*Number of chains, and amounts of private-brand and total sales for all chains reporting amounts of private-brand sales in specified years, by size of chain*

Number of stores per chain	1919			1922			1925		
	Number of chains	Total net sales	Private-brand sales	Number of chains	Total net sales	Private-brand sales	Number of chains	Total net sales	Private-brand sales
2–5	13	$13, 437, 000	$4, 732, 000	26	$26, 524, 000	$7, 883, 000	43	$30, 721, 000	$7, 588, 000
6–10	3	2, 291, 000	283, 000	10	6, 424, 000	1, 785, 000	16	18, 988, 000	12, 583, 000
11–25	3	15, 103, 000	7, 167, 000	10	19, 114, 000	9, 625, 000	11	31, 407, 000	22, 311, 000
26–50	4	18, 812, 000	1, 643, 000	6	34, 737, 000	4, 259, 000	8	18, 226, 000	10, 222, 000
51–100	1	4, 433, 000	4, 122, 000	2	10, 390, 000	9, 618, 000	10	82, 483, 000	20, 581, 000
101–500	1	11, 487, 000	230, 000	2	22, 957, 000	1, 509, 000	6	122, 991, 000	25, 211, 000
501–1,000									
1,001 and over	1	61, 874, 000	5, 780, 000	1	72, 485, 000	6, 374, 000	1	72, 517, 000	5, 885, 000
Total	26	127, 437, 000	23, 957, 000	57	192, 631, 000	41, 053, 000	95	377, 333, 000	104, 381, 000
A. & P. and Kroger							2	556, 259, 000	122, 544, 000
1,001 and over (including A. & P. and Kroger)							3	628, 776, 000	128, 429, 000
Total (including A. & P. and Kroger)							97	933, 592, 000	226, 925, 000

Number of stores per chain	1928			1929			1930		
	Number of chains	Total net sales	Private-brand sales	Number of chains	Total net sales	Private-brand sales	Number of chains	Total net sales	Private-brand sales
2–5	54	$107, 979, 000	$20, 798, 000	97	$106, 280, 000	$14, 226, 000	98	$95, 401, 000	$10, 809, 000
6–10	34	27, 541, 000	16, 982, 000	43	66, 792, 000	22, 613, 000	50	66, 383, 000	18, 512, 000
11–25	35	40, 322, 000	17, 034, 000	41	71, 719, 000	23, 299, 000	45	78, 914, 000	26, 758, 000
26–50	23	82, 542, 000	50, 782, 000	26	59, 553, 000	20, 603, 000	29	67, 185, 000	14, 835, 000
51–100	15	58, 891, 000	21, 724, 000	15	57, 448, 000	17, 896, 000	17	66, 088, 000	23, 698, 000
101–500	18	371, 882, 000	80, 286, 000	21	537, 189, 000	91, 884, 000	23	563, 942, 000	93, 686, 000
501–1,000	4	97, 499, 000	20, 899, 000	7	433, 555, 000	93, 638, 000	9	537, 264, 000	118, 481, 000
1,001 and over	4	483, 472, 000	31, 171, 000	5	483, 631, 000	230, 296, 000	3	384, 134, 000	212, 748, 000
Total	187	1, 270, 128, 000	259, 676, 000	255	1, 815, 567, 000	514, 455, 000	274	1, 859, 311, 000	519, 527, 000
A. & P. and Kroger	2	1, 167, 241, 000	236, 182, 000	2	1, 325, 254, 000	248, 060, 000	2	1, 318, 245, 000	251, 130, 000
1,001 and over (including A. & P. and Kroger)	6	1, 650, 713, 000	267, 353, 000	7	1, 808, 285, 000	478, 296, 000	5	1, 702, 379, 000	463, 878, 000
Total (including A. & P. and Kroger)	189	2, 437, 369, 000	495, 858, 000	257	3, 040, 821, 000	762, 455, 000	276	3, 177, 556, 000	770, 657, 000

TABLE 7.—*Stores operated by identical chains reporting amounts of private-brand sales for three and for four years, respectively, by kind of chain*

Kind of chain	46 chains					77 chains			
	Chains	Stores in—				Chains	Stores in—		
		1925	1928	1929	1930		1928	1929	1930
Grocery	5	576	831	918	933	9	2,523	2,616	2,615
Grocery and meat	4	68	70	97	93	10	2,809	3,042	3,581
Confectionery	6	87	170	177	197	8	215	217	235
Drug	7	201	372	514	612	13	424	582	689
Tobacco	3	1,147	1,124	1,048	1,011	3	1,124	1,048	1,011
Variety ($1 limit)	2	242	410	483	562	2	410	483	562
Men's ready-to-wear	2	7	32	25	26	5	56	60	63
Men's furnishings	1	2	2	3	3	1	2	3	3
Women's accessories	3	11	22	28	44	3	22	28	44
Hats and caps	1	2	2	2	2	2	14	14	12
Men's shoes	2	146	168	157	161	3	257	240	243
Women's shoes	3	50	83	88	92	4	87	93	97
Men's and women's shoes	4	260	503	562	580	8	523	586	601
Dry goods and apparel	1	2	3	3	3	2	9	17	18
Department store	1	3	3	3	3	3	238	540	569
Musical instruments	1	3	4	4	4	1	4	4	4
Total	46	2,807	3,799	4,112	4,326	77	8,717	9,573	10,347
A. & P. and Kroger	2	16,890	20,437	20.994	20,903	2	20,437	20,994	20,903
Grocery and meat (including A. & P. and Kroger)	6	16,958	20,507	21,091	20,996	12	23,246	24,036	24,484
Total (including A. & P. and Kroger)	48	19,697	24,236	25,106	25,229	79	29,154	30,567	31,250

TABLE 8.—*List of all commodities reported under private label by seven leading grocery and meat chains, together with the frequency reported, 1931*

Commodity	Number of chains reporting	Commodity	Number of chains reporting
Beans, canned	7	Lentils	5
Catsup	7	Maple sirup	5
Coffee	7	Mustard	5
Corn, canned	7	Pumpkin, canned	5
Flour	7	Salmon, canned	5
Jelly	7	Spices	5
Peaches, canned	7	Spinach, canned	5
Peas, canned	7	Succotash, canned	5
Sandwich spread	7	Toilet paper	5
Tea	7	Vinegar	5
Tomatoes, canned	7	Apple butter	4
Asparagus, canned	6	Apple sauce, canned	4
Bread	6	Barley, package	4
Butter	6	Beef, dried	4
Chili sauce	6	Berries, canned	4
Extracts	6	Bluing	4
Mayonnaise	6	Cherries, canned	4
Olives	6	Cocoa	4
Peanut butter	6	Flour:	
Pears, canned	6	Buckwheat	4
Pineapple, canned	6	Pancake	4
Preserves	6	Gelatin, flavored	4
Rice	6	Ginger ale	4
Ammonia	5	Grape juice	4
Apricots, canned	5	Milk, evaporated	4
Bacon	5	Relish	4
Beets, canned	5	Root beer	4
Eggs	5	Salad dressing	4
Kraut, canned	5	Salt	4

Commodity	Number of chains reporting
Spaghetti	4
Tapioca	4
Beans, dried	3
Brooms	3
Candy	3
Cornmeal	3
Flour:	
Graham	3
Pastry	3
Fruit salad	3
Grapefruit, canned	3
Ham	3
Honey	3
Macaroni	3
Mincemeat	3
Oats	3
Olive oil	3
Peas, dried	3
Pork and beans, canned	3
Shrimp, canned	3
Soap powder	3
Soda water	3
Sweet potatoes, canned	3
Tuna fish, canned	3
Baking powder	2
Cakes	2
Carrots, canned	2
Clotheslines	2
Cocoanut, package	2
Codfish	2
Cookies	2
Crackers	2
Cream of tartar	2
Currants	2
Dates	2
Doughnuts	2
Dressing, Thousand Island	2
Farina	2
Flour, rye	2
Fruit cake	2
Lard	2
Marshmallow cream	2
Milk, condensed	2
Noodles	2
Nuts, shelled	2
Pickles	2
Polish, furniture	2
Prunes	2
Prunes, canned	2
Rubbers, jar	2
Salad oil	2
Sardines	2
Sausage	2
Soap chips	2
Starch	2
Vegetables, mixed, canned	2
Waxed paper	2
Beef, smoked	1
Bird food	1
Breakfast food	1
Brown bread, canned	1
Carrots and peas, canned	1
Cheese	1
Chili con carne	1
Cider	1
Coaster wagons	1
Corn flakes	1
Cottonseed oil	1
Cranberry sauce	1
Cream, toilet	1
Disinfectant	1
Dressing, French	1
Flour, potato	1
Frankfurters	1
Herring, kippered	1
Hominy	1
Machine oil	1
Marmalade	1
Matches	1
Milk and cream, fresh	1
Molasses	1
Mops	1
Oleomargarine	1
Pimentoes	1
Peroxide	1
Polish, silver cream	1
Powder, talcum	1
Raisins	1
Rolls	1
Sal soda	1
Snacks, kippered	1
Soap	1
Sirup:	
Beverage	1
Malt	1
Tablets, writing	1
Toothpaste	1
Wall-paper cleaner	1
Washboards	1

Number of items reported 154
Number of times reported 479

TABLE 9.—*List of all commodities reported under private label by five leading dollar-limit variety chains, together with the frequency reported, 1931*

Commodity	Number of chains reporting	Commodity	Number of chains reporting
Hosiery	5	Flash lights	1
Hair nets	4	Flash-light unit cells	1
Sanitary napkins	4	Food choppers	1
Bias tape	3	Footballs	1
Razor blades	3	Golf sticks	1
Safety pins	3	Grinders, bench	1
Shirts	3	Hair switches	1
Batteries	2	Hammers	1
Candy	2	Hand drills	1
Cutlery	2	Hatchets	1
Elastic	2	Hydrometers	1
Garters	2	Jacks, auto	1
Golf balls	2	Linen, table	1
Polish, furniture	2	Maps	1
Powder puffs	2	Needles, phonograph	1
Shaving creams	2	Overshoes	1
Shoe laces	2	Paints and varnishes	1
Snap fasteners	2	Pencils	1
Stationery	2	Penknives	1
Thread	2	Pliers	1
Tooth paste	2	Records, phonograph	1
Tubes, radio	2	Ribbons	1
Underwear	2	Sanitary belts	1
Vacuum bottles	2	Scales, family	1
Aluminum goods	1	Shirts, work	1
Blankets	1	Shoes	1
Braces, ratchet bit	1	Snips, tinners'	1
Brushes	1	Spark plugs	1
Caps, men's	1	Ties, men's	1
Clocks, alarm	1	Tire pumps, auto	1
Coffee	1	Toilet preparations	1
Collars, men's	1	Toothbrushes	1
Combs	1	Tubes, inner	1
Dinner ware	1	Vises, bench	1
Dress shields	1	Water-wave nets	1
Enamel ware	1	Wrenches	1

TABLE 10.—*Numbers and proportions of private-brand-owning chains, and stores operated December 31, 1930, reporting on private-brand mark-up policy in 1931, by kind of chain*

Kind of chain	Number reporting on mark-up policy		Percentage of private brand-owning chains [1]	
	Chains, 1931	Stores operated Dec. 31, 1930	Chains, 1931	Stores operated Dec. 31, 1930
Grocery	43	9,608	100.0	100.0
Grocery and meat	52	17,102	94.5	52.0
Meat	4	149	100.0	100.0
Confectionery	11	142	55.0	32.2
Drug	71	1,235	94.7	96.3
Tobacco	20	1,156	100.0	100.0
Variety:				
$1 limit	12	2,045	92.3	52.1
$5 limit	1	53	100.0	100.0
Unlimited	---	---	---	---
Men's ready-to-wear	9	80	60.0	46.5
Women's ready-to-wear	3	27	75.0	27.6
Men's and women's ready-to-wear	3	39	60.0	81.3
Men's furnishings	2	21	100.0	100.0
Women's accessories	3	30	42.9	33.3
Hats and caps	6	66	75.0	52.4
Millinery	2	305	100.0	100.0
Men's shoes	4	246	80.0	80.7
Women's shoes	6	212	54.5	85.1
Men's and women's shoes	24	1,074	88.9	96.6
Dry goods	2	49	100.0	100.0
Dry goods and apparel	9	217	90.0	13.0
Department store	6	31	66.7	3.2
General merchandise	2	16	100.0	100.0
Furniture	2	38	100.0	100.0
Musical instruments	4	61	66.7	85.9
Hardware	3	14	100.0	100.0
Total	304	34,016	86.6	62.0

[1] See Table 4 for chain and Table 5 for store figures of private-brand ownership.

TABLE 11.—*Numbers and proportions of private-brand-owning chains, and stores operated December 31, 1928, reporting on private-brand-pricing policy in 1929–30, by kind of chain*

Kind of chain	Number reporting on pricing policy		Percentage of private-brand-owning chains [1]	
	Chains, 1929–30	Stores operated Dec. 31, 1928	Chains, 1929–30	Stores operated Dec. 31, 1928
Grocery	52	7,657	81.3	86.6
Grocery and meat	62	30,265	83.8	96.5
Meat	2	67	50.0	62.6
Confectionery	2	23	8.7	4.1
Drug	49	881	65.3	86.0
Tobacco	9	1,564	69.2	97.8
Variety ($1 limit)	4	2,152	50.0	80.9
Men's ready-to-wear	8	48	33.3	18.2
Men's and women's ready-to-wear	2	40	40.0	62.5
Men's furnishings	5	49	83.3	87.5
Women's accessories	3	25	33.3	23.1
Hats and caps	7	114	53.8	33.5
Men's shoes	3	111	50.0	35.0
Women's shoes	3	17	37.5	8.0
Men's and women's shoes	10	150	32.3	15.4
Dry goods	2	8	100.0	100.0
Dry goods and apparel	8	1,069	66.7	97.8
Department store	10	472	76.9	96.5
General merchandise	3	93	42.9	73.8
Furniture	1	3	3.3	1.9
Musical instruments	3	45	42.9	55.6
Total	248	44,853	61.1	89.2

[1] See Table 4 for chain and Table 5 for store figures of private-brand ownership for kinds of chains included in this table.

TABLE 12.—*Numbers and proportions of chains reporting on national advertising of private brands, 1929–30, and stores operated by them December 31, 1928, by kind of chain*

Kind of chain	Number of reports of private-brand ownership, in 23 kinds of business		Number of reports on national advertising of private brands, in 23 kinds of business		Proportions reporting on national advertising of private brands	
	Chains	Stores operated	Chains	Stores operated	Chains	Stores operated
Grocery	64	8,840	60	8,397	93.8	95.0
Grocery and meat	74	31,361	72	31,308	97.3	99.8
Meat	4	107	3	57	75.0	53.3
Confectionery	23	561	16	435	69.6	77.5
Drug	75	1,024	72	1,016	96.0	99.2
Tobacco	13	1,600	13	1,600	100.0	100.0
Variety ($1 limit)	8	2,660	8	2,660	100.0	100.0
Men's ready-to-wear	24	264	20	213	83.3	80.7
Women's ready-to-wear	3	131	2	110	66.7	84.0
Men's and women's ready-to-wear	5	64	5	64	100.0	100.0
Men's furnishings	6	56	6	56	100.0	100.0
Women's accessories	9	108	9	108	100.0	100.0
Hats and caps	13	340	11	211	84.6	62.1
Millinery	2	19	1	15	50.0	78.9
Men's shoes	6	317	5	312	83.3	98.4
Women's shoes	8	212	8	212	100.0	100.0
Men's and women's shoes	31	972	26	857	83.9	88.2
Dry goods	2	8	2	8	100.0	100.0
Dry goods and apparel	12	1,093	11	1,090	91.7	99.7
Department store	13	489	10	471	76.9	96.3
General merchandise	7	126	6	112	85.7	88.9
Furniture	1	3	1	3	100.0	100.0
Musical instruments	7	81	6	67	85.7	82.7
Total	410	50,436	373	49,382	91.0	97.9

O

72D CONGRESS } SENATE { DOCUMENT
2d Session } { No. 170

CHAIN STORES

Quality of Canned Vegetables and Fruits

(Under Brands of Manufacturers, Chains, and Other Distributors)

LETTER

FROM THE

CHAIRMAN OF THE FEDERAL TRADE COMMISSION

TRANSMITTING

IN RESPONSE TO SENATE RESOLUTION No. 224, SEVENTIETH CONGRESS, REPORT OF THE FEDERAL TRADE COMMISSION RELATIVE TO QUALITY OF CANNED VEGETABLES AND FRUITS (UNDER BRANDS OF MANUFACTURERS, CHAINS, AND OTHER DISTRIBUTORS)

JANUARY 10 (calendar day, JANUARY 13), 1933.—Referred to the Committee on the Judiciary and ordered to be printed

---

UNITED STATES
GOVERNMENT PRINTING OFFICE
WASHINGTON : 1933

SENATE RESOLUTION NO. 228

SUBMITTED BY MR. BROOKHART

IN THE SENATE OF THE UNITED STATES,
June 8 (calendar day, June 10), 1932.

Resolved, That the reports which may hereafter be filed with the Secretary of the Senate, pursuant to Senate Resolution No. 224, Seventieth Congress, first session, relative to the investigation by the Federal Trade Commission of chain stores, be printed, with accompanying illustrations, as Senate documents.

Attest:

EDWIN P. THAYER, *Secretary.*

Chain-store reports of the Federal Trade Commission so far submitted to the Senate are:

Title	Senate Document No.	Price per copy
SEVENTY-SECOND CONGRESS, FIRST SESSION		*Cents*
Cooperative Grocery Chains	12	15
Wholesale Business of Retail Chains	29	5
Sources of Chain-Store Merchandise	30	10
Scope of the Chain-Store Inquiry	31	5
Chain-Store Leaders and Loss Leaders	51	10
Cooperative Drug and Hardware Chains	82	5
Growth and Development of Chain Stores	100	10
SEVENTY-SECOND CONGRESS, SECOND SESSION		
Chain-Store Private Brands	142	10
Short Weighing and Over Weighing in Chain and Independent Grocery Stores	153	5
Sizes of Stores of Retail Chains	156	5
Quality of Canned Vegetables and Fruits (under Brands of Manufacturers, Chains, and Other Distributors)	170	5

These reports may be obtained at prices above noted from

THE SUPERINTENDENT OF DOCUMENTS,
WASHINGTON, D. C.

CONTENTS

TEXT TABLES

APPENDIX TABLES

ACKNOWLEDGMENT

For the general direction and supervision of the inquiry into the chain-store industry, the commission acknowledges the services of Mr. Francis Walker, chief economist, and Mr. W. H. S. Stevens, assistant chief economist. As contributing especially to the preparation of this report on quality of canned vegetables and fruits (under brands of manufacturers, chains, and other distributors), the commission desires to mention Mr. John S. Biggs; Mr. Byron P. Parry, examiner in charge of the inquiry; and Mr. Kenneth S. Boardman.

LETTER OF TRANSMITTAL

Federal Trade Commission,
Washington, January 13, 1933.

The President of the Senate,
United States Senate, Washington, D. C.

Dear Sir: I have the honor to transmit herewith a report of the Federal Trade Commission, entitled "Quality of Canned Vegetables and Fruits (under Brands of Manufacturers, Chains, and Other Distributors)," submitted in pursuance of Senate Resolution 224, Seventieth Congress, first session. This is the eleventh report of a series of reports covering a study on the subject of chain stores.

By direction of the commission.

W. E. Humphrey, *Chairman.*

LETTER OF SUBMITTAL

Federal Trade Commission,
Washington, D. C.

To the Senate of the United States:

This report is submitted in partial response to Senate Resolution 224, Seventieth Congress, first session, directing the commission to conduct an inquiry into the chain-store system of marketing and distribution.

In connection with its study in five cities of the comparative buying and selling prices of chain and independent grocery stores, the commission, in three of the five cities, Des Moines, Memphis, and Detroit, purchased samples of certain brands of canned fruits and canned vegetables for grading. While the samples purchased were obtained solely with the needs of the price study in view the results of the grading are presented in this report because no adequate data regarding the quality of commodities under chain-store and other labels are available. Furthermore, reductions in appropriations rendered it impossible to carry through rather extensive plans for further work on the question of quality of chain and other brands of commodities. It is believed that the results presented in this report are representative of the situation in the three cities covered.

In all, samples were obtained in the 3 cities for 511 items of canned fruits and canned vegetables. Each sample consisted of three cans, two of which were graded by the warehouse division of the United States Department of Agriculture, the standards used being those promulgated by the department or those customarily employed by it in commercial grading. The merchandise purchased represents the brands of chains, manufacturers, both national advertisers and others, wholesalers and cooperative chains.

RESULTS OF GRADING CANNED VEGETABLES

In all, 396 cans of vegetables were graded. Of these, 85 were canned spinach and pumpkin which do not have the same standards as other vegetables. The results of the grading showed that excluding these two kinds of vegetables, the brands of the chains were only slightly below those of nationally advertising manufacturers in the proportion of their cans grading "fancy," "extra standard," and "standard," respectively. They make a slightly better showing than nonnationally advertising manufacturers in the "fancy" grade and show a materially higher proportion for "extra standard." Compared with wholesalers, the chains show a distinctly higher proportion in "fancy" and a somewhat lower proportion in "extra standard." Chains lead the cooperatives slightly in proportions of their brands of canned vegetables grading "fancy" but for the "extra standard" grade the brands of the cooperatives had a much higher ratio.

For canned spinach and pumpkin the cooperative chains made the outstanding showing, three-fourths of their cans grading "fancy." All of the chain brands of these canned vegetables graded "standard." The nonnationally advertising manufacturers have a higher proportion of "fancy" than do the nationally advertising manufacturers.

RESULTS OF GRADING CANNED FRUITS

A total of 621 cans of fruit was graded. The proportion of the chain brands of fruits which graded "fancy" was slightly higher than the average; although below the proportions for brands of both wholesalers and nationally advertising manufacturers. In the proportion of brands grading "choice" the chains substantially exceeded the figures shown by any other group. None of the chain brands of canned fruits graded "seconds."

As with canned vegetables there were marked differences in the grades of manufacturers who advertise nationally and those who do not, the former being the higher in quality. There was also the same general close correspondence in the grades of the chains and the nationally advertising manufacturers. Furthermore, the comparisons of the grade scores indicate that the chains compare favorably with these and other distributors in the quality of their private brands of canned vegetables and fruits.

VARIATIONS IN GRADES

Wide variations in the quality of canned vegetables and fruits packed under identical labels were found in the case of a number of brands. This type of variation was found alike in the brands of chains, manufacturers, wholesalers, and cooperatives.

WM. E. HUMPHREY, *Chairman.*

QUALITY OF CANNED VEGETABLES AND FRUITS

(Under Brands of Manufacturers, Chains, and Other Distributors)

Section 1. Origin and scope of the report.

Introduction.—This report dealing with the quality of chain-store brands of canned goods in comparison with those of other distributors and of manufacturers, is submitted in further response to Senate Resolution 224, Seventieth Congress, first session, which, among other things, directed the commission to report in full to the Senate "the advantages or disadvantages of chain-store distribution * * * as shown by * * * quality of goods and services rendered by chain stores and other distributors," etc.

In considering the representativeness of this study of the quality of canned vegetables and canned fruits, it is important that it be realized that the methods and procedure followed were dictated by the requirements of an extensive study of chain and independent prices and margins and that the data procured were not intended to constitute the only study of this subject made by the commission. The original plans for the chain-store inquiry called for a much more extensive study of this subject. Reductions in appropriations rendered it impossible to carry through the rather extensive plans for this work. It is not expected, therefore, at the time of this writing that it will be possible to do anything further with this subject. No adequate data of the quality of commodities under chain-store and other labels, however, are available and a careful examination of the material obtained in the work on the price and margin study led to the conclusion that this information was sufficiently representative of the situation, at least in three cities, to justify its presentation. A full description of the methods used in the selection of the commodities is given below, these methods, as has already been stated, being determined primarily by the requirements of the price and margin study and not in accordance with any predetermined plan for the analysis of quality.

In connection with the price and margin study in three cities, Des Moines, Iowa; Memphis, Tenn.; and Detroit, Mich., the commission purchased samples of a number of brands of canned fruits and vegetables on which the retail selling prices and wholesale or chain-store purchase costs had been obtained by its agents. These brands of canned goods include those of manufacturers, wholesalers, chain stores and cooperative chains. The purpose of these purchases was to compare the prices and margins of these goods sold through independent retailers with the prices and margins of goods of corresponding quality sold through chain stores. As the private brands of chain stores are not, as a rule, sold through independent retailers and those of wholesalers and cooperative chains are not distributed through chain stores, while the same brands of manufacturers are not always distributed in a particular city through both independent and chain stores, it was necessary, in order to make the different items priced comparable with one another, that the goods in question for all these types of distributors should be accurately graded, and it was for the purpose of this grading that the cans in question were purchased.

The pressure of other problems, particularly in the earlier stages of the chain-store inquiry when the pricing work in Washington and Cincinnati was being conducted and when the staff of people available was very small, prevented the purchasing of samples for testing either in Washington or Cincinnati. Samples of a different pack could have been purchased in these cities at later dates but this was not done because of the possible variations in quality and the fact that the prices and costs obtained in the price and margin study had been for those of the packs of an earlier period.

Selection of samples.—The general method followed in the selection and purchase of canned goods in the three cities specified may be illustrated by a summary of the procedure in the city of Des Moines. In the preliminary survey of that city for the price and margin study, an agent of the commission obtained from each wholesale dealer, from each chain-store headquarters, and from each cooperative chain headquarters a complete list of the canned vegetables and canned fruits customarily carried in stock, including its own private brands.

Twenty-four individual retail grocers well distributed over all sections of the city were then questioned on this subject and a complete list was made of all the principal brands of canned vegetables and fruits carried by each of them in Nos. 1, 2, 2½, and 3 cans, together with a notation of the grade claimed for each brand and of the brand's relative importance according to the estimation of the retailer. During the first three days of the regular pricing work, schedules were obtained from 57 individual retail dealers and from three chain stores. Using these 60 schedules and the information previously obtained in the preliminary survey from wholesale dealers, chain stores, cooperative chains and the 24 retail grocers, a selected list was prepared of 176 items of canned fruits and vegetables sold under the brands of manufacturers, wholesalers, and cooperative chains and 26 items sold under the private brands of the regular chains. In so far as the goods sold through independent retailers were concerned, this list included each item of any brand of canned fruits or vegetables which was found in 3 per cent or more of the stores covered in the preliminary canvass and in the first three days of the retail pricing. This list was then extended to include one or more items under the private brands of each large wholesaler and of each cooperative group whose brands did not appear on the basis of 3 per cent of the retail stores. After the list had been prepared, it was necessary to cut out some items in order that the total number should not exceed a reasonable maximum. The items thus eliminated were selected with a view to disturbing as little as possible the original distribution of the brands, commodities, and classes of dealers.

Sample obtained, Des Moines.—When finally completed, the list included approximately 230 items of canned fruits and vegetables under the labels mentioned and the commission placed orders for these samples, each sample consisting of three cans, two for actual testing and the other to be held as a reserve sample. The dealers with whom these orders were placed, however, were able to supply only 171 or about three-fourths of the samples ordered and in one instance, only one can of the commodity was furnished instead of the three ordered. Of the samples obtained on these orders, 53 were under the brands of manufacturers, 57 were under the private brands of wholesalers, 20 under the private brands of regular chains, and 41 under the private brands of cooperative chains. The failure to procure a higher proportion of the samples ordered was due in part to the fact that it was not possible to place the orders until more than two months after the close of the pricing period for which the brand names had been obtained. The merchandise involved does not flow steadily from producer to the consumer and the brands purchased by distributors vary considerably from time to time.

The data obtained from Des Moines are shown in Appendix Table 1.

Sample obtained, Memphis.—The representativeness of the sample obtained in Memphis is in some respects hardly as satisfactory as that for Des Moines, although the samples in that city were purchased almost immediately after the close of the retail pricing work. A list for the city of Memphis was prepared in a manner similar to that for Des Moines and orders were placed for 3-can samples of approximately 170 items. Samples were obtained of 80 items under brands of manufacturers,[1] 18 under the private brands of wholesalers, 1 under the private brand of a chain, and 12 under those of cooperatives. Detailed data secured from the Memphis sample are shown in Appendix Table 2.

Sample obtained, Detroit.—For Detroit, the commission procured a somewhat better distribution of private-brand samples among the different groups of owners than was obtained at either of the other cities except for the fact that no cooperative group brands were sold in this city at the time of the study in question. The list for this city consisted of approximately 230 items. On these orders samples were obtained for 147 manufacturer's brand items,[2] 48 wholesaler's brand items, and 34 chain-store brand items. The basic data are shown in Appendix Table 3.

Total sample.—For all three cities, orders were placed for a total of approximately 630 items of brands of goods which were moving in quantities at the time the grocery commodities were priced in retail stores in the three cities in question. For reasons previously explained, however, samples were obtained only for 511 items or about 80 per cent of the total number ordered. In view of the methods employed in the selection of the commodities and the care taken to make the list comprehensive, it is believed that the commodities in question, considered as a whole, are adequately representative of the brands of these products that were being distributed in the three cities covered by this survey.

Packers represented.—The merchandise purchased showing the manufacturer's or packer's labels represents the products of 27 packers of canned fruits and 47 packers of canned vegetables, several companies packing both products being counted in both lists. The sample also includes products distributed under the brands of 6

[1] Only one can could be obtained of one sample.
[2] Only one can could be obtained for each of three of these samples.

wholesale dealers, 3 large chains, each operating more than 500 stores, and 3 of the largest cooperative chains. The manufacturers include California Packing Corporation, Hunt Bros. Packing Co., Libby, McNeil & Libby, Curtice Bros. Co., Snider Packing Corporation, Hawaiian Pineapple Co., Pratt-Low Preserving Co., William R. Roach & Co., and others not so well known. Wholesalers or manufacturing wholesalers whose products are represented in the sample are Francis H. Leggett, Reid, Murdoch & Co., Chas. Hewitt & Sons, J. T. Fargason, Lee & Cady, and Weideman Grocery Co. Canned goods sold under chain-store private labels which are represented in the sample include brands of the Great Atlantic & Pacific Tea Co., the National Tea Co., and Kroger Grocery & Baking Co., while those of the cooperative chains include brands of the Independent Grocers Alliance, Grocers Wholesale Co., and the Red and White Corporation.

Grading procedure.—The samples of canned fruits and vegetables purchased as described above were submitted to the warehouse division of the Department of Agriculture for testing, in order to have the grade of the product sold under each brand officially determined. As mentioned, each sample purchased consisted of three cans, with a few exceptions. Two cans of each sample were graded by the department and the third was retained by the Federal Trade Commission.

The standards used in grading these samples were those customarily employed by the warehouse division of the United States Department of Agriculture in grading commercial samples examined by it under authority of the provisions of the United States warehouse act.[3]

Section 2. Results of grading canned fruits and vegetables.

It should be pointed out that it was not possible to find brands of all four types of distributors for some products. The cooperative chains in the three cities covered by this study did not have any private brands of canned grapefruit.

With the exception of peeled apricots and fruits for salad the chains are represented in each commodity under consideration. In view of the fact that the important consideration is a comparison of chain brands with brands of other types of distributors, the lack of some commodities under the brand of some one or another of these other kinds of distributors is not serious since at least some comparison can still be made.

Canned vegetables.—The number of cans of vegetables under the brands of chains, cooperative chains, wholesalers, manufacturers who advertise nationally and other manufacturers, which were graded, and the distribution of these cans by grades are shown in Table 1. The basic data by cities are shown in Appendix Tables 1, 2, and 3 and are consolidated by products in Appendix Tables 4 and 5.

---

[3] For example, under the Department of Agriculture regulations:

"The grades of canned tomatoes are ascertained by considering the following factors, the importance of each of which has been expressed numerically and the maximum number of credits allowable for each factor are as follows:

	Points
Percentage of whole tomatoes	20
Solidity	20
Color	20
Absence of defects (skins, cores, blemishes, extraneous matters, etc.)	20
Flavor	20
Total	100

It was deemed desirable to show separately the grading results of those manufacturers who advertised nationally and those manufacturers who did not so advertise. Data of the Crowell Publishing Co.[4] and the Curtis Publishing Co.[5] were used to determine which of the manufacturers represented in the commission's sample were national advertisers. Based on their listings, two companies packing both canned fruits and canned vegetables are national advertisers, five other concerns packing canned vegetables are in this category as are three other companies packing canned fruits.

Canned spinach and pumpkin are shown separately in Table 1 because there is no "extra standard" grade for these products in the Department of Agriculture standards. Thus the minimum score limit of "fancy" is lower by 5 points and the maximum for "standard" is higher by 10 points for these two products than for the other canned vegetables graded.

TABLE 1.—*Distribution, by grades of cans of vegetables, of various types of brand owners*

Grades of canned vegetables	Manufacturers			Distributors			All groups combined
	National advertisers	Other	Total	Wholesalers	Chains	Cooperatives	
Except spinach and pumpkin: [1]							
Fancy	11	14	25	3	7	3	38
Extra standard	30	25	55	32	21	15	123
Standard	23	51	74	29	16	8	127
Substandard	3	13	16	1	4		21
No grade	1	1	2				2
Fancy and extra standard combined	41	39	80	35	28	18	161
Standard and substandard combined	26	64	90	30	20	8	148
All grades combined	68	104	172	65	48	26	311
Spinach and pumpkin:							
Fancy	5	5	10	4		12	26
Standard	23	8	31	12	8	4	55
Substandard				4			4
All grades combined	28	13	41	20	8	16	85

[1] See text.

Of the 396 cans of vegetables graded by the Department of Agriculture for the commission, 96, or 24.2 per cent, were under brands of nationally advertising manufacturers and 117, or 29.6 per cent, were under the brands of other manufacturers. The wholesalers were next in representation, having 21.5 per cent of the total number of cans followed by the regular chains with 14.1 per cent and the cooperative chains, 10.6 per cent.

Of the 311 cans of vegetables excluding spinach and pumpkin, 127 graded "standard" and only 38 cans were of the highest or "fancy" grade. There were 21 cans grading "substandard" distributed among three types of distributors, viz, manufacturers 16 cans (of which 3 were those of national advertisers while 13 were from other manufacturers), chains 4 cans, and wholesalers 1 can.

[4] National Markets and National Advertising, 1930.
[5] Leading Advertisers, 1931 (figures for 1930).

As the manufacturers have the largest proportion of total cans of vegetables it is logical that their proportions of cans under each grade should be the highest as shown in the upper part of Table 2.

TABLE 2.—*Percentage distribution, by grades of canned vegetables, of various types of brand owners*

Grades of canned vegetables	Manufacturers			Distributors			All groups combined
	National advertisers	Other	Total	Wholesalers	Chains	Cooperatives	
Except spinach and pumpkin:							
Fancy	29.0	36.8	65.8	7.9	18.4	7.9	100.0
Extra standard	24.4	20.3	44.7	26.0	17.1	12.2	100.0
Standard	18.1	40.2	58.3	22.8	12.6	6.3	100.0
Substandard	14.3	61.9	76.2	4.8	19.0		100.0
No grade	50.0	50.0	100.0				100.0
Fancy and extra standard combined	25.5	24.2	49.7	21.7	17.4	11.2	100.0
Standard and substandard combined	17.6	43.2	60.8	20.3	13.5	5.4	100.0
All grades combined	21.9	33.4	55.3	20.9	15.4	8.4	100.0
Spinach and pumpkin:							
Fancy	19.2	19.2	38.4	15.4		46.2	100.0
Standard	41.8	14.6	56.4	21.8	14.6	7.2	100.0
Substandard				100.0			100.0
All grades combined	33.0	15.3	48.3	23.5	9.4	18.8	100.0

Of the 85 cans of spinach and of pumpkin, 28 cans, or 33 per cent, were brands of nationally advertising manufacturers; 13, or 15.3 per cent, of other manufacturers; 20, or 23.5 per cent, of wholesalers; 8, or 9.4 per cent, of chains; and 16, or 18.8 per cent, of cooperatives.

The proportions of cans of vegetables under each type of brand owner falling in each grade are shown in the following table.

TABLE 3.—*Percentage distribution, by types of brand owners, of grades of canned vegetables*

Grades of canned vegetables	Manufacturers			Distributors			All groups combined
	National advertisers	Other	Total	Wholesalers	Chains	Cooperatives	
Except spinach and pumpkin:							
Fancy	16.2	13.5	14.5	4.6	14.6	11.5	12.2
Extra standard	44.1	24.0	32.0	49.2	43.7	57.7	39.6
Standard	33.8	49.0	43.0	44.6	33.4	30.8	40.8
Substandard	4.4	12.5	9.3	1.6	8.3		6.8
No grade	1.5	1.0	1.2				.6
Fancy and extra standard combined	60.3	37.5	46.5	53.8	58.3	69.2	51.8
Standard and substandard combined	38.2	61.5	52.3	46.2	41.7	30.8	47.6
All grades combined	100.0	100.0	100.0	100.0	100.0	100.0	100.0
Spinach and pumpkin:							
Fancy	17.9	38.5	24.4	20.0		75.0	30.6
Standard	82.1	61.5	75.6	60.0	100.0	25.0	64.7
Substandard				20.0			4.7
All grades combined	100.0	100.0	100.0	100.0	100.0	100.0	100.0

From this table it appears that, as regards all vegetables except spinach and pumpkin, the chains are only slightly below nationally advertising manufacturers in the proportions of their cans grading "fancy," "extra standard," and "standard," respectively. They make a slightly better showing than nonnationally advertising manufacturers in the "fancy" grade, and show a materially higher proportion for "extra standard." Compared with wholesalers, the chains show a distinctly higher proportion in "fancy" and a somewhat lower proportion in "extra standard," but combining the two grades the chains show 58.3 per cent in contrast with 53.8 per cent for wholesalers. Chains lead cooperatives slightly in the proportions graded "fancy" (14.6 and 11.5 per cent, respectively) but for the "extra standard" grade the cooperatives show so high a ratio (57.7 per cent) as to become the leader in the combined proportions of "fancy" and "extra standard" (69.2 per cent, compared with 60.3 per cent for nationally advertising manufacturers, 58.3 per cent for chains, 53.8 per cent for wholesalers, and 37.5 per cent for other manufacturers).

For spinach and pumpkin the cooperatives make the outstanding showing, three-fourths of their samples grading "fancy" and the rest "standard." None of the chain samples of these two commodities were in the "fancy" grade, all being "standard." The other manufacturers' group shows a higher percentage of "fancy" (38.5) than do the nationally advertising manufacturers (17.9 per cent), which is in marked contrast to the proportions shown for all other kinds of vegetables.

Canned fruits.—Table 4 shows the distribution among the several specified types of brand owners of the specified grades of canned fruits, and Table 5 the proportions of each grade secured from each type of brand owner.

TABLE 4.—*Distribution, by grades of cans of fruit, of various types of brand owners*

Grades of canned fruits	Manufacturers			Distributors			All groups combined
	National advertisers	Other	Total	Wholesalers	Chains	Cooperatives	
Fancy	67	15	82	46	14	11	153
Choice	147	41	188	88	34	37	347
Standard	34	26	60	16	6	12	94
Seconds	2	5	7	8		3	18
No grade	4	2	6	2		1	9
Fancy and choice combined	214	56	270	134	48	48	500
Standard and seconds combined	36	31	67	24	6	15	112
All grades combined	254	89	343	160	54	64	621

Of the 621 cans of fruit graded by the Department of Agriculture for the commission, 254, or over 40 per cent, were under manufacturers' nationally advertised labels; 89, or one-seventh, were packed by nonnationally advertising manufacturers; 160, or more than one-fourth, by wholesalers; and 54 and 64 respectively, or about one-tenth, by chains and by cooperatives.

TABLE 5.—*Percentage distribution, by grades of canned fruits, of various types of brand owners*

Grades of canned fruits	Manufacturers			Distributors			All groups combined
	National advertisers	Other	Total	Wholesalers	Chains	Cooperatives	
Fancy	43.8	9.8	53.6	30.1	9.1	7.2	100.0
Choice	42.4	11.8	54.2	25.3	9.8	10.7	100.0
Standard	36.2	27.6	63.8	17.0	6.4	12.8	100.0
Seconds	11.1	27.8	38.9	44.4		16.7	100.0
No grade	44.5	22.2	66.7	22.2		11.1	100.0
Fancy and choice combined	42.8	11.2	54.0	26.8	9.6	9.6	100.0
Standard and seconds combined	32.1	27.7	59.8	21.4	5.4	13.4	100.0
All grades combined	40.9	14.3	55.2	25.8	8.7	10.3	100.0

One hundred and fifty-three of the 621 cans of fruit graded were "fancy" and 347 were "choice." An appreciably higher proportion of the total number of cans graded fell in these two classes than in the case of canned vegetables. Conversely, only 94 and 18 out of 621 cans of fruits were "standard" and "seconds," respectively, as contrasted with 127 and 21 out of 311 cans of vegetables.[6]

Table 6 gives the proportions of the cans of each type of brand owner which fall in each of the grades.

TABLE 6.—*Percentage distribution, by types of brand owners, of grades of canned fruits*

Grades of canned fruits	Manufacturers			Distributors			All groups combined
	National advertisers	Other	Total	Wholesalers	Chains	Cooperatives	
Fancy	26.4	16.8	23.9	28.7	25.9	17.2	24.6
Choice	57.8	46.1	54.8	55.0	63.0	57.8	55.9
Standard	13.4	29.2	17.5	10.0	11.1	18.7	15.1
Seconds	.8	5.6	2.0	5.0		4.7	2.9
No grade	1.6	2.3	1.8	1.3		1.6	1.5
Fancy and choice combined	84.2	62.9	78.7	83.7	88.9	75.0	80.5
Standard and seconds combined	14.2	34.8	19.5	15.0	11.1	23.4	18.0
All grades combined	100.0	100.0	100.0	100.0	100.0	100.0	100.0

The proportion of chain-store brands of fruits grading "fancy" (25.9 per cent) was slightly higher than the average (24.6 per cent), although the chain proportions are below both nationally advertising manufacturers (26.4 per cent) and wholesalers (28.7 per cent). In the proportion of brands grading "choice" the chains substantially exceeded the figures shown by any other group. Their proportion of brands grading "choice" and "fancy" combined (88.9 per cent) was not only above the general average (80.5 per cent) but was also higher than that of the nationally advertising manufacturers (84.2

[6] Not including spinach and pumpkin.

per cent), and appreciably higher than the proportions for wholesalers (83.7 per cent), cooperative chains (75 per cent) and other manufacturers (62.9 per cent). In canned fruits, none of the chain store private brands graded "seconds."

As was the case with canned vegetables there were marked differences in the grades of manufacturers who advertised nationally and those who did not, the former being the higher in quality. There was also the same general close correspondence in the grades of the regular chains and the nationally advertising manufacturers.

It has been noted that the canned vegetables covered by the test, in general, are of a lower grade than canned fruits; 47.6 per cent of the brands of canned vegetables tested [7] were graded as either "substandard" or "standard" as compared with only 18.0 per cent for brands of canned fruits.

As stated later, wide variations in the quality of canned vegetables and fruits packed under identical labels were found in the case of a number of brands. This type of variation was found alike in the brands of chains, of manufacturers, of wholesalers, and of cooperatives.

Canned fruits and vegetables combined.—The number of cans of fruits and vegetables from all sources graded by the Department of Agriculture was 1,017 of which 85 were on a different basis of grading.[8] Table 7 shows the distribution of the 932 comparably scored cans by grades for each type of distributor. It combines the data hitherto shown separately for each kind of product in Tables 1 and 4.

TABLE 7.—*Combined distribution, by grades of cans of vegetables*[1] *and fruits of various types of brand owners*

Grades of canned vegetables and fruits	Manufacturers			Distributors			All types combined
	National advertisers	Other	Total	Wholesalers	Chains	Cooperatives	
Fancy	78	29	107	49	21	14	191
Choice or extra standard	177	66	243	120	55	52	470
Standard	57	77	134	45	22	20	221
Substandard or seconds	5	18	23	9	4	3	39
No grade	5	3	8	2		1	11
Two upper grades combined	255	95	350	169	76	66	661
Standard and substandard combined	62	95	157	54	26	23	260
All grades combined	322	193	515	225	102	90	932

[1] Spinach and pumpkin excluded. See text.

Table 8 shows the percentage distribution of each grade among the several types of brand owners. In effect it combines the data of Tables 2 and 5.

[7] Spinach and pumpkin excluded.
[8] Spinach and pumpkin.

TABLE 8.—*Percentage distribution, by grades of canned vegetables and fruits, of various types of brand owners*

Grades of canned vegetables and fruits	Manufacturers			Distributors			All groups combined
	National advertisers	Other	Total	Wholesalers	Chains	Cooperatives	
Fancy	40.8	15.2	56.0	25.7	11.0	7.3	100.0
Choice or extra standard	37.7	14.0	51.7	25.5	11.7	11.1	100.0
Standard	25.8	34.8	60.6	20.4	10.0	9.0	100.0
Substandard or seconds	12.8	46.2	59.0	23.1	10.2	7.7	100.0
No grade	45.4	27.3	72.7	18.2		9.1	100.0
Two upper grades combined	38.6	14.4	53.0	25.5	11.5	10.0	100.0
Standard and substandard combined	23.9	36.5	60.4	20.8	10.0	8.8	100.0
All grades combined	34.6	20.7	55.3	24.1	10.9	9.7	100.0

The purpose of the above tables is to show the combined results of the grading of canned fruits and canned vegetables. While the terminology used for grades of canned fruits is not identical with that for canned vegetables in that "extra standard" instead of "choice" and "substandard" instead of "seconds" are used in grading the latter, these two terms represent the second and the fourth highest grade for canned vegetables and canned fruits respectively.[9]

The proportions of cans of fruits and vegetables from each type of distributor falling within each grade are shown in Table 9, which also shows the combined percentages of the two top grades and also of the two lower grades.

TABLE 9.—*Percentage distribution, by types of brand owners, of grades of canned vegetables and fruits*

Grades of canned vegetables and fruits	Manufacturers			Distributors			All groups combined
	National advertisers	Other	Total	Wholesalers	Chains	Cooperatives	
Fancy	24.2	15.0	20.8	21.8	20.6	15.5	20.5
Choice or extra standard	54.9	34.2	47.2	53.3	53.9	57.8	50.4
Standard	17.7	39.9	26.0	20.0	21.6	22.2	23.7
Substandard or seconds	1.6	9.3	4.5	4.0	3.9	3.4	4.2
No grade	1.6	1.6	1.5	.9		1.1	1.2
Two upper grades combined	79.1	49.2	68.0	75.1	74.5	73.3	70.9
Standard and substandard combined	19.3	49.2	30.5	24.0	25.5	25.6	27.9
All grades combined	100.0	100.0	100.0	100.0	100.0	100.0	100.0

Slightly over 70 per cent of the canned fruits and vegetables obtained from all types of distributors were of the two highest grades. The nationally advertising manufacturers had the highest proportion of cans in the two top grades (79.1 per cent) followed by wholesalers (75.1 per cent), chains (74.5 per cent), cooperative chains (73.3 per cent), with the nonnationally advertising manufacturers last, their

[9] The scoring range for fruits of "choice" grade is 80-89 except for fruits for salad, which are graded on the basis of the score of the component fruits. The scoring range for "extra standard" vegetables is 75 to 89 except for spinach and pumpkin for which vegetables there is no extra standard grade.

proportion (49.2 per cent) being materially below that for all groups combined.

In respect to "fancy" grade canned fruits and vegetables combined the chains ranked third, the proportion of cans of this type of distributor in this grade being 20.6 per cent as compared with an average percentage of 20.5 per cent for all types of brand owners. The nationally advertising manufacturers with 24.2 per cent grading "fancy" had the highest percentage, followed by the wholesalers with 21.8 per cent, chains with 20.6, the cooperative chains with 15.5, and the other manufacturers with 15.0 per cent.

The nonnationally advertising manufacturers had the largest proportion (39.9 per cent) of canned fruits and vegetables combined grading "standard," the other types of brand owners being well below the average for all groups combined, 23.7 per cent.

The nationally advertising manufacturers had but 1.6 per cent of their cans with a grade of "substandard" or "seconds," the cooperative chains 3.4 per cent, the chains 3.9 per cent, and the wholesalers 4 per cent. The average for all types was 4.2 per cent. Nonnationally advertising manufacturers with 9.3 per cent had the largest proportion of cans falling within these, the lowest grades of edible canned vegetables and fruits, respectively. The nationally advertising manufacturers show the best results when the two highest grades combined or the two lowest grades combined are considered whereas the brands of other manufacturers make the poorest showing in these same combinations of grades.

Section 3. Official scores of canned vegetables and canned fruits.

Appendix Table 6 shows the official grades, the range of official scores, and the average official score of the combined samples of canned vegetables purchased in the three cities, by kinds of owner of the brands. Corresponding information for canned fruits is shown in Appendix Table 7.

Analysis of the actual numerical grades permits more exact comparisons than are possible in the preceding data of the number of cans of a given type of brand owner falling in a certain grade. For example, two types of brand owners might show approximately equal proportions of their respective totals as grading "fancy," but within this general grade there might be a variation of several points in the actual average scores.

In this comparison "substandard" vegetables and "seconds" of fruits are omitted since no numerical values were assigned to some of the samples which fell in this grade.

Average scores using all products having uniform ranges in grading.—The average scores, by kinds of distributors and for the three grades of canned vegetables and of canned fruits are shown in Table 10 for all products on which the scoring range was the same within a grade.

The average scores in this table are the simple averages of all the individual scores within the given grades on all products which have uniform ranges of scores within these grades. Because of this qualification spinach and pumpkin are excluded from the canned vegetables, and grapefruit and fruits for salad from the canned fruits. In this analysis no attempt is made to limit the comparison to those products of which samples were secured from each type of brand owner. The aim, rather, is to present the data of Tables 1 and 4 in somewhat greater refinement. In those tables the samples were segregated into broad groups of the four general grades; here the average score is presented for each grade (except "substandard" and "seconds") to permit more exact scrutiny of the results.

TABLE 10.—*Average scores, by grades of canned vegetables and canned fruits, for specified brand-owning groups (all samples secured)* [1]

Grades of—	Manufacturers	Distributors		
		Wholesalers	Chains	Cooperatives
Canned vegetables:				
Fancy	91.1	91.3	91.4	93.0
Extra standard	82.9	83.5	82.3	81.2
Standard	72.2	74.3	70.9	73.0
3 grades combined	79.1	79.7	79.6	80.0
Canned fruits:				
Fancy	91.1	91.7	91.2	91.5
Choice	85.5	85.6	86.7	85.6
Standard	76.4	74.3	75.5	75.1
3 grades combined	84.7	85.6	86.6	84.2

[1] All samples secured on products having uniform scoring ranges in grades. Spinach and pumpkin excluded from vegetables, and grapefruit and fruits for salad from fruits.

Of the canned vegetables graded "fancy" the cooperatives show an average score almost two points per cent higher than that of manufacturers which in itself is only slightly below the averages for wholesalers and chains. For "fancy" fruits the wholesalers are the highest (91.7); cooperatives are second, 91.5, chains third, 91.2 and manufacturers again the lowest.

Wholesalers show the best average score for "extra standard" vegetables (83.5) while chains lead in "choice" fruits (86.7). In the "standard" grade the wholesalers again lead in vegetables with 74.3, while the manufacturers with 76.4 show the best average score in fruits. Chains are the lowest (70.9) for "standard" grade vegetables, but next to the highest (75.5) for fruits of standard grade.

Combining all the scores for all the samples included in this comparison the chains are in third place (79.6) for vegetables but show the highest average (86.6) for fruits. Cooperatives show the high average (80) for vegetables, but the low (84.2) for fruits.

While no extensive variations would be expected, because of the grade limits, the general uniformity tends to indicate, that based on these data, chains compare favorably with other distributors in the quality of their canned vegetables and fruits.

Average scores using only products represented for each type of brand owner.—In the preceding comparison all products were used on which there is a uniform range in grading. In it, there are a number of instances where one or more types of brand owners are not represented in the sample.

Although improbable, it still is possible that certain specific commodities tend to average lower scores within a grade than do other commodities. The inclusion of such a commodity, should the entire sample of it have been obtained from a single type of brand owner, might materially lower the average score of that type. In the same way, omission of such a commodity from a particular type of brand owner might inflate the average of that type in comparison with the other types. To test these possibilities, and to minimize this potential bias Table 11 shows average grades by brand owners based solely on those individual products of which one or more samples, falling in the particular grade, were secured from each type of brand owner. The basic figures are those in Appendix Tables 6 and 7 where data are shown under a specified grade for all four types of brand owners as indicated by footnote 2 in Table 6 and footnote 3 in Table 7.

TABLE 11.—*Average scores, by grades of canned vegetables and canned fruits, for specified brand-owning groups (including only those products in which all groups had representation in the given grade)*

Grades of—	Manufacturers	Distributors		
		Wholesalers	Chains	Cooperatives
Canned vegetables:				
Fancy (1 product)	90.5	92.0	92.3	94.0
Extra standard (4 products)	82.7	83.4	81.3	81.2
Standard (4 products)	72.2	74.3	70.9	73.0
3 grades combined	77.1	79.4	77.7	79.6
Canned fruits:				
Fancy (4 products)	91.1	91.8	91.1	91.6
Choice (7 products)	85.6	85.6	86.7	85.5
Standard (1 product)	75.0	68.0	75.0	79.0
3 grades combined	86.2	86.6	87.2	86.4

The ranges between the average scores of each type of distributor are wider for canned vegetables of "fancy" and "extra standard" grades than is the case with the two top grades of canned fruits. In canned vegetables grading "fancy" the average score of the chain brands was 92.3, the range being from 90.5 for the manufacturers' brands to 94 for the cooperatives. The cooperatives had the lowest average score of canned vegetables of "extra standard" grade (81.2) the other extreme of the range for this grade being 83.4 for wholesalers' brands. The range of the average scores for "standard" grade brands of canned vegetables was from 70.9 for chain brands to 74.3 for wholesalers' brands.

In the case of canned fruits as appears from the table the differences between brand owners in respect to average scores in both "fancy" and "choice" grades are slight. The wholesalers' brands with 91.8 had the highest average score in the "fancy" grade while the lowest, 91.1, was for the brands of both manufacturers and chains. The range was nearly as small for "choice" grade, 86.7 for the chains and 85.5 for the cooperatives. In the "standard" grade, however, a wider range appears, 79 being the average for the cooperatives and 68 for the wholesalers; chains and manufacturers each showing an average of 75.

From these average scores it seems that the average quality of the private brands of canned fruits of chains compares favorably with those of other types of distributors. To put it another way, there is little to choose between the brands of canned fruits of "fancy" and "choice" grades put out by the four kinds of distributors, but in the "standard" grade where the range of average scores is widest, the chains tie with manufacturers for second highest and thus compare favorably with those of the other three types of brand owners. In no grade of canned vegetables is the average score of the chains the highest of the four kinds of distributors, it being second in "fancy" grade, the third in "extra standard" grade, and lowest in "standard" grade. The breadth of the ranges of the average scores in grades of canned vegetables and the location of the average scores of the chains within these ranges, lead to the conclusion that the chains do not show up so well in canned vegetables in comparison with the other types of distributors as they do in the case of canned fruits.

Section 4. Variations in grades.

The influence of the number of samples purchased of the various brands of canned vegetables and canned fruits is illustrated by Tables 12 and 13, which show for the four types of distributors the tendency for the items tested to vary in grade as the number of samples purchased increases. These tables are based upon Appendix Tables 1, 2, and 3.

TABLE 12.—*Distribution, according to uniformity of grades, of samples of canned vegetables [1] of various types of brand owners*

Samples per brand and brand owner	Number of cans graded showing—											
	No variation in grades					Variations in grades						All cans graded
	Fancy	Extra standard	Standard	Substandard	Total	Fancy	Extra standard	Standard	Substandard	No grade	Total	
Single sample (2 cans):												
Manufacturer	12	[2] 26	44	8	[2] 90		2	4	3	1	10	[2] 100
Wholesaler		22	10		32		3	3			6	38
Chain	4	10	14	2	30	1	3		2		6	36
Cooperative	2	10	4		16	1	3	2			6	22
Total	18	[2] 68	72	10	[2] 168	2	11	9	5	1	28	[2] 196
2 samples (4 cans):												
Manufacturer						6	8	7	2		23	23
Wholesaler			4		4	3	5	3	1		12	16
Chain		4			4	2	4	2			8	12
Cooperative							2	2			4	4
Total		4	4		8	11	19	14	3		17	55
3 or more samples:												
Manufacturer						7	16	19	3	1	46	46
Wholesaler			[3] 5		5		2	4			6	11
Total			5		5	7	18	23	3	1	52	57
All samples combined:												
Manufacturer	12	[2] 26	44	8	[2] 90	13	26	30	8	2	79	[2] 169
Wholesaler		22	19		41	3	10	10	1		24	65
Chain	4	14	14	2	34	3	7	2	2		14	48
Cooperative	2	10	4		16	1	5	4			10	26
Total	18	[2] 72	81	10	[2] 181	20	48	46	11	2	127	[2] 308

[1] Spinach and pumpkin not included.
[2] 3 single-can samples excluded.
[3] 1 sample contained only 1 can, but is included with other 4 cans of same brand.

TABLE 13.—*Distribution, according to uniformity of grades, of samples of canned fruits of various types of brand owners*

Samples per brand and brand owner	Number of cans graded showing—											All cans graded
	No variation in grades					Variations in grades						
	Fancy	Choice	Standard	Seconds	Total	Fancy	Choice	Standard	Seconds	No grade	Total	
Single sample (2 cans):												
Manufacturer	16	[1] 50	32	4	[1] 102	3	8	4	1	4	20	[1] 122
Wholesaler	16	32	4	8	60	2	2	------	------	------	4	64
Chain	8	22	2	------	32	------	------	------	------	------	------	32
Cooperative	6	14	8	2	30	2	3	1	1	1	8	38
Total	46	[1] 118	46	14	[1] 224	7	13	5	2	5	32	[1] 256
2 samples (4 cans):												
Manufacturer	4	12	8	------	24	5	16	9	2	------	32	56
Wholesaler	4	16	------	------	20	6	20	12	------	2	40	60
Chain	------	4	4	------	8	5	3	------	------	------	8	16
Cooperative	------	4	------	------	4	3	10	3	------	------	16	20
Total	8	36	12	------	56	19	49	24	2	2	96	152
3 or more samples:												
Manufacturer	6	6	------	------	12	48	95	7	------	2	152	164
Wholesaler	------	------	------	------	------	18	18	------	------	------	36	36
Chain	------	------	------	------	------	1	5	------	------	------	6	6
Cooperative	------	6	------	------	6	------	------	------	------	------	------	6
Total	6	12	------	------	18	67	118	7	------	2	194	212
All samples combined:												
Manufacturer	26	[1] 68	40	4	[1] 138	56	119	20	3	6	204	[1] 342
Wholesaler	20	48	4	8	80	26	40	12	------	2	80	160
Chain	8	26	6	------	40	6	8	------	------	------	14	54
Cooperative	6	24	8	2	40	5	13	4	1	1	24	64
Total	60	[1] 166	58	14	[1] 298	93	180	36	4	9	322	[1] 620

[1] 1 single can sample excluded.

Tables 14 and 15 show, respectively, for vegetables and fruits the proportional uniformity of the grades of the several types of brand owners, both as a whole and according to the number of samples secured of a particular brand. In general there is evident a marked tendency for variation in grades to occur with an increase in the number of samples graded. Thus, as shown in Table 14, of the single samples (2 cans) the proportions of cans showing no variation range from 72.7 for cooperatives to 90 per cent for manufacturers. In contrast, in the two sample (4 can) brands, none of the brands of manufacturers and of cooperatives, and only one-fourth and one-third, respectively, of the brands of wholesalers and chains were uniform in grade. Three or more samples of a single brand of vegetables were secured only in manufacturers' and wholesalers' brands. There were grade variations in all of the manufacturers' brands and in more than half of those of wholesalers.

Recognizing the tendency toward greater variation with increasing numbers of samples graded, it still seems that on the whole the chains' standing is not unfavorable. For all samples combined, on the available data, more than 70 per cent of the chain samples of canned vegetables showed no variation in grades, while only 53.2 per cent of those of manufacturers, 61.5 per cent of cooperatives', and 63.1 per cent of wholesalers' were in this category.

TABLE 14.—*Percentage distribution, according to uniformity of grades, of samples of canned vegetables of various types of brand owners*

Samples per brand and brand owner	Percentage of number of cans graded showing—											All cans graded
	No variation in grades					Variations in grades						
	Fancy	Extra standard	Standard	Substandard	Total	Fancy	Extra standard	Standard	Substandard	No grade	Total	
Single sample (2 cans):												
Manufacturer	12.0	26.0	44.0	8.0	90.0	-------	2.0	4.0	3.0	1.0	10.0	100.0
Wholesaler	-------	57.9	26.3	-------	84.2	-------	7.9	7.9	-------	------	15.8	100.0
Chain	11.1	27.7	38.9	5.6	83.3	2.8	8.3	-------	5.6	------	16.7	100.0
Cooperative	9.1	45.4	18.2	-------	72.7	4.6	13.6	9.1	-------	------	27.3	100.0
Total	9.2	34.7	36.7	5.1	85.7	1.0	5.6	4.6	2.6	.5	14.3	100.0
2 samples (4 cans):												
Manufacturer	-------	-------	-------	-------	-------	26.1	34.8	30.4	8.7	------	100.0	100.0
Wholesaler	-------	-------	25.0	-------	25.0	18.8	31.2	18.8	6.2	------	75.0	100.0
Chain	-------	33.3	-------	-------	33.3	16.7	33.3	16.7	-------	------	66.7	100.0
Cooperative	-------	-------	-------	-------	-------	-------	50.0	50.0	-------	------	100.0	100.0
Total	-------	7.3	7.3	-------	14.6	20.0	34.5	25.5	5.4	------	85.4	100.0
3 or more samples:												
Manufacturer	-------	-------	-------	-------	-------	15.2	34.8	41.3	6.5	2.2	100.0	100.0
Wholesaler	-------	-------	45.4	-------	45.4	-------	18.2	36.4	-------	------	54.6	100.0
Total	-------	-------	8.8	-------	8.8	12.3	31.6	40.3	5.3	1.7	91.2	100.0
All samples combined:												
Manufacturer	7.1	15.4	26.0	4.7	53.2	7.7	15.4	17.8	4.7	1.2	46.8	100.0
Wholesaler	-------	33.9	29.2	-------	63.1	4.6	15.4	15.4	1.5	------	36.9	100.0
Chain	8.3	29.2	29.2	4.1	70.8	6.3	14.7	4.1	4.1	------	29.2	100.0
Cooperative	7.6	38.5	15.4	-------	61.5	3.9	19.2	15.4	-------	------	38.5	100.0
Total	5.8	23.4	26.3	3.3	58.8	6.5	15.6	14.9	3.6	.6	41.2	100.0

As regards canned fruits, as shown in Table 15, the chains also make a distinctly favorable showing. All of their single sample (2-can) brands graded were uniform in grade within the sample; as compared with 93.7 per cent for wholesalers, 83.6 per cent for manufacturers, and 79.0 per cent for cooperatives.

Of the two sample (4-can) brands graded, one-half of the chains', 42.8 per cent of the manufacturers', one-third of the wholesalers', and only one-fifth of the cooperatives' brands were uniform in grade.

Taking the combined results, nearly three-fourths (74.1 per cent) of the chains', less than two-thirds (62.5 per cent) of the cooperatives', one-half of the wholesalers', and only four-tenths (40.4 per cent) of the manufacturers' brands graded were free from variation in grades within each sample graded.

TABLE 15.—*Percentage distribution, according to uniformity of grades, of samples of canned fruits of various types of brand owners*

Samples per brand and brand owner	Percentage of cans graded showing—											All cans graded
	No variations in grades					Variations in grades					Total	
	Fancy	Choice	Standard	Seconds	Total	Fancy	Choice	Standard	Seconds	No grade		
Single sample (2 cans):												
Manufacturer	13.1	41.0	26.2	3.3	83.6	2.5	6.5	3.3	0.8	3.3	16.4	100.0
Wholesaler	25.0	50.0	6.2	12.5	93.7	3.1	3.1	------	------	------	6.2	[1] 99.9
Chain	25.0	68.8	6.2	------	100.0	------	------	------	------	------	------	100.0
Cooperative	15.8	36.9	21.0	5.3	79.0	5.3	7.9	2.6	2.6	2.6	21.0	100.0
Total	18.0	46.1	18.0	5.4	87.5	2.7	5.0	2.0	.8	2.0	12.5	100.0
2 samples (4 cans):												
Manufacturer	7.1	21.4	14.3	------	42.8	8.9	28.6	16.1	3.6	------	57.2	100.0
Wholesaler	6.7	26.6	------	------	33.3	10.0	33.3	20.0	------	3.3	66.6	[1] 99.9
Chain	------	25.0	25.0	------	50.0	31.3	18.7	------	------	------	50.0	100.0
Cooperative	------	20.0	------	------	20.0	15.0	50.0	15.0	------	------	80.0	100.0
Total	5.3	23.7	7.9	------	36.9	12.5	32.2	15.8	1.3	1.3	63.1	100.0
3 or more samples:												
Manufacturer	3.7	3.7	------	------	7.4	29.2	57.9	4.3	------	1.2	92.6	100.0
Wholesaler	------	------	------	------	------	50.0	50.0	------	------	------	100.0	100.0
Chain	------	------	------	------	------	16.7	83.3	------	------	------	100.0	100.0
Cooperative	------	100.0	------	------	100.0	------	------	------	------	------	------	100.0
Total	2.8	5.7	------	------	8.5	31.6	55.7	3.3	------	.9	91.5	100.0
All samples combined:												
Manufacturer	7.6	19.9	11.7	1.2	40.4	16.4	34.8	5.8	.9	1.7	59.6	100.0
Wholesaler	12.5	30.0	2.5	5.0	50.0	16.2	25.0	7.5	------	1.3	50.0	100.0
Chain	14.8	48.2	11.1	------	74.1	11.1	14.8	------	------	------	25.9	100.0
Cooperative	9.4	37.5	12.5	3.1	62.5	7.8	20.3	6.2	1.6	1.6	37.5	100.0
Total	9.7	26.8	9.3	2.3	48.1	15.0	29.0	5.8	.6	1.5	51.9	100.0

[1] Adjusted to 99.9 per cent.

Tables 14 and 15 also show the detail of the distribution of brand samples which graded uniformly, together with the proportions of graded cans which showed variations within a sample. These figures should be considered in relation to Tables 3 and 6 if the relative showing on brand uniformity by grades is sought. For example, taking "fancy" vegetables the proportions of the respective totals graded were (Table 3): Manufacturer, 14.5 per cent; wholesaler, 4.6 per cent; chains, 14.6 per cent; and cooperatives, 11.5, while corresponding proportions of the totals graded "fancy" which showed no variations in grade were manufacturer, 7.1 per cent; wholesaler, none; chain, 8.3 per cent; and cooperative, 7.6 per cent.

Somewhat similar results appear in comparing the percentages of Table 15 with those of Table 6. On the whole there seems to be a greater tendency toward uniformity of grade in "choice" than in "fancy" fruits, which also holds to a considerable extent for the corresponding grades of canned vegetables.

APPENDIX

TABLE 1.—*Grades of canned vegetables and fruits, selected brands, based on samples purchased in Des Moines, Iowa, in July, 1930*

A. VEGETABLES

General information				Facts found on official grading						
Brand	Size of can	Owner of brand	Sample bought from—	Identity of can	Score	Grade [1]	Net weight stated on label	Net weight found	Solids	Liquids
TOMATOES							*Ounces*	*Ounces*	*Ounces*	*Ounces*
110-A	2	Manufacturer	Regular chain	A	79	Standard	19	19.95	11.36	8.59
				B	81	Extra standard	19	19.95	11.66	8.29
147	2	do	Independent dealer	A	66	Substandard	19	19.95	9.66	10.29
				B	74	Standard	19	19.70	10.86	8.84
102	2	do	do	A	69	Substandard	19	20.20	9.66	10.54
				B	70	Standard	19	20.20	10.58	9.62
285-B	2	Wholesaler	Wholesaler	A	85	Extra standard	19	20.20	13.36	6.84
				B	89	do	19	20.45	13.16	7.29
285-C	2	do	do	A	77	Standard	19	20.70	10.86	9.84
				B	82	Extra standard	19	20.20	13.04	7.16
301-C	2	Regular chain	Regular chain	A	76	Standard	19	20.20	13.64	6.56
				B	71	do	19	20.45	13.64	6.81
327-B	2	do	do	A	65	Substandard	19	18.95	8.76	10.19
				B	79	Extra standard	19	19.95	11.96	7.99
401-A	2	Cooperative	Cooperative	A	91	Fancy	19	20.20	14.16	6.04
				B	87	Extra standard	19	20.20	14.16	6.04
401-B	2	do	do	A	81	do	19	20.45	12.16	8.29
				B	77	Standard	19	20.45	10.86	9.59
434-A	2	do	do	A	76	Extra standard	19	19.95	11.64	8.31
				B	71	Standard	19	19.45	10.86	8.59
GREEN BEANS, WHOLE										
145	2	Manufacturer	Regular chain	A	91	Fancy	19	20.45	11.50	8.95
				B	90	do	19	20.70	13.25	7.45
110-A	2	do	do	A	86	Extra standard	19	19.70	12.00	7.70
				B	85	do	19	19.95	12.00	7.95
285-C	2	Wholesaler	Wholesaler	A	85	do	19	20.45	10.75	9.70
				B	87	do	19	20.20	11.75	8.45
271-A	2	do	do	A	74	Standard	19	19.95	11.00	8.95
				B	81	Extra standard	19	20.95	10.75	10.20
434-A	2	Cooperative	Cooperative	A	94	Fancy	20	20.20	12.20	8.00
				B	94	do	20	20.45	12.75	7.70

GREEN BEANS, CUT										
138	2	Manufacturer	Regular chain	A	69	Standard	19	20.70	12.25	8.45
				B	69	do	19	20.70	12.00	8.70
168	2	do	Independent dealer	A	64	do	19	20.45	15.50	4.95
				B	63	do	19	20.45	13.75	6.70
285-C	2	Wholesaler	Wholesaler	A	71	do	19	20.20	13.00	7.20
				B	71	do	19	20.20	12.75	7.45
285-B	2	do	do	A	69	do	20	20.20	12.75	7.45
				B	69	do	20	20.20	12.75	7.45
327-B	2	Regular chain	Regular chain	A	84	Extra standard	19	20.45	12.25	8.20
				B	85	do	19	20.20	12.75	7.45
301-C	2	do	do	A	65	Standard	19	19.95	10.25	9.70
				B	65	do	19	20.20	10.50	9.70
401-B	2	Cooperative	Cooperative	A	77	Extra standard	19	20.70	12.75	7.95
				B	77	do	19	20.45	12.50	7.95
401-C	2	do	do	A	64	Standard	19	19.70	13.25	6.45
				B	64	do	19	19.95	12.25	7.70
SWEET CORN, CREAM STYLE										
110-A	2	Manufacturer	Regular chain	A	92	Fancy	20	20.55	20.55	
				B	91	do	20	20.75	20.75	
110-A	2	do	Wholesaler	A	87	Extra standard	20	21.25	21.25	
				B	85	do	20	21.50	21.50	
110-A	2	do	Regular chain	A		None [2]	20	21.50	21.50	
				B	79	Standard	20	21.50	21.50	
167-A	2	do	Wholesaler	A	84	do	20	21.25	21.25	
				B	87	Extra standard	20	21.50	21.50	
167-A	2	do	do	A	79	Substandard	20	21.25	21.25	
				B	79	do	20	20.75	20.75	
102	2	do	Independent dealer	A	74	Standard	20	21.00	21.00	
				B	70	do	20	20.50	20.50	
139	2	do	do	A	70	do	20	21.00	21.00	
				B	70	do	20	21.00	21.00	
122	2	do	Regular chain	A	69	do	20	20.50	20.50	
				B	68	do	20	21.25	21.25	
271-A	2	Wholesaler	Wholesaler	A	83	Extra standard	20	21.75	21.75	
				B	83	do	20	21.75	21.75	
285-C	2	do	do	A	82	do	20	20.95	20.95	
				B	81	do	20	20.70	20.70	
285-B	2	do	do	A	80	Standard	20	21.75	21.75	
				B	78	do	20	21.50	21.50	
285-D	2	do	do	A	76	do	20	21.50	21.50	
				B	78	do	20	21.75	21.75	
285-A	2	do	do	A	74	do	20	20.75	20.75	
				B	74	do	20	20.50	20.50	
285-A	2	do	do	A	72	do	20	21.25	21.25	
				B	71	do	20	21.25	21.25	

[1] For some of the items in this table the score shown seems to warrant a grade higher than that given, but in each of these cases the number of points scored under some factor was too low to permit the higher grade, regardless of the total score for the can.

[2] Not graded on account of foreign matter in can.

TABLE 1.—*Grades of canned vegetables and fruits, selected brands, based on samples purchased in Des Moines, Iowa, in July, 1930*—Continued

A. VEGETABLES—Continued

General information				Facts found on official grading						
Brand	Size of can	Owner of brand	Sample bought from—	Identity of can	Score	Grade [1]	Net weight stated on label	Net weight found	Solids	Liquids
SWEET CORN, CREAM STYLE—continued							Ounces	Ounces	Ounces	Ounces
285-A	2	Wholesaler	Wholesaler	A [2]	74	Standard	20	21.25	21.25	-----
327-C	2	Regular chain	Regular chain	A	91	Fancy	20	20.25	20.25	-----
				B	91	do	20	20.50	20.50	-----
327-B	2	do	do	A	89	Extra standard	20	21.00	21.00	-----
				B	84	do	20	20.75	20.75	-----
327-A	2	do	do	A	70	Standard	20	20.75	20.75	-----
				B	70	do	20	20.75	20.75	-----
401-B	2	Cooperative	Cooperative	A	87	Extra standard	20	21.00	21.00	-----
				B	87	do	20	21.50	21.50	-----
401-A	2	do	do	A	80	do	20	22.00	22.00	-----
				B	79	do	20	21.00	21.00	-----
434-A	2	do	do	A	81	Standard	20	21.00	21.00	-----
				B	81	do	20	21.25	21.25	-----
PEAS										
145	2	Manufacturer	Regular chain	A	92	Fancy	20	20.95	13.16	7.79
				B	92	do	20	20.95	12.86	8.09
130	2	do	Independent dealer	A	68	Standard	20	21.20	14.36	6.84
				B	67	do	20	21.70	14.06	7.64
285-C	2	Wholesaler	Wholesaler	A	88	Extra standard	20	21.20	14.16	7.04
				B	88	do	20	21.20	13.36	7.84
285-A	2	do	do	A	87	do	20	21.20	13.16	8.04
				B	85	do	20	21.20	13.16	8.04
285-B	2	do	do	A	79	do	20	21.45	14.16	7.29
				B	79	do	20	21.20	14.16	7.04
327-A	2	Regular chain	Regular chain	A	77	do	20	20.95	13.56	7.39
				B	78	do	20	20.95	13.86	7.09
327-B	2	do	do	A	74	Standard	20	20.95	13.06	7.89
				B	74	do	20	20.95	12.86	8.09
327-D	2	do	do	A	71	do	20	20.95	13.86	7.09
				B	71	do	20	20.95	14.06	6.89
301-C	2	do	do	A	74	do	20	21.70	14.26	7.44
				B	72	do	20	21.45	14.36	7.09
401-B	2	Cooperative	Cooperative	A	84	Extra standard	20	20.70	12.96	7.74
				B	83	do	20	20.95	13.36	7.59

401-A	2	do	do	A	82	do	20	20.45	13.04	7.41
				B	81	do	20	20.45	12.76	7.69
434-A	2	do	do	A	73	Standard	20	21.45	13.56	7.89
				B	73	do	20	21.45	13.86	7.59
SPINACH [4]										
110-A	2	Manufacturer	Regular chain	A	86	Fancy	19	18.95	12.96	5.99
				B	77	Standard	19	19.45	12.66	6.79
110-A	2½	do	do	A	81	do	27	28.95	19.16	9.79
				B	81	do	27	29.45	18.36	11.09
285-C	2½	Wholesaler	Wholesaler	A	89	Fancy	27	29.45	19.36	10.09
				B	89	do	27	28.95	16.86	12.09
285-C	2	do	do	A	73	Standard	19	20.20	12.96	7.24
				B	73	do	19	19.70	10.86	8.84
285-A	2	do	do	A	82	do	19	19.45	12.76	6.69
				B	80	do	19	19.45	12.72	6.73
285-A	2½	do	do	A	83	Substandard	27	29.70	18.36	11.34
				B	81	do	27	29.70	20.16	9.54
271-A	2½	do	do	A	82	Standard	27	28.70	17.26	11.44
				B	80	do	27	28.20	20.86	7.34
327-A	2½	Regular chain	Regular chain	A	75	do	27	27.45	20.16	7.29
				B	75	do	27	28.20	16.16	12.04
401-A	2½	Cooperative	Cooperative	A	87	Fancy	27	28.70	18.66	10.04
				B	87	do	27	28.70	22.96	5.74
401-A	2	do	do	A	86	do	19	18.45	13.16	5.29
				B	85	do	19	18.45	13.56	4.89
434-A	2½	do	do	A	89	do	27	28.20	19.46	8.74
				B	89	do	27	27.45	19.46	7.99
434-A	2	do	do	A	78	Standard	19	18.95	12.16	6.79
				B	78	do	19	18.70	13.06	5.64
PUMPKIN										
110-A	2	Manufacturer	Regular chain	A	89	Fancy	19	20.50	20.50	
				B	88	do	19	20.25	20.25	
178	2	do	Independent dealer	A	87	do	20	21.00	21.00	
				B	87	do	20	21.00	21.00	
176	2	do	Regular chain	A	73	Standard	19	20.75	20.75	
				B	72	do	19	20.75	20.75	
285-C	2	Wholesaler	Wholesaler	A	80	do	20	21.00	21.00	
				B	71	do	20	21.50	21.50	
327-B	2	Regular chain	Regular chain	A	74	do	19	20.75	20.75	
				B	77	do	19	21.25	21.25	
401-A	2	Cooperative	Cooperative	A	88	Fancy	20	21.00	21.00	
				B	88	do	20	20.75	20.75	
401-B	2	do	do	A	76	Standard	19	19.00	19.00	
				B	72	do	19	19.75	19.75	
434-A	2	do	do	A	89	Fancy	20	20.75	20.75	
				B	87	do	20	21.00	21.00	

[1] See note 1, page 19.
[3] Only 1 can purchased.
[4] No "extra standard" grade for spinach and pumpkin in U. S. D. A. grading standards.

TABLE 1.—*Grades of canned vegetables and fruits, selected brands, based on samples purchased in Des Moines, Iowa, in July, 1930*—Continued

B. FRUITS

General information				Facts found on official grading						
Brand	Size of can	Owner of brand	Sample bought from—	Identity of can	Score	Grade [1]	Net weight stated on label	Net weight found	Solids	Liquids
PEACHES, Y. C., HALVED							*Ounces*	*Ounces*	*Ounces*	*Ounces*
110-A	2½	Manufacturer	Wholesaler	A	89	Choice	30	30.20	19.90	10.30
				B	92	do	30	30.45	21.10	9.35
110-A	2½	do	do	A	88	do	30	30.20	20.20	10.00
				B	80	do	30	23.95	16.30	7.65
110-A	1-T	do	do	A	86	do	16	17.10	10.40	6.70
				B	83	do	16	17.35	11.10	6.25
153-A	2½	do	Independent dealer	A	83	do	28	29.95	20.80	9.15
				B	82	do	28	30.45	19.40	11.05
136	1-T	do	Regular chain	A	78	Standard	15	16.60	12.20	4.40
				B	75	do	15	16.60	12.90	3.70
285-C	2½	Wholesaler	Wholesaler	A	91	Fancy	30	30.70	18.30	12.40
				B	91	do	30	31.20	21.00	10.20
285-B	2½	do	do	A	86	Choice	30	29.95	22.00	7.95
				B	84	do	30	30.20	22.00	8.20
285-E	2½	do	do	A	83	do	30	30.20	19.00	11.20
				B	83	do	30	31.20	19.80	11.40
271-A	2½	do	do	A	92	Fancy	30	30.70	21.00	9.70
				B	89	Choice	30	30.70	18.90	11.80
271-B	1-T	do	do	A	87	do	15	17.35	10.70	6.65
				B	86	do	15	16.60	10.90	5.70
271-B	2½	do	do	A	74	Standard	30	29.95	20.86	9.09
				B	90	Choice	30	30.45	20.35	10.10
327-C	2½	Regular chain	Regular chain	A	92	Fancy	30	31.95	21.40	10.55
				B	92	do	30	31.20	21.20	10.00
327-B	2½	do	do	A	90	do	30	31.45	21.30	10.15
				B	92	do	30	31.45	21.80	9.65
401-A	1-T	Cooperative	Ccoperative	A	89	Choice	16	17.35	12.30	5.05
				B	89	do	16	17.35	10.80	6.55
401-A	2½	do	do	A	87	do	28	31.45	20.36	11.09
				B	88	do	28	31.95	19.70	12.25
401-B	2½	do	do	A	84	do	28	30.95	20.50	10.45
				B	86	do	28	31.20	19.80	11.40
434-A	2½	do	do	A	84	do	30	31.20	18.10	13.10
				B	84	do	30	31.20	18.00	13.20

PEACHES, Y. C., SLICED										
110-A	2½	Manufacturer	Wholesaler	A	87	do	30	28.70	21.66	7.04
				B	89	do	30	30.45	20.81	9.64
110-A	1-T	do	do	A	89	do	16	17.10	11.30	5.80
				B	87	do	16	16.60	11.00	5.60
146-B	2½	do	Regular chain	A	85	do	29	29.45	22.00	7.45
				B	80	do	29	30.45	21.80	8.65
106	2½	do	do	A	70	Standard	30	30.45	17.70	12.75
				B	73	do	30	31.20	17.90	13.30
271-A	2½	Wholesaler	Wholesaler	A	90	Fancy	30	30.45	19.26	11.19
				B	93	do	30	31.20	18.66	12.54
271-B	1-T	do	do	A	84	Choice	15	18.60	10.15	8.45
				B	80	do	15	17.85	11.76	6.09
271-B	2½	do	do	A	72	Standard	30	31.20	19.70	11.50
				B	84	Choice	30	30.95	19.90	11.05
285-C	2½	do	do	A	87	do	30	30.95	20.10	10.85
				B	87	do	30	31.45	19.90	11.55
285-C	1-T	do	do	A	74	Standard	15	17.10	10.80	6.30
				B	73	do	15	17.35	11.60	5.75
285-B	2½	do	do	A	82	do	30	29.70	20.50	9.20
				B	84	Choice	30	30.45	18.30	12.15
285-B	1-T	do	do	A	72	Standard	15	17.10	11.60	5.50
				B	73	do	15	17.10	12.00	5.10
285-E	2½	do	do	A	68	Seconds	30	28.95	21.80	7.15
				B	64	do	30	29.20	22.70	6.50
401-A	2½	Cooperative	Cooperative	A	92	Fancy	28	31.20	17.40	13.80
				B	94	do	28	31.20	15.70	15.50
401-A	1-T	do	do	A	83	Choice	16	17.35	11.60	5.75
				B	83	do	16	17.35	11.60	5.75
434-A	2½	do	do	A	89	do	30	31.45	18.50	12.95
				B	89	do	30	31.45	19.30	12.15
APRICOTS, PEELED										
166	2½	Manufacturer	Regular chain	A	78	Standard	29	30.20	18.70	11.50
				B	76	do	29	30.45	19.30	11.15
271-A	2½	Wholesaler	Wholesaler	A	92	Fancy	30	31.45	20.20	11.25
				B	90	do	30	31.70	21.20	10.50
401-A	2½	Cooperative	Cooperative	A	90	Choice	29	31.45	18.40	13.05
				B	87	do	29	30.95	20.00	10.95
APRICOTS, UNPEELED										
163-A	1-T	Manufacturer	Regular chain	A	90	Fancy	17	17.35	9.80	7.55
				B	86	Choice	17	18.10	11.00	7.10
110-A	2½	do	Wholesaler	A	88	do	30	31.45	[5] 14.50	[5] 16.95
				B	87	do	30	30.70	17.00	13.70
110-A	1-T	do	do	A	87	do	16	17.35	9.30	8.05
				B	86	do	16	17.60	10.00	7.60
110-C	2½	do	do	A	78	Standard	29	31.20	16.60	14.60
				B	78	do	29	31.20	16.40	14.80

[1] See note 1, page 19.

[5] These weights look as if they had been reversed, but the field notes made at the time of grading show the "drained weight" as 14.502. Weight of the syrup was computed later by subtraction.

TABLE 1.—*Grades of canned vegetables and fruits, selected brands, based on samples purchased in Des Moines, Iowa, in July, 1930*—Continued

B. FRUITS—Continued

General information				Facts found on official grading						
Brand	Size of can	Owner of brand	Sample bought from—	Identity of can	Score	Grade [1]	Net weight stated on label	Net weight found	Solids	Liquids
							Ounces	*Ounces*	*Ounces*	*Ounces*
APRICOTS, UNPEELED—contd.										
146-B	1-T	Manufacturer	Regular chain	A	70	Seconds	16	16.85	10.30	6.55
				B	77	do	16	16.85	9.10	7.75
285-C	1-T	Wholesaler	Wholesaler	A	88	Choice	15	17.60	10.60	7.00
				B	88	do	15	17.85	9.80	8.05
285-E	2½	do	do	A	68	Seconds	30	30.20	18.20	12.00
				B	68	do	30	30.20	17.50	12.70
271-B	1-T	do	do	A	81	do	15	17.25	12.80	4.45
				B	77	do	15	17.10	10.30	6.80
327-B	2½	Regular chain	Regular chain	A	88	Choice	30	31.20	18.20	13.00
				B	88	do	30	31.20	17.80	13.40
434-A	2½	Cooperative	Cooperative	A	85	do	30	31.70	17.10	14.60
				B	86	do	30	31.95	[6] 17.35	[6] 14.60
401-A	1-T	do	do	A	85	do	15	17.60	12.60	5.00
				B	82	do	15	18.10	12.30	5.80
PEARS										
110-A	2½	Manufacturer	Wholesaler	A	87	do	30	31.20	19.10	12.10
				B	85	do	30	30.70	19.10	11.60
110-A	2	do	Regular chain	A	86	do	20	20.20	13.10	7.10
				B	88	do	20	20.20	12.50	7.70
110-A	1-T	do	Wholesaler	A	85	do	16	17.10	10.30	6.80
				B	85	do	16	17.10	11.40	5.70
105	1-T	do	Regular chain	A	83	do	15	17.10	11.10	6.00
				B	85	do	15	17.10	11.10	6.00
111	2½	do	Independent dealer	A	67	Seconds	30	31.20	17.50	13.70
				B	77	Standard	30	30.20	20.80	9.40
271-A	2½	Wholesaler	Wholesaler	A	94	Fancy	30	30.95	18.20	12.75
				B	92	do	30	30.95	18.00	12.95
271-A	1-T	do	do	A	93	do	15	17.60	10.60	7.00
				B	92	do	15	17.60	9.80	7.80
285-C	2½	do	do	A	95	do	30	30.95	23.00	7.95
				B	92	do	30	31.45	17.00	14.45
285-C	1-T	do	do	A	90	Choice	15	17.60	10.50	7.10
				B	87	do	15	17.85	11.30	6.55
285-E	2½	do	do	A	61	Seconds	29	29.95	19.10	10.85
				B	59	do	29	30.20	19.00	11.20

327-B	2½	Regular chain	Regular chain	A	88	Choice	30	30.20	18.80	11.40
				B	91	do	30	30.95	20.10	10.85
401-A	2½	Cooperative	Cooperative	A	92	Fancy	29	31.45	18.40	13.05
				B	86	Choice	29	29.95	17.80	12.15
401-A	1-T	do	do	A	80	do	16	16.85	9.30	7.55
				B	86	do	16	16.85	9.70	7.15
401-B	2½	do	do	A	85	do	28	29.95	18.00	11.95
				B	88	do	28	30.20	19.70	10.50
434-A	2½	do	do	A	75	Standard	29	30.45	19.80	10.65
				B	75	do	29	29.95	21.00	8.95
PINEAPPLE, SLICED										
110-A	2	Manufacturer	Wholesaler	A	92	Fancy	20	20.95	14.50	6.45
				B	93	do	20	21.20	14.30	6.90
110-A	2	do	Regular chain	A	91	do	20	20.95	14.90	6.05
				B	89	Choice	20	20.95	14.90	6.05
110-B	2	do	Wholesaler	A	90	do	20	20.95	14.40	6.55
				B	86	do	20	20.45	13.40	7.05
285-C	½	Wholesaler	do	A	89	do	9	9.60	6.10	3.50
				B	83	do	9	9.35	6.00	3.35
285-E	2½	do	do	A	70	Standard	30	30.70	17.60	13.10
				B	72	do	30	30.70	18.10	12.60
327-B	2	Regular chain	Regular chain	A	86	Choice	20	20.95	14.90	6.05
				B	85	do	20	21.45	14.20	7.25
401-A	2	Cooperative	Cooperative	A	90	Fancy	20	20.70	16.50	4.20
				B	90	do	20	20.70	14.90	5.80
401-B	2	do	do	A	76	Standard	20	20.20	13.50	6.70
				B	78	do	20	20.45	14.20	6.25
PINEAPPLE, CRUSHED										
110-A	2	Manufacturer	Wholesaler	A	91	Fancy	20	21.45	13.26	8.19
				B	90	do	20	21.70	14.46	7.24
110-A	½	do	do	A	87	Choice	9	9.35	5.46	3.89
				B	90	Fancy	9	9.85	6.96	2.89
110-A	2	do	Regular chain	A	87	Choice	20	21.45	13.56	7.89
				B	87	do	20	21.45	13.96	7.49
271-A	[7] 3 x 4	Wholesaler	Wholesaler	A	91	Fancy	14	15.55	11.26	4.29
				B	91	do	14	15.55	10.76	4.79
285-C	2	do	do	A	89	Choice	20	21.70	14.66	7.04
				B	91	do	20	21.20	14.66	6.54
285-A	2	do	do	A	88	do	21	21.45	13.96	7.49
				B	89	do	21	21.45	15.16	6.29
327-B	2½	Regular chain	Regular chain	A	90	do	30	30.70	19.66	11.04
				B	91	Fancy	30	31.95	19.86	12.09
327-B	2	do	do	A	83	Choice	20	20.45	14.46	5.99
				B	86	do	20	21.20	15.56	5.64
401-A	2	Cooperative	Cooperative	A	--------	None [2]	20	21.20	14.46	6.74
				B	86	Choice	20	21.70	14.86	6.84

[1] See note 1, page 19.
[2] Not graded on account of foreign matter in can.
[6] Interpolated for use in computing averages—The field notes do not show the "drained weights" for this can.
[7] An off-size can—about 1½.

TABLE 1.—*Grades of canned vegetables and fruits, selected brands, based on samples purchased in Des Moines, Iowa, in July, 1930*—Continued

B. FRUITS—Continued

General information				Facts found on official grading						
Brand	Size of can	Owner of brand	Sample bought from—	Identity of can	Score	Grade [1]	Net weight stated on label	Net weight found	Solids	Liquids
							Ounces	*Ounces*	*Ounces*	*Ounces*
SWEET CHERRIES (WHITE)										
110-A	2½	Manufacturer	Regular chain	A	81	Choice	30	30.95	19.00	11.95
				B	81	do	30	30.70	19.00	11.70
285-C	2½	Wholesaler	Wholesaler	A	91	Fancy	30	31.20	19.00	12.20
				B	91	do	30	31.70	17.60	14.10
271-A	2½	do	do	A	84	Choice	30	31.70	17.60	14.10
				B	87	do	30	31.70	17.20	14.50
434-A	2½	Cooperative	Cooperative	A	84	do	31	31.20	17.40	13.80
				B	83	do	31	31.20	17.00	14.20
401-A	2½	do	do	A	86	do	28	30.70	17.40	13.30
				B	86	do	28	30.95	17.40	13.55
401-B	2½	do	do	A	70	Standard	30	29.70	20.40	9.30
				B	66	Seconds	30	29.70	21.40	8.30
GRAPEFRUIT										
133	2	Manufacturer	Regular Chain	A		Choice	20	20.95	11.80	9.15
				B		do	20	20.70	12.36	8.34
285-A	2	Wholesaler	Wholesaler	A		Fancy	20	21.45	11.36	10.09
				B		do	20	20.45	10.36	10.09
FRUITS FOR SALAD [8]										
110-A	1-T	Manufacturer	Regular chain	A		Fancy	16	17.10	11.80	5.30
				B		do	16	17.35	11.40	5.95
101	1-T	do	do	A		do	16	17.60	12.40	5.20
				B		do	16	17.60	13.00	4.60
285-A	1-T	Wholesaler	Wholesaler	A		Choice	15	17.85	10.10	7.75
				B		do	15	17.60	11.00	6.60
285-C	1-T	do	do	A		do	15	17.60	10.80	6.80
				B		do	15	17.85	10.60	7.25
271-A	1-T	do	do	A		Fancy	15	17.60	11.60	6.00
				B		do	15	18.10	11.20	6.90
271-B	1-T	do	do	A		do	15	17.85	9.10	8.75
				B		Choice	15	17.60	10.10	7.50
104-B	1-T	Manufacturer	Regular chain	A		do	15	17.85	10.70	7.15
				B		Fancy	15	17.85	10.20	7.65

Brand	Size of can	Owner of brand	Sample bought from—	Identity of can	Score	Grade	Net weight stated on label	Net weight found	Solids	Liquids
434-A	1-T	Cooperative	Cooperative	A		do	16	17.85	12.30	5.55
				B		do	16	17.85	11.00	6.85
401-A	1-T	do	do	A		Choice	16	17.10	10.30	6.80
				B		Fancy	16	16.85	9.40	7.45

[1] See note 1, page 19.

[8] To time of grading no official grades had been promulgated; grades are best estimates which Department of Agriculture representatives could make, using standards for component fruits.

TABLE 2.—*Grades of canned vegetables and fruits, selected brands, based on samples purchased in Memphis, Tenn., in November, 1930*

A. VEGETABLES

General information				Facts found on official grading						
Brand	Size of can	Owner of brand	Sample bought from—	Identity of can	Score	Grade [1]	Net weight stated on label	Net weight found	Solids	Liquids
TOMATOES							*Ounces*	*Ounces*	*Ounces*	*Ounces*
162	2	Manufacturer	Regular chain	A	77	Standard	19	20.70	10.16	10.54
				B	89	Extra standard	19	20.95	13.66	7.29
170	2	do	do	A	85	do	19	19.95	13.86	6.09
				B	81	do	19	20.20	12.06	8.14
113-A	2	do	do	A	75	Standard	19	20.45	13.16	7.29
				B	68	do	19	19.45	10.16	9.29
119	2	do	do	A	71	do	19	20.20	10.86	9.34
				B	67	do	19	19.95	11.66	8.29
113-B	2	do	do	A	67	Substandard	19	20.20	13.36	6.84
				B	64	do	19	18.45	11.16	7.29
158	2	do	Independent dealer	A [2]	69	Standard	19	20.70	11.36	9.34
158	1-P	do	do	A	69	Substandard	10	10.60	6.16	4.44
				B	68	do	10	11.10	6.06	5.04
257-B	2	Wholesaler	Wholesaler	A	81	Extra standard	19	19.20	12.46	6.74
				B	89	do	19	20.20	13.96	6.24
257-A	2	do	do	A	77	do	19	19.70	11.06	8.64
				B	72	Standard	19	19.70	10.36	9.34
GREEN BEANS, WHOLE										
162	2	Manufacturer	Regular chain	A	91	Fancy	19	20.45	12.36	8.09
				B	91	do	19	19.95	12.36	7.59
170	2	do	do	A	85	Extra standard	19	20.70	12.86	7.84
				B	85	do	19	20.70	12.16	8.54
114	2	do	Wholesaler	A [3] B	83	do	19	19.70	11.86	7.84

[1] For some of the items in this table the score shown seems to warrant a grade higher than that given, but in each of these cases the number of points scored under some factor was too low to permit the higher grade, regardless of the total score for the can.

[2] Only 1 can purchased.

[3] This can is listed under "Cut beans," below.

TABLE 2.—*Grades of canned vegetables and fruits, selected brands, based on samples purchased in Memphis, Tenn., in November, 1930*—Contd.

A. VEGETABLES—Continued

General information				Facts found on official grading						
Brand	Size of can	Owner of brand	Sample bought from—	Identity of can	Score	Grade [1]	Net weight stated on label	Net weight found	Solids	Liquids
							Ounces	*Ounces*	*Ounces*	*Ounces*
GREEN BEANS, CUT										
117	2	Manufacturer	Regular chain	A	76	Extra standard	19	20.20	14.06	6.14
				B	76	do	19	20.20	14.06	6.14
114	2	do	Wholesaler	A	79	do	19	20.20	12.16	8.04
				B						
174	2	do	do	A	69	Standard	19	20.70	11.86	8.84
				B	70	do	19	20.70	12.16	8.54
165	2	do	Independent dealer	A	71	do	19	20.20	12.16	8.04
				B	69	do	19	19.95	12.86	7.09
SWEET CORN, CREAM STYLE										
137	2	do	Wholesaler	A	90	Fancy	20	20.95	20.95	----
				B	90	do	20	20.95	20.95	----
150	2	do	Regular chain	A	85	Extra standard	20	20.95	20.95	----
				B	85	do	20	21.20	21.20	----
PEAS										
162	2	do	do	A	94	Fancy	20	20.70	13.66	7.04
				B	92	do	20	20.70	13.46	7.24
170	2	do	do	A	91	do	20	20.45	13.46	6.99
				B	91	do	20	20.70	13.16	7.54
170	2	do	do	A	82	Extra standard	20	20.20	13.26	6.94
				B	78	do	20	20.20	12.96	7.24
140	2	do	Independent dealer	A	91	Fancy	20	20.95	13.66	7.29
				B	91	do	20	21.20	13.56	7.64
114	2	do	Wholesaler	A	87	Extra standard	20	20.70	14.16	6.54
				B	86	do	20	20.45	14.16	6.29
174	2	do	do	A	86	do	20	21.20	13.66	7.54
				B	86	do	20	20.95	12.76	8.19
107-A	2	do	Regular chain	A	84	do	20	20.20	12.66	7.54
				B	----	None [5]	20	20.70	13.16	7.54
107-B	2	do	Independent dealer	A	78	Standard	20	21.20	12.86	8.34
				B	78	do	20	21.20	12.66	8.54
154-B	2	do	Regular chain	A	82	Extra standard	20	21.20	14.56	6.64
				B	82	do	20	21.20	14.26	6.94
154-A	2	do	do	A	75	Standard	20	21.45	13.00	8.45
				B	75	do	20	21.20	13.86	7.34

177	2	do	Independent dealer	A	71	do	20	21.95	13.01	8.94
				B	73	do	20	21.45	15.66	5.79
162	2	do	Regular chain	A	69	do	20	20.70	14.14	6.56
				B	71	do	20	20.70	14.14	6.56
161-B	2	do	do	A	65	Substandard	20	21.95	15.16	6.79
				B	65	do	20	21.20	14.86	6.34
257-B	2	Wholesaler	Wholesaler	A	90	Fancy	20	20.70	14.06	6.64
				B	87	Extra Standard	20	20.70	13.46	7.24
257-B	2	do	do	A	75	Standard	20	20.20	13.30	6.90
				B	74	do	20	20.20	13.30	6.90
434-A	2	Cooperative	Cooperative	A	79	Extra standard	20	19.95	13.26	6.69
				B	78	do	20	20.20	14.96	5.24
SPINACH [a]										
110-A	2½	Manufacturer	Wholesaler	A	85	Fancy	27	30.45	19.60	10.85
				B	85	do	27	30.20	19.00	11.20
110-A	2	do	do	A	79	Standard	19	19.45	13.00	6.45
				B	79	do	19	19.45	14.30	5.15
169	2½	do	do	A	81	do	25	26.95	20.00	6.95
				B	81	do	25	27.45	21.70	5.75
110-E	2½	do	Regular chain	A	77	do	27	29.45	20.70	8.75
				B	76	do	27	29.70	18.00	11.70
110-E	[illegible]	do	do	A	84	do	19	19.20	13.00	6.20
				B	84	do	19	19.45	13.50	5.95
146-A	2½	do	do	A	73	do	27	27.70	20.10	7.60
				B	74	do	27	27.20	20.30	6.90
146-A	2	do	do	A	77	do	18	18.45	12.10	6.35
				B	77	do	18	18.45	12.10	6.35
257-B	2½	Wholesaler	Wholesaler	A	75	do	27	27.20	20.50	6.70
				B	73	do	27	27.45	20.00	7.45
434-A	2½	Cooperative	Cooperative	A	88	Fancy	27	27.20	20.56	6.64
				B	88	do	27	27.70	19.60	8.10

B. FRUITS

PEACHES, Y. C., HALVED										
146-A	2½	Manufacturer	Regular chain	A	91	Fancy	30	30.45	21.00	9.45
				B	90	do	30	30.20	21.00	9.20
146-A	1-T	do	do	A	84	Choice	16	17.10	12.00	5.10
				B	80	do	16	16.60	12.80	3.80
110-E	2½	do	do	A	89	do	30	31.20	22.00	9.20
				B		None	30	30.45	22.50	7.95
110-A	2½	do	Wholesaler	A	85	Choice	30	30.20	20.30	9.90
				B	83	do	30	30.70	23.10	7.60
110-A	1-T	do	do	A	77	Standard	16	17.10	13.10	4.00
				B	72	do	16	16.85	12.00	4.85
110-D	2½	do	do	A	70	do	29	30.20	19.30	10.90
				B	75	do	29	29.70	21.50	8.20

[a] See note 4, page 21.
[1] See note 1, page 27.
[4] This can is listed under "Whole beans," above.
[5] Not graded on account of foreign matter in can.
[6] Not graded on account of flavor.

TABLE 2.—*Grades of canned vegetables and fruits, selected brands, based on samples purchased in Memphis, Tenn., in November, 1930*—Contd.

B. FRUITS—Continued

General information				Facts found on official grading							
Brand	Size of can	Owner of brand	Sample bought from—	Identity of can	Score	Grade [1]	Net weight stated on label	Net weight found	Solids	Liquids
PEACHES, Y. C., HALVED—continued							*Ounces*	*Ounces*	*Ounces*	*Ounces*
153-B	2½	Manufacturer	Regular chain	A	64	Seconds	28	28.95	21.20	7.75
				B	64	do	28	29.45	22.70	6.75
257-B	2½	Wholesaler	Wholesaler	A	84	Choice	30	30.95	20.30	10.65
				B	80	do	30	30.45	22.00	8.45
257-B	1-T	do	do	A	84	do	16	17.35	10.50	6.85
				B	84	do	16	17.10	11.40	5.70
353-C	2½	Regular chain	Regular chain	A	87	do	30	30.45	20.30	10.15
				B	87	do	30	30.95	22.50	8.45
434-A	2½	Cooperative	Cooperative	A	86	do	30	31.20	21.00	10.20
				B	85	do	30	29.95	20.90	9.05
434-A	1-T	do	do	A	85	do	16	17.35	11.70	5.65
				B	85	do	16	17.35	12.80	4.55
PEACHES, Y. C., SLICED										
146-A	2½	Manufacturer	Regular chain	A	90	Fancy	30	30.95	19.30	11.65
				B	91	do	30	31.45	18.80	12.65
146-A	1-T	do	do	A	90	do	16	18.10	9.70	8.40
				B		None [6]				
146-B	1-T	do	do	A	79	Standard	16	16.19	10.90	5.29
				B	79	do	16	16.19	10.70	5.49
110-E	2½	do	do	A	82	Choice	30	30.95	20.00	10.95
				B	86	do	30	30.20	20.60	9.60
110-E	1-T	do	do	A	78	Standard	16	17.10	10.60	6.50
				B	78	do	16	17.85	11.30	6.55
110-A	2½	do	Wholesaler	A	81	Choice	30	28.95	18.15	10.80
				B	88	do	30	30.95	21.16	9.79
110-A	1-T	do	do	A	74	Standard	16	17.35	10.96	6.39
				B	71	do	16	17.35	10.26	7.09
110-D	2½	do	do	A	73	do	29	30.95	21.56	9.39
				B	71	do	29	30.45	21.96	8.49
110-D	1-T	do	do	A	69	do	16	17.10	12.36	4.74
				B	72	do	16	17.10	10.96	6.14
257-B	2½	Wholesaler	do	A	91	Fancy	30	27.80	19.91	7.89
				B	90	do	30	27.75	20.16	7.59

257-B	1-T	do	do	A		None [6]	16	17.85	10.00	7.85
				B		do	16	17.85	10.00	7.85
434-A	1-T	Cooperative	Cooperative	A	79	Standard	15	16.85	10.16	6.69
				B	79	do	15	16.60	11.06	5.54
467-B	1-T	do	do	A	72	do	16	16.60	11.50	5.10
				B	72	do	16	17.35	11.30	6.05
467-A	1-T	do	do	A	61	Seconds	16	16.35	12.30	4.05
				B	61	do	16	16.60	12.80	3.80
APRICOTS, PEELED										
110-E	2½	Manufacturer	Regular chain	A	89	Choice	30	31.20	19.70	11.50
				B	89	do	30	31.70	20.80	10.90
110-A	2½	do	Wholesaler	A	87	do	30	30.95	19.70	11.25
				B	83	do	30	30.70	18.70	12.00
110-D	2½	do	do	A	74	Standard	29	29.70	19.10	10.60
				B	73	do	29	30.95	17.30	13.65
467-A	1-T	Cooperative	Cooperative	A	85	Choice	15	17.35	11.60	5.75
				B	91	Fancy	15	17.85	11.10	6.75
APRICOTS, UNPEELED										
110-E	2	Manufacturer	Regular chain	A	87	Choice	20	20.45	13.00	7.45
				B	88	do	20	20.70	12.70	8.00
110-A	1-T	do	Wholesaler	A	86	do	16	16.60	9.76	6.84
				B	83	do	16	16.85	10.20	6.65
110-D	1-T	do	do	A	81	Choice	16	17.35	10.60	6.75
				B	82	do	16	17.35	10.10	7.25
146-A	1-T	do	Regular chain	A	77	Standard	16	17.35	11.50	5.85
				B	81	Choice	16	17.35	9.90	7.45
257-B	1-T	Wholesaler	Wholesaler	A	68	Standard	16	17.35	9.60	7.75
				B	68	do	16	17.35	10.60	6.75
434-A	1-T	Cooperative	Cooperative	A	80	Choice	16	17.35	10.50	6.85
				B	79	Standard	16	17.85	10.60	7.25
PEARS										
110-E	2	Manufacturer	Regular chain	A	89	Choice	20	20.95	13.20	7.75
				B	88	do	20	20.70	12.50	8.20
110-A	2½	do	Wholesaler	A	81	do	30	29.95	21.40	8.55
				B	81	do	30	30.20	21.60	8.60
110-A	1-T	do	do	A	83	do	16	16.60	11.20	5.40
				B	83	do	16	17.35	11.50	5.85
110-D	1-T	do	do	A	75	Standard	16	16.60	10.70	5.90
				B	74	do	16	16.85	10.70	6.15
146-A	2½	do	Regular chain	A	89	Choice	30	29.95	20.20	9.75
				B	81	do	30	30.95	20.70	10.25
146-A	1-T	do	do	A	80	Choice	16	16.85	10.50	6.35
				B	75	Standard	16	16.60	12.20	4.40
112	2½	do	Independent dealer	A	55	Seconds	30	29.45	21.70	7.75
				B	([7])	do	30	30.95	28.66	2.29
257-B	2½	Wholesaler	Wholesaler	A	83	Choice	29	30.20	19.70	10.50
				B	80	do	29	30.70	17.00	13.70
257-B	1-T	do	do	A	82	do	16	16.85	9.20	7.65
				B	82	do	16	16.85	9.50	7.35

[1] See note 1, page 27. [6] Not graded on account of flavor. [7] Graded "seconds" as edible fruit, although no core calculated

Table 2.—*Grades of canned vegetables and fruits, selected brands, based on samples purchased in Memphis, Tenn., in November, 1930*—Contd.

B. FRUITS—Continued

General information				Facts found on official grading						
Brand	Size of can	Owner of brand	Sample bought from—	Identity of can	Score	Grade [1]	Net weight stated on label	Net weight found	Solids	Liquids
PINEAPPLE, SLICED							*Ounces*	*Ounces*	*Ounces*	*Ounces*
146-A	2	Manufacturer	Regular chain	A	92	Fancy	20	21.20	14.70	6.50
				B	81	Choice	20	20.95	13.50	7.45
257-B	2	Wholesaler	Wholesaler	A	90	Fancy	20	20.95	12.90	8.05
				B	93	do	20	21.45	14.20	7.25
467-C	2	Cooperative	Cooperative	A	88	Choice	20	21.45	14.30	7.15
				B	89	do	20	21.45	14.80	6.65
PINEAPPLE, CRUSHED										
110-A	2½	Manufacturer	Wholesaler	A	92	Fancy	30	29.95	19.86	10.09
				B	92	do	30	32.20	19.86	12.34
110-A	1-F	do	do	A	90	do	9	9.35	5.90	3.45
				B	90	do	9	9.60	5.80	3.80
110-A	2	do	do	A	87	Choice	20	21.45	14.56	6.89
				B	87	do	20	21.20	13.66	7.54
110-D	2½	do	do	A	82	do	30	30.45	18.46	11.99
				B	82	do	30	30.70	19.46	11.24
110-D	2	do	do	A	80	do	20	21.20	13.96	7.24
				B	80	do	20	21.45	13.96	7.49
146-A	2	do	Regular chain	A	91	Fancy	20	20.70	14.96	5.74
				B	88	Choice	20	21.20	13.56	7.64
146-A	2½	do	do	A	90	Fancy	30	31.45	19.56	11.89
				B	88	Choice	30	30.95	17.96	12.99
146-A	1-F	do	do	A	80	do	9	9.35	6.16	3.19
				B	83	do	9	9.60	6.26	3.34
257-B	1-F	Wholesaler	Wholesaler	A	88	do	9	9.60	6.44	3.16
				B	88	do	9	9.85	6.16	3.69
257-B	2	do	do	A	72	Standard	20	20.45	14.86	5.59
				B	72	do	20	20.45	13.44	7.01
257-A	1-F	do	do	A	80	Choice	9	9.85	5.56	4.29
				B	80	do	9	9.60	6.06	3.54
467-C	2	Cooperative	Cooperative	A	92	Fancy	20	20.95	14.84	6.11
				B	91	do	20	21.45	14.36	7.09
434-A	2	do	do	A	73	Standard	20	19.95	14.96	4.99
				B	73	do	20	20.45	14.76	5.69

SWEET CHERRIES (WHITE)										
110-E	2½	Manufacturer	Regular chain	A	80	Choice	30	30.45	19.45	11.00
				B	80	do	30	30.45	19.05	11.40
146-A	2½	do	do	A	77	do	30	30.45	19.05	11.40
				B	77	do	30	30.45	19.07	11.38
110-A	2½	do	Wholesaler	A	90	Fancy	30	32.20	19.75	12.45
				B	90	do	30	32.20	19.35	12.85
257-B	2½	Wholesaler	do	A	86	Choice	31	29.95	16.40	13.55
				B	86	do	31	31.45	17.40	14.05
FRUITS FOR SALADS [8]										
146-A	2	Manufacturer	Regular chain	A		Fancy	20	21.20	14.80	6.40
				B		do	20	20.45	17.10	3.35
110-A	2	do	Wholesaler	A		do	20	20.70	13.60	7.10
				B		do	20	20.70	16.10	4.60
110-E	2	do	Regular chain	A		do	20	20.20	14.00	6.20
				B		do	20	20.45	15.00	5.45
257-B	2	Wholesaler	Wholesaler	A		do	20	21.45	14.00	7.45
				B		do	20	21.45	14.80	6.65

[1] See note 1, page 27.

[8] See note 8, Appendix Table 1.

TABLE 3.—*Grades of canned vegetables and fruits, selected brands, based on samples purchased in Detroit, Mich., in March and April, 1931*

A. VEGETABLES

General information				Facts found on official grading						
Brand	Size of can	Owner of brand	Sample bought from—	Identity of can	Score	Grade [1]	Net weight stated on label	Net weight found	Solids	Liquids
							Ounces	*Ounces*	*Ounces*	*Ounces*
TOMATOES										
110-A	2	Manufacturer	Wholesaler	A	79	Extra standard	19	20.45	13.28	7.17
				B	75	do	19	20.20	11.53	8.67
110-A	2	do	Regular chain	A	74	Standard	19	18.95	12.23	6.72
				B	81	Extra standard	19	19.20	12.88	6.32
110-A	2	do	Wholesaler	A	71	Standard	19	19.45	11.18	8.27
				B	80	Extra standard	19	19.70	10.83	8.87
110-A	2	do	Regular chain	A	76	do	19	19.95	11.33	8.62
				B	72	Standard	19	19.20	12.38	6.82

[1] For some of the items in this table the score shown seems to warrant a grade higher than that given, but in each of these cases the number of points scored under some factor was too low to permit the higher grade, regardless of the total score for the can.

TABLE 3.—*Grades of canned vegetables and fruits, selected brands, based on samples purchased in Detroit, Mich., in March and April, 1931*—Con.

A. VEGETABLES—Continued

General information				Facts found on official grading							
Brand	Size of can	Owner of brand	Sample bought from—	Identity of can	Score	Grade [1]	Net weight stated on label	Net weight found	Solids	Liquids
TOMATOES—continued							*Ounces*	*Ounces*	*Ounces*	*Ounces*
110-A	2	Manufacturer	Regular chain	A	76	Substandard	19	18.20	8.03	10.17
				B	73	Standard	19	19.70	12.13	7.57
167-A	2	do	Wholesaler	A	87	Extra standard	19	20.20	13.68	6.52
				B	85	do	19	19.95	12.98	6.97
142	2	do	do	A	85	do	19	20.45	15.58	4.87
				B	78	do	19	20.45	12.88	7.57
175	2	do	Regular chain	A	74	Standard	19	19.95	12.43	7.52
				B	73	do	19	20.20	13.88	6.32
103	2	do	Wholesaler	A	71	do	19	19.95	12.78	7.17
				B	72	do	19	19.20	14.18	5.02
129	2	do	do	A	55	Substandard	19	20.45	10.83	9.62
				B	60	Standard	19	19.95	10.48	9.47
171	2	do	Regular chain	A	63	Substandard	19	18.95	9.53	9.42
				B	60	do	19	19.95	6.38	13.57
160	2	do	do	A	60	do	19	19.45	10.98	8.47
				B	57	do	19	19.45	9.22	10.23
215-B	2	Wholesaler	Wholesaler	A	89	Extra standard	19	20.95	15.03	5.92
				B	85	do	19	20.45	12.43	8.02
271-A	2½	do	Independent dealer	A	78	do	30	29.70	17.43	12.27
				B	78	do	30	29.70	18.13	11.57
271-A	2	do	do	A	82	do	19	20.20	14.68	5.52
				B	72	Substandard	19	20.45	9.18	11.27
353-B	2	Regular chain	Regular chain	A	79	Extra standard	19	20.70	13.78	6.92
				B	75	do	19	20.20	13.58	6.62
353-A	2	do	do	A	71	Substandard	19	19.95	12.28	7.67
				B	79	Extra standard	19	20.20	12.30	7.90
GREEN BEANS, WHOLE										
167-A	2	Manufacturer	Wholesaler	A	90	Fancy	19	20.45	11.15	9.30
				B	90	do	19	20.70	12.10	8.60
271-A	2	Wholesaler	Independent dealer	A	92	do	19	19.70	14.50	5.20
				B	92	do	19	19.70	15.65	4.05
301-A	2	Regular chain	Regular chain	A	93	do	19	20.45	11.70	8.75
				B	90	do	19	20.20	11.80	8.40
353-A	2	do	do	A	89	Extra standard	20	20.20	10.80	9.40
				B	94	Fancy	20	19.95	10.75	9.20

327-A	2	do	do	A	89	Extra standard	19	20.20	11.50	8.70
				B	87	do	19	20.20	12.50	7.70
GREEN BEANS, CUT										
180	2	Manufacturer	do	A	81	do	19	20.20	12.30	7.90
				B	80	do	19	20.20	13.15	7.05
152	2	do	Wholesaler	A	80	do	19	20.70	11.45	9.25
				B	79	do	19	20.45	11.15	9.30
160	2	do	Regular chain	A	63	Standard	19	20.45	12.80	7.65
				B	63	do	19	20.45	12.55	7.90
115	2	do	do	A	61	do	19	20.45	12.95	7.50
				B	61	do	19	20.45	13.45	7.00
271-A	2	Wholesaler	Independent dealer	A	72	Extra standard	19	19.70	12.20	7.50
				B	83	do	19	19.70	11.80	7.90
215-B	2	do	Wholesaler	A	68	Standard	19	20.20	11.50	8.70
				B	68	do	19	20.20	11.15	9.05
353-B	2	Regular chain	Regular chain	A	68	do	19	20.20	12.60	7.60
				B	65	do	19	19.20	12.60	6.60
353-D	2	do	do	A	61	Substandard	19	20.20	12.95	7.25
				B	62	do	19	20.20	12.40	7.80
SWEET CORN, CREAM STYLE										
152	2	Manufacturer	Wholesaler	A	84	Extra standard	20	20.45	20.45	
				B	82	do	20	20.45	20.45	
152	2	do	do	A	84	Standard	20	20.45	20.45	
				B	79	do	20	20.70	20.70	
110-A	2	do	Regular chain	A	79	Extra standard	20	20.70	20.70	
				B	79	do	20	21.20	21.20	
110-A	2	do	Wholesaler	A	77	Standard	20	21.20	21.20	
				B	78	do	20	20.95	20.95	
110-A	2	do	Regular chain	A	76	do	20	20.70	20.70	
				B	76	do	20	20.70	20.70	
110-A	2	do	Wholesaler	A	76	do	20	20.70	20.70	
				B	75	do	20	20.70	20.70	
110-A	2	do	do	A	74	do	20	21.20	21.20	
				B	73	do	20	20.95	20.95	
156	2	do	Regular chain	A [2]	81	Extra standard	20	20.70	20.70	
127	2	do	do	A	78	Standard	20	20.95	20.95	
				B	75	do	20	20.70	20.70	
161-A	2	do	do	A	74	do	20	21.95	21.95	
				B	75	do	20	21.20	21.20	
167-A	2	do	Wholesaler	A	74	do	20	21.20	21.20	
				B	75	do	20	20.70	20.70	
167-A	2	do	do	A	70	do	20	21.20	21.20	
				B	70	do	20	21.95	21.95	
180	2	do	Regular chain	A	70	do	20	20.45	20.45	
				B	69	do	20	20.70	20.70	
229-B	2	Wholesaler	Wholesaler	A	79	do	20	21.20	21.20	
				B	79	do	20	21.20	21.20	
229-B	2	do	do	A	78	do	20	20.70	20.70	
				B	80	do	20	20.70	20.70	

[1] See note 1, page 33.
[2] Only 1 can purchased.

TABLE 3.—*Grades of canned vegetables and fruits, selected brands, based on samples purchased in Detroit, Mich., in March and April, 1931*—Con.

A. VEGETABLES—Continued

General information				Facts found on official grading						
Brand	Size of can	Owner of brand	Sample bought from—	Identity of can	Score	Grade [1]	Net weight stated on label	Net weight found	Solids	Liquids
							Ounces	*Ounces*	*Ounces*	*Ounces*
SWEET CORN, CREAM STYLE—con.										
271-A	2	Wholesaler	Independent dealer	A	75	Standard	20	20.45	20.45	
				B	75	do	20	20.45	20.45	
271-A	2	do	do	A	71	do	20	20.95	20.95	
				B	76	do	20	20.70	20.70	
353-A	2	Regular chain	Regular chain	A	80	Extra standard	20	20.70	20.70	
				B	82	do	20	20.70	20.70	
353-A	2	do	do	A	73	Standard	20	21.20	21.20	
				B	75	do	20	20.95	20.95	
327-B	2	do	do	A	80	Extra standard	20	20.20	20.20	
				B	80	do	20	20.45	20.45	
PEAS										
110-A	2	Manufacturer	do	A	90	Fancy	20	20.70	13.90	6.80
				B	90	do	20	20.95	13.00	7.95
110-A	2	do	do	A	89	Extra standard	20	20.95	13.30	7.65
				B	91	Fancy	20	20.95	13.45	7.50
110-A	2	do	Wholesaler	A	89	Extra standard	20	20.20	12.50	7.70
				B	91	Fancy	20	20.70	12.75	7.95
110-A	2	do	do	A	90	do	20	20.70	13.35	7.35
				B	89	Extra standard	20	20.20	14.45	5.75
110-A	2	do	Regular chain	A	87	do	20	21.20	13.50	7.70
				B	87	do	20	20.95	13.50	7.45
167-A	2	do	Wholesaler	A	92	Fancy	20	21.45	14.65	6.80
				B	94	do	20	21.20	14.20	7.00
167-A	2	do	do	A	83	Extra standard	20	21.20	14.15	7.05
				B	84	do	20	21.20	14.55	6.65
167-B	2	do	do	A	79	Standard	20	20.95	13.40	7.55
				B	79	do	20	21.20	13.90	7.30
154-C	2	do	Regular chain	A	83	Extra standard	20	21.45	13.95	7.50
				B	81	do	20	20.95	13.65	7.30
180	2	do	do	A	82	do	20	21.20	15.25	5.95
				B	81	do	20	21.20	15.10	6.10
180	2	do	do	A	81	Standard	20	20.70	14.10	6.60
				B	82	do	20	20.45	14.15	6.30
134	2	do	do	A	69	do	20	21.70	16.45	5.25
				B	66	do	20	21.45	17.00	4.45

271-A	2	Wholesaler	Independent dealer	A	86	Extra standard	20	20.70	13.25	7.45
				B	88	do	70	20.45	14.55	5.90
215-B	2	do	Wholesaler	A	87	do	20	20.45	13.10	7.35
				B	87	do	20	20.45	13.10	7.35
215-C	2	do	do	A	79	do	20	21.20	14.20	7.00
				B	76	Standard	20	20.95	13.30	7.65
353-A	2	Regular chain	Regular chain	A	91	Fancy	20	20.70	13.10	7.60
				B	89	Extra standard	20	20.95	12.90	8.05
353-A	2	do	do	A	82	do	20	20.95	13.10	7.85
				B	90	Fancy	20	20.70	13.50	7.20
301-A	2	do	do	A	81	Extra standard	20	20.95	13.40	7.55
				B	81	do	20	20.20	13.20	7.00
SPINACH [a]										
135-A	2	Manufacturer	Wholesaler	A	89	Fancy	19	18.45	14.06	4.39
				B	90	do	19	18.45	14.11	4.34
135-A	2½	do	do	A	84	Standard	27	28.20	20.01	8.19
				B	85	Fancy	27	27.45	19.16	8.29
110-F	2½	do	do	A	83	Standard	27	28.95	18.78	10.17
				B	82	do	27	28.45	18.81	9.64
110-A	2½	do	Regular chain	A	82	do	27	28.95	19.68	9.27
				B	78	do	27	29.45	21.01	8.44
110-A	2½	do	Wholesaler	A	77	do	27	29.45	19.53	9.92
				B	76	do	27	28.95	19.16	9.79
110-A	2½	do	Regular chain	A	73	do	27	28.95	20.48	8.47
				B	74	do	27	29.20	21.71	7.49
124	2	do	do	A	80	do	18	19.20	15.26	3.94
				B	78	do	18	18.95	15.68	3.27
172	2½	do	Wholesaler	A	79	do	27	29.20	21.03	8.17
				B	73	do	27	28.95	20.41	8.54
157	2	do	do	[2] A	79	do	19	17.45	12.41	5.04
271-A	2½	Wholesaler	Independent dealer	A	85	Fancy	30	28.20	20.86	7.34
				B	87	do	30	28.70	19.91	8.79
243	2	do	Wholesaler	A	83	Standard	19	18.95	14.11	4.84
				B	80	do	19	18.70	13.91	4.79
243	2½	do	do	A	71	Substandard	27	28.70	17.61	11.09
				B	71	do	27	28.70	18.41	10.29
353-A	2	Regular chain	Regular chain	A	78	Standard	19	18.45	12.48	5.97
				B	79	do	19	18.45	12.96	5.49
301-A	2½	do	do	A	79	do	27	27.70	18.68	9.02
				B	76	do	27	27.45	19.06	8.39

B.—FRUITS

PEACHES, Y. C., HALVED							*Ounces*	*Ounces*	*Ounces*	*Ounces*
135-A	2½	Manufacturer	Wholesaler	A	95	Fancy	30	30.45	20.10	10.35
				B	93	do	30	30.45	21.10	9.35
110-F	2½	do	do	A	88	Choice	30	30.70	19.40	11.30
				B	91	Fancy	30	30.70	18.80	11.90

See note 1, page 33.

[2] Only one can purchased.

[a] See note 4, page 21.

TABLE 3.—*Grades of canned vegetables and fruits, selected brands, based on samples purchased in Detroit, Mich., in March and April, 1931*—Con.

B. FRUITS—Continued

General information				Facts found on official grading						
Brand	Size of can	Owner of brand	Sample bought from—	Identity of can	Score	Grade [1]	Net weight stated on label	Net weight found	Solids	Liquids
							Ounces	*Ounces*	*Ounces*	*Ounces*
PEACHES, Y. C., HALVED—con.										
110-A	2½	Manufacturer	Regular chain	A	89	Choice	30	29.95	20.90	9.05
				B	91	do	30	29.95	20.60	9.35
110-A	2½	do	do	A	90	do	30	29.70	21.30	8.40
				B	89	do	30	30.95	21.30	9.65
110-A	2½	do	Wholesaler	A	89	do	30	30.45	21.25	9.20
				B	87	do	30	30.20	21.25	8.95
110-A	2½	do	Regular chain	A	84	do	30	29.45	20.70	8.75
				B	89	do	30	30.70	18.60	12.10
104-A	2½	do	do	A	88	do	30	31.20	20.70	10.50
				B	88	do	30	31.20	20.50	10.70
132-A	2½	do	do	A [2]	90	do	30	29.45	18.90	10.55
135-B	2½	do	Wholesaler	A	79	Standard	29	30.45	21.90	8.55
				B	79	do	29	29.45	20.40	9.05
110 G	1-T	do	do	A	83	do	16	16.35	11.30	5.05
				B	83	do	16	16.10	11.50	4.60
271-A	1-T	Wholesaler	Independent dealer	A	85	Choice	15	17.85	10.90	6.95
				B	84	do	15	18.10	11.00	7.10
271-A	2½	do	do	A	82	do	30	29.70	22.30	7.40
				B	85	do	30	30.45	21.90	8.55
229-A	2½	do	Wholesaler	A	85	do	30	29.95	20.10	9.85
				B	92	do	30	29.95	21.00	8.95
229-A	1-T	do	do	A	84	do	15	17.85	12.05	5.80
				B	87	do	15	17.60	12.00	5.60
243	1-T	do	do	A	88	do	16	17.60	11.70	5.90
				B	87	do	16	17.10	12.30	4.80
327-E	2½	Regular chain	Regular chain	A	91	do	30	30.95	21.40	9.55
				B	88	do	30	29.95	20.80	9.15
353-A	2½	do	do	A	89	do	30	30.70	20.10	10.60
				B	86	do	30	30.70	21.00	9.70
301 C	2½	do	do	A	78	Standard	29	29.95	19.80	10.15
				B	75	do	29	29.70	22.80	6.90
301-C	2½	do	do	A	75	do	29	28.70	21.20	7.50
				B	75	do	29	28.95	21.70	7.25

PEACHES, Y. C., SLICED										
110-A	2½	Manufacturer	Wholesaler	A	93	Choice	30	30.70	20.30	10.40
				B	93	do	30	30.45	20.75	9.70
110-A	2½	do	Regular chain	A	91	do	30	29.45	20.90	8.55
				B	91	do	30	30.45	19.40	11.05
110-A	2½	do	do	A	88	do	30	31.45	18.60	12.85
				B	91	do	30	29.70	20.00	9.70
110-A	1-T	do	do	A	86	do	16	17.60	10.70	6.90
				B	87	do	16	16.85	11.10	5.75
110-A	2½	do	do	A	85	do	30	30.95	20.55	10.40
				B	85	do	30	30.95	20.00	10.95
110-A	1-T	do	do	A	85	do	16	17.10	11.10	6.00
				B	84	do	16	16.60	11.60	5.00
110-A	2	do	Wholesaler	A	82	do	20	20.95	13.70	7.25
				B	83	do	20	20.95	14.60	6.35
110 A	1-T	do	do	A	88	do	16	17.60	11.80	5.80
				B	88	Standard	16	16.85	12.20	4.65
135-A	2½	do	do	A	93	Fancy	30	32.45	17.70	14.75
				B	92	do	30	29.95	20.60	9.35
135-A	1-T	do	do	A	89	Choice	16	17.10	10.30	6.80
				B	88	do	16	16.85	11.50	5.35
110-F	2½	do	do	A	87	do	30	30.45	20.50	9.95
				B	86	Standard	30	29.45	22.20	7.25
128	2½	do	Regular chain	A	89	Choice	30	31.95	19.40	12.55
				B	89	do	30	32.20	19.80	12.40
146-A	1-T	do	Wholesaler	A	87	do	16	17.60	11.75	5.85
				B	85	do	16	18.35	9.75	8.60
104-B	1-T	do	do	A	86	do	15	16.85	10.50	6.35
				B	85	do	15	16.60	11.30	5.30
135-B	2½	do	do	A	88	Standard	29	30.20	21.40	8.80
				B	86	do	29	29.45	19.50	9.95
135-B	1-T	do	do	A	84	do	16	16.85	11.40	5.45
				B	83	do	16	16.85	11.70	5.15
110-G	1-T	do	do	A	87	Choice	16	17.35	10.55	6.80
				B		None [3]	16	16.85	11.00	5.85
229-A	2½	Wholesaler	do	A	84	Choice	30	31.45	18.60	12.85
				B	88	do	30	31.20	18.60	12.60
229-A	1-T	do	do	A	88	Standard	15	17.10	9.80	7.30
				B	90	Choice	15	17.10	10.20	6.90
243	1-T	do	do	A	92	Fancy	16	18.35	10.60	7.75
				B	91	do	16	17.10	11.40	5.70
243	2½	do	do	A	88	Choice	30	30.70	18.20	12.50
				B	89	do	30	29.95	20.90	9.05
243	2½	do	do	A	84	do	30	30.45	20.80	9.65
				B	84	do	30	31.45	19.60	11.85
243	2	do	do	A	80	do	20	20.70	13.50	7.20
				B	92	do	20	21.70	14.70	7.00
271-A	1-T	do	Independent dealer	A	81	do	15	17.10	11.30	5.80
				B	81	do	15	17.10	11.40	5.70
271-A	2½	do	do	A	82	do	30	30.70	21.70	9.00
				B	88	do [4]	30	31.20	19.90	11.30

[1] See note 1, page 33. [2] Only 1 can purchased. [3] Not graded on account of flavor. [4] This can, while grading choice, gave evidence of being old merchandise, one end being distended.

TABLE 3.—*Grades of canned vegetables and fruits, selected brands, based on samples purchased in Detroit, Mich., in March and April, 1931*—Con.

B. FRUITS—Continued

General information				Facts found on official grading						
Brand	Size of can	Owner of brand	Sample bought from—	Identity of can	Score	Grade [1]	Net weight stated on label	Net weight found	Solids	Liquids
PEACHES, Y. C., SLICED—contd.							*Ounces*	*Ounces*	*Ounces*	*Ounces*
353-A	2½	Regular chain	Regular chain	A	90	Fancy	30	31.20	18.20	13.00
				B	90	do	30	30.70	17.90	12.80
353-B	1-T	do	do	A	85	Choice	15	17.10	9.80	7.30
				B	88	do	15	16.85	10.30	6.55
327-E	2½	do	do	A	92	do	30	30.95	19.30	11.65
				B	87	do	30	31.45	20.80	10.65
APRICOTS, PEELED										
132-B	1-T	Manufacturer	do	A	75	Standard	15	16.85	9.70	7.15
				B	75	do	15	16.85	10.20	6.65
163-A	2½	do	do	A	80	Choice	30	30.95	19.00	11.95
				B	81	do	30	31.70	18.50	13.20
135-B	2½	do	Wholesaler	A	77	Standard	29	31.20	19.60	11.60
				B	76	do	29	30.70	20.00	10.70
APRICOTS, UNPEELED										
110-F	2½	do	do	A	85	Choice	30	31.20	17.20	14.00
				B	86	do	30	30.70	18.70	12.00
110-G	1-T	do	do	A	75	Standard	16	17.10	11.10	6.00
				B	74	do	16	17.10	11.20	5.90
132-B	1-T	do	Regular chain	A	86	Choice	15	17.60	9.20	8.40
				B	87	do	15	17.85	9.20	8.65
146-B	2½	do	Wholesaler	A	73	Standard	29	29.20	18.20	11.00
				B	70	do	29	30.45	19.50	10.95
163-B	1-F	do	Regular chain	A	81	Choice	14	14.10	7.60	6.50
				B	81	do	14	14.35	7.60	6.75
271-A	2½	Wholesaler	Independent dealer	A	94	Fancy	30	32.20	16.70	15.50
				B	90	do	30	32.95	17.50	15.45
271-A	1-T	do	do	A	87	Choice	15	18.35	10.10	8.25
				B	87	do	15	18.10	10.10	8.00
243	1-T	do	Wholesaler	A	84	do	16	17.85	11.30	6.55
				B	84	do	16	17.85	10.50	7.35
327-B	2½	Regular chain	Regular chain	A	84	do	30	32.70	17.30	15.40
				B	85	do	30	32.70	17.00	15.70
301-C	2½	do	do	A	72	Standard	29	30.95	18.80	12.15
				B	78	do	29	30.70	17.90	12.80

PEARS										
110-A	2½	Manufacturer	do	A	92	Fancy	30	30.45	18.80	11.65
				B	92	do	30	30.45	19.60	10.85
110-A	2	do	do	A	90	do	20	20.20	13.60	6.60
				B	90	do	20	20.20	13.30	6.90
110-A	2	do	Wholesaler	A	91	do	20	20.20	12.60	7.60
				B	86	Choice	20	20.45	13.20	7.25
110-A	2	do	Regular chain	A	90	do	20	20.20	13.90	6.30
				B	88	do	20	20.20	13.40	6.80
110-A	2½	do	do	A	89	do	30	31.20	18.70	12.50
				B	88	do	30	30.95	18.80	12.15
110-A	2	do	do	A	86	do	20	20.20	12.80	7.40
				B	87	do	20	20.20	12.50	7.70
110-A	2½	do	Wholesaler	A	82	do	30	29.95	20.00	9.95
				B	83	do	30	30.20	19.60	10.60
110-F	2½	do	do	A	90	do	30	30.20	19.70	10.50
				B	90	do	30	29.95	19.70	10.25
159-B	1-T	do	Regular chain	A	84	do	15	17.10	12.20	4.90
				B	84	do	15	17.10	11.00	6.10
149-B	2½	do	do	A	77	Standard	30	30.70	19.20	11.50
				B	73	do	30	30.70	20.40	10.30
149-A	2½	do	do	A	81	do	28	30.70	18.40	12.30
				B		None [3]	28	30.70	19.40	11.30
135-A	2½	do	Wholesaler	A	87	Choice	30	30.70	20.30	10.40
				B	91	do	30	30.70	20.80	9.90
135-A	1-T	do	do	A	84	do	16	16.85	10.50	6.35
				B	85	do	16	16.85	10.50	6.35
271-A	2½	Wholesaler	Independent dealer	A	94	Fancy	30	30.20	19.20	11.00
				B	90	do	30	29.95	18.80	11.15
271-A	2	do	do	A	90	do	20	20.20	12.00	8.20
				B	89	do	20	20.45	13.60	6.85
271-A	1-T	do	do	A	88	Choice	15	17.35	10.00	7.35
				B	83	do	15	17.10	10.50	6.60
243	2	do	Wholesaler	A	93	do	20	20.95	12.80	8.15
				B	90	do	20	20.95	14.20	6.75
243	1-T	do	do	A	76	Standard	16	16.85	10.80	6.05
				B	83	do	16	16.35	11.20	5.15
327-B	2½	Regular chain	Regular chain	A	95	Fancy	30	30.70	19.30	11.40
				B	90	do	30	30.20	17.90	12.30
353-A	2½	do	do	A	93	do	29	30.45	21.20	9.25
				B	90	do	29	30.45	19.40	11.05
PINEAPPLE, SLICED										
110-A	2	Manufacturer	do	A	96	do	20	21.45	[5] 14.40	7.05
				B	96	do	20	21.70	14.40	7.30
110-A	2	do	Wholesaler	A	91	do	20	21.20	14.90	6.30
				B	91	do	20	21.20	14.80	6.40
110-A	2½	do	Regular chain	A	90	do	30	31.20	21.20	10.00
				B	90	Choice	30	31.45	21.50	9.95
110-A	2	do	do	A	90	Fancy	20	21.20	14.90	6.30
				B	90	do	20	20.95	14.20	6.75

[1] See note 1, page 33.

[3] Not graded on account of flavor.

[5] Interpolated for the purpose of computing averages.

TABLE 3.—*Grades of canned vegetables and fruits, selected brands, based on samples purchased in Detroit, Mich., in March and April, 1931*—Con.

B. FRUITS—Continued

General information				Facts found on official grading							
Brand	Size of can	Owner of brand	Sample bought from—	Identity of can	Score	Grade[1]	Net weight stated on label	Net weight found	Solids	Liquids
							Ounces	*Ounces*	*Ounces*	*Ounces*
PINEAPPLE, SLICED—continued										
110-A	2½	Manufacturers	Regular chain	A	87	Choice	30	31.70	21.50	10.20
				B	88	do	30	31.70	22.50	9.20
110-A	2½	do	Wholesaler	A	87	do	30	30.95	22.70	8.25
				B	87	do	30	31.20	21.70	9.50
110-A	2½	do	Regular chain	A	85	do	30	31.20	20.20	11.00
				B	83	do	30	31.20	20.20	11.00
146-A	2	do	Wholesaler	A	88	do	20	20.45	14.50	5.95
				B	90	do	20	20.45	14.20	6.25
131-A	2	do	do	A	90	Fancy	20	20.95	15.20	5.75
				B	90	do	20	21.20	14.70	6.50
131-B	2½	do	Regular chain	A	90	do	30	30.70	20.10	10.60
				B	87	Choice	30	31.20	20.60	10.60
131-D	2½	do	Wholesaler	A	81	do	30	30.95	19.30	11.65
				B	82	do	30	30.70	19.50	11.20
131-D	2	do	do	A	75	Standard	20	20.45	14.10	6.35
				B	75	do	20	20.45	13.80	6.65
110-F	2	do	do	A	90	Fancy	20	21.20	14.10	7.10
				B	90	do	20	21.70	14.20	7.50
141	2½	do	Regular chain	A	86	Choice	30	31.45	20.80	10.65
				B	87	do	30	32.20	21.40	10.80
271-A	2½	Wholesaler	Independent dealer	A	95	Fancy	30	31.70	20.90	10.80
				B	85	Choice	30	30.95	20.20	10.75
243	2½	do	Wholesaler	A	85	do	30	30.70	19.70	11.00
				B	87	do	30	30.20	20.10	10.10
353-A	2½	Regular chain	Regular chain	A	90	Fancy	30	31.70	20.80	10.90
				B	90	do	30	31.95	20.50	11.45
353-A	2	do	do	A	92	do	20	21.20	14.70	6.50
				B	88	Choice	20	20.95	15.10	5.85
301-C	2½	do	do	A	85	do	30	31.20	22.30	8.90
				B	82	do	30	31.45	20.40	11.05
327-E	2	do	do	A	87	do	20	20.20	14.20	6.00
				B	86	do	20	20.20	14.20	6.00

PINEAPPLE, CRUSHED										
131-C	2½	Manufacturer	Regular chain	A	91	Fancy	30	31.20	18.46	12.74
				B	91	do	30	31.45	16.36	15.09
110-F	2	do	Wholesaler	A	90	do	20	21.20	14.25	6.95
				B	91	do	20	21.20	15.05	6.15
131-D	2	do	do	A	83	Choice	20	21.20	14.95	6.25
				B	87	do	20	21.20	13.95	7.25
215-B	2	Wholesaler	do	A	90	do	20	20.95	13.86	7.09
				B	91	do	20	21.45	14.96	6.49
327-B	2	Regular chain	Regular chain	A	87	do	20	21.20	13.16	8.04
				B	89	do	20	21.95	14.06	7.89
353-B	2	do	do	A	81	do	20	21.20	15.76	5.44
				B	88	do	20	21.70	12.66	9.04
SWEET CHERRIES (WHITE)										
110-A	2	Manufacturer	Wholesaler	A	86	do	20	20.70	12.70	8.00
				B	86	do	20	20.70	13.40	7.30
110-A	2	do	do	A	86	do	20	20.95	12.90	8.05
				B	86	do	20	20.95	12.70	8.25
110-A	1-T	do	do	A	86	do	16	16.85	10.20	6.65
				B	86	do	16	16.85	10.80	6.05
110-A	1-T	do	Regular chain	A	83	do	16	17.10	10.50	6.60
				B	83	do	16	16.85	10.00	6.85
110-A	2	do	do	A	82	do	20	19.95	12.20	7.75
				B	80	do	20	19.95	12.30	7.65
110-A	1-T	do	do	A	81	do	16	17.35	9.70	7.65
				B	81	do	16	18.10	10.40	7.70
135-A	2	do	Wholesaler	A	83	do	20	20.70	11.70	9.00
				B	88	do	20	20.95	12.60	8.35
135-A	1-T	do	do	A	84	do	16	17.85	9.80	8.05
				B	87	do	16	17.85	10.10	7.75
159-A	1-T	do	Regular chain	A	86	do	16	18.10	10.40	7.70
				B	85	do	16	17.85	9.40	8.45
151	2	do	Wholesaler	A	74	Standard	19	21.20	12.80	8.40
				B	65	do	19	20.70	12.80	7.90
271-A	1-T	Wholesaler	Independent dealer	A	81	Choice	15	17.35	9.70	7.65
				B	81	do	15	17.60	9.40	8.20
353-A	2½	Regular chain	Regular chain	A	84	do	30	31.95	19.40	12.55
				B	84	do	30	31.95	19.40	12.55
GRAPEFRUIT										
109	2	Manufacturer	do	A		do	20	20.20	12.50	7.70
				B		do	20	20.70	13.15	7.55
144-B	2	do	do	A		do	20	21.20	13.35	7.85
				B		do	20	20.95	12.65	8.30
125	2	do	Wholesaler	A		do	20	20.70	11.50	9.20
				B		do	20	21.20	12.40	8.80
123	2	do	do	A		do	20	20.95	12.90	8.05
				B		None[6]	20	19.70	10.80	8.90

[1] See note 1, page 33.
[6] Not graded on account of low drained weight.

Table 3.—*Grades of canned vegetables and fruits, selected brands, based on samples purchased in Detroit, Mich., in March and April, 1931*—Con.

B. FRUITS—Continued

General information				Facts found on official grading						
Brand	Size of can	Owner of brand	Sample bought from—	Identity of can	Score	Grade [1]	Net weight stated on label	Net weight found	Solids	Liquids
GRAPEFRUIT—continued							*Ounces*	*Ounces*	*Ounces*	*Ounces*
133	2	Manufacturer	Wholesaler	A		Choice	20	20.45	11.20	9.25
				B		Standard	20	20.95	11.50	9.45
133	2	do	Regular chain	A		None [3]	20	20.45	11.60	8.85
				B		Standard	20	21.20	12.80	8.40
116	2	do	do	A		do	20	20.95	13.30	7.65
				B		do	20	20.70	13.80	6.90
144-A	2	do	do	A		do	20	21.95	11.50	10.45
				B		do	20	21.70	9.70	12.00
271-A	2	Wholesaler	Independent dealer	A		Choice	20	21.20	12.18	9.02
				B		do	20	20.45	12.50	7.95
243	2	do	Wholesaler	A		do	20	20.70	11.45	9.25
				B		do	20	21.20	11.95	9.25
353-A	2	Regular chain	Regular chain	A		do	20	20.45	13.20	7.25
				B		do	20	20.70	12.90	7.80
FRUITS FOR SALAD [7]										
110-A	2½	Manufacturer	Wholesaler	A		Fancy	30	30.70	20.75	9.95
				B		do	30	31.45	19.90	11.55
110-A	1-T	do	do	A		do	16	17.85	12.00	5.85
				B		do	16	17.10	11.60	5.50
110-A	2½	do	Regular chain	A		do	30	29.95	21.85	8.10
				B		do	30	30.20	21.75	8.45
110-A	1-T	do	do	A		do	16	17.35	11.25	6.10
				B		do	16	17.35	10.90	6.45
110-A	1-T	do	do	A		do	16	17.35	12.10	5.25
				B		do	16	17.35	12.20	5.15
110-A	1-T	do	do	A		Choice	16	17.10	12.35	4.75
				B		Fancy	16	17.10	12.05	5.05
146-A	2½	do	Wholesaler	A		do	30	30.70	18.91	11.79
				B		do	30	31.45	20.40	11.05
146-A	1-T	do	do	A		do	16	17.85	10.40	7.45
				B		do	16	17.10	11.80	5.30
101	2½	do	Regular chain	A		do	30	31.45	20.20	11.25
				B		do	30	31.45	22.65	8.80
135-A	1-T	do	Wholesaler	A		do	16	16.85	11.05	5.80
				B		do	16	17.85	11.65	6.20

110-F	1-T	do	do	A		do	16	16.85	11.55	5.36
				B		do	16	17.35	11.25	6.10
104-B	1-T	do	Regular chain	A		do	15	17.85	11.75	6.10
				B		do	15	17.85	11.15	6.70
104-B	2½	do	do	A		do	29	31.45	20.00	11.45
				B		Choice	29	31.70	20.50	11.20
271-A	2½	Wholesaler	Independent dealer	A		Fancy	30	29.95	21.72	8.23
				B		do	30	30.70	22.65	8.05
271-A	1-T	do	do	A		do	15	17.85	11.20	6.65
				B		Choice	15	17.25	9.45	7.80
243	2½	do	Wholesaler	A		Fancy	30	31.45	20.45	11.00
				B		do	30	31.70	19.55	12.15
243	1-T	do	do	A		do	15	17.35	11.60	5.75
				B		do	15	17.85	10.40	7.45
229-B	2½	do	do	A		do	30	32.20	22.65	9.55
				B		do	30	32.20	21.65	10.55

[1] See note 1, page 33.
[3] Not graded on account of flavor.
[7] See note 8, Appendix Table 1.

TABLE 4.—*Summary of the results of grading the samples of canned vegetables purchased in Des Moines, Memphis, and Detroit*

BRANDS OF MANUFACTURERS

Brand	Product	Total	Fancy	Extra standard	Standard	Substandard	No grade
	Except spinach and pumpkin:						
102	Tomatoes	2			1	1	
	Sweet corn, cream style	2			2		
103	Tomatoes	2			2		
107-A	Peas	2		1			1
107-B	Do	2			2		
110-A (NA)[1]	Tomatoes	12		6	5	1	
	Green beans, whole	2		2			
	Sweet corn, cream style	16	2	4	9		1
	Peas	10	5	5			
113-A	Tomatoes	2			2		
113-B	Do	2				2	
	Green beans:						
114 (NA)	Whole	1		1			
	Cut	1		1			
	Peas	2		2			
115	Green beans, cut	2			2		
117	Do	2		2			
119	Tomatoes	2			2		
122	Sweet corn, cream style	2			2		
127	Do	2			2		
129	Tomatoes	2			1	1	
130	Peas	2			2		
134	Do	2			2		
137	Sweet corn, cream style	2	2				
138	Green beans, cut	2			2		
139	Sweet corn, cream style	2			2		
140	Peas	2	2				
142	Tomatoes	2		2			
145	Green beans, whole	2	2				
	Peas	2	2				
147	Tomatoes	2			1	1	
150 (NA)	Sweet corn, cream style	2		2			
152	Green beans, cut	2		2			
	Sweet corn, cream style	4		2	2		
154-A	Peas	2			2		
154-B	Do	2		2			
154-C	Do	2		2			
156	Sweet corn, cream style	1		1			
158	Tomatoes	3			1	2	
160	Do	2				2	
	Green beans, cut	2			2		
161-A	Sweet corn, cream style	2			2		
161-B	Peas	2				2	
162	Tomatoes	2		1	1		
	Green beans, whole	2	2				
	Peas	4	2		2		
165	Green beans, cut	2			2		
167-A (NA)	Tomatoes	2		2			
	Green beans, whole	2	2				
	Sweet corn, cream style	8		1	5	2	
	Peas	4	2	2			
167-B (NA)	Do	2			2		
168	Green beans, cut	2			2		
170	Tomatoes	2		2			
	Green beans, whole	2		2			
	Peas	4	2	2			
171	Tomatoes	2				2	
174 (NA)	Green beans, cut	2			2		
	Peas	2		2			
175	Tomatoes	2			2		
177	Peas	2			2		
180	Green beans, cut	2		2			
	Sweet corn, cream style	2			2		
	Peas	4		2	2		
	Total	172	25	55	74	16	2
	Spinach and pumpkin:						
110-A (NA)	Spinach	14	3		11		
	Pumpkin	2	2				
110-E (NA)	Spinach	4			4		
110-F (NA)	Do	2			2		
124	Do	2			2		
135-A	Do	4	3		1		
146-A (NA)	Do	4			4		

[1] The abbreviation (NA) indicates those manufacturers who are national advertisers.

TABLE 4.—*Summary of the results of grading the samples of canned vegetables purchased in Des Moines, Memphis, and Detroit*—Continued

BRANDS OF MANUFACTURERS—Continued

Brand	Product	Total	Fancy	Extra standard	Standard	Substandard	No grade
	Spinach and pumpkin:						
157	Spinach	1			1		
169	Do	2			2		
172 (NA)	Do	2			2		
176	Pumpkin	2			2		
178	Do	2	2				
	Total	41	10		31		

BRANDS OF WHOLESALERS

Brand	Product	Total	Fancy	Extra standard	Standard	Substandard	No grade
	Except spinach and pumpkin:						
215-B	Tomatoes	2		2			
	Green beans, cut	2			2		
	Peas	2		2			
215-C	do	2		1	1		
229-B	Sweet corn, cream style	4			4		
257-A	Tomatoes	2		1	1		
257-B	do	2		2			
	Peas	4	1	1	2		
271-A	Tomatoes	4		3		1	
	Green beans, whole	4	2	1	1		
	Green beans, cut	2		2			
	Sweet corn, cream style	6		2	4		
	Peas	2		2			
285-A	Sweet corn, cream style	5			5		
	Peas	2		2			
285-B	Tomatoes	2		2			
	Green beans, cut	2			2		
	Sweet corn, cream style	2			2		
	Peas	2		2			
285-C	Tomatoes	2		1	1		
	Green beans, whole	2		2			
	Green beans, cut	2			2		
	Sweet corn, cream style	2		2			
	Peas	2		2			
285-D	Sweet corn, cream style	2			2		
	Total	65	3	32	29	1	
	Spinach and pumpkin:						
243	Spinach	4			2	2	
257-B	do	2			2		
271-A	do	4	2		2		
285-A	do	4			2	2	
285-C	do	4	2		2		
	Pumpkin	2			2		
	Total	20	4		12	4	

BRANDS OF CHAINS

Brand	Product	Total	Fancy	Extra standard	Standard	Substandard	No grade
	Except spinach and pumpkin:						
301-A	Green beans, whole	2	2				
	Peas	2		2			
301-C	Tomatoes	2			2		
	Green beans, cut	2			2		
	Peas	2			2		
327-A	Green beans, whole	2		2			
	Sweet corn, cream style	2			2		
	Peas	2		2			
327-B	Tomatoes	2		1		1	
	Green beans, cut	2		2			
	Sweet corn, cream style	4		4			
	Peas	2			2		
327-C	Sweet corn, cream style	2	2				
327-D	Peas	2			2		
353-A	Tomatoes	2		1		1	
	Green beans, whole	2	1	1			
	Sweet corn, cream style	4		2	2		
	Peas	4	2	2			
353-B	Tomatoes	2		2			
	Green beans, cut	2			2		
353-D	do	2				2	
	Total	48	7	21	16	4	

TABLE 4.—*Summary of the results of grading the samples of canned vegetables purchased in Des Moines, Memphis, and Detroit*—Continued

BRANDS OF CHAINS—Continued

Brand	Product	Total	Fancy	Extra standard	Standard	Substandard	No grade
	Spinach and pumpkin:						
310-A	Spinach	2			2		
327-A	do	2			2		
327-B	Pumpkin	2			2		
353-A	Spinach	2			2		
	Total	8			8		

BRANDS OF COOPERATIVES

Brand	Product	Total	Fancy	Extra standard	Standard	Substandard	No grade
	Except spinach and pumpkin:						
410-A	Tomatoes	2	1	1			
	Sweet corn, cream style	2		2			
	Peas	2		2			
401-B	Tomatoes	2		1	1		
	Green beans, cut	2		2			
	Sweet corn, cream style	2		2			
	Peas	2		2			
401-C	Green beans, cut	2			2		
434-A	Tomatoes	2		1	1		
	Green beans, whole	2	2				
	Sweet corn, cream style	2			2		
	Peas	4		2	2		
	Total	26	3	15	8		
	Spinach and pumpkin:						
401-A	Spinach	4	4				
	Pumpkin	2	2				
401-B	do	2			2		
434-A	Spinach	6	4		2		
	Pumpkin	2	2				
	Total	16	12		4		

TABLE 5.—*Summary of the results of grading the samples of canned fruits purchased in Des Moines, Memphis, and Detroit*

BRANDS OF MANUFACTURERS

Brand	Product	Total	Fancy	Choice	Standard	Seconds	No grade
101	Fruits for salad	4	4				
104-A	Peaches, halved	2		2			
104-B	Peaches, sliced	2		2			
	Fruits for salad	6	4	2			
105	Pears	2		2			
106	Peaches, sliced	2			2		
109	Grapefruit	2		2			
110-A (NA)[1]	Peaches, halved	18		16	2		
	Peaches, sliced	24		21	3		
	Apricots, peeled	2		2			
	Apricots, unpeeled	6		6			
	Pears	24	5	19			
	Pineapple, sliced	18	10	8			
	Pineapple, crushed	12	7	5			
	Sweet cherries (white)	16	2	14			
	Fruits for salad	16	15	1			
110-B (NA)	Pineapple, sliced	2		2			
110-C (NA)	Apricots, unpeeled	2			2		
110-D (NA)	Peaches, halved	2			2		
	Peaches, sliced	4			4		
	Apricots, peeled	2			2		
	Apricots, unpeeled	2		2			
	Pears	2			2		
	Pineapple, crushed	4		4			
110-E (NA)	Peaches, halved	2		1			1
	Peaches, sliced	4		2	2		
	Apricots, peeled	2		2			
	Apricots, unpeeled	2		2			
	Pears	2		2			
	Sweet cherries (white)	2		2			
	Fruits for salad	2	2				
110-F (NA)	Peaches, halved	2	1	1			
	Peaches, sliced	2		1	1		
	Apricots, unpeeled	2		2			
	Pears	2		2			
	Pineapple, sliced	2	2				
	Pineapple, crushed	2	2				
	Fruits for salad	2	2				
110-G (NA)	Peaches, halved	2			2		
	Peaches, sliced	2		1			1
	Apricots, unpeeled	2			2		
111	Pears	2			1	1	
112	do	2				2	
116	Grapefruit	2			2		
123	do	2		1			1
125 (NA)	do	2		2			
128	Peaches, sliced	2		2			
131-A (NA)	Pineapple, sliced	2	2				
131-B (NA)	do	2	1	1			
131-C (NA)	Pineapple, crushed	2	2				
131-D (NA)	Pineapple, sliced	4		2	2		
	Pineapple, crushed	2		2			
132-A	Peaches, halved	1		1			
132-B	Apricots, peeled	2			2		
	Apricots, unpeeled	2		2			
133 (NA)	Grapefruit	6		3	2		1
135-A	Peaches, halved	2	2				
	Peaches, sliced	4	2	2			
	Pears	4		4			
	Sweet cherries (white)	4		4			
	Fruits for salad	2	2				
135-B	Peaches, halved	2			2		
	Peaches, sliced	4			4		
	Apricots, peeled	2			2		
136	Peaches, halved	2			2		
141	Pineapple, sliced	2		2			
144-A	Grapefruit	2			2		
144-B	do	2		2			
146-A (NA)	Peaches, halved	4	2	2			
	Peaches, sliced	6	3	2			1
	Apricots, unpeeled	2		1	1		
	Pears	4		3	1		
	Pineapple, sliced	4	1	3			
	Pineapple, crushed	6	2	4			
	Sweet cherries (white)	2		2			
	Fruits for salad	6	6				

[1] The abbreviation (NA) indicates those manufacturers who are national advertisers.

TABLE 5.—*Summary of the results of grading the samples of canned fruits purchased in Des Moines, Memphis, and Detroit*—Continued

BRANDS OF MANUFACTURERS—Continued

Brand	Product	Total	Fancy	Choice	Standard	Seconds	No grade
146-B (NA)	Peaches, sliced	4		2	2		
	Apricots, unpeeled	4			2	2	
149-A	Pears	2			1		1
149-B	do	2			2		
151	Sweet cherries (white)	2			2		
153-A	Peaches, halved	2		2			
153-B	do	2				2	
159-A	Sweet cherries (white)	2		2			
159-B	Pears	2		2			
163-A	Apricots, peeled	2		2			
	Apricots, unpeeled	2	1	1			
163-B	do	2		2			
166	Apricots, peeled	2			2		
	Total	343	82	188	60	7	6

BRANDS OF WHOLESALERS

Brand	Product	Total	Fancy	Choice	Standard	Seconds	No grade
215-B	Pineapple, crushed	2		2			
229-A	Peaches, halved	4		4			
	Peaches, sliced	4		3	1		
229-B	Fruits for salad	2	2				
243	Peaches, halved	2		2			
	Peaches, sliced	8	2	6			
	Apricots, unpeeled	2		2			
	Pears	4		2	2		
	Pineapple, sliced	2		2			
	Grapefruit	2		2			
	Fruits for salad	4	4				
257-A	Pineapple, crushed	2		2			
257-B	Peaches, halved	4		4			
	Peaches, sliced	4	2				2
	Apricots, unpeeled	2			2		
	Pears	4		4			
	Pineapple, sliced	2	2				
	Pineapple, crushed	4		2	2		
	Sweet cherries (white)	2		2			
	Fruits for salad	2	2				
271-A	Peaches, halved	6	1	5			
	Peaches, sliced	6	2	4			
	Apricots, peeled	2	2				
	Apricots, unpeeled	4	2	2			
	Pears	10	8	2			
	Pineapple, sliced	2	1	1			
	Pineapple, crushed	2	2				
	Sweet cherries (white)	4		4			
	Grapefruit	2		2			
	Fruits for salad	6	5	1			
271-B	Peaches, halved	4		3	1		
	Peaches, sliced	4		3	1		
	Apricots, unpeeled	2				2	
	Fruits for salad	2	1	1			
285-A	Pineapple, crushed	2		2			
	Grapefruit	2	2				
	Fruits for salad	2		2			
285-B	Peaches, halved	2		2			
	Peaches, sliced	4		1	3		
285-C	Peaches, halved	2	2				
	Peaches, sliced	4		2	2		
	Apricots, unpeeled	2		2			
	Pears	4	2	2			
	Pineapple, sliced	2		2			
	Pineapple, crushed	2		2			
	Sweet cherries (white)	2	2				
	Fruits for salad	2		2			
285-E	Peaches, halved	2		2			
	Peaches, sliced	2				2	
	Apricots, unpeeled	2				2	
	Pears	2				2	
	Pineapple, sliced	2			2		
	Total	160	46	88	16	8	2

TABLE 5.—*Summary of the result s of grading the samples of canned fruits purchased in Des Moines, Memphis, and Detroit*—Continued

BRANDS OF CHAINS

Brand	Product	Total	Fancy	Choice	Stand-ard	Seconds	No grade
301-C	Peaches, halved	4			4		
	Apricots, unpeeled	2			2		
	Pineapple, sliced	2		2			
327-B	Peaches, halved	2	2				
	Apricots, unpeeled	4		4			
	Pears	4	2	2			
	Pineapple, sliced	2		2			
	Pineapple, crushed	6	1	5			
327-C	Peaches, halved	2	2				
327-E	do	2		2			
	Peaches, sliced	2		2			
	Pineapple, sliced	2		2			
353-A	Peaches, halved	2		2			
	Peaches, sliced	2	2				
	Pears	2	2				
	Pineapple, sliced	4	3	1			
	Sweet cherries (white)	2		2			
	Grapefruit	2		2			
353-B	Peaches, sliced	2		2			
	Pineapple, crushed	2		2			
353-C	Peaches, halved	2		2			
	Total	54	14	34	6		

BRANDS OF COOPERATIVES

Brand	Product	Total	Fancy	Choice	Stand-ard	Seconds	No grade
401-A	Peaches, halved	4		4			
	Peaches, sliced	4	2	2			
	Apricots, peeled	2		2			
	Apricots, unpeeled	2		2			
	Pears	4	1	3			
	Pineapple, sliced	2	2				
	Pineapple, crushed	2		1			1
	Sweet cherries (white)	2		2			
	Fruits for salad	2	1	1			
401-B	Peaches, halved	2		2			
	Pears	2		2			
	Pineapple, sliced	2			2		
	Sweet cherries (white)	2			1	1	
434-A	Peaches, halved	6		6			
	Peaches, sliced	4		2	2		
	Apricots, unpeeled	4		3	1		
	Pears	2			2		
	Pineapple, crushed	2			2		
	Sweet cherries (white)	2		2			
	Fruits for salad	2	2				
467-A	Peaches, sliced	2				2	
	Apricots, peeled	2	1	1			
467-B	Peaches, sliced	2			2		
467-C	Pineapple, sliced	2		2			
	Pineapple, crushed	2	2				
	Total	64	11	37	12	3	1

TABLE 6.—*Canned vegetables: Official grades, range of official score and average official score, by groups of owners of the brands, of the samples which were purchased in the three cities, combined* [1]

Product and type of brand owner	Fancy			Extra standard			Standard		
	Number of cans graded	Range of official score	Average official score	Number of cans graded	Range of official score	Average official score	Number of cans graded	Range of official score	Average official score
Tomatoes:									
Brands of manufacturers	-------	-------	-------	13	75–89	[2] 81.7	18	60–79	[2] 71.7
Brands of wholesalers	-------	-------	-------	11	77–89	[2] 83.2	2	72–77	[2] 74.5
Brands of regular chains	-------	-------	-------	4	75–79	[2] 78.0	2	71–76	[2] 73.5
Brands of cooperatives	1	91	91.0	3	76–87	[2] 81.3	2	71–77	[2] 74.0
Green beans, whole:									
Brands of manufacturers	6	90–91	[2] 90.5	5	83–86	84.8	-------	-------	-------
Brands of wholesalers	2	92–92	[2] 92.0	3	81–87	84.3	1	74	74.0
Brands of regular chains	3	90–94	[2] 92.3	3	87–89	88.3	-------	-------	-------
Brands of cooperatives	2	94–94	[2] 94.0	-------	-------	-------	-------	-------	-------
Green beans, cut:									
Brands of manufacturers	-------	-------	-------	7	76–81	[2] 78.7	12	61–71	[2] 66.0
Brands of wholesalers	-------	-------	-------	2	72–83	[2] 77.5	6	68–71	[2] 69.3
Brands of regular chains	-------	-------	-------	2	84–85	[2] 84.5	4	65–68	[2] 65.8
Brands of cooperatives	-------	-------	-------	2	77–77	[2] 77.0	2	64–64	[2] 64.0
Sweet corn, cream style:									
Brands of manufacturers	4	90–92	90.8	10	79–87	[2] 83.4	28	68–84	[2] 74.3
Brands of wholesalers	-------	-------	-------	4	81–83	[2] 82.3	17	71–80	[2] 75.9
Brands of regular chains	2	91–91	91.0	6	80–89	[2] 82.5	4	70–75	[2] 72.0
Brands of cooperatives	-------	-------	-------	4	79–87	[2] 83.3	2	81–81	[2] 81.0
Peas:									
Brands of manufacturers	15	90–94	91.5	20	78–89	[2] 84.4	16	66–82	[2] 73.8
Brands of wholesalers	1	90	90.0	12	79–88	[2] 85.0	3	74–76	[2] 75.0
Brands of regular chains	2	90–91	90.5	6	77–89	[2] 81.3	6	71–74	[2] 72.7
Brands of cooperatives	-------	-------	-------	6	78–84	[2] 81.2	2	73–73	[2] 73.0
Spinach: [3]									
Brands of manufacturers	6	85–90	86.7	-------	-------	-------	29	73–84	78.6
Brands of wholesalers	4	85–89	87.5	-------	-------	-------	10	73–83	78.1
Brands of regular chains	-------	-------	-------	-------	-------	-------	6	75–79	77.0
Brands of cooperatives	8	85–89	87.4	-------	-------	-------	2	78–78	78.0
Pumpkin: [3]									
Brands of manufacturers	4	87–89	87.8	-------	-------	-------	2	72–73	72.5
Brands of wholesalers	-------	-------	-------	-------	-------	-------	2	71–80	75.5
Brands of regular chains	-------	-------	-------	-------	-------	-------	2	74–77	75.5
Brands of cooperatives	4	87–89	88.0	-------	-------	-------	2	72–76	74.0

[1] A blank indicates that no sample of the given product was found in that grade for the given group.

[2] Indicates comparably graded products (see note 3), samples of which were obtained from each type of brand owner. Only data so indicated were used in Table 11.

[3] These data are not included in Tables 10 and 11 because of differences in the range of scores used in grading. For spinach and pumpkin fancy grade might range from 85–100 and standard from 70 to 85, there being no official extra standard grade used in the scoring of these products.

TABLE 7.—*Canned fruits: Official grades, range of official score, and average official score, by groups of owners of the brands, of the samples which were purchased in the three cities, combined* [1]

Product and type of brand owner	Fancy			Choice			Standard		
	Number of cans graded	Range of official score	Average official score	Number of cans graded	Range of official score	Average official score	Number of cans graded	Range of official score	Average official score
Peaches, halved:									
Brands of manufacturers	5	90–95	92.0	25	[2] 80–92	[3] 86.6	10	70–83	77.1
Brands of wholesalers	3	91–92	91.3	22	80–92	[4] 85.4	1	74	74.0
Brands of regular chains	4	90–92	91.5	6	86–91	[3] 88.0	4	75–78	75.8
Brands of cooperatives				12	84–89	[3] 86.0			
Peaches, sliced:									
Brands of manufacturers	5	90–93	[3] 91.2	35	80–93	[3] 86.8	18	69–88	77.9
Brands of wholesalers	6	90–93	[3] 91.2	19	80–92	[3] 85.1	7	72–88	76.3
Brands of regular chains	2	90–90	[3] 90.0	4	85–92	[3] 88.0			
Brands of cooperatives	2	92–94	[3] 93.0	4	83–89	[3] 86.0	4	72–79	75.5
Apricots, peeled:									
Brands of manufacturers				6	80–89	84.8	8	73–78	75.5
Brands of wholesalers	2	90–92	91.0						
Brands of regular chains									
Brands of cooperatives	1	91	91.0	3	85–90	87.3			
Apricots, unpeeled:									
Brands of manufacturers	1	90	90.0	18	81–88	[3] 84.9	7	70–78	[3] 75.0
Brands of wholesalers	2	90–94	92.0	6	84–88	[3] 86.3	2	68–68	[3] 68.0
Brands of regular chains				4	84–88	[3] 86.3	2	72–78	[3] 75.0
Brands of cooperatives				5	80–86	[3] 83.6	1	79	[3] 79.0
Pears:									
Brands of manufacturers	5	90–92	[3] 91.0	34	80–91	[3] 85.7	7	73–81	76.0
Brands of wholesalers	10	89–95	[3] 92.1	10	80–93	[3] 85.8	2	76–83	79.5
Brands of regular chains	4	90–95	[3] 92.0	2	88–91	[3] 89.5			
Brands of cooperatives	1	92	[3] 92.0	5	80–88	[3] 85.0	2	75–75	75.0
Pineapple, sliced:									
Brands of manufacturers	16	90–96	[3] 91.4	18	81–90	[3] 86.3	2	75–75	75.0
Brands of wholesalers	3	90–95	[3] 92.7	5	83–89	[3] 85.8	2	70–72	71.0
Brands of regular chains	3	90–92	[3] 90.7	7	82–88	[3] 85.6			
Brands of cooperatives	2	90–90	[3] 90.0	2	88–89	[3] 88.5	2	76–78	77.0
Pineapple, crushed:									
Brands of manufacturers	13	90–92	[3] 90.7	15	80–88	[3] 84.5			
Brands of wholesalers	2	91–91	[3] 91.0	10	80–91	[3] 87.4	2	72–72	72.0
Brands of regular chains	1	91	[3] 91.0	7	81–90	[3] 86.3			
Brands of cooperatives	2	91–92	[3] 91.5	1	86	[3] 86.0	2	73–73	73.0
Sweet cherries (white):									
Brands of manufacturers	2	90–90	90.0	24	77–88	[3] 83.1	2	65–74	69.5
Brands of wholesalers	2	91–91	91.0	6	81–87	[3] 84.2			
Brands of regular chains				2	84–84	[3] 84.0			
Brands of cooperatives				4	83–86	[3] 84.8	1	70	70.0
Grapefruit:									
Brands of manufacturers				10			6		
Brands of wholesalers	2			4					
Brands of regular chains				2					
Brands of cooperatives									
Fruits for salad:									
Brands of manufacturers	35			3					
Brands of wholesalers	14			6					
Brands of regular chains									
Brands of cooperatives	3			1					

[1] A blank indicates that no sample of the given product was found in that grade for the given group.
[2] In some instances a can might have a numerical score entitling it to a grade of "Fancy", for example, but because of a marked deficiency on some one point was graded "Choice." Thus the highest "Choice" may exceed the lowest "Fancy." See Note 1, Appendix Table 1.
[3] Indicates products, samples of which were obtained from each type of brand owner. Only data so indicated were used in Table 11.

O

72D CONGRESS } SENATE { DOCUMENT
2d Session } { No. 153

CHAIN STORES

Short Weighing and Over Weighing in Chain and Independent Grocery Stores

---

LETTER

FROM THE

CHAIRMAN OF THE FEDERAL TRADE COMMISSION

TRANSMITTING

IN RESPONSE TO SENATE RESOLUTION No. 224
SEVENTIETH CONGRESS, REPORT OF THE FEDERAL
TRADE COMMISSION RELATIVE TO SHORT
WEIGHING AND OVER WEIGHING IN
CHAIN AND INDEPENDENT
GROCERY STORES

DECEMBER 8 (calendar day, DECEMBER 15), 1932.—Referred to the Committee on the Judiciary and ordered to be printed

---

UNITED STATES
GOVERNMENT PRINTING OFFICE
WASHINGTON : 1933

SENATE RESOLUTION NO. 228

SUBMITTED BY MR. BROOKHART

IN THE SENATE OF THE UNITED STATES,
June 8 (calendar day, June 10), 1932.

Resolved, That the reports which may hereafter be filed with the Secretary of the Senate, pursuant to Senate Resolution No. 224, Seventieth Congress, first session, relative to the investigation by the Federal Trade Commission of chain stores, be printed, with accompanying illustrations, as Senate documents.

Attest:

EDWIN P. THAYER, *Secretary.*

Chain-store reports of the Federal Trade Commission so far submitted to the Senate are:

Title	Senate Document No.	Price per copy
SEVENTY-SECOND CONGRESS, FIRST SESSION		
		Cents
Cooperative Grocery Chains	12	15
Wholesale Business of Retail Chains	29	5
Sources of Chain-Store Merchandise	30	10
Scope of the Chain-Store Inquiry	31	5
Chain-Store Leaders and Loss Leaders	51	10
Cooperative Drug and Hardware Chains	82	5
Growth and Development of Chain Stores	100	10
SEVENTY-SECOND CONGRESS, SECOND SESSION		
Chain-Store Private Brands	142	In press
Short Weighing and Over Weighing in Chain and Independent Grocery Stores	153	5

These reports may be obtained at prices above noted from

THE SUPERINTENDENT OF DOCUMENTS

WASHINGTON, D. C.

CONTENTS

APPENDICES

TEXT TABLES

APPENDIX TABLES

ACKNOWLEDGMENT

For the general direction and supervision of the inquiry into the chain-store industry, the commission acknowledges the services of Mr. Francis Walker, chief economist, and Mr. W. H. S. Stevens, assistant chief economist. As contributing especially to the preparation of this report on Short Weighing and Over Weighing in Chain and Independent Grocery Stores, the commission desires to mention Mr. Arthur Connors and Mr. Byron P. Parry, examiner in charge of the inquiry.

LETTER OF TRANSMITTAL

FEDERAL TRADE COMMISSION,
Washington, December 15, 1932.

To the PRESIDENT OF THE SENATE,
Washington, D. C.

DEAR SIR: I have the honor to transmit herewith a report of the Federal Trade Commission entitled "Short Weighing and Over Weighing in Chain and Independent Grocery Stores," submitted in pursuance to Senate Resolution 224, Seventieth Congress, first session. This is the ninth report of a series of reports covering a study of the subject of chain stores.

By direction of the commission.

W. E. HUMPHREY, *Chairman.*

LETTER OF SUBMITTAL

FEDERAL TRADE COMMISSION,
Washington, D. C., December 15, 1932.

To the Senate of the United States:

Under Senate Resolution 224, Seventieth Congress, first session, the commission was directed to make an inquiry into the chain-store system of marketing and distribution, including, among other things, "the advantages or disadvantages of chain-store distribution in comparison with those of other types of distribution." This report on Short Weighing and Over Weighing in Chain and Independent Grocery Stores deals with the subject of weights given on five bulk commodities purchased in chain and independent stores and was undertaken because of a charge frequently made that chain grocery stores obtain an advantage over independent stores through the short weighing of bulk commodities.

It is often stated that in weighing out bulk commodities exact net weights can not be achieved in a large percentage of cases but that over a long period the shortages and overages will balance each other. Both shortages and overages are likely to occur when clerks weigh out bulk merchandise hurriedly while other customers are waiting to be served, or when the weight of a unit of the article sold is comparatively large.

SCOPE OF INVESTIGATION

To determine the extent to which the chain stores short weigh commodities sold in bulk and also to determine whether this practice occurs more often in chain than in independent stores, five bulk articles were purchased for weighing from both kinds of stores without disclosing by whom and for what purpose such purchases were being made. The commodities purchased were navy beans, dried prunes, Lima beans, light-weight sweetened crackers, and sugar. The quantities of the commodities bought varied from one-half pound to 4 pounds.

The purchases were made in four cities each having a population of over 100,000. To make the study representative the cities selected were located in different sections of the country; one in New England, one in the Middle Atlantic States, one in the South, and one in the Middle West. In each of these cities there were one or more of the five largest chain-store systems and also one or more local chains as well as one or more cooperative chains with their membership of independent grocers. Practically all stores in the four cities were shopped, hence all types of stores in all types of neighborhoods are represented. In the four cities a total of 1,691 stores was shopped for the five bulk commodities.

Of the total number of stores shopped, 702, or 41.5 per cent, belonged to 11 different grocery or grocery and meat chains; 320, or 18.9 per cent, were independent stores affiliated with 11 cooperative chains; and 669, or 39.6 per cent, were independent stores without cooperative affiliations. As certain of the 11 chains operated stores in more than one of the four cities the city comparisons are for 14 groups of chain stores.

PROPORTION OF SHORT, OVER, AND EXACT WEIGHT PURCHASES

On all purchases from chains in the four cities 50.3 per cent of the items were short in weight. On all purchases from independent and cooperative retailers 47.8 per cent were short weight. Overweights were obtained on only 34.1 per cent of the total purchases from chain stores as compared with 43.8 per cent of the purchases from independents and cooperative chains combined. Exact weights, however, were given on 15.6 per cent of the items purchased from chains but on only 8.4 per cent of those bought from cooperatives and independents combined.

AMOUNTS OF TOTAL SHORT OR OVER WEIGHT

The short weights (not including over weights) on total purchases from chains (0.987 of 1 per cent) were substantially below those of independents and cooperative chains combined (1.265 per cent).

However, the total net shortage (the difference between total quantities short weight and over weight) on all items purchased from chain stores was slightly over three-tenths of 1 per cent (0.321 of 1 per cent) of the total quantity bought, as compared with a net overage for independents of 0.143 of 1 per cent. The overages and shortages from cooperatives exactly balanced. Combining the cooperative and independent dealer purchases the result is a net overage of 0.096 of 1 per cent.

While the size of the shortage for chains may seem insignificant to many, it would amount to 3.41 per cent on the investment in these bulk commodities, figured on the basis of the average stock turn of grocery and meat chains of 10.61 times per annum.

The turnover of certain other bulk commodities such as fresh meats and produce is probably much higher than the average, and these commodities constitute a substantial proportion of the total business of most chains selling groceries. A shortage of weight of the size found in this test, if it were applicable to all bulk commodities weighed by the chains, would obviously result in an increase in the rate of return on the investment in such commodities, and probably, because of their large volume, on total investment as well.

VARIATIONS IN CHAIN AND INDEPENDENT WEIGHTS BY CITIES

It should not be inferred that all chain stores gave short net weights or that all independent stores gave net overweights. In city No. 1 the chains gave short weights less frequently than either the cooperatives or independents. In the other three cities, the former were more frequently short than the latter. In no one of the four cities did the chains give overages more frequently than shortages although the cooperatives did so in one city, the independents in two, and the cooperatives and independents combined in two.

In city No. 1 the chains had a net overage in the total quantities purchased but gave net shortages in the other three. The cooperatives likewise gave a net overage in only one city (No. 4) and were short in the other three.

The independents, excluding cooperatives, on the other hand had a net shortage in total weight purchased in only one city and a net overage in three. Cooperatives and independents combined had net shortages in two cities and net overages in two.

Short weighing was found to be much more prevalent in city No. 2 for every group of distributors than it was in any other city. That city was the only one of the four in which every one of the three groups of distributors had a net shortage. The combined chain distributors in that city with a net shortage of over 1 per cent (1.044 per cent) and 61.7 per cent of the total items purchased underweight, were responsible for a higher proportion of short-weight purchases and a higher net shortage than any other group of distributors tabulated in any of the four cities.

VARIATIONS IN WEIGHTS BETWEEN CHAINS

The proportion of purchases from the several chains which were short weight exceeded the proportion of purchases which were overweight in all but two of the 14 separate chain comparisons. For any chain the lowest proportion of short weights was 38.6 per cent of the total purchases made from it; the highest was 69.5. In most cases, overweights for the chains ranged from 30 to 40 per cent of the total items purchased. Eleven chains, or nearly 80 per cent of them, gave net shortages on the total quantities bought and in two cities, none of the chains had a net overage.

Of the 14 chain groups shopped in the four cities, there were only three which had net overages, the highest of which was 0.212 of 1 per cent of the total weight purchased. The range of net shortages for the different chain groups was from 0.036 of 1 per cent to 1.73 per cent.

VARIATIONS IN WEIGHTS BETWEEN COOPERATIVE CHAINS

The proportion of short weights given by cooperative chains exceeded the proportion of overweights in 5 of the 8 cooperative groups as compared with 12 out of 14 chain groups. The smallest proportion of short weights given by any cooperative was 37.8 per cent of the total number of items purchased from it, and the largest was 61.5 per cent. The proportion of overweight purchases from the various cooperatives ranged from 32.2 per cent to 53.2 per cent of the total number of purchases. The total quantities bought from each of 5 of the 8 cooperative groups of stores showed a net shortage in weight, while those from each of the remaining 3 showed a net overage. The largest net shortage in weight for any one of these cooperative groups was 0.722 of 1 per cent of the quantity purchased; the largest net overage, 1.047 per cent.

SHORT WEIGHTS AND OVERWEIGHTS BY COMMODITIES

The chain stores were more frequently short weight than either the independent stores or cooperatives on two of the five items, navy beans and sweetened crackers, and were more frequently short than their independent competitors on dried prunes as well. On sugar and Lima beans, the reverse was found, the chains giving short weights less frequently than their independent or cooperative competitors. Except on Lima beans, however, where the difference is very slight, the proportion of chain purchases which were short weight always exceeded the proportion which was overweight. The showing for the independents and cooperatives was slightly better, both of these types of distributors giving more overages than shortages on prunes and Lima beans. On sweetened crackers and sugar, however, the independents and cooperatives as well as the chains had substantially lower proportions of overages than shortages.

In actual net weight each type of distributor gave net overages on prune and Lima bean purchases and net short weights on sweetened crackers. On navy beans the chains gave a net short weight and the other type of distributors a net overweight, the reverse being true on sugar where the chains had a slight net overage and the other types of distributors were net short. Except in the case of sugar where the chains had a slight overage, the overweights given by the chains were less and the shortages greater than was true of cooperative and independent distributors combined. The general and comparatively high shortages on sweetened crackers are possibly explained in part by the fact that this was relatively the most expensive article purchased in the various stores and also the one which was perhaps at the same time the least susceptible of accurate weighing.

EFFECT OF WEIGHING AND PACKAGING BY DISTRIBUTORS ON WEIGHING RESULTS

Since it is sometimes contended that preweighed bulk purchases reflect more clearly the attitude of grocery stores in the matter of accurate weights, considerable interest attaches to the weight of such bulk items—that is, those items weighed by employees in advance of sale. A total of 795 items, or 12 per cent of total purchases (6,640 items) made were preweighed, and nearly two-thirds (64.4 per cent) of these were obtained from chains. As has been often alleged short weights occurred more frequently on these preweighed items than on items weighed at the time of sale. For the chains the proportion of preweighed items which were short in weight was 59 per cent, as compared with 50.3 per cent on both preweighed and other items. For independents and cooperatives combined, the difference was much more striking, the proportion of shortages on preweighed items being 65 per cent as against only 47.8 per cent on the total items purchased from those dealers. The chains therefore had a considerably smaller proportion of short weights on preweighed items than the independents or cooperatives separately or combined. They also gave exact weights on a larger proportion of items.

The buyer of commodities weighed and packaged in advance of sale stands about two chances out of three that he will get short weights from either the independent dealer or the cooperative and only a slightly better chance in the chain store. Furthermore, the net shortage on these preweighed items is much greater, on the average, than is the case with items weighed at the time of purchase. On preweighed items the net shortage represented slightly over eight-tenths of 1 per cent (0.813) of the quantity purchased as compared with less than one-tenth of 1 per cent (0.091) on total quantities of all goods bought. Between chains and independent and cooperative chain dealers the difference in the size of the shortages on preweighed items was markedly in favor of the chains. The chains were net short 0.719 of 1 per cent of the total weight of the preweighed items bought as compared with 1.005 per cent for the independents and cooperatives combined.

SHORT WEIGHTS AND OVER WEIGHTS EXCLUDING PREWEIGHED COMMODITIES

Even after the exclusion of the preweighed items, the chains show, as they did in the case of total purchases, an appreciably higher proportion of exact weights, a somewhat higher proportion of short weights and an appreciably lower proportion of overweights than do the other types of distributors.

Similarly, a comparison of the amounts of net overages and shortages for all purchases, excluding those preweighed, with the amounts of such net overages and shortages for all commodities purchased showed a net shortage for the chains of two-tenths of 1 per cent while the net overage for the cooperatives and independents combined was slightly over two-tenths of 1 per cent, the net difference amounting to about four-tenths of 1 per cent in favor of the independent stores.

By the commission.

W. E. Humphrey, *Chairman.*

SHORT WEIGHING AND OVER WEIGHING IN CHAIN AND INDEPENDENT GROCERY STORES

Section 1. Origin of this report.

Introduction.—This report has been prepared in partial response to Resolution 224 of the United States Senate in the Seventieth Congress, first session, authorizing the chain-store inquiry and directing specifically that the commission inquire into and report to the Senate respecting, among other things—

(*c*) The advantages or disadvantages of chain-store distribution in comparison with those of other types of distribution as shown by prices, costs, profits, and margins, quality of goods and services rendered by chain stores and other distributors or resulting from integration, managerial efficiency, low overhead, or other similar causes.

No allegation of the advantages or disadvantages of chain stores has perhaps aroused more controversy or is of more general interest than the claim that chain grocery stores obtain an advantage over independent stores through the short weighing of customers, particularly in the sale of bulk commodities.

During the past several years the charge that store managers of grocery chains intentionally give short weight has been frequently made. It has also been charged that some of these chains operate under a policy whereby the store manager is given little or no shrinkage or shortage allowance and must therefore give short weights in order to come out even. This practice of the store managers, it is sometimes contended, is known to chain-store operators and is tacitly, though not definitely, approved by them. Some trade papers and antichain organizations have made much of instances of short weights in chain grocery stores. There have been reported cases of short weights in these stores which have resulted in court convictions; other cases have been dismissed by the courts, the latter in some instances causing criticism from some sources of both the chains and courts.

It is often stated that in weighing out bulk commodities exact net weights can not be achieved in a large percentage of cases but that in the long run the shortages and overages will offset or balance each other. Shortages or overages are likely to occur to some extent, particularly during a busy time when clerks have to weigh out bulk merchandise hurriedly while other customers are waiting to be served. Then, too, there are always some clerks who do not take sufficient care to arrive at exact weights. This report, in response to the Senate resolution, presents an analysis of chain-store weights given in sales of bulk merchandise in comparison with weights given by independent stores in order to answer two questions: (1) Do the grocery stores, both chain and independent, short weigh the public in the sales of bulk commodities? (2) What is the extent of such short weighing, if any, in these two types of establishments?

In this study, data on purchases of bulk commodities that were weighed out and packaged in the store in advance are recorded and compiled both separately from and combined with merchandise weighed at the time of purchase. Preweighed bulk purchases, it is sometimes contended, reflect more clearly the attitude of chain grocery stores, or any other kind of stores, in the matter of accurate weights since the weighing of such articles is presumably done either at the warehouse or during the clerk's spare time when careful attention can be given to exactness of weights.

Section 2. Chain policies in relation to alleged short weighing of grocery products.

Relation of store employees to short weighing.—Short weighing may be due to the dishonesty of the store employees. Thus, the proprietor of an eastern wholesale grocery house says:

> There is just one thing which may defeat the chain and that is stealing. All merchants are confronted with this problem, but I believe the chains are teaching their employees dishonesty and that will act as a boomerang and just injure themselves in the end. They pay very low wages and yet expect a manager to be responsible for all shortages. We have been in the fresh-meat business for about 12 years and in that time have had to fire 25 butchers. I have had some of them acknowledge that they all practice a short-weight system and sell inferior goods, whenever they can, for the price of better goods so they can make some money on the side. And yet, some of the crooked butchers I have fired were hired by the chain stores.

To a similar effect is the following statement of the manager of a middle western wholesale grocery house:

> In this city there have been found as high as 50 cases of theft in one week in chain stores. This consists of giving short weights.

In cases of this character, the chain itself probably is not the sole beneficiary of the short weighing. The consumer is overcharged but the difference which he pays goes into the pockets of the employees. Some of the chains, not only in the grocery and grocery and meat business, but also in other lines, employ a staff of people to visit the stores and check up on weights, prices, etc., in an effort to reduce this individual dishonesty. Thus, one large grocery chain reports:

> We have two or three secret-service people of our own working out of the head office. These are women to visit the stores to buy and notice the count, weight, price, etc. They are not known to the managers.

Similarly, an official of a large grocery and meat chain said:

> To a certain extent overcharging or dishonesty may be checked up in the following ways: We use spotters spasmodically to make purchases in some stores. Customers may notice overcharges or other unsatisfactory service and complain. * * *
>
> In the meat department everything is in pounds and ounces and it is easier for a man to knock down in meats than in the grocery department where most items are in standard packages. It is very easy to overcharge a few cents in weighing out meat. This is not a case of fundamental dishonesty, but the tradition in the meat business everywhere has been to take advantage of any discrepancies in favor of the meat man or the house. It is done all the time.

Chain attitude toward short weighing.—One large eastern chain in handling grocery products reports:

> We have discharged some managers from time to time for overcharging, dishonesty or knocking-down, and when it is a clear case they are never re-hired.

In another chain, the following detailed statement of policy in cases involving short weighing was supplied to an agent of the commission:

We consider that an employee charged with giving short weights is thereby charged with having violated our instructions, and we do not ordinarily furnish counsel. Exceptions have been made, however, in cases where it was evident that an organized attempt was being made to discredit us in the eyes of the public. In general, our attitude has been that if an employee is charged with an offense of this kind, he must make his own defense and if found guilty stand the penalty himself as having violated our instructions in any failure to give full weight.

In dealing with such cases as have arisen in which employees were charged with short weighing by local authorities, our local officers have endeavored in each case to ascertain whether the shortage was intentional, or whether it was the result of hurried or careless weighing on the part of the employee, or his assistants, or whether packages were delivered short weight by the manufacturer or packer. Instances of this latter have occurred and were not discovered until they had been put on sale.

Where the employee has had a previous good record, and our supervision has been convinced that there was no dishonesty on his part, as might happen through the carelessness of an employee or even through too-hurried weighing on his part, the employee has sometimes been retained. Where there has been evidence of dishonesty or continued carelessness, however, employees have been dismissed not only when convicted by local authorities, but also in cases detected by our own inspection and supervision where local authorities were not involved.

A very large grocery chain in the Middle West issued a bulletin containing the following instructions regarding short weight to managers during July, 1930:

Daily we are apprised of the extraordinary activities of various authorities on checking up on short weighting customers. In some of the outlying suburban and country towns some of our competitors have been heavily fined and given much adverse publicity.

We want to repeat here our policy of accuracy of weight. Overweight loses profit for your store. Underweight loses trade for your store besides creating the danger of an arrest and prosecution with its attendant bad publicity.

We urge all our managers to constantly check their clerks and particularly their extra help in order to assure accuracy of weights in every store at all times.

In another circular of instructions the same company adds:

Under these circumstances it behooves every chain-store manager and clerk to be more careful than ever to carry the oft-repeated policy of exact weights and measures and particular attention must be paid to the element of shrinkage after being weighed on merchandise weighed up in advance to the sale. In order to cope with this situation in a positive manner we suggest that you continue the policy of weighing small quantity of the merchandise up in advance so as to enable you to serve the public promptly during the rush periods but that you do not actually close the bag until you have reweighed it in the presence of the customer, thus assuring them of correct weight and eliminating any suspicion or playing into the hands of opponents of the chain store by any instances of short weight.

Store managers will please see to it that all employees adhere strictly to this rule of correct weights at all times. District managers will pay particular attention to this feature of merchandising at every visit.

At another time this company repeats:

Accuracy of weights is demanded by our company, the customer, the city sealer, the * * * Department of Agriculture, common sense, and the future of our business.

Effect of shortage allowances.—It is also claimed that there is a tendency to short weigh in the chain stores because the chain stores do not make allowances to store managers for waste, spoilage, and shrinkage, and that it is in consequence necessary for the store manager to short weigh or overcharge in some other manner in order to make up the difference. In some instances apparently it is true that the chain does not make a definite allowance for shortages of the character specified. For example, store managers in one of the large grocery chains are informed that they must account for the retail price of all goods sent them. However, this chain goes on to say:

We have no definite shortage allowance, but figure that it should run about one-half of 1 per cent or less. If it runs over this figure, we investigate to discover the reasons which may be errors by the store manager in not taking credits properly, selling at too low prices, putting money in the wrong pocket, etc.

In other words, though no definite allowance is made for shortages in billing, the stores and the managers are supposed to account for the quantities billed; some shortage is expected and so long as it is not excessive, headquarters disregards it. This policy is apparently characteristic also of some of the largest grocery and meat chains in the United States. One of these very large chains reports:

We have no definite allowance for shortage, nor is there any maximum limit as to the credit that will be allowed. The only rule is that all claims for shortage or damage shall be put through on a regular credit form, which must be approved by the assistant superintendent and forwarded to the office. The assistant superintendent knows the conditions in the territory and knows whether or not the credit asked is within reason. Should a store manager have unusual shortages or losses, it would indicate the necessity of checking up on his efficiency as a store manager.

Differences in the territories, in the seasons, and in the weather, and in the kind of merchandise handled have a direct bearing on the rate of loss. Occasionally, too, the merchandise received on a purchase may prove not to be in good condition and may incur heavy spoilage losses. In any case, the manager makes out his credit and the assistant superintendent has access to all the facts when it is submitted to him for approval.

In another one of these very large chains—

A store is usually allowed between 1 and 1½ per cent on sales for either overage or shortage. If it is more than 1½ per cent, we insist upon a recheck of the store, and when the recheck is taking place all office records are rechecked and all charges reextended—a complete survey is made. Then if the shortage still exists after a second recheck, the man is cautioned, and if it is repeated he is generally dismissed, unless the facts can be qualified. In some cases the store manager is not responsible for shortages, such as people breaking into the store and stealing out of the back room. Of course, all of those things are investigated before the man is dismissed for shortages.

There are still other chains, however, which employ a system of more or less definite allowances. In one of the largest chains—

On bulk stuff the stores are allowed certain prearranged amounts of shrinkage. For instance, we will bill out 100 pounds of rice as 97 pounds; 100 pounds of potatoes as 97 pounds; 43 pounds of apples as 40 pounds.

On fruits and vegetables a special shrinkage sheet is prepared setting forth the allowances on these lines; all merchandise of this nature is billed to the stores so that a manager can return to us 100 per cent of what he is charged. As a matter of fact, he should be able to return more than this per cent because the amount of allowance is high.

Another chain of a few hundred stores says that—

The allowance for shortage and shrinkage on produce is 7½ per cent, but no allowance is made on any other kind of merchandise. * * * How much allowance will be made on the rest of the merchandise, upon which no allowance is technically made, depends upon the kind of store and the type of manager. If the shortage appears unreasonable it is investigated.

While yet another chain states that—

Shortage allowances vary from season to season, being higher in summer than winter, and from store to store. They range from 3 to 5 per cent.

The seasonal difference in allowances for spoilage for another grocery and meat chain "runs around 2½ to 3 per cent during the winter and around 3 to 4 per cent in the summer."

According to the chain-store officials, therefore, allowances are made for some shortage either directly or indirectly. This tends to rebut the allegation that store managers are under any compulsion from the system in use either to underweigh or resort to similar practices. In further rebuttal of this allegation, several chain-store officials also point out that in grocery products overages in favor of the store managers frequently occur and that these, in any case, tend to offset the shortages.

One of the commonest forms of such overages, of course, arises from the splitting by customers of combinations of two or more units sold at an odd-cent price. This source of overages to the store is thus described by one of the large chains:

On a great many commodities, particularly, such staples as butter and eggs, the custom of "odd-pricing" prevails. For example, if butter is priced at 57 cents a pound, one-half pound would sell for 29 cents and one-quarter pound for 15 cents, so that there would be a tendency for a manager to receive an amount greater than that for which he was charged. The same thing occurs on items priced two for 25 cents, three for 25 cents, etc., when only one is sold to a customer.

A second source of such overages reported by the same chain is that—

In billing the stores we make some allowance for shrinkage, particularly on produce items, such as potatoes, apples, etc. Potatoes are supposed to weigh 120 pounds to the sack and we bill them out at 117 pounds. Apples are supposed to weigh 40 pounds to the box and we bill them out at 38. There are quite a number of items that are handled in this manner.

Thirdly, according to another chain—

In the grocery business there is generally a slight overage brought about through billing by the dozen or case and retailing by the piece. This would run from one-tenth to one-fourth of 1 per cent.

Again, according to a leading grocery and meat chain—

There is a tendency on some commodities, such as roasted coffee, to increase in weight while they are in the stores due to absorption of moisture, particularly during damp weather.

Finally, the last-mentioned chain reports:

Our warehouse accounting figures regularly show a deficit which we refer to as "warehouse shrinkage" and which is largely accounted for by items shipped to stores which are not properly charged.

Section 3. Plan of investigation.

To determine the extent to which the chain stores short weigh commodities sold in bulk, and also to determine whether this practice occurs more often in chain than in independent stores, it was necessary to purchase these articles for weighing from both kinds of stores without disclosing by whom and for what purpose such purchases were being made.

In order to make the study representative, it was regarded as fundamental that it should be made in more than one city. In part, this decision was dictated by the fact that most of the largest chains handling groceries occupy rather well-defined geographical areas and that more than two are not frequently found in any except the largest cities. It seemed essential to include in the study some four or five of the largest chains and also important to obtain adequate representation of so-called local or regional chains as well as of cooperative chain organizations. Because of the limitations of time and expense, the selection of very large cities for the study would have involved the shopping of limited areas in each with the possible uncertainty of the representativeness of the selection.

A selection of cities of a more moderate size, however, would permit the shopping of practically all stores in each city. Giving consideration to all these factors, it seemed best to conduct the work in cities of this character and for this purpose, after considerable study, four such cities, each with a population of over 100,000 inhabitants, were selected; one in New England, one in the Middle Atlantic States, one in the South and one in the Middle West. The cities in question contained a considerable number of stores belonging to five of the largest chains selling groceries, each of which operates more than 1,000 stores.

Although none of these cities are exceptionally large, the chain-store business is excellently represented in each of them. In each there are stores of three or more chain-store systems and two or more cooperative chains. In each city there are two of the five above-mentioned chains with over 1,000 stores which handle groceries and also one or more localized or regional chains. In all four cities combined, there are 11 chain-store systems. As certain of the 11 chains operated stores in more than one of the four cities, the city comparisons are for 14 groups of chain stores. In order to avoid disclosing more specifically the chains involved, the cities included in this test are identified only by numbers and the chains, only by letters.

After some consideration, the bulk products finally selected for purchase in the chain and independent stores located in these four cities were (1) navy beans, (2) dried prunes, (3) Lima beans, (4) lightweight sweetened crackers, (5) sugar. In making this selection, the primary consideration was the comparatively general availability of these five commodities in bulk form in most stores. The weight factor also played a part in the choice, various commodities such as potatoes and other vegetables and fruits being rejected on account of the difficulty of exact weighing. In the case of three of these commodities, sugar, navy and Lima beans, the weight of each grain or bean is small so that close or exact weights can be readily given by a store manager. In the case of the other two commodities, only the smallest size prunes obtainable were bought in each store and only lightweight sweetened crackers, such as vanilla wafers, were purchased in order to reduce as far as possible unavoidable variances from exact weights due to the weight of an individual unit. If a store did not carry a stock of lightweight sweetened crackers, no crackers of any kind were purchased in that store.

As Government regulations do not permit purchases of over $1 in a store without procuring receipts therefor, it was necessary that the commodities should be as low priced as possible in order to buy a variety of them and still stay within this price limitation. Perishability and convenience of handling also played a part in the selection since the purchases made had to be handled, stored, packed, and ultimately shipped to Washington for salvage. Moreover the facilities of the field staff for handling and storing were obviously of the most limited character. While it was felt that some sample purchases of meat, cheese, butter, lard, and fresh vegetables would be extremely desirable in the study of chain-store weights, the physical difficulties in handling such merchandise seemed to render it impracticable. Furthermore, it is difficult for a grocer to cut an exact pound of cheese, meat, or butter with the result that the customer is often charged a few cents over or under the price per pound, thereby greatly complicating the weight computations involved in a study of weights. Moreover, the salvage value of such perishable products would be practically nil since Government regulations prevent the distribution of products locally or their donation to local charities or organizations immediately after they have served their purpose. All merchandise obtained in this study was shipped to the General Supply Committee, Washington, D. C., for sale or other disposition.

Of the four cities studied, the tests were conducted in one city in May, 1930, and the other three cities in April and May, 1932. In the first city in which the study was made, the purchases included 1 pound each of navy beans, dried prunes and Lima beans, one-half pound of sweetened crackers, and 2 pounds of sugar. The same products were purchased in the other three cities but the decline of commodity prices made it possible to increase the quantities of two of them. Instead of 1 pound of navy beans, the shoppers were instructed to buy three pounds. Similarly, the quantity of sweetened crackers purchased was increased to 1 pound. While a half-pound purchase of this article is common, it was thought that a larger quantity might furnish a fairer test in an article containing a relatively small number of units per pound or half pound.

All commodities were found at times packaged under manufacturers' or distributors' brands in some of the stores. In most cases, however, these articles could also be obtained in bulk. For example, granulated sugar is frequently found in 2-pound cartons under Domino, Jack Frost, or other brands. It can also, however, generally be obtained in bulk. It was not an uncommon experience in shopping in a store to hear a customer call for and insist on obtaining the bulk instead of the packaged article.

Section 4. Method of purchasing.

In making the weight investigation two experienced women shoppers did most of the buying although the drivers of the automobiles used by the workers shopped some stores, particularly when two stores were located close together. The two agents assigned to check the weights of the products bought also did some shopping during the morning hours.

Each of the drivers of the automobiles was given a street map of the section of the city assigned to him. The driver and the shopper acompanying him were instructed to shop every chain and independent grocery store in the area except the very small, poorly stocked stores or stores in foreign or colored neighborhoods where it was believed an agent's visit might attract undue attention and suspicion. The shoppers were instructed to shop only the side of the streets bounding the area assigned to them, leaving the other side of the boundary streets to be shopped by agents having the adjoining areas. The driver was instructed to drive the length of one street in his area, shopping every grocery store on the way, including all corner stores but no stores located on cross streets. Cross streets were covered in the same way, except that the corner stores already shopped were of course omitted. Each driver checked off the streets on the map of the area assigned to him as the shopping was completed. The greatest precaution was taken to avoid shopping the same store twice.

The automobile carrying the shoppers was parked at such a distance that it could not be seen from the store. The shopper walked from the car to the store and made the purchases as any customer would do. She was instructed not to look at the scales nor stand near the scales while the purchases were being made, nor pay any particular attention to the clerk, nor watch or examine any additions or listing of articles by the clerk. Usually she was engaged in locating in the store other articles on the shopping list to determine, if possible, in advance whether or not they would be offered to her in packaged form; or she might be examining other articles on display. Occasionally she asked a price of some article not on her shopping list. All purchases were made in as natural or casual a manner as possible, so as not to attract any attention to herself or her purchases. The shopper was instructed to be particularly alert in observing salesmen, supervisors of chains, collectors, or customers who might observe the purchase of the same list of articles in more than one store.

The shopper was required to ask the price of each article purchased either before buying it or while it was being put up. In some stores the shopper soon learned that she might expect to have the clerk offer her some particular product or products in ready packaged form, as for example, sugar or prunes. In such a case she was instructed to delay asking the price until she found out if she could get the product in bulk. If the clerk handed out a ready-packaged product, the shopper could ask for the product in bulk, and then ask the price of the packaged article and decide not to take it. In this way the price might appear to be the reason for deciding not to take the article. If a store carried sugar only in cartons packaged at the refinery the shopper declined it with some comment that she did not especially need sugar that day or she did not want to carry it. No packaged articles were purchased except when it was felt that a refusal would arouse suspicion.

It was necessary that the shopper know the price of every article purchased when she left the store. In most stores where a full list of articles was secured the clerk either inclosed a list of prices printed by the cash register or adding machine, or listed the prices of the articles on the outer sack, or made out a bill of sale on the regular store form. After leaving each store the shopper was thus able to compare immediately prices quoted orally by the clerk with those recorded on the various memoranda, thereby checking any incorrect additions or "short changing." All sales slips and additions were marked for identification with the name and address of the store and preserved.

The shopper carried the articles to the automobile where the driver assisted in filling out a form report with the name and address of the store and the price of each article. The form was then inclosed in the sack containing the purchases from that store. The driver also marked the name and address of the store on the outer bag close to any additions made thereon by the clerk.

Section 5. Method of weighing.

In two of the cities headquarters offices for the weighing and recording of weights were established in vacant rooms in the post-office buildings; in the other two cities, where space in the post offices could not be obtained, hotel sample rooms were used. As soon as the shoppers returned with their purchases to the headquarters office two examiners of the commission's staff immediately began weighing the purchases, both examiners carefully observing each and every weight recorded.

The scale used was of the "equal arm" type registering both over and under weights accurate to one-eighth of an ounce. This scale, manufactured by the Exact Weight Scale Co., is of a kind used by many city inspectors of weights and measures. The accuracy of the scale and the weights used was checked by the United States Bureau of Standards prior to starting the work in 1930 and again before the work was resumed in 1932.

Frequent tests (and adjustments when necessary) were made of the balance of the scale to make sure that the pointer came to rest at all times at exact zero when both pans were empty. In weighing the purchases a weight or weights equivalent to the quantity of the article requested was placed on one pan of the scale and the commodity in the sack or bag as purchased on the other. The indicator or pointer showed on the chart of the scale the gross amount over or under the requested weight. This gross shortage or overage was observed by two persons and recorded. The product was then weighed without the container and the net weight observed and recorded in the same way.

Readings of the scale chart on both the overage and shortage side that fell half way between the one-eighth ounce markings were recorded as of the next higher one-eighth unit. For example, an overage of one-sixteenth of an ounce was recorded as one-eighth ounce overweight, while a shortage of one-sixteenth of an ounce was recorded as one-eighth of an ounce underweight. This procedure had the effect of balancing such over and under readings as fell at half way points on the scale. All purchases were weighed and recorded within two hours after their delivery at the headquarters and most of them within half that time. Purchases were made during all hours of the day from early morning until late afternoon and during busy Saturday mornings as well as during slack business hours.

Section 6. Stores shopped and purchases made in four cities.

City No. 1.—Agents of the commission shopped for the five bulk commodities in 319 stores in city No. 1 during seven days in April and May, 1932. City No. 1 is located in an Eastern State. The 319 stores shopped included all the grocery and grocery and meat stores in the city except a comparatively few located in strictly foreign and colored neighborhoods, and a few small low-class stores carrying very limited stocks, which could hardly be classed as grocery stores. Purchases were made from 117 stores belonging to three grocery and meat chains, which number represented 36.7 per cent of the total stores shopped in the city. The two larger chains operated 47 and 52 stores respectively, and a smaller chain, more sectional in the area over which it extends, operated 18 stores.

Of the 202 independent stores in the city 28 were members of one cooperative chain [1] while 28 other stores were affiliated with two other cooperative chains. Eleven stores were associated in a fourth and loosely organized cooperative, not all the stores of which could be identified. The results for the 56 stores identifiable as belonging to the first three cooperative chains are individually tabulated. The 11 stores of the fourth, however, are included with the independent stores because of the comparatively insignificant extent of their cooperative functions. The cooperative chain stores, numbering 56, comprise 17.5 per cent of the total stores shopped and the independent stores, 45.8 per cent.

A total of 1,273 purchases of the five different bulk commodities was made in 319 stores in city No. 1. Failure to find some of the articles, notably sugar, prunes, and Lima beans, in bulk in some stores reduced the average number of items obtained to four per store. A total of 523 purchases, or 41.1 per cent, was made from chain stores; while 219 purchases, or 17.2 per cent, were made from cooperative chains; and 531 items, or 41.7 per cent, were bought from independent stores.

City No. 2.—A total of 328 stores was shopped for the five bulk commodities in city No. 2 during seven days in May, 1932. This city is located in New England. As in other cities, agents of the commission shopped all grocery or grocery and meat stores in the city except those in neighborhoods that were predominantly foreign or colored. Some decidedly inferior stores were also omitted because women shoppers were very much out of place in them, and would be likely to attract attention to the work. Also, such stores as were omitted are not especially representative of the grocery stores of the city.

Three grocery and meat chains operate together a total of 128 stores, or 39 per cent, of the total stores shopped in city No. 2. The two larger chains operate 59 and 50 stores respectively while a smaller more localized chain operates 19 stores. Two other chains of two stores each were found, but are not included in the tabulations because the number of purchases was considered too small to be of significance either separately or combined.

---

[1] A cooperative chain is defined as an association of independent retailers acting cooperatively either by themselves or with a wholesaler to obtain advantages in buying, advertising, or in the performance of other merchandising functions or activities. See report of the Federal Trade Commission on Cooperative Grocery Chains.

Of the 200 independent stores shopped in the city, 42 belong to one cooperative chain while 15 others are members of two other cooperative chains. The 57 independent stores belonging to cooperative groups comprise 17.4 per cent of the total stores shopped in the city. Included in the group of 143 strictly independent stores are 9 stores belonging to two loosely organized cooperative groups whose retail stores could not in all cases be identified. The independent group comprised 43.6 per cent of all the stores in the city.

A total of 1,108 purchases of the five different commodities, or approximately 3.4 purchases per store was made in the 328 stores in city No. 2. The average number of purchases was fewer per store in city No. 2 than in city No. 1 due to the failure to find as many commodities in bulk form, especially Lima beans, which product was procurable in bulk from only 10 of the 128 chain stores shopped. A total of 410 purchases, or 37 per cent of all purchases made, was bought from chain stores; while 197 purchases, or 17.8 per cent, were made from cooperative chains; and 501 purchases, or 45.2 per cent, were made from independent stores.

City No. 3.—This city, located in the Middle West, was the largest city in which the five bulk commodities were purchased. Agents of the commission shopped in 604 stores in this city, excepting, as in other cities, only the stores in foreign or colored neighborhoods and a few very low class stores.

The proportion of chain stores found in this city was higher than in any other city in which purchases were made. A total of 309 stores belonging to five grocery and meat chains shopped in this city comprised 51.2 per cent of the total number of stores shopped. One large chain operated 163 stores in the city; two others of wider geographical distribution, operated 77 and 61 stores, respectively; and two small local chains operated respectively five and three stores.

One cooperative chain with 44 member stores and another with 37 members comprised 13.4 per cent of the total stores shopped. The independent stores in the city numbering 214 made up 35.4 per cent of the total number of stores shopped for accurate weights.

A total of 2,570 purchases of the five bulk commodities was made in the 604 stores in city No. 3. The average number of items obtainable in each store was 4.3 which was a slightly larger average than was found in city No. 1 (4.0) and considerably above the average found in city No. 2 (3.4). A total of 1,371 purchases, or 53.4 per cent, was made from chain stores; while 371 purchases, or 14.4 per cent, were made from cooperative chain stores; and 828 purchases, or 32.2 per cent, were bought from independent stores.

City No. 4.—The same five bulk commodities were purchased during nine days in May, 1930, in 440 stores in city No. 4 which is located in a Southern State. As in the other three cities, the stores shopped in this city included all the grocery and grocery and meat stores in the city except those located in strictly colored or foreign neighborhoods and a few small, low-class stores carrying such poor stocks that they could scarcely be classed as grocery stores.

While the same commodities were purchased in city No. 4 as in the other three cities, the weights of two of the articles purchased differed from those purchased in the other places. This city was the first one shopped and the original purchase schedule called for 1 pound of navy beans and one-half pound of sweetened crackers. Subsequently in the other three cities the quantity of navy beans purchased was increased to 3 pounds and the quantity of crackers to 1 pound. It was found that short weights occurred less frequently on the 1-pound purchases of navy beans from chain or from cooperative and independent stores combined in city No. 4 than when bought in 3-pound lots in any of the other three cities. The actual percentage of net shortage, however, was somewhat greater in city No. 4 than in two of the cities but less than half what it was in the other one of the four. While purchases of the light-weight sweetened crackers are common, in one-half pound lots, it was believed that a 1-pound purchase permitted a fairer test of the accuracy of weights in a commodity having a relatively high unit weight.

In city No. 4 three grocery and meat chains operated a total of 148 stores or 33.6 per cent of the total stores shopped in the city. The largest chain operated 56 stores; and each of the other two operated 52 and 40 stores.

Two cooperative chains numbering 71 and 55 stores comprised 28.6 per cent of all the stores in the city. Independent stores numbering 166 made up the other 37.8 per cent of the stores.

A total of 1,689 purchases of the five different bulk commodities was made in the 440 stores shopped in the city. The average number of purchases per store was 3.8. A total of 642 purchases, or 38 per cent, was made from chain stores; while 486, or 28.8 per cent, were made from cooperative chains; and 561 articles, or 33.2 per cent, were bought from independent stores.

Section 7. Chain and independent store weights in four cities combined.

Proportions of short, over, and exact [2] weight purchases.—In the four cities covered by the inquiry into chain and independent store weights, 1,691 stores were shopped for the five bulk commodities. Table 1 shows the total number of chain, cooperative chain, and independent stores in the four cities shopped and the proportion of total purchases found to be short in net weight, over net weight, or of exact net weight.

TABLE 1.—*Proportion of short weights, overweights, and exact weights on bulk commodities purchased at 702 chain and 989 independent stores in four cities, 1930 and 1932*

Store group	Number of stores shopped	Number of items purchased	Average number of items per store	Purchases showing—		
				Short weight	Overweight	Exact weight
				Per cent	*Per cent*	*Per cent*
Chains	702	2,946	4.2	50.3	34.1	15.6
Cooperatives	320	1,273	4.0	47.1	43.9	9.0
Independents	669	2,421	3.6	48.1	43.8	8.1
Cooperatives and independents	989	3,694	3.7	47.8	43.8	8.4
Total	1,691	6,640	3.9	48.9	39.5	11.6

[2] In summarizing the results of this study the term "exact weight" has been used to indicate the weight when the pointer of the scale came to rest at zero as accurately as two observers could determine.

Of the total number of stores shopped, 702, or 41.5 per cent, belonged to 11 different grocery or grocery and meat chains; 320, or 18.9 per cent, were independent stores affiliated with 11 cooperative chains; and 669, or 39.6 per cent, were independent stores without cooperative affiliations.[3]

In these four cities, chain stores gave exact net weights nearly twice as frequently as either cooperative or independent stores. All chains together weighed out the exact quantities asked for on 15.6 per cent of the purchases made as compared with 9.0 per cent exact weights obtained from cooperative chain stores and 8.1 per cent from other independents. From cooperatives and independents together exact net weights were obtained on 8.4 per cent of the purchases.

While chains more frequently gave exact weights than cooperative and other independent stores both separately and combined, they also more frequently gave short and less frequently overweight than did the independents. Of the total purchases made in all chain stores, 50.3 per cent were short of the net weight requested, while cooperative and independent stores together were short on 47.8 per cent of the purchases made. Overweight purchases from chain stores amounted to only 34.1 per cent of the total purchases made from them, whereas overweight purchases from all independents amounted to 43.8 per cent.

Quantity of total short or total overweights.—While the proportion of short, over, and exact net weights obtained from different kinds of stores is of considerable interest, the actual quantity of the deviation from exact weights is of greater importance. Table 2 shows the actual quantity and percentage of net shortages or overages on all purchases of the five bulk commodities from all chain, cooperative chain, and independent stores.

TABLE 2.—*Quantity and percentage of net shortage (—) or overage (+) on bulk commodities purchased at 702 chain and 989 independent stores in four cities, 1930 and 1932*

Store group	Net weight requested	Total net shortage (—) or overage (+)	Total net shortage (—) or overage (+)
	Pounds	*Ounces*	*Per cent*
Chains	4, 489½	—230⅜	—0. 321
Cooperatives	1, 799½	0	0
Independents	3, 716½	+85	+ . 143
Cooperatives and independents	5, 516	+85	+ . 096
Total	10, 005½	—145⅜	— . 091

In the four cities in which the shopping experiment was carried out, all chain stores together gave short weights amounting to 230⅜ ounces net, or 14.4 pounds, on total purchases of 4,489½ pounds. This quantity shortage, expressed in percentage, means that all chain stores were net short on an average 0.321 per cent of the requested or exact net weight of the total items purchased of them.

[3] A few of the 669 independent stores were known to have some cooperative chain affiliation but identification could not in all cases be determined.

The cooperative chain stores, on the other hand, exactly balanced net shortages with net overages on purchases amounting to 1,799½ pounds while independent stores were 85 ounces, or 0.143 per cent, net overweight on total purchases of 3,716½ pounds. For cooperative and independents combined, the total net overage was 85 ounces, or 0.096 per cent, on total purchases supposed to weigh 5,516 pounds. From the above figures it will be seen that the total net weight spread or difference between chain and independent stores (including cooperatives) was nearly one-half of 1 per cent (0.417 per cent) in favor of the independent stores on the total purchases made from both types of stores.

While the size of the shortage for chains may seem insignificant to many, it amounts to 3.41 per cent on the investment in these commodities, figured on the basis of average stock turn of grocery and meat chains, 10.61 times per annum. Moreover, the turnover of certain bulk commodities such as fresh meats and produce is probably much higher than the average and these commodities constitute a substantial proportion of the total business of most chains selling groceries. A shortage of weight of this magnitude, therefore, if applicable to the total business in commodities weighed by the chain would exercise a very favorable effect on the rate of return on the investment in such commodities, and probably, because of their volume, on total investment as well.

In the preceding table the shortage or overage figures are net figures. The following table shows for all stores of each type the total short weights and the total overweights and the percentages of both short weights and overweights based on the total quantities purchased. Corresponding figures for each chain, cooperative chain, and independent store group in each of the four cities are found in Appendix Table 1.

TABLE 3.—*Quantity and percentage of total net shortage and overage on bulk commodities purchased at 702 chain and 989 independent stores in four cities, 1930 and 1932*

Store group	Total short weight		Total overweight		Total net shortage (−) or overage (+)
	Ounces	*Per cent*	*Ounces*	*Per cent*	*Per cent*
Chains	708¾	0.987	478⅜	0.666	−0.321
Cooperatives	365⅜	1.269	365⅜	1.269	±.000
Independents	750¾	1.262	835¾	1.405	+.143
Cooperatives and independents	1,116⅛	1.265	1,201⅛	1.361	+.096
Total	1,824⅞	1.140	1,679½	1.049	−.091

While shortages and overages obtained are treated in this report as offsetting each other in so far as they do accomplish that end, it is, nevertheless, of some interest to note the average short weights of the stores that gave short weights without relation to the over weights.

The average total shortage, based on total weights purchased, occurring in 50.3 per cent of the total purchases from chain stores, amounted to nearly 1 per cent (0.987) as compared with an average of 0.321 per cent when overages are included in the calculation. Cooperative chain stores, 47.1 per cent of the purchases from which were short of exact net weight, had a corresponding total shortage of 1.269 per cent, although when overages are also considered these stores gave exact net weights on total purchases. The data for independent stores, 48.1 per cent of the purchases from which were short weight, show a total shortage of 1.263 per cent as compared with a net overage of 0.143 per cent. The total shortage given by all cooperative and independent stores combined was 1.265 per cent, as compared with a total shortage of 0.987 per cent given by all chain stores.

Section 8. Variations in chain and independent weights by cities.

From the above it should not be inferred that all chain stores gave short net weights or that all independent stores gave overweights. There were important variations not only between the chains and independents from city to city but also between chains and between independents in the same or different cities.

The following table presents the results of the weighing in each of the four cities for each of four groups of distributors—chain, cooperative, independent, and independent and cooperative combined:

TABLE 4.—*Proportion of short weights, overweights, and exact weights on total number of bulk commodities purchased at chain, cooperative chain, and independent stores in each of four cities, 1930 and 1932*

City	Number of stores shopped	Number of items purchased	Purchases showing— Short weight	Over-weight	Exact weight
			Per cent	*Per cent*	*Per cent*
City No. 1:					
Chains	117	523	42.2	37.7	20.1
Cooperatives	56	219	50.2	43.8	6.0
Independents	146	531	44.6	48.6	6.8
Cooperatives and independents	202	750	46.3	47.2	6.5
City No. 2:					
Chains	128	410	61.7	27.6	10.7
Cooperatives	57	197	59.4	33.5	7.1
Independents	143	501	58.3	34.7	7.0
Cooperatives and independents	200	698	58.6	34.4	7.0
City No. 3:					
Chains	309	1,371	52.1	33.5	14.4
Cooperatives	81	371	48.5	40.7	10.8
Independents	214	828	47.6	43.1	9.3
Cooperatives and independents	295	1,199	47.9	42.4	9.7
City No. 4:					
Chains	148	642	46.0	36.6	17.4
Cooperatives	126	486	39.5	50.6	9.9
Independents	166	561	43.2	48.1	8.7
Cooperatives and independents	292	1,047	41.4	49.3	9.3

In city No. 1 the chains gave short weights less frequently than the cooperatives and independents, separately or combined. In the other three cities the chains were more frequently short than either the independents or cooperatives, separately or combined. In no one of the four cities did the chains show overages more frequently than shortages, although this was found in the cooperatives in one city, in the independents in two, and in the cooperatives and independents combined in two.

In city No. 1 the chains had a net overage but gave net shortages in the other three. The cooperatives had a net overage only in city No. 4 and were short in the other three. (Table 5.)

TABLE 5.—*Quantity and percentage of net shortage (—) or overage (+) on total quantity of bulk commodities purchased at chain, cooperative chain, and independent stores in each of four cities, 1930 and 1932*

City	Net weight requested	Total net shortage (—) or overage (+)	Total net shortage (—) or overage (+)
City No. 1:	*Pounds*	*Ounces*	*Per cent*
Chains	837	+¾	+0.006
Cooperatives	363	−1¼	−.022
Independents	881¼	+73¾	+.523
Cooperatives and independents	1,244¼	+72½	+.364
City No. 2:			
Chains	716	−119⅝	−1.044
Cooperatives	343	−33¼	−.606
Independents	858	−49⅛	−.358
Cooperatives and independents	1,201	−82⅜	−.429
City No. 3:			
Chains	2,288½	−91½	−.250
Cooperatives	598	−36	−.376
Independents	1,376¾	+2⅝	+.012
Cooperatives and independents	1,974¾	−33⅜	−.106
City No. 4:			
Chains	648	−20	−.193
Cooperatives	495½	+70½	+.889
Independents	600½	+57¾	+.601
Cooperatives and independents	1,096	+128¼	+.731

The independents, excluding cooperatives, on the other hand, had a net shortage in only one city and a net overage in three. Data for cooperatives and independents combined show net shortages in two cities and net overages in two. The net chain overage in city No. 1 was less than that of the independents or independents and cooperatives combined. In city No. 2 the chain shortage was greater than that of the independents or the independents and cooperatives combined. In city No. 3 it was less than that of the cooperatives. In city No. 4 only the chains showed a shortage. City No. 2 is interesting because of the sharp contrast shown by the weighing results in that city as compared with the other three. In the first place, short weighing was very much more prevalent in that city for every group of distributors than it was in any other city. In the other three cities, the highest proportion of short weights shown for any group was only 52.1 per cent for the chains in city No. 3 and the proportion was as low as 39.5 per cent for the cooperatives in city No. 4. In city No. 2, however, the lowest proportion of short weight purchases was 58.3 per cent for the independents and the highest, 61.7 per cent for the chains. A second point which is worth noting about the figures for this city is the fact that it was the only one of the four cities in which every one of the four groups of distributors had a net shortage. Further, this was the only one of the four cities in which any one of the four groups of distributors had a net shortage of more than 1 per cent. Finally, the chain distributors in that city, with a net shortage of over 1 per cent (1.044 per cent) were responsible for a higher proportion of short weight purchases and a higher net shortage than any other group of distributors tabulated in any of the four cities.

Section 9. Variations in weights between chains.

Although there are no such wide variations in the weighing results for individual chain-store systems as there are between the chain and the independent distributors, there are enough differences between these chains, both among cities and within the same city to warrant some discussion. The following table, therefore, presents the weighing results for each chain in each of the four cities which were shopped by agents of the commission.

TABLE 6.—*Quantity and percentage of net shortage (—) or overage (+) on five bulk commodities purchased at 702 chain stores in four cities, 1930 and 1932*

	Number of stores shopped	Number of items purchased	Purchases showing—			Net weight requested	Total net shortage (—) or overage (+)	Total net shortage (—) or overage (+)
			Short weight	Overweight	Exact weight			
			Per cent	*Per cent*	*Per cent*	*Pounds*	*Ounces*	*Per cent*
City No. 1:								
Chain A	47	193	38. 8	39. 4	21. 8	314	+3¾	+0. 075
Chain B	52	252	42. 9	37. 3	19. 8	398	+4½	+. 071
Chain C	18	78	48. 7	34. 6	16. 7	125	—7½	—. 375
City No. 2:								
Chain A	59	177	69. 5	23. 7	6. 8	304	—84⅛	—1. 730
Chain B	50	171	56. 7	30. 4	12. 9	310	—27⅛	—. 547
Chain C	19	62	53. 2	30. 7	16. 1	102	—8⅜	—. 513
City No. 3:								
Chain A	61	276	55. 1	27. 9	17. 0	448	—36⅛	—. 504
Chain B	77	351	69. 2	18. 5	12. 3	598	—93⅞	—. 981
Chain C	163	707	42. 0	43. 4	14. 6	1, 181½	+40⅛	+. 212
Chain D	5	24	66. 7	25. 0	8. 3	39	—1½	—. 240
Chain E	3	13	46. 1	38. 5	15. 4	22	—⅛	—. 036
City No. 4:								
Chain A	56	251	38. 6	36. 3	25. 1	260½	—8	—. 192
Chain B	52	199	56. 3	37. 7	6. 0	183	—4¾	—. 162
Chain C	40	192	44. 8	35. 9	19. 3	204½	—7¼	—. 222
Total	702	2, 946	50. 3	34. 1	15. 6	4, 489½	—230⅜	—. 321

The proportion of short weights shown for individual chains exceeds the proportion of overweights in all 14 comparisons except chain A in city No. 1 and chain C in city No. 3. The lowest proportion of short weights reported for any chain is 38.6 per cent for chain A in city No. 4, the highest is 69.5 for chain A in city No. 2. For the chains, in most cases, overweights range from 30 to 40 per cent of the total number of items purchased from them. Chain C in city No. 3 is the only one from which purchases were overweight in excess of 40 per cent of the total purchases made. For four other chains, however, three of which are in city No. 3, overweights were found in less than 30 per cent of the purchases made from them.

Of the 14 chain groups shopped in the four cities, reports show net overages for only three of them—two in city No. 1 and one in city No. 3. Eleven chain groups, therefore, or nearly 80 per cent of them, had net shortages, and in two cities, none of the chains had any net overages. The highest overage for the three chains having overages is slightly over one-fifth of 1 per cent (0.212) for chain C in city No. 3. The range of net shortages for the chains having them is from 0.036 per cent for chain E in city No. 3 to 1.730 per cent for chain A in city No. 2. By far the highest net shortages are those shown for the chains in city No. 2. Both chains B and C had a net shortage of over one-half of 1 per cent and chain C had nearly 2 per cent (1.730). In only one instance, chain B (0.981 per cent) in city No. 3 was as large a net shortage found for any chain in any city as was found for any one of the chains in city No. 2.

Section 10. Variations in weights between cooperative chains.

Cooperative grocery chains which have come into prominence in all parts of the country during the past several years had about as much variation from exact weights in bulk commodities as the centrally owned chains. Table 7 shows the results of the weighing tests for each cooperative chain (or group of cooperative chains in two instances, where the number of stores in such chains was small) in each of the four cities shopped.

TABLE 7.—*Quantity and percentage of net shortage (—) or overage (+) on five bulk commodities purchased at 320 cooperative chain stores in four cities, 1930 and 1932*

	Number of stores shopped	Number of items purchased	Purchases showing—			Net weight requested	Total net shortage (—) or overage (+)	Total net shortage (—) or overage (+)
			Short weight	Over-weight	Exact weight			
			Per cent	*Per cent*	*Per cent*	*Pounds*	*Ounces*	*Per cent*
City No. 1:								
Cooperative chain D	28	113	42.5	53.1	4.4	184	+10¼	+0.348
Other cooperatives	28	106	58.5	34.0	7.5	179	—11½	—.402
City No. 2:								
Cooperative chain D	42	143	61.5	32.2	6.3	251	—29	—.722
Other cooperatives	15	54	53.7	37.0	9.3	92	—4¼	—.289
City No. 3:								
Cooperative chain F	37	159	46.5	45.3	8.2	260	—2¼	—.054
Cooperative chain G	44	212	50.0	37.3	12.7	338	—33¾	—.624
City No. 4:								
Cooperative chain D	71	267	37.8	53.2	9.0	268	+44⅞	+1.047
Cooperative chain E	55	219	41.5	47.5	11.0	227½	+25⅝	+.704
Total	320	1,273	47.1	43.9	9.0	1,799½	±0	±.000

The proportion of short weights given by cooperative chains exceded the proportion of overweights in 5 of the 8 cooperative groups as compared with 12 out of 14 chain groups. The smallest proportion of short weights found for any cooperative was 37.8 per cent for cooperative chain D in city No. 4 and the largest was 61.5 per cent for cooperative chain D in city No. 2. The average proportion of short weights for all cooperatives was 47.1 per cent as compared with the chain figure of 50.3 per cent.

The proportion of overweights ranged from 32.2 per cent for cooperative chain D in city No. 2 to 53.2 per cent for cooperative chain D in city No. 4 and averaged 43.9 per cent. This average figure of 43.9 per cent was 9.8 points per cent higher than the proportion of overweights (34.1 per cent) shown for all chains.

Of the eight cooperative chain groups only three had net overages, one in city No. 1 and two in city No. 4. The largest net overage was 1.047 per cent shown for cooperative chain D in city No. 4. The other two overages were 0.704 per cent and 0.348 per cent, respectively. Five cooperative chain groups had net shortages, and in two cities all of the cooperatives had shortages. The range of net shortages for these cooperative groups was from 0.054 per cent for cooperative chain F in city No. 3 to 0.722 per cent for cooperative chain D in city No. 2.

Section 11. Short weights and overweights by commodities.

Proportions of short weights and overweights.—For all stores combined the largest proportions of short weights were given on navy beans (55.5 per cent) and sweetened crackers (55.4 per cent). On both prunes and Lima beans the proportion was between 40 and 42 per cent, while on sugar it was 46.4 per cent. On both prunes and Lima beans the proportion of overweight purchases exceeded the proportion of short-weight purchases. The highest proportion of exact net weights (15 per cent) was shown on sugar purchases.

TABLE 8.—*Proportion of short weights, over weights, and exact weights on specified bulk commodities purchased at 702 chain and 989 independent stores in four cities, 1930 and 1932*

Commodity	Number of stores shopped	Number of items purchased	Purchases showing—		
			Short weight	Over-weight	Exact weight
			Per cent	*Per cent*	*Per cent*
Navy beans:					
Chains	702	679	64.3	26.1	9.6
Cooperatives	320	294	45.2	46.6	8.2
Independents	669	611	50.6	43.2	6.2
Cooperatives and independents	989	905	48.8	44.3	6.9
Total	1,691	1,584	55.5	30.5	18.0
Prunes, dried:					
Chains	702	499	42.3	40.7	17.0
Cooperatives	320	200	43.0	46.5	10.5
Independents	669	324	40.4	52.2	7.4
Cooperatives and independents	989	524	41.4	50.0	8.6
Total	1,691	1,023	41.8	45.5	12.7
Lima beans:					
Chains	702	560	39.1	40.4	20.5
Cooperatives	320	261	42.5	49.4	8.1
Independents	669	493	42.2	48.9	8.9
Cooperatives and independents	989	754	42.3	49.1	8.6
Total	1,691	1,314	41.0	45.3	13.7
Crackers, sweetened:					
Chains	702	699	57.1	30.5	12.4
Cooperatives	320	299	54.9	37.1	8.0
Independents	669	563	53.7	37.8	8.5
Cooperatives and independents	989	862	54.1	37.6	8.3
Total	1,691	1,561	55.4	34.4	10.2
Sugar:					
Chains	702	509	42.6	36.6	20.8
Cooperatives	320	219	48.0	40.6	11.4
Independents	669	430	50.0	40.0	10.0
Cooperatives and independents	989	649	49.3	40.2	10.5
Total	1,691	1,158	46.4	38.6	15.0

The chain stores were more frequently short weight than either the independent stores or cooperatives, separately or combined, on two of the five items, namely, navy beans and sweetened crackers, and were more frequently short than their independent competitors on dried prunes as well. On sugar and Lima beans the reverse was found, the chains giving short weights less frequently than their independent or cooperative competitors. Except on Lima beans, however, where the difference was very slight, the proportion of chain purchases which was short weight always exceeded the proportion which was overweight. The showing for the independents and cooperatives was slightly better, both of these types of distributors giving more overages than shortages on prunes and Lima beans. On sweetened crackers and sugar, however, the independents and cooperatives as well as the chains had substantially lower proportions of overages than shortages.

Total quantities of short weights and overweights.—The following table shows the actual quantities of shortages and overages for chains, independents, and cooperatives on each of the five commodities purchased in the various chain and independent stores.

TABLE 9.—*Quantity and percentage of net shortage (—) or overage (+) on specified bulk commodities purchased at 702 chain and 989 independent stores in four cities, 1930 and 1932*

Commodity	Net weight requested	Total net shortage (—) or overage (+)	Total net shortage (—) or overage (+)
	Pounds	*Ounces*	*Per cent*
Navy beans:			
Chains	1,783	−171	−0.599
Cooperatives	661	+1¾	+.017
Independents	1,543	+46⅞	+.190
Cooperatives and independents	2,204	+48⅝	+.138
Total	3,987	−122⅜	−.192
Prunes, dried:			
Chains	500½	+17¼	+.215
Cooperatives	201	+12⅛	+.377
Independents	323	+75⅞	+1.468
Cooperatives and independents	524	+88	+1.050
Total	1,024½	+105¼	+.642
Lima beans:			
Chains	561	+27⅛	+.302
Cooperatives	261	+24¾	+.593
Independents	493	+58⅝	+.743
Cooperatives and independents	754	+83⅜	+.691
Total	1,315	+110½	+.525
Crackers, sweetened:			
Chains	625	−119⅛	−1.191
Cooperatives	238½	−27¾	−.727
Independents	497½	−94⅜	−1.186
Cooperatives and independents	736	−122⅛	−1.037
Total	1,361	−241¼	−1.108
Sugar:			
Chains	1,020	+15⅜	+.094
Cooperatives	438	−10⅞	−.155
Independents	860	−2	−.015
Cooperatives and independents	1,298	−12⅞	−.062
Total	2,318	+2½	+.007

An examination of this table shows for each type of distributor net overages on prune and Lima-bean purchases and net short weights on sweetened crackers. On navy beans, the chains had a net short weight and the other types of distributors, net overages, the reverse being true on sugar where the chains had a slight net overage and the other distributors were short on an average. Except in the case of sugar, where the chains show a slight overage, the overages for the chains were less and the shortages greater than for the cooperative and independent distributors combined. Taking the cooperatives and independents separately, however, the shortage for chains was greater on sweetened crackers by a very narrow margin than the shortage for independents. The general and comparatively high shortages on sweetened crackers are possibly explained in part by the fact that this article was relatively the most expensive one purchased in the various stores and also probably the one which was most difficult to weigh accurately.

Section 12. Weights by commodities and cities.

The commodities on the shopper's list that had proportionately the greatest number of shortages varied not only with the type of distributor but also with the city.

City No. 1.—For all chain stores in city No. 1 the proportion of short weights for each article bought varied from 20.9 per cent on prunes to 60.5 per cent on navy beans. (Appendix Table 2.) Cooperative chain and independent stores combined had a range of net shortages on the total number of purchases that varied from 37 per cent on Lima beans to 55.7 per cent on sugar.

Net weights obtained from chain stores ranged from over one-half of 1 per cent (0.521) short on sweetened crackers purchased in 1-pound lots from 117 stores to 1.271 per cent overweight on dried prunes purchased in like quantity from 91 stores. Independent and cooperative stores combined gave weights that ranged from 0.265 per cent short on crackers purchased in 174 stores to 1.865 per cent overweight on prunes purchased in 93 stores.

Chain stores in city No. 1 gave more short net weights on navy beans (the article purchased in largest quantity in each store) than on other products, while cooperatives and independents showed a tendency to short weight more often on sugar. The greatest quantity of net shortage, however, did not occur on the article most frequently found underweight. Except for the cooperative chain group, the commodity showing the greatest short weight was sweetened crackers, due perhaps to the fact that crackers was the most expensive article on the list and also because of the relatively greater weight of a unit of the article.

Both chain and independent stores gave a higher percentage of overweights on dried prunes than on other articles. The cooperative chain stores gave more overweights on Lima beans, and the largest percentage of overweight purchases from independent and cooperative chain stores combined also occurred on Lima beans. The largest net overages, however, were obtained from all types of stores on dried prunes. The frequent overweights on purchases of dried prunes from each store group may have been due to the fact that the dried prune is of a more perishable character than any of the other articles on the shopper's list, and also because the shopping was done during the late spring when fresh fruits were displacing prunes, with the result that some grocers may have been closing out their stocks of prunes for the season.

Notwithstanding that the greatest overweights occurred on prunes bought in chain stores, exact weights were also obtained most often on this same article bought from the same stores. Independents and cooperatives combined did not show much variation in the proportion of exact weights given on the five different articles, the proportion ranging from 5.2 per cent on crackers to 7.3 per cent on both navy and Lima beans.

Individually all three chains had the largest percentage of net shortages on the 3-pound purchases of navy beans.[4] In actual net weight shortage chains A and C gave the largest underweight on crackers and chain B on navy beans.

Chains A and C gave exact net weights on Lima beans more often than on any other article, while chain B sold exact weights of dried prunes more frequently than other articles.

The most frequent as well as the largest total net overweights for each of the three chains were on dried prunes except for chain A which, while giving the largest net overweight on prunes, gave overweights more frequently on sugar.

City No. 2.—In city No. 2 as well as in city No. 1 (Appendix Table 3) chain stores gave more short weights on the 3-pound purchases of navy beans than on the other products. According to commodities, the frequency of short weights varied among chains from 48.6 per cent on sugar to 75.2 per cent on navy beans. Among cooperative and independent stores combined shortages varied from 51.1 per cent on Lima beans to 65.5 per cent on sweetened crackers.

Weights obtained from chain stores in this city ranged from an average net shortage of 0.042 per cent on 74 purchases of sugar in 2-pound lots to 2.891 per cent short on Lima beans 1 pound of which was obtained from each of 10 stores. Independent and cooperative stores combined gave net weights that ranged from 1.776 per cent short on sweetened crackers purchased from 165 stores to 0.29 per cent overweight on purchases of dried prunes made in 89 stores.

The chains gave a higher percentage of overweights (33.8) on the purchases of bulk sugar than on the other articles while cooperatives and independents gave their overweights (41.6 per cent) most often on dried prunes. Exact net weights were obtained most frequently from chains on Lima beans and also from cooperatives and independents combined.

Again, as in city No. 1, it may be said that all three chains in city No. 2 had the largest percentage of shortages (other than in commodities purchased one or two times[5]) in the 3-pound purchases of navy beans. In actual net shortage chain A gave the largest underweight on sweetened crackers and chains B and C on Lima beans.[6]

[4] Not shown in tables in this report.

[5] Two chains gave a higher percentage of shortages in Lima beans, but from 1 chain only 1 purchase was made and from the other only 2 purchases.

[6] Not shown in tables in this report.

Chains A and C gave exact net weights on sugar more often than on any other article; and chain B gave exact net weights on dried prunes more frequently than on other articles.

Of the five products purchased, chain A gave net overweights most frequently and in largest amounts on sugar; chain B, on dried prunes; and chain C gave overweights most frequently on dried prunes but in largest quantity on sugar.

City No. 3.—Net weights of the various commodities obtained in chain stores in city No. 3 ranged from an average of 1.287 per cent short on 307 1-pound purchases of sweetened crackers to 0.347 per cent overweight on 294 1-pound purchases of Lima beans (Appendix Table 4). All independent stores combined gave weights that ranged from 1.836 per cent short on 1-pound purchases of sweetened crackers bought in 271 stores to 0.803 per cent overweight on 1-pound purchases of dried prunes bought in 181 stores.

In this city, like the two previously discussed, chain stores gave short weights on navy beans purchased in 3-pound quantities more frequently than on any of the other articles purchased in smaller quantities. The proportion of short net-weight purchases obtained from all chain stores in city No. 3 varied from 42.9 per cent on Lima beans to 67.3 per cent on navy beans.

Cooperative and independent stores combined had a proportion of shortages that ranged from 39.2 per cent on dried prunes to 59.8 per cent on sweetened crackers. Both chain stores and all independents together had the largest short weights on sweetened crackers, the former being 1.287 per cent short in weight and the latter 1.836 per cent short.

Overages occurred most frequently with both chain and independent stores on dried prunes. The largest average net overage (0.347 per cent) given by chains was on Lima beans. Independents and cooperatives combined gave their largest overweights (0.803 per cent) on dried prunes. Exact weights were obtained from chains in this city most often on Lima beans and from independents on sugar.

Each of the chains in city No. 3, except chain E with only three stores, had the largest percentage of shortages on the 3-pound purchases of navy beans.[7] This was practically the same situation that was found in the two cities previously discussed. All chains gave their largest short weights on sweetened crackers.

The three larger chains gave exact net weights most frequently on a variety of articles which included Lima beans, prunes, and sugar. Overweights were most frequently given by each of the three large chains on dried prunes. Two of these chains also gave the largest amount of overweight on dried prunes; the other one did not average a net overweight on any article.

Two of the stores belonging to chain B in city No. 3 were designated and used by that chain as training stores for clerks. Both were large stores in thickly settled parts of the city, and in them more than the usual number of clerks was employed. In each of

[7] Not shown in tables in this report.

these stores the five bulk articles were obtained by agents of the commission. A check on the weights obtained showed a net shortage on every article purchased except one. These shortages ranged from one-eighth ounce on 2 pounds of sugar to 1⅜ ounces on sweetened crackers. Three of the shortages were for three-eighths ounces, two were for one-half ounce, one was one-fourth ounce short, and another was three-fourths of an ounce short. The single overweight was one-eighth ounce on a 1-pound purchase of dried prunes. In one of the stores a student clerk weighed the purchases; in the other store it was not ascertained whether the weighing was done by a student or by a regular clerk in the store. This chain, it may be noted, gave short net weights on 69.2 per cent of the total purchases made from it, net overweights on 18.5 per cent of the purchases, and exact net weights on 12.3 per cent. The total net shortage on 351 items purchased from stores belonging to this chain was about 1 per cent (0.981).

City No. 4.—Chain store weights in city No. 4 ranged from 1.403 per cent short on sweetened crackers purchased in one-half pound lots from 147 stores to 0.251 per cent overweight on Lima beans purchased in 1 pound lots from 143 stores. (Appendix Table 5.) Independent and cooperative stores combined gave weights that ranged from 0.084 per cent short on sugar purchased in 2-pound lots from 176 stores to 1.369 per cent overweight on navy beans bought in 1-pound lots from 254 stores.

For all chain stores in city No. 4 the proportion of short weights for each of the bulk articles purchased varied from 33.6 per cent on Lima beans to 55.8 per cent on sweetened crackers. Cooperative chain and independent stores combined had a narrower range of shortages, namely, from 39.1 per cent on dried prunes to 43.7 per cent on sweetened crackers.

Chain stores gave the largest percentage of short net weights (55.8) on sweetened crackers, the most expensive article on the list. This was in contrast to the chains of the other three cities which gave the largest percentages of net shortages on the 3-pound purchases of navy beans. Cooperatives and independents in this city likewise gave the largest percentage of net shortages (43.7) on sweetened crackers although on total purchases this article was overweight. The chains also gave the largest shortage on sweetened crackers, which was 1.403 per cent short of exact net weight. Cooperatives and independents combined gave short weights on but one item, sugar, which was found to be 0.084 per cent short of exact net weight.

As a whole, chain stores gave a higher percentage of overweights (45.4) on Lima beans than on other items. Cooperative chains gave the largest proportion of overweights (61.8) on navy beans and independents on dried prunes with a percentage of overweight amounting to 55.4 per cent.

On purchases from chain stores exact net weights occurred most often on sugar, about one-third of the purchases of which was exact net weight. Cooperatives and independents combined also had the largest percentage of exact net weights on sugar, with 12.5 per cent of all purchases from them registering exact weight.

Two of the three chains gave individually the largest percentages of net shortages on sweetened crackers, while the third had a larger percentage on navy beans.[8] Each of the three chains in this instance also gave the largest amount of net shortage on the items most frequently found short. Each of the three chains was most frequently overweight on Lima beans, purchases of which showed the largest total net overage from two chains while the other chain had a larger overage on dried prunes. Two chains gave exact net weights most frequently on sugar; the other on Lima beans.

Section 13. Effect of preweighing by distributors on weighing results.

Proportions of short, over, and exact weight purchases.—Of the 6,640 items purchased in the 1,691 stores in all four cities 795 items, or 12 per cent of the total purchases, were preweighed—i. e., weighed up and sacked in the stores during the clerks' spare time or, in the case of the chain stores, weighed up and sacked in the chain-store warehouse.

Nearly two-thirds (64.4 per cent) of the 795 preweighed items, or 512, were obtained from the 702 chain stores. Only 283 items were obtained from the 989 cooperative chain and independent stores.

The articles bought preweighed included chiefly navy and Lima beans and sugar. Dried prunes and crackers were rarely found packaged in advance.

Table 10 shows the number of preweighed items obtained from chain, cooperative chain, and independent stores and the percentage of purchases showing short, over, and exact net weights.

TABLE 10.—*Proportion of short weights, overweights, and exact weights on preweighed bulk commodities purchased at 702 chain and 989 independent stores in four cities, 1930 and 1932*

Store group	Number of stores shopped	Number of items purchased	Purchases showing—		
			Short weight	Overweight	Exact weight
			Per cent	*Per cent*	*Per cent*
Chains	702	512	59.0	22.3	18.7
Cooperatives	320	99	65.7	22.2	12.1
Independents	669	184	64.7	25.5	9.8
Cooperatives and independents	989	283	65.0	24.4	10.6
Total	1,691	795	61.1	23.0	15.9

The first point of interest to be noted about this table is that chain stores which gave exact net weights on 15.6 per cent of the purchases made from them by the commission (Table 1) had only a slightly higher percentage of exact weights (18.7) on preweighed goods. Cooperatives and independents likewise did not appreciably increase the proportion of their exact weights on preweighed goods. On total purchases the percentage of exact weights obtained from these stores was 8.4 per cent; on preweighed goods the percentage of exact weights was 10.6.

[8] Not shown in tables in this report.

Proportion of net shortages.—The most significant point shown by these comparisons, however, is that chain, cooperative, and independent stores in the four cities combined gave appreciably larger proportions of short net weights on preweighed goods than were given on total purchases bought from them. This difference in proportion of short weights was much more marked in the case of the independents than in that of the chains. The former weighed out 64.7 per cent of the preweighed goods short of exact net weight as compared with only 48.1 per cent of short net weights on all purchases made of them. (Table 1.) The latter, however, gave short weights on 59 per cent of the preweighed goods as compared with 50.3 per cent on total purchases. Similarly, the percentage of overweight for each type of stores was correspondingly less on preweighed goods than on total purchases. In other words, the buyer of commodities weighed and packaged in advance by the independent and cooperative stores stands about two chances out of three that he will get short weight and only slightly better in the chain stores.

The actual net shortage figures on preweighed goods (Table 11), however, are of much more significance than the proportion of shortages on such purchases. The importance of this from the consumer's point of view lies in the fact that the net shortage in these preweighed items seems considerably higher on the average than in the case of items weighed at the time of purchase, amounting for all types of stores studied to slightly over eight-tenths of 1 per cent.

TABLE 11.—*Quantity and percentage of net shortage (−) or overage (+) on preweighed bulk commodities purchased at 702 chain and 989 independent stores in four cities, 1930 and 1932*

Store group	Net weight requested,	Total net shortage (−) or overage (+)	Total net shortage (−) or overage (+)
	Pounds	*Ounces*	*Per cent*
Chains	1,047	−120⅜	−0.719
Cooperatives	176	−30⅜	−1.079
Independents	340	−52⅝	−0.967
Cooperatives and independents	516	−83	−1.005
Total	1,563	−203⅜	−0.813

This figure compares with a net overage of nearly one-tenth of 1 per cent (0.091) on all purchases made from all stores by the commission as shown in Table 2.

Not only did the chain stores give lower proportions of short weights on commodities preweighed at the warehouse or store but they also gave an appreciably lower percentage of net weight short than in the case of their independent and cooperative competitors. This appears from the preceding table which shows that the independent and cooperative stores were short nearly three-tenths of 1 per cent more than the chains on such items.

Chains as a whole were 0.719 per cent and cooperative chain and independent stores combined, 1.005 per cent short of exact net weight on the five preweighed bulk articles as compared with a total net shortage of 0.321 per cent for the former on all purchases of the five bulk articles made from their stores and an overage of 0.096 per cent for the latter.

Cooperative chains as a whole were somewhat shorter in net weights than the combined independent stores in this comparison.

Short net weights on preweighed navy beans on sale by Chain B, City No. 3.—Among the preweighed articles bought and tested for accurate weights in city No. 3 were 21 four-pound purchases of navy beans. Chain B in that city advertised a sale of this commodity in the newspapers at a price of 9 cents for 4 pounds. Purchases of this commodity in 4-pound lots are included with the preweighed articles in Table 11. They are also considered separately in Table 12.

TABLE 12.—*Quantity and proportion of net shortage (—) on 21 purchases of preweighed navy beans advertised at 9 cents in 4-pound quantities by chain B in city No. 3, 1932*

Date	Number of items purchased	Purchases showing—			Net weight requested	Total net shortage	Total net shortage
		Short weight	Overweight	Exact weight			
		Per cent	*Per cent*	*Per cent*	*Pounds*	*Ounces*	*Per cent*
May 16	3	100.0	0	0	12	−3⅝	−1.888
May 17	2	100.0	0	0	8	−2½	−1.953
May 18	1	100.0	0	0	4	−¾	−1.172
May 19	5	100.0	0	0	20	−2½	−.781
May 20	7	100.0	0	0	28	−6	−1.339
May 21	3	66.7	33.3	0	12	−⅞	−.456
Total	21	95.2	4.8	0	84	−16¼	−1.209

Not a single exact net weight was obtained in this sale of preweighed navy beans. Of the 21 purchases made, 20 were short of exact net weight and only one was overweight by one-half ounce. Net shortages ranged from one-fourth ounce to 1⅝ ounces on the 20 short-weight purchases. The total net shortage on the 84 pounds purchased from 21 stores of chain B was 16¼ ounces, or 1.209 per cent.

Comparison of net weights on total purchases and preweighed purchases.—The following table presents a comparison of the net overages and shortages on all commodities purchased with those shown on items weighed and packaged in advance by distributors for each chain and each of the larger cooperatives separately and for all the independents in each of the four cities. The detail of the figures for total purchases, by product and kind of store, appears in Appendix Tables 2 to 5. The detail for the commodities weighed and packaged in advance will be found in Appendix Tables 6 to 9.

TABLE 13.—*A comparison of net shortage (—) or overage (+) on total purchases of five bulk commodities with preweighed purchases of the same commodities, by kind of stores, 1930 and 1932*

Kind of store	Per cent shortage (—) or overage (+)	
	On total purchases	On preweighed purchases
CHAINS		
City No. 1:		
Chain A	+0.075	−0.932
Chain B	+.071	+.012
Chain C	−.375	−.052
City No. 2:		
Chain A	−1.730	−1.846
Chain B	−.547	−.911
Chain C	−.513	−2.930
City No. 3:		
Chain A	−.504	−.418
Chain B	−.981	−1.120
Chain C	+.212	−.067
Chain D	−.240	−.781
Chain E	−.036	−.879
City No. 4:		
Chain A	−.192	−.205
Chain B	−.162	−1.172
Chain C	−.222	−.250
Total chains	−.321	−.719
COOPERATIVE CHAINS		
City No. 1:		
Cooperative chain D	+.348	+.521
Other cooperatives	−.402	−1.823
City No. 2:		
Cooperative chain D	−.722	−.806
Other cooperatives	−.289	−1.683
City No. 3:		
Cooperative chain F	−.054	−1.429
Cooperative chain G	−.624	−.460
City No. 4:		
Cooperative chain D	+1.047	−1.637
Cooperative chain E	+.704	−.355
Total cooperative chains	±.000	−1.079
INDEPENDENTS [1]		
City No. 1	+.523	−1.382
City No. 2	−.358	−1.755
City No. 3	+.012	−.425
City No. 4	+.601	−1.087
Total independents	+.143	−.967

[1] Not including cooperatives.

With the exception of one chain and one cooperative, every one of these two types of distributors had net shortages on preweighed goods and the combined results for independents in each of the four cities were also net shortages.

Individually as well as in the total figures, the chains present a much better showing as regards the amount of shortages than either the cooperative or the independent stores in the commodities weighed and packaged by distributors. Only 4 out of the 14 chain comparisons showed a net shortage of as much as 1 per cent as compared with 3 out of 4 cities in which the independents exceeded this figure and 4 out of 8 instances of the same result in the case of the cooperatives.

The highest net short weight found, however, was in chain C in city No. 2 and was practically 3 per cent. As has already been pointed out, there was a decidedly greater proportion of short weighing in this city on the part of each of the three types of distributors than appeared in the other three cities either separately or combined.

It is not, therefore, surprising to find that four of the five largest net short weights on preweighed goods occurred in that city. The second largest of these was chain A in that city with a net shortage of 1.846 per cent. The independent stores in that city had a net shortage of 1.755 per cent and the miscellaneous small cooperatives located there were 1.683 per cent short.

Comparing the figures for all commodities with those for commodities weighed up in advance, it appears that every distributor or group of distributors shown in Table 13 gave consumers less favorable weights on the latter group of items, excepting chain C and cooperative chain D in city No. 1 and chain A and cooperative chain G in city No. 3. In the total purchases of all items there was only one case of a net shortage of over 1 per cent as compared with 11 instances of shortages of this size on preweighed commodities.

Section 14.—Short weights and overweights excluding commodities preweighed by distributors.

Combined results.—As indicated at the beginning of the preceding section, about 64 per cent of the total items weighed in advance by distributors were purchased by the commission in chain establishments. This section also showed that the weighing results of chain distributors were definitely more favorable to consumers for such goods than the results for other distributors. Because of this situation, it is desirable to compare the results for chains with those for other types of distributors, excluding the items weighed and packaged in advance by distributors. The following table, therefore, presents the proportions of short, over, and exact weight purchases made by the commission from the chain, cooperative, and independent distributors and from cooperatives and independents combined.

TABLE 14.—*Proportion of short weights, overweights, and exact weights on bulk commodities (excluding preweighed articles) purchased at 702 chain and 989 independent stores in four cities, 1930 and 1932*

Store group	Number of nonpreweighed items purchased	Purchases showing—		
		Short weight	Overweight	Exact weight
		Per cent	*Per cent*	*Per cent*
Chains	2,434	48.5	36.6	14.9
Cooperatives	1,174	45.5	45.7	8.8
Independents	2,237	46.8	45.2	8.0
Cooperatives and independents	3,411	46.3	45.4	8.3
Total	5,845	47.2	41.8	11.0

As before the exclusion of the preweighed items (Table 1), the chains have an appreciably higher proportion of exact weights, a somewhat higher proportion of short weights and an appreciably lower proportion of overweights than do the other types of distributors.

Similarly, a comparison of the amounts of net overages and shortages for all purchases, excluding those preweighed by distributors, with the amounts of such net overages and shortages for all commodities purchased, shows a picture less favorable to the consumer for the chains than for the independents despite the exclusion of the preweighed articles. The net shortage for the chains still amounts to two-tenths of 1 per cent while the net overage for the cooperatives and independents combined is slightly over two-tenths of 1 per cent, the net difference amounting to about four-tenths of 1 per cent in favor of the consumer at the independent stores.

TABLE 15.—*Quantity and percentage of net shortage (—) or overage (+) on bulk commodities (excluding preweighed articles) purchased at 702 chain and 989 independent stores in four cities, 1930 and 1932*

Store group	Net weight requested	Total net shortage (—) or overage (+)	Total net shortage (—) or overage (+)
	Pounds	*Ounces*	*Per cent*
Chains	3,442½	—110	—0.200
Cooperatives	1,623½	+30⅜	+.117
Independents	3,376½	+137⅝	+.255
Cooperatives and independents	5,000	+168	+.210
Total	8,442½	+58	+.043

Results by cities.—In a comparison of the results, excluding preweighed articles, from city to city, there is little to indicate a much more favorable showing to the consumer for the chains as compared with the independents than in the case of all purchases made (Table 4). This appears from the following table which shows the proportion of short weight, overweight, and exact weight for chains, cooperatives, independents, and cooperatives and independents combined in each of the four cities studied.

TABLE 16.—*Proportion of short weights, overweights, and exact weights on total number of bulk commodities (excluding preweighed articles) purchased at chain, cooperative chain, and independent stores in each of four cities, 1930 and 1932*

City	Number of items purchased	Purchases showing—		
		Short weight	Over-weight	Exact weight
		Per cent	*Per cent*	*Per cent*
City No. 1:				
Chains	433	40.9	40.9	18.2
Cooperatives	207	49.8	44.9	5.3
Independents	499	42.3	50.7	7.0
Cooperatives and independents	706	44.5	49.0	6.5
City No. 2:				
Chains	308	56.8	32.5	10.7
Cooperatives	176	58.5	34.7	6.8
Independents	468	56.6	35.9	7.5
Cooperatives and independents	644	57.1	35.6	7.3
City No. 3:				
Chains	1,153	50.7	35.1	14.2
Cooperatives	328	45.4	43.3	11.3
Independents	740	46.7	44.5	8.8
Cooperatives and independents	1,068	46.3	44.1	9.6
City No. 4:				
Chains	540	45.4	38.7	15.9
Cooperatives	463	38.6	52.1	9.3
Independents	530	42.3	49.4	8.3
Cooperatives and independents	993	40.6	50.6	8.8

In city No. 1 the proportion of short weights given by the chains was definitely less than that of any other type of distributor, and in city No. 2 it was less than for the cooperatives though insignificantly higher than for the independents. In the other two cities the proportion of short weighing was appreciably higher in the chains. There was no case in which the proportion of overweights given by the chains for any of these four cities was higher than the proportion of short weights, although in city No. 1 it happens that the short weight and overweight percentages for this type of distributor were exactly equal. The independents in city No. 1, however, and both independents and cooperatives in city No. 4 had definitely higher proportions of overweights than of short weights. In each of the four cities the exact-weight percentages for the chain stores were very much higher than the exact-weight percentages of the other types of distributors.

In the amounts of net overages and shortages in these four cities the chains also gave less favorable results to the consumer than the independents in practically every instance.

TABLE 17.—*Quantity and percentage of net shortage (—) or overage (+) on total quantity of bulk commodities (excluding preweighed articles) purchased at chain, cooperative chain, and independent stores in each of four cities, 1930 and 1932*

City	Net weight requested	Total net shortage (—) or overage (+)	Total net shortage (—) or overage (+)
	Pounds	*Ounces*	*Per cent*
City No. 1:			
Chains	642	+13⅜	+0.130
Cooperatives	339	+3½	+.065
Independents	816¼	+88⅛	+.675
Cooperatives and independents	1,155¼	+91⅝	+.496
City No. 2:			
Chains	461	—64⅝	—.876
Cooperatives	298	—25⅝	—.537
Independents	789	—29¾	—.236
Cooperatives and independents	1,087	—55⅜	—.318
City No. 3:			
Chains	1,835½	—45¼	—.154
Cooperatives	523	—24⅛	—.288
Independents	1,216¾	+13½	+.069
Cooperatives and independents	1,739¾	—10⅝	—.038
City No. 4:			
Chains	504	—13½	—.167
Cooperatives	463½	+76⅝	+1.033
Independents	554½	+65¾	+.741
Cooperatives and independents	1,018	+142⅜	+.874

Only in one of the four cities (city No. 1) do the figures for the chains show a net overage. Although this overage is greater than that of the cooperatives, it is very much below that for the independents and also for the independents and cooperatives combined. For city No. 2 net shortages are shown for all types of distributors, but the net shortage for the chains is very much higher than for the other types. For city No. 3 the chain shortage shown is less than the shortage of the cooperatives, but for the independents here an overage is shown and for cooperatives and independents combined, a shortage is shown which is less than that of the chain stores. For city No. 4 the data show a slight net shortage for chains as compared with relatively heavy overages for the other types of distributors.

Section 15. Short changing and overcharging in chain and independent stores.

In connection with the weight study all shoppers were instructed to note carefully all cases of short changing or overcharging, as well as undercharging, and also the inclusion in the bill of any items not purchased, that might occur in making the purchases from any chain, cooperative chain, or independent stores in the four cities. The information thus obtained was intended to determine the truth of the statement made by some persons that, besides giving short weights, chain stores also on occasion make short change or overcharge the customer to offset losses from shrinkage or shortage on merchandise, to create stock gains or overages to offset future shortages, or otherwise to obtain an extra profit.

It is not believed that these data are conclusive on the subject of overcharging or short changing, since they are confined to averages on approximately four inexpensive items purchased in each store. Under regulations governing official expenditures, individual purchases can not exceed $1 in any one place unless a receipt is obtained. In this inquiry it was deemed inexpedient to obtain receipts both from a standpoint of time involved and the necessity to avoid attracting attention to the work. The cost of the items purchased was, therefore, kept under $1 in each store. This restriction was also a factor in limiting the character of the commodities bought. It is believed that if intentional errors are at times made in additions or in making change, such discrepancies would in all probability be more numerous and larger on purchases involving a larger number of articles and on a bill of larger amount.

The results of this part of the inquiry show remarkably few cases of short changing or of charging more for purchases than the prices orally quoted. Shoppers were either short changed or overcharged in only 8 chain stores out of a total of 702 shopped. In each of 4 of these stores the amount of the overcharge was 1 cent; in 2 stores it was 2 cents and 3 cents, respectively; and in each of 2 other stores the overcharge was 10 cents. Two chain stores undercharged the shopper, or short changed themselves, by 1 cent and 5 cents. In another chain store the clerk, intentionally or unintentionally, charged for 3 pounds of navy beans requested but apparently meant to weigh out only 2 pounds. This incident, however, was offset in another chain store where 3 pounds were given but only 2 pounds were charged for.

Out of 320 cooperative chain stores shopped the purchaser was short changed only twice, once for 6 cents and another time for 10 cents. On one occasion the clerk charged the shopper for 3 pounds of navy beans but apparently weighed up the merchandise at 2 pounds. On the other hand, eight cooperative chain stores, either intentionally as a courtesy refund [9] or unintentionally, short changed

[9] By the term "courtesy refund" is meant a deduction from the amount of the bill of 1 or 2 cents in cases where the amount of the purchases resulted in an odd cent or 2.

themselves or undercharged the shopper. In each of five of these stores the undercharge was for 1 cent; in a sixth store the amount was 3 cents; in a seventh, 5 cents; and in the eighth, 10 cents.

Independent stores (numbering 669 shopped in the four cities) gave short change or overcharged the shopper in 12 instances, amounting to a total of 43 cents, and short changed themselves eleven times for 23 cents. Among the 12 cases of short changing or overcharging 2 were for 1 cent each, 5 were for 2 cents each, 2 were for 3 cents, and 1 each was for 7 cents, 8 cents, and 10 cents. Six of the eleven cases of undercharging the shopper were given as courtesy refunds. Of the other 5 cases, 2 were for 1 cent, 2 were for 2 cents, and 1 was for 10 cents. One other store in this group apparently weighed out the requested 3 pounds of navy beans, yet charged for only 2 pounds.

A more detailed statement of this information gathered in each of the four cities is found in Appendix I.

APPENDIX I

Short Changing and Overcharging in Chain and Independent Stores in Each of Four Cities

CITY NO. 1

Chain stores.—In city No. 1 only 2 chain stores out of 117 shopped made incorrect charges for the articles purchased. A clerk in one store charged 10 cents on the bill for 1 pound of dried prunes although he had previously quoted the price to the shopper at 9 cents. In another store belonging to the same chain, however, the clerk added 1 cent to the price quoted on one article but reduced the price quoted on another article by 2 cents, thus charging the shopper 1 cent less for the five articles purchased than the prices quoted.

Cooperative stores.—Four cooperative stores out of 56 shopped in city No. 1 gave incorrect change. Three of the stores short changed themselves 1 cent each. In one of the stores the under charge was intentional as a courtesy refund. In a fourth store sweetened crackers quoted at 28 cents per pound were added on the bill at 25 cents. No cooperative chain store in this city made an overcharge.

Independent stores.—Eleven independent stores out of 146 shopped in this city were inaccurate in making change or in additions of the items. In five stores the inaccuracy favored the shopper; in six cases the store benefited.

In four stores the shopper was given a 1-cent courtesy refund, as, for example, when the bill totaled 66 cents the clerk or store owner remarked that 65 cents was sufficient. In a fifth store the clerk short changed himself 2 cents.

Six stores in the same city overcharged the shopper, 4 of them by 2 cents each, 1 by 3 cents, and 1 by 8 cents. Two charged an extra 2 cents for sweetened crackers over the quoted or marked price. Another clerk quoted sugar at 9 cents, yet charged 11 cents for it. The other 3 favored themselves by inaccurate additions or in making change in the amounts of 2 cents, 3 cents, and 8 cents, respectively.

CITY NO. 2

Chain stores.—Shoppers found no cases of incorrect additions of purchases or short changing in shopping 128 chain stores in this city. One chain store, however, charged for 3 pounds of navy beans but gave only seven-eighths of an ounce over 2 pounds. This sale was offset by a second chain that charged for only 2 pounds but gave net weight of one-eighth ounce less than 3 pounds.

Cooperative stores.—An overcharge of 10 cents, due either to the incorrect addition of three items or short changing, was made on a list of three articles purchased in 1 store out of 57 cooperatives shopped in this city.

Independent stores.—A clerk in one independent store itemized sweetened crackers 1 cent below the quoted or marked price. In another independent store a charge was made for only 2 pounds of navy beans, although the 3 pounds requested were given.

CITY NO. 3

Chain stores.—Four chain stores out of 309 shopped in city No. 3 gave short change or overcharged the shopper—two by 1 cent each and one by 10 cents. A clerk in a fourth chain store included an item in his addition at 12 cents which had been quoted to the shopper at 10 cents. A clerk in a fifth chain store made an error of 5 cents in favor of the shopper in itemizing the purchases.

Cooperative stores.—Out of 81 cooperative stores shopped in this city no short changing or overcharging occurred. In one store, although 3 pounds of navy beans were requested and paid for, only 2¼ ounces over 2 pounds net were given.

Independent stores.—One independent store overcharged the shopper 10 cents, charging 58 cents on a bill that totaled 48 cents; a second store gave a courtesy refund of 2 cents on purchases amounting to 67 cents. These were the only two irregularities found among 214 independent stores in this city.

CITY NO. 4

Chain stores.—Three chain stores out of 148 chain stores shopped in city No. 4 short changed or overcharged the shopper, in one instance by 1 cent, in another by 3 cents, and in a third by 10 cents. In the latter case the clerk added four items to make 55 cents instead of 45 cents. No cases of undercharging the shopper occurred among the chains in this city.

Cooperative stores.—Out of 126 cooperative chain stores shopped in city No. 4 one overcharged the shopper 6 cents. In this store navy beans quoted by the clerk at 10 cents per pound were added in the bill at 13 cents, and 1 pound of Lima beans quoted at 17 cents was added in the same bill at 20 cents. In the same city four cooperative chain stores short changed themselves or made errors in additions favorable to the shopper. In two stores the errors amounted to 1 cent in each; in another store, 5 cents; and in another, 10 cents.

Independent stores.—Five cases of short changing or overcharging the shopper and four cases in which the shopper was not charged the full amount of the bill were found in shopping 166 independent stores in city No. 4. In each of two stores the overcharge or short charge was 1 cent; in a third, 2 cents; in a fourth, 3 cents; and in the fifth, 7 cents. In one store the price of 1 pound of Lima beans quoted at 17 cents was set down on the bill at 18 cents; in another store 25 cents was charged for one pound of dried prunes quoted at 18 cents.

In two of the four stores where the full amount of the bill was not charged the amounts were for 1 cent each. In one of these two cases the undercharge was intentionally made as a courtesy refund. In a third store the total bill presented for three items obtained was 2 cents below total quoted prices, and in the fourth store the grocer short changed himself 10 cents.

APPENDIX II

Appendix Tables

Table 1.—*Quantity and percentage of total shortage and overage and net shortage or overage on bulk commodities purchased at chain, cooperative chain, and independent stores in four cities, 1930 and 1932*

Kind of store	Total short weight		Total overweight		Net shortage (−) or overage (+) [1]
	Ounces	*Per cent*	*Ounces*	*Per cent*	*Per cent*
CHAINS					
City No. 1:					
Chain A	32¾	0.652	36½	0.727	+0.075
Chain B	25	.393	29½	.463	+.071
Chain C	20¼	1.013	12¾	.638	−.375
City No. 2:					
Chain A	105½	2.169	21⅜	.439	−1.730
Chain B	48¼	.973	21⅛	.426	−.547
Chain C	15⅛	.927	6¾	.414	−.513
City No. 3:					
Chain A	77	1.074	40⅞	.570	−.504
Chain B	126⅛	1.318	32¼	.337	−.981
Chain C	114½	.606	154⅝	.818	+.212
Chain D	6¾	1.082	5¼	.841	−.240
Chain E	3¾	1.065	3⅝	1.030	−.036
City No. 4:					
Chain A	34⅜	.825	26⅜	.633	−.192
Chain B	62⅞	2.147	58⅛	1.985	−.162
Chain C	36½	1.116	29¼	.894	−.222
Total chains	708¾	.987	478⅜	.666	−.321
COOPERATIVE CHAINS					
City No. 1:					
Cooperative chain D	28½	.968	38¾	1.316	+.348
Other cooperatives	40	1.397	28½	.995	−.402
City No. 2:					
Cooperative chain D	52½	1.307	23½	.585	−.722
Other cooperatives	19⅜	1.316	15⅛	1.028	−.289
City No. 3:					
Cooperative chain F	56	1.346	53¾	1.292	−.054
Cooperative chain G	71⅜	1.320	37⅝	.696	−.624
City No. 4:					
Cooperative chain D	54⅞	1.280	99¾	2.327	+1.047
Cooperative chain E	42¾	1.174	68⅜	1.878	+.704
Total cooperative chains	365⅝	1.269	365⅝	1.269	±.000
INDEPENDENTS [2]					
City No. 1	153⅛	1.086	226⅞	1.609	+.523
City No. 2	186½	1.359	137⅜	1.001	−.358
City No. 3	281⅛	1.276	283¾	1.288	+.012
City No. 4	130	1.353	187¾	1.954	+.601
Total independents	750¾	1.263	835¾	1.405	+.143
Total cooperatives and independents	1,116⅛	1.265	1,201⅛	1.361	+.096
All stores	1,824⅞	1.140	1,679½	1.049	−.091

[1] The percentages in column 5 are exact net figures which do not in all cases represent the exact difference between columns 2 and 4 due to adjusting third place figures.
[2] Not including cooperatives.

TABLE 2.—*Proportion and quantity of net shortage (—) or overage (+) on specified bulk commodities purchased at 117 chain and 202 independent stores in city No. 1, 1932*

Commodity	Number of stores shopped	Number of items purchased	Purchases showing— Short weight	Overweight	Exact weight	Net weight requested	Total net shortage (—) or overage (+)	Total net shortage (—) or overage (+)
			Per cent	*Per cent*	*Per cent*	*Pounds*	*Ounces*	*Per cent*
Navy beans:								
Chains	117	114	60.5	27.2	12.3	340	−18⅜	−0.338
Cooperatives	56	50	48.0	44.0	8.0	150	+2¼	+.094
Independents	146	128	48.5	44.5	7.0	382¼	+24¾	+.405
Cooperatives and independents	202	178	48.3	44.4	7.3	532¼	+27	+.317
Total	319	292	53.1	37.7	9.2	872¼	+8⅝	+.062
Prunes, dried:								
Chains	117	91	20.9	51.6	27.5	91	+18½	+1.271
Cooperatives	56	26	42.3	46.2	11.5	26	+4¾	+1.142
Independents	146	67	37.3	58.2	4.5	67	+23	+2.146
Cooperatives and independents	202	93	38.7	54.8	6.5	93	+27¾	+1.865
Total	319	184	29.9	53.3	16.8	184	+46¼	+1.571
Lima beans:								
Chains	117	113	33.6	41.6	24.8	113	+9⅝	+.532
Cooperatives	56	48	41.7	56.2	2.1	48	+7½	+.977
Independents	146	117	35.0	55.6	9.4	117	+26	+1.389
Cooperatives and independents	202	165	37.0	55.7	7.3	165	+33½	+1.269
Total	319	278	35.6	50.0	14.4	278	+43⅛	+.970
Crackers, sweetened:								
Chains	117	117	51.3	35.9	12.8	117	−9¾	−.521
Cooperatives	56	51	51.0	47.0	2.0	51	−2½	−.306
Independents	146	123	48.8	44.7	6.5	123	−4⅞	−.248
Cooperatives and independents	202	174	49.4	45.4	5.2	174	−7⅜	−.265
Total	319	291	50.2	41.6	8.2	291	−17⅛	−.368
Sugar:								
Chains	117	88	39.8	34.1	26.1	176	+¾	+.027
Cooperatives	56	44	65.9	25.0	9.1	88	−13¼	−.941
Independents	146	96	51.0	43.8	5.2	192	+4⅞	+.159
Cooperatives and independents	202	140	55.7	37.9	6.4	280	−8⅜	−.187
Total	319	228	49.6	36.4	14.0	456	−7⅝	−.105

Table 3.—*Proportion and quantity of net shortage (—) or overage (+) on specified bulk commodities purchased at 128 chain and 200 independent stores in city No. 2, 1932*

Commodity	Number of stores shopped	Number of items purchased	Purchases showing—			Net weight requested	Total net shortage (—) or overage (+)	Total net shortage (—) or overage (+)
			Short weight	Over-weight	Exact weight			
			Per cent	*Per cen*	*Per cent*	*Pounds*	*Ounces*	*Per cent*
Navy beans:								
Chains	128	117	75.2	17.1	7.7	347	−73¾	−1.328
Cooperatives	57	56	57.1	37.5	5.4	167	−5⅜	−.201
Independents	143	135	59.2	34.1	6.7	405	−10	−.154
Cooperatives and independents	200	191	58.6	35.1	6.3	572	−15⅜	−.168
Total	328	308	64.9	28.3	6.8	919	−89⅛	−.606
Prunes, dried:								
Chains	128	81	53.1	33.3	13.6	82	−10½	−.800
Cooperatives	57	21	57.1	38.1	4.8	21	−3	−.893
Independents	143	68	51.5	42.6	5.9	68	+7⅛	+.655
Cooperatives and independents	200	89	52.8	41.6	5.6	89	+4⅛	+.290
Total	328	170	52.9	37.7	9.4	171	−6⅜	−.233
Lima beans:								
Chains	128	10	70.0	10.0	20.0	10	−4⅝	−2.891
Cooperatives	57	36	50.0	33.3	16.7	36	−2½	−.434
Independents	143	95	51.6	40.0	8.4	95	−1	−.066
Cooperatives and independents	200	131	51.1	38.2	10.7	131	−3½	−.167
Total	328	141	52.5	36.2	11.3	141	−8⅛	−.360
Crackers, sweetened:								
Chains	128	128	61.7	31.3	7.0	128	−29¾	−1.453
Cooperatives	57	49	73.5	22.4	4.1	49	−18⅜	−2.344
Independents	143	116	62.1	33.6	4.3	116	−28½	−1.536
Cooperatives and independents	200	165	65.5	30.3	4.2	165	−46⅞	−1.776
Total	328	293	63.8	30.7	5.5	293	−76⅝	−1.634
Sugar:								
Chains	128	74	48.6	33.8	17.6	149	−1	−.042
Cooperatives	57	35	54.3	40.0	5.7	70	−4	−.357
Independents	143	87	64.4	25.3	10.3	174	−16¾	−.602
Cooperatives and independents	200	122	61.5	29.5	9.0	244	−20¾	−.532
Total	328	196	56.6	31.1	12.3	393	−21¾	−.346

Table 4.—*Proportion and quantity of net shortage (—) or overage (+) on specified bulk commodities purchased at 309 chain and 295 independent stores in city No. 3, 1932*

Commodity	Number of stores shopped	Number of items purchased	Purchases showing— Short weight	Over-weight	Exact weight	Net weight requested	Total net shortage (—) or overage (+)	Total net shortage (—) or overage (+)
			Per cent	*Per cent*	*Per cent*	*Pounds*	*Ounces*	*Per cent*
Navy beans:								
Chains	309	306	67.3	24.5	8.2	954	−68⅝	−0.448
Cooperatives	81	78	53.9	33.3	12.8	234	−26⅜	−.704
Independents	214	204	49.5	44.6	5.9	611¾	+7¾	+.079
Cooperatives and independents	295	282	50.7	41.5	7.8	845¾	−18⅝	−.138
Total	604	588	59.4	32.6	8.0	1,799¾	−87	−.302
Prunes, dried:								
Chains	309	197	44.2	40.1	15.7	198	+8½	+.268
Cooperatives	81	66	36.4	50.0	13.6	67	+2	+.187
Independents	214	115	40.9	52.2	6.9	115	+21⅜	+1.162
Cooperatives and independents	295	181	39.2	51.4	9.4	182	+23⅜	+.803
Total	604	378	41.8	45.5	12.7	380	+31⅞	+.524
Lima beans:								
Chains	309	294	42.9	38.4	18.7	295	+16⅜	+.347
Cooperatives	81	79	41.8	50.6	7.6	79	+⅜	+.030
Independents	214	175	41.1	48.6	10.3	175	+20⅛	+.719
Cooperatives and independents	295	254	41.3	49.2	9.5	254	+20½	+.504
Total	604	548	42.2	43.4	14.4	549	+36⅞	+.420
Crackers, sweetened:								
Chains	309	307	58.0	28.3	13.7	306½	−63⅛	−1.287
Cooperatives	81	78	66.7	25.6	7.7	78	−16⅝	−1.332
Independents	214	193	57.0	31.6	11.4	193	−63	−2.040
Cooperatives and independents	295	271	59.8	29.9	10.3	271	−79⅝	−1.836
Total	604	578	58.8	29.1	12.1	577½	−142¾	−1.545
Sugar:								
Chains	309	267	43.8	39.7	16.5	535	+15⅛	+.177
Cooperatives	81	70	41.4	45.7	12.9	140	+4⅝	+.206
Independents	214	141	45.4	42.5	12.1	282	+16⅜	+.363
Cooperatives and independents	295	211	44.1	43.6	12.3	422	+21	+.311
Total	604	478	43.9	41.4	14.7	957	+36⅛	+.236

TABLE 5.—*Proportion and quantity of net shortage (—) or overage (+) on specified bulk commodities purchased at 148 chain and 292 independent stores in city No. 4, 1930*

Commodity	Number of stores shopped	Number of items purchased	Purchases showing—			Net weight requested	Total net shortage (—) or overage (+)	Total net shortage (—) or overage (+)
			Short weight	Overweight	Exact weight			
Navy beans:			*Per cent*	*Per cent*	*Per cent*	*Pounds*	*Ounces*	*Per cent*
Chains	148	142	52.1	35.9	12.0	142	−10½	−0.462
Cooperatives	126	110	31.8	61.8	6.4	110	+31¼	+1.776
Independents	166	144	45.8	48.6	5.6	144	+24⅜	+1.058
Cooperatives and independents	292	254	39.8	54.3	5.9	254	+55⅝	+1.369
Total	440	396	44.2	47.7	8.1	396	+45⅛	+.712
Prunes, dried:								
Chains	148	130	47.7	38.5	13.8	129½	+¾	+.036
Cooperatives	126	87	44.8	46.0	9.2	87	+8⅜	+.602
Independents	166	74	32.4	55.4	12.2	73	+24⅜	+2.087
Cooperatives and independents	292	161	39.1	50.3	10.6	160	+32¾	+1.279
Total	440	291	43.0	45.0	12.0	289½	+33½	+.723
Lima beans:								
Chains	148	143	33.6	45.4	21.0	143	+5¾	+.251
Cooperatives	126	98	40.8	51.0	8.2	98	+19⅜	+1.236
Independents	166	106	43.4	50.0	6.6	106	+13½	+.796
Cooperatives and independents	292	204	42.2	50.5	7.3	204	+32⅞	+1.007
Total	440	347	38.6	48.4	13.0	347	+38⅝	+.696
Crackers, sweetened:								
Chains	148	147	55.8	29.9	14.3	73½	−16½	−1.403
Cooperatives	126	121	41.3	46.3	12.4	60½	+9¾	+1.007
Independents	166	131	45.8	44.3	9.9	65½	+2	+.191
Cooperatives and independents	292	252	43.7	45.2	11.1	126	+11¾	+.583
Total	440	399	48.1	39.6	12.3	199½	−4¾	−.149
Sugar:								
Chains	148	80	36.2	31.2	32.6	160	+½	+.020
Cooperatives	126	70	40.0	45.7	14.3	140	+1¾	+.078
Independents	166	106	43.4	45.3	11.3	212	−6½	−.192
Cooperatives and independents	292	176	42.0	45.5	12.5	352	−4¾	−.084
Total	440	256	40.2	41.0	18.8	512	−4¼	−.052

TABLE 6.—*Proportion and quantity of net shortage (—) or overage (+) on preweighed bulk commodities purchased at chain and independent stores in city No. 1, 1932*

Store group	Number of stores shopped	Number of preweighed items purchased	Purchases showing—			Net weight requested	Total net shortage (—) or overage (+)	Total net shortage (—) or overage (+)
			Short weight	Overweight	Exact weight			
			Per cent	*Per cent*	*Per cent*	*Pounds*	*Ounces*	*Per cent*
Chain A	47	36	55.6	11.1	33.3	83	−12⅜	−0.932
Chain B	52	33	39.4	27.3	33.3	67	+⅛	+.012
Chain C	18	21	52.4	33.3	14.3	45	−⅜	−.052
Cooperative chain D	28	3	0	66.7	33.3	6	+½	+.521
Other cooperatives	28	9	77.8	11.1	11.1	18	−5¼	−1.823
Independents	146	32	81.3	15.6	3.1	65	−14⅜	−1.382
Total	319	134	57.5	20.9	21.6	284	−31¾	−.699
Total chains	117	90	48.9	22.2	28.9	195	−12⅝	−.405
Total cooperatives	56	12	58.3	25.0	16.7	24	−4¾	−1.237
Total cooperatives and independents	202	44	75.0	18.2	6.8	89	−19⅛	−1.343

TABLE 7.—*Proportion and quantity of net shortage (—) or overage (+) on preweighed bulk commodities purchased at chain and independent stores in city No. 2, 1932*

Store group	Number of stores shopped	Number of preweighed items purchased	Purchases showing—			Net weight requested	Total net shortage (—) or overage (+)	Total net shortage (—) or overage (+)
			Short weight	Overweight	Exact weight			
			Per cent	*Per cent*	*Per cent*	*Pounds*	*Ounces*	*Per cent*
Chain A	59	38	89.4	5.3	5.3	102	−30⅛	−1.846
Chain B	50	59	69.5	18.6	11.9	145	−21⅛	−.911
Chain C	19	5	60.0	0	40.0	8	−3¾	−2.930
Cooperative Chain D	42	15	73.3	20.0	6.7	32	−4⅛	−.806
Other cooperatives	15	6	50.0	33.3	16.7	13	−3½	−1.683
Independents	143	33	81.8	18.2	0	69	−19⅜	−1.755
Total	328	156	76.3	15.4	8.3	369	−82	−1.389
Total chains	128	102	76.5	12.7	10.8	255	−55	−1.348
Total cooperatives	57	21	66.7	23.8	9.5	45	−7⅝	−1.059
Total cooperatives and independents	200	54	75.9	20.4	3.7	114	−27	−1.480

TABLE 8.—*Proportion and quantity of net shortage (—) or overage (+) on preweighed bulk commodities purchased at 309 chain and 295 independent stores in city No. 3, 1932*

Store group	Number of stores shopped	Number of preweighed items purchased	Purchases showing—			Net weight requested	Total net shortage (—) or overage (+)	Total net shortage (—) or overage (+)
			Short weight	Overweight	Exact weight			
			Per cent	*Per cent*	*Per cent*	*Pounds*	*Ounces*	*Per cent*
Chain A	61	22	50.0	18.2	31.8	43	−2⅞	−0.418
Chain B	77	101	77.2	12.9	9.9	224	−40⅛	−1.120
Chain C	163	90	41.1	41.1	17.8	176	−1⅞	−.067
Chain D	5	1	100.0	----------	----------	2	−¼	−.781
Chain E	3	4	75.0	25.0	----------	8	−1⅛	−.879
Cooperative Chain F	37	22	81.8	18.2	----------	41	−9⅜	−1.429
Cooperative Chain G	44	21	61.9	23.8	14.3	34	−2½	−.460
Independents	214	88	54.6	31.8	13.6	160	−10⅞	−.425
Total	604	349	59.9	26.4	13.7	688	−69	−.627
Total chains	309	218	59.6	25.2	15.2	453	−46¼	−.638
Total cooperatives	81	43	72.1	20.9	7.0	75	−11⅞	−.990
Total cooperatives and independents	295	131	60.3	28.2	11.5	235	−22¾	−.605

Table 9.—*Proportion and quantity of net shortage (—) or overage (+) on preweighed bulk commodities purchased at 148 chain and 292 independent stores in city No. 4, 1930*

Store group	Number of stores shopped	Number of pre-weighed items purchased	Purchases showing— Short weight	Over-weight	Exact weight	Net weight requested	Total net shortage (—) or overage (+)	Total net shortage (—) or overage (+)
			Per cent	*Per cent*	*Per cent*	*Pounds*	*Ounces*	*Per cent*
Chain A	56	41	36.6	31.7	31.7	61	−2	−0.205
Chain B	52	7	71.4	14.3	14.3	8	−1½	−1.172
Chain C	40	54	55.6	22.2	22.2	75	−3	−.250
Cooperative chain D	71	16	62.4	18.8	18.8	21	−5½	−1.637
Cooperative chain E	55	7	42.8	28.6	28.6	11	−⅝	−.355
Independents	166	31	58.1	25.8	16.1	46	−8	−1.087
Total	440	156	51.9	25.0	23.1	222	−20⅝	−.581
	148	102	49.0	25.5	25.5	144	−6½	−.282
Total chains	126	23	56.6	21.7	21.7	32	−6⅛	−1.196
Total cooperatives								
Total cooperatives and independents	292	54	57.4	24.1	18.5	78	−14⅛	−1.132

O

GETTING AND SPENDING: The Consumer's Dilemma

An Arno Press Collection

Babson, Roger W[ard]. **The Folly of Instalment Buying.** 1938

Bauer, John. **Effective Regulation of Public Utilities.** 1925

Beckman, Theodore N. and Herman C. Nolen. **The Chain Store Problem.** 1938

Berridge, William A., Emma A. Winslow and Richard A. Flinn. **Purchasing Power of the Consumer.** 1925

Borden, Neil H. **The Economic Effects of Advertising.** 1942

Borsodi, Ralph. **The Distribution Age.** 1927

Brainerd, J. G[rist], editor. **The Ultimate Consumer.** 1934

Carson, Gerald. **Cornflake Crusade.** [1957]

Cassels, John M[acIntyre]. **A Study of Fluid Milk Prices.** 1937

Caveat Emptor. 1976

Cherington, Paul Terry. **Advertising as a Business Force.** 1913

Clark, Evans. **Financing the Consumer.** 1933

Cook, James. **Remedies and Rackets:** The Truth About Patent Medicines Today. [1958]

Cover, John H[igson]. **Neighborhood Distribution and Consumption of Meat in Pittsburgh.** [1932]

Federal Trade Commission. **Chain Stores.** 1933

Ferber, Robert and Hugh G. Wales, editors. **Motivation and Market Behavior.** 1958

For Richer or Poorer. 1976

Grether, Ewald T. **Price Control Under Fair Trade Legislation.** 1939

Harding, T. Swann. **The Popular Practice of Fraud.** 1935

Haring, Albert. **Retail Price Cutting and Its Control by Manufacturers.** [1935]

Harris, Emerson P[itt]. **Co-operation:** The Hope of the Consumer. 1918

Hoyt, Elizabeth Ellis. **The Consumption of Wealth.** 1928

Kallen, Horace M[eyer]. **The Decline and Rise of the Consumer.** 1936

Kallet, Arthur and F. J. Schlink. **100,000,000 Guinea Pigs:** Dangers in Everyday Foods, Drugs, and Cosmetics. 1933

Kyrk, Hazel. **A Theory of Consumption.** [1923]

Laird, Donald A[nderson]. **What Makes People Buy.** 1935

Lamb, Ruth deForest. **American Chamber of Horrors:** The Truth About Food and Drugs. [1936]

Lambert, I[saac] E. **The Public Accepts:** Stories Behind Famous Trade-Marks, Names, and Slogans. [1941]

Larrabee, Carroll B. **How to Package for Profit.** 1935

Lough, William H. **High-Level Consumption.** 1935

Lyon, Leverett S[amuel]. **Hand-to-Mouth Buying.** 1929

Means, Gardiner C. **Pricing Power and the Public Interest.** [1962]

Norris, Ruby Turner. **The Theory of Consumer's Demand.** 1952

Nourse, Edwin G. **Price Making in a Democracy.** 1944

Nystrom, Paul H[enry]. **Economic Principles of Consumption.** [1929]

Pancoast, Chalmers Lowell. **Trail Blazers of Advertising.** 1926

Pasdermadjian, H[rant]. **The Department Store.** 1954

Pease, Otis. **The Responsibilities of American Advertising.** 1958

Peixotto, Jessica B[lanche]. **Getting and Spending at the Professional Standard of Living.** 1927

Radin, Max. **The Lawful Pursuit of Gain.** 1931

Reid, Margaret G. **Consumers and the Market.** 1947

Rheinstrom, Carroll. **Psyching the Ads.** [1929]

Rorty, James. **Our Master's Voice:** Advertising. [1934]

Schlink, F. J. **Eat, Drink and Be Wary.** [1935]

Seldin, Joseph J. **The Golden Fleece:** Selling the Good Life to Americans. [1963]

Sheldon, Roy and Egmont Arens. **Consumer Engineering.** 1932

Stewart, Paul W. and J. Frederic Dewhurst. **Does Distribution Cost Too Much?** 1939

Thompson, Carl D. **Confessions of the Power Trust.** 1932

U. S. National Commission on Food Marketing. **Food From Farmer to Consumer.** 1966

U. S. Senate Subcommittee on Anti-Trust and Monopoly of the Committee on the Judiciary. **Administered Prices.** 1963

Waite, Warren C[leland] and Ralph Cassady, Jr. **The Consumer and the Economic Order.** 1939

Washburn, Robert Collyer. **The Life and Times of Lydia E. Pinkham.** 1931

Wiley, Harvey W[ashington]. **The History of a Crime Against the Food Law.** [1929]

Wright, Richardson [Little]. **Hawkers and Walkers in Early America.** 1927

Zimmerman, Carle C[lark]. **Consumption and Standards of Living.** 1936